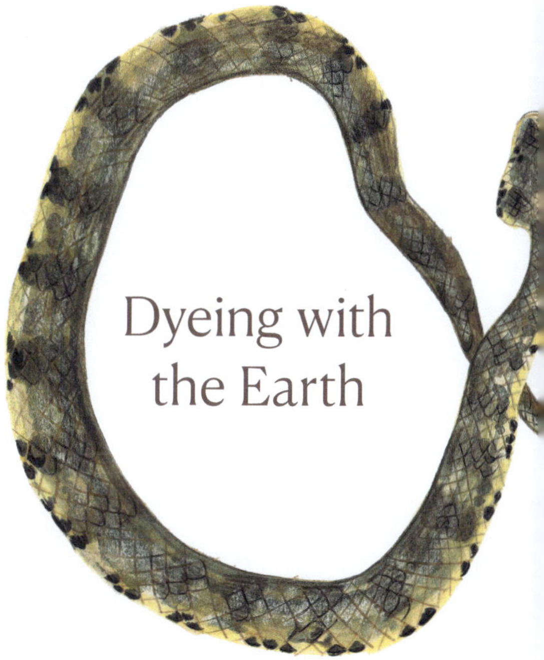

Dyeing with the Earth

ハブ 30.11.18

On the road on the way to Toguchi.

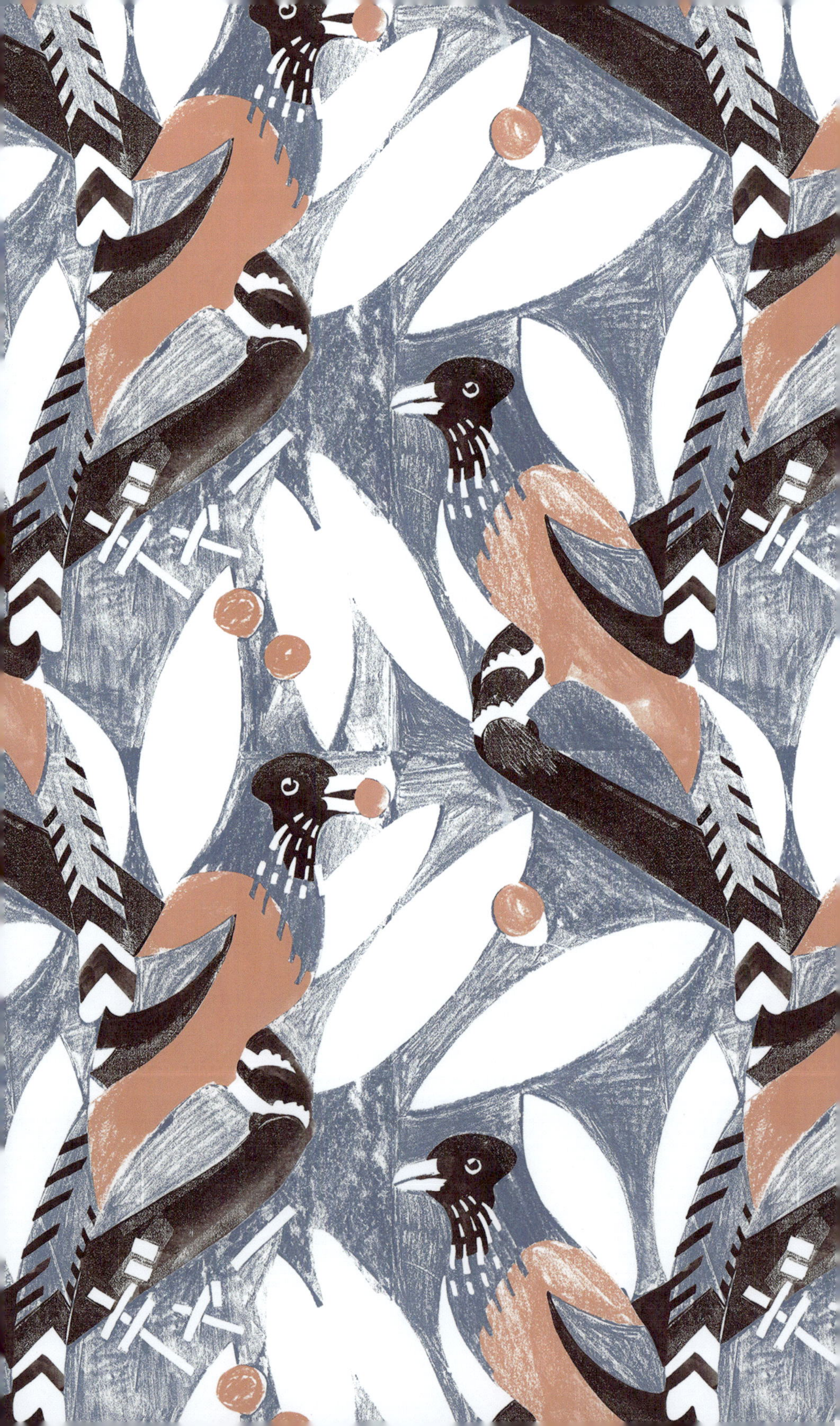

Charlotte Linton

Dyeing with the Earth

Textiles, Tradition, & Sustainability in Contemporary Japan

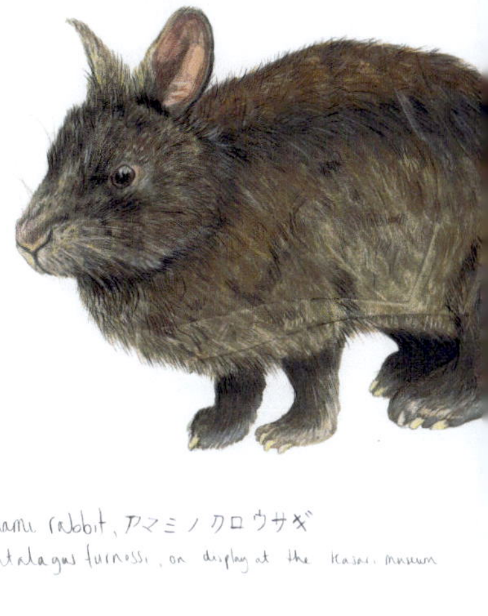

Duke University Press *Durham and London* 2025

Printed in the United States of America on acid-free paper ∞
Project Editor: Lisa Lawley
Designed by Courtney Leigh Richardson
Typeset in Garamond Premier Pro, Canela, and Alegreya Sans
by Westchester Publishing Services

Library of Congress Cataloging-in-Publication Data
Names: Linton, Charlotte, [date] author.
Title: Dyeing with the earth : textiles, tradition, and sustainability
in contemporary Japan / Charlotte Linton.
Other titles: Textiles, tradition, and sustainability in contemporary
Japan
Description: Durham : Duke University Press, 2025. | Includes
bibliographical references and index.
Identifiers: LCCN 2025001892 (print)
LCCN 2025001893 (ebook)
ISBN 9781478032212 (paperback)
ISBN 9781478028987 (hardcover)
ISBN 9781478061199 (ebook)
Subjects: LCSH: Dyes and dyeing—Textile fibers—Japan—Amami
Ōshima. | Textile industry—Japan—Amami Ōshima. | Kimonos—
Japan—Amami Ōshima. | Textile crafts—Japan—Amami Ōshima. |
Textile industry—Environmental aspects—Japan—Amami Ōshima.
Classification: LCC TT854.3 .L568 2025 (print) | LCC TT854.3 (ebook)
LC record available at https://lccn.loc.gov/2025001892
LC ebook record available at https://lccn.loc.gov/2025001893

Cover art: Background image showing the Kanai Kougei workshop and the craftsman Kazuhito Kanai, 2018. Drawings of *sharinbai* blossoms, Ryūkyū indigo, and a praying mantis. Courtesy of Charlotte Linton.

Frontispieces: (*page ii*) Textile print designed by the author during a period of ethnographic research in Amami Ōshima. The design depicts the *rurikakesu* (Lidth's jay), found only in the Amami Islands. The word *giyā* is repeated in katakana text to describe the shrill noise of their call. (*page iii*) A taxidermy Amami black rabbit from the collection of a local folk museum.

Publication of this book was supported by the AAS First Book Subvention Program of the Association for Asian Studies.

Contents

リュウキュウアオヘビ 16.11.17
Ryūkyū Green Snake

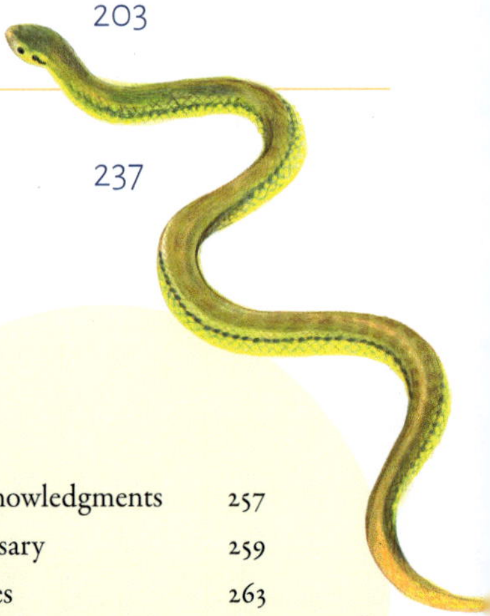

Introduction

I first met Koki in 2017, around three months into fieldwork while I was working at Kanai Kougei, a traditional *dorozome* (mud-dyeing) workshop on the island of Amami Ōshima, in southern Japan (figure I.1).[1] Koki was learning about the production of the Amamian kimono cloth *Oshima tsumugi*, whose yarns are dyed using the dorozome technique, and had dropped by to introduce himself to the workshop's *shachō* (company president), Kazuhito Kanai.[2] In his crisp white T-shirt and black jeans, Koki's Tokyo style stood in contrast to that of the workshop's staff in our tattered dyeing overalls. In conversation, Koki and I quickly discovered we had both studied fashion at Central Saint Martins in London only a few years apart. When I interviewed him later, we discussed our shared interest in eco-friendly fashion and tried to establish when we became aware of a discourse around sustainability within the fashion industry. Koki recalled:

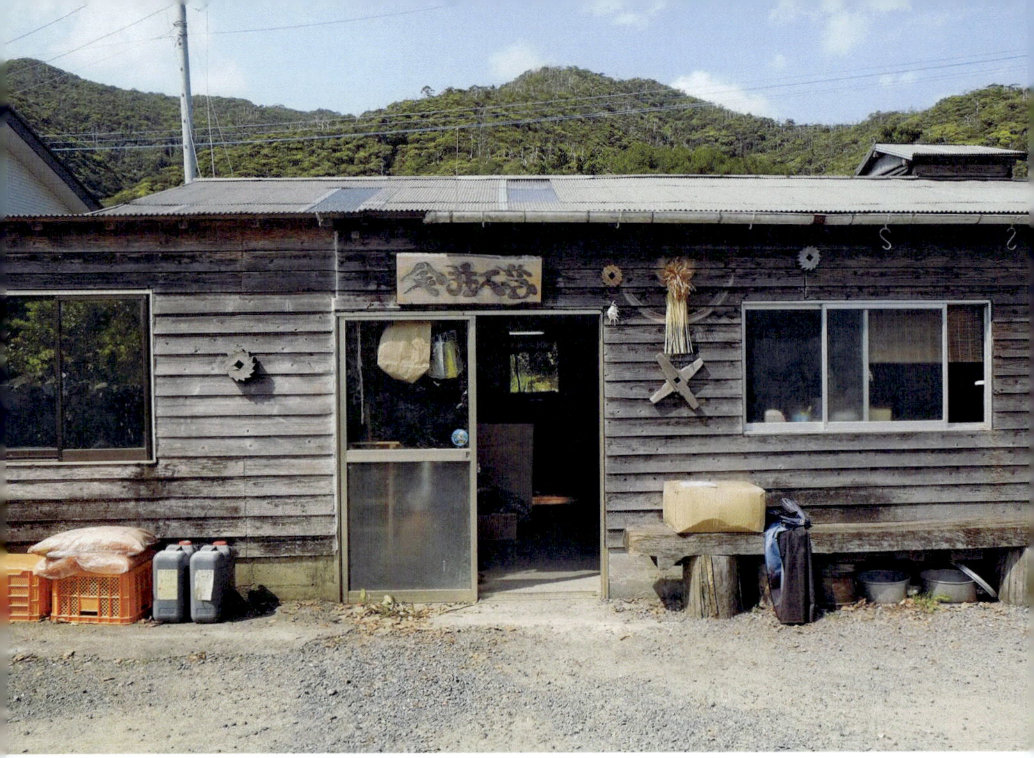

Figure 1.1 *The Kanai Kougei workshop.*

> I remember one American girl [in college], she was publicly speaking [out] about [sustainability]. . . . Then the financial crisis happened, and for me personally there were many things happening, and then at the end, the nuclear disaster happened . . . and also the Dhaka building collapsed in Bangladesh, that was huge . . . and you started to realize "Okay, this is really messed up." I couldn't really believe it—what kind of world are we living in? Maybe we need to focus on better things. But then I'm not going to become a volunteer, ditching everything I've studied. So, I try to at least maintain what I find, where good happens in my own industry.

Koki emphasized that this awareness, which began while we were studying between 2002 and 2011, grew steadily with a string of financial, environmental, and human rights disasters including the 2013 collapse of the Rana Plaza factory in Dhaka, Bangladesh, where at least 1,134 people producing garments for global fashion chains lost their lives (De Neve and Prentice 2017, 3). This was a landmark moment for the fashion and textile industry and highlighted the terrible working conditions in many producing regions.[3] Three months later, the *New York Times* published a photo-essay that investigated water pollution in Dhaka caused by local factories producing pharmaceuticals and leather but also textiles and garments (Yardley 2013). Journalist Jim Yardley reported that many factories were dumping untreated industrial wastewater into canals, destroying paddies, killing fish, and contaminating crops. The canals' water—whose color, Yardley stated, changed according to fashion tastes—was so polluted that the fumes were making local children sick. The *New York Times* article is perhaps representative of the rising awareness among the public and media of the meeting point apparent in mass textile production of exploitative labor practices and the extensive impact of environmental damage. But the article also failed to elaborate on the effects felt within the wider ecosystems that constitute the environment. This is perhaps due to the absence of any visible wildlife to have survived the industrial onslaught; as of 2019, the Bangladeshi government declared three rivers in the Dhaka region "biologically dead" (Chowdhury 2019).

The fashion and textile industries are said to be one of the world's top water polluters.[4] The intensive use of chemicals and heavy metals in industrial dyeing processes is a significant part of the problem (Greenpeace International 2011; Greenpeace Germany 2021a and 2021b), but the production of textiles spans from plant cultivation and raw fiber extraction to yarn and garment production and includes all of the finishing processes in between. Add to that shipping, use, and disposal, and the fashion industry is estimated to be responsible for 4 percent of global carbon dioxide emissions (Berg et al. 2020, 5) and 35 percent of microplastic pollution, while 92 million tons of global textiles are disposed of annually (Niinimäki et al. 2020, 189). The unprecedented threat of the climate crisis and ecosystem degradation has advanced calls to address the sustainability of the fashion and textile industries. The debate has thus moved from the emphasis on human rights and consumer and commercial responsibilities that occurred after the Rana Plaza disaster in 2013 to one that also considers the rights of other species and ecosystems, recognizing that issues arising from unethical consumption are not mutually exclusive.

For Koki, the regularity of life-changing events happening at a global scale, and the questionable ethics of an industry he had committed to, spawned a persistent anxiety that prompted him to relocate to Amami from Tokyo to pursue a career in traditional craft. During my ten years of industry experience designing for luxury brands in London, Paris, and New York, I, too, became increasingly conscious of how globalization had closed the physical and cultural divide between factories in the Global South and design studios in the Global North. I watched (and participated in) the designing of four garment and accessories collections a year, which used exciting colors and fancy finishes to capture the whims of the market. Manufacturing agents in countries such as China and India were required to meet quality standards and ethical regulations via the brand's in-house corporate social responsibility policies, yet outsourced factories—and ultimately the health and well-being of workers and ecosystems—were at the same time being squeezed by studio managers to lower production costs to increase the brand's profit margins.[5] The demands that mass manufacturing and high levels of consumerism had on the environment and labor force sat uncomfortably with me, and so in New York my interest in craft expanded, taking me to MONO JAPAN, an annual trade show of contemporary Japanese craft held in the Netherlands. It was here that I participated in a group dorozome workshop with Yukihito Kanai, thirty-eight, son of the Shachō and second-generation dyer from Kanai Kougei.[6]

Yukihito-san had traveled six thousand miles to promote his family's business and Amamian culture and had brought with him to Europe the "earth" of Amami.[7] Dorozome uses a liquid made from the boiled wood of a local tree and Amamian mud to create shades from red brick to chocolate black with which to color textiles. The process was compelling, and Amami, a paradise of nature cloaked in subtropical rainforest and surrounded by coral reefs, provided craftworkers with abundant materials. Having made the move to academia, I asked Yukihito-san there and then whether I might come to Kanai Kougei, work as an unpaid apprentice, and carry out twelve months of ethnography in Amami. With an area of 712.35 square kilometers and a population of around 63,000 people, Amami is a small but immensely biodiverse island located in the Ryūkyū archipelago with an average mean temperature of 70 degrees Fahrenheit (figures I.2 and I.3). As a former stop on the historic trading routes between mainland Japan, the former Okinawan Ryūkyū kingdom, Taiwan, and China, culturally it borrows from these dominant forces.[8] Yet as an island it developed its own social and cultural practices. Examples include a popular music genre called *shima-uta*; a form of religious practice led by female priestesses known as *noro* and *yuta*; the island's own variant of the Japanese language, *shimayumuta*; and a kimono cloth claiming a lineage of 1,300 years—Oshima tsumugi (figure I.4). In recent years Amami's rich cultural and environmental heritage has drawn migrants moving from mainland Japanese cities looking for slower lifestyles and lower costs of living with access to culture, nature, and community.[9] Epitomizing contemporary Amamian cool, being a place that straddles the history and future of Japanese craft, Kanai Kougei has become a magnet for these migrants and increasingly a number of global brands.

While Koki had migrated to Amami to engage in learning the techniques involved in weaving a complex and beautiful traditional silk textile, what made Kanai Kougei of interest to me was its approach to evolving local traditions to make them relevant to contemporary markets and concerns. While it was a booming business in the mid-twentieth century employing twenty thousand residents, today the *tsumugi* industry exists precariously, having faced significant

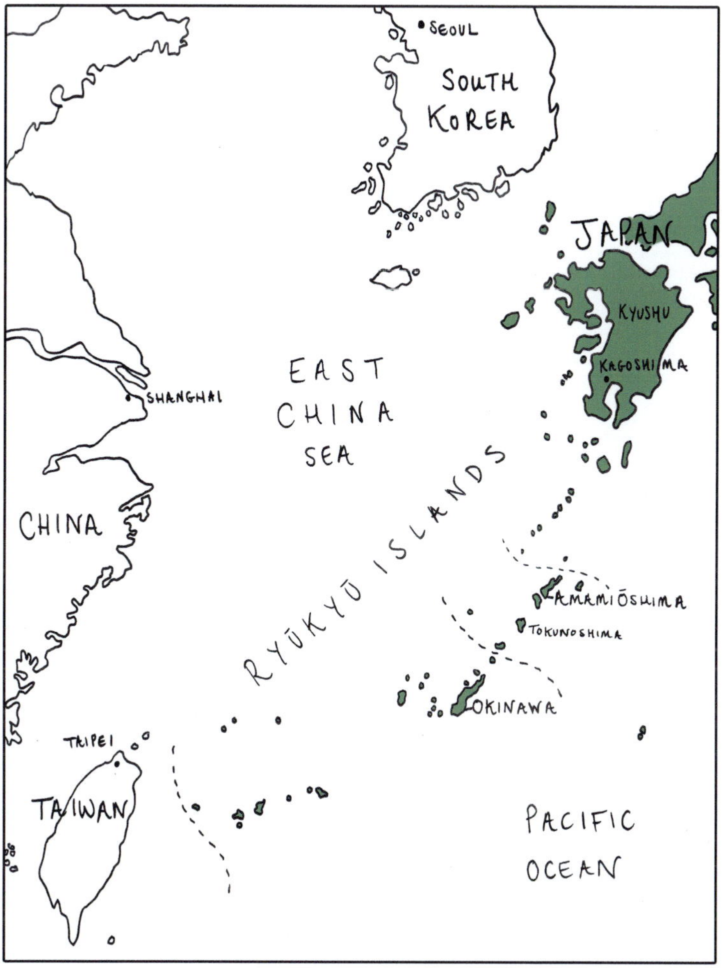

Figure I.2 *The Ryūkyū Islands, with dotted lines indicating the boundaries of the island groups.*

economic difficulties since Japan's economic downturn in the 1990s alongside changing cultural norms around wearing kimono. Kanai Kougei continues to participate in and support tsumugi production, but, to sustain its business and the future of the craft, the workshop has established a contemporary apparel business and joined a growing number of companies across Japan offering their own products and services directly to customers. This means that *kusakizome* (dyeing with plant and tree materials) is available as a technique for hire.

In line with the emergent interest in traditional, "eco-friendly" techniques, a shift in concern has occurred in regard to ways the industry colors cloth (Woodcock

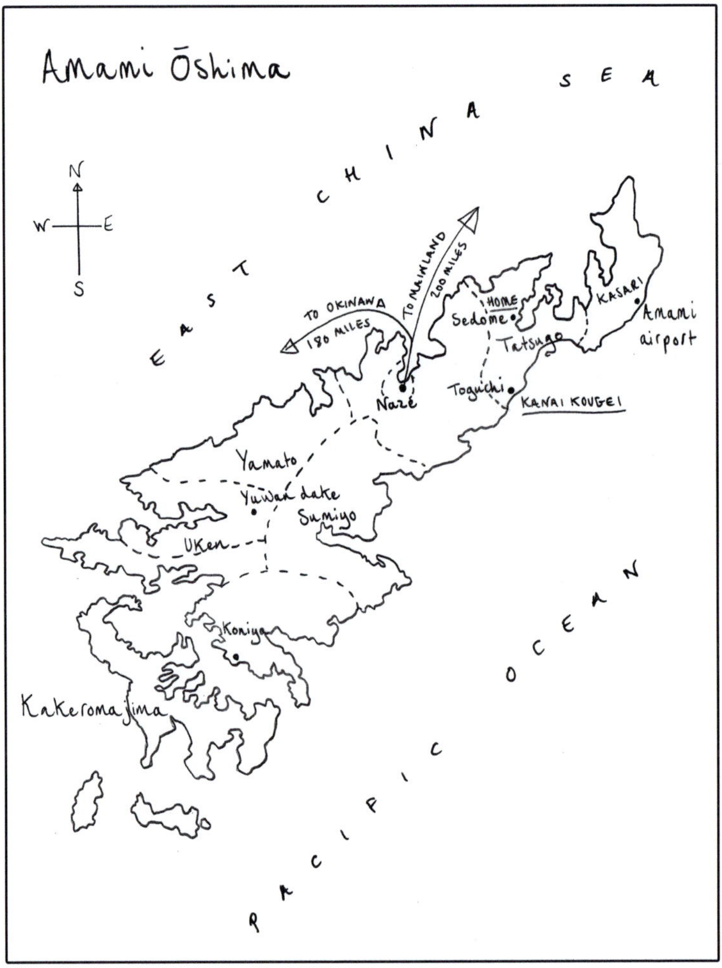

Figure 1.3 *A map of Amami Ōshima showing key sites.*

2021). Designers and brands of fashion and home wares have begun to question the impact of synthetic colorants for human and ecosystem health and are commissioning the dyeing of textiles in geographic areas recognized for their local industries.[10] These narrators from outside of the craft community reference historically important materials and processes and their strong links with local culture and nature, which emanate from the site of production.[11] In 1856, during the midst of the Industrial Revolution in Europe, the petrochemical dye industry was kick-started when British chemist William Henry Perkin accidentally synthesized "mauvine" from coal tar, but before that, globally sourced organic materials

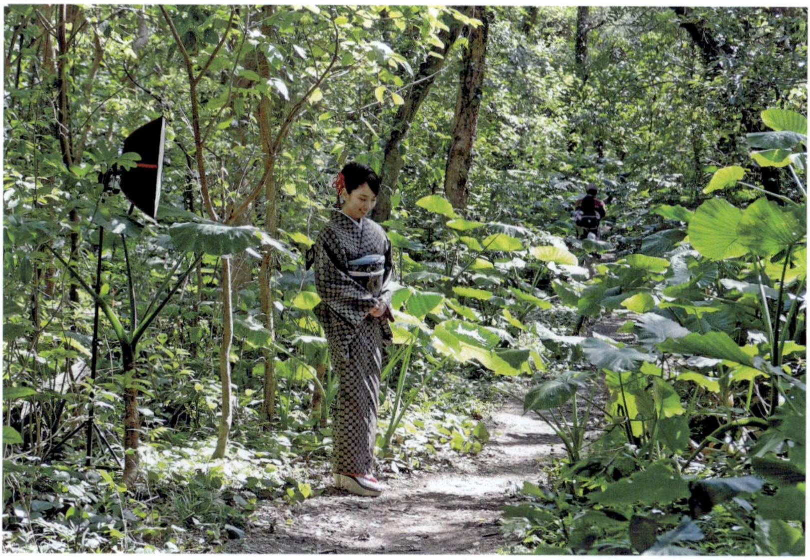

Figure 1.4 *An Oshima tsumugi photo shoot.*

were used to color the world's cloth (see Schneider 1987, 427–31).[12] Synthetic dyes replaced natural variants because they were more economically efficient and stable and offered vibrant new colors to a growing consumer market (see chapter 2). Throughout the Global North, many traditional textile processes have been superseded by industrial variants, but despite reduced output, Japan's regionally specific textiles have remained relatively resilient, including the use of natural dyestuffs in their production. This can be attributed to Japan's late industrialization, which occurred predominantly within the last century and accelerated after World War II. But a combination of government cultural preservation measures, the willingness of craftspeople to adapt to new materials and technologies, and the importance of craft as visual cues for national identity has meant the country's textile traditions continue to be held in high regard, making Japan a significant site for study.

The participation of a number of young Japanese dye craftspeople in MONO JAPAN—some of whom feature in this book—led me to consider how small-scale traditional craft, historically defined by its territorial region (Thomas et al. 2013), fits within the global picture. These pre-fieldwork encounters demonstrated that, while niche and local, the natural dyeing community is an international network. But in contrast to the production dynamics happening at the corporation scale, the people I encountered were a "community of practice" (Lave and

Wenger 1991) sharing knowledge, contacts, materials, debates, ideas, and ideals.[13] In their classic work on the anthropology of textiles, *Cloth and Human Experience*, Annette Weiner and Jane Schneider (1989, 3) state that cloth is "a convincing analog for the regenerative and degenerative processes of life, and as a great connector, binding humans not only to each other but to the ancestors of their past and the progeny of the future." Rather than by coincidence, it was because of the global discourse on sustainability and its intersection with traditional craft that Koki and I met at Kanai Kougei that day. Uncertainty about the future was generating a catalyst for change within our industry, and as I discovered, the most interesting developments were happening at the grassroots level.

By reviving kusakizome at a precarious time for their industry, the craftspeople at Kanai Kougei are engaging with global environmental issues and the preservation of Japan's traditional craft techniques on their own terms. Yet this raises critical questions: What does it mean for small-scale traditional craft processes, reliant on local materials, natural resources, and labor, to be propelled into a global market? How do the custodians of a craft negotiate the expectations and demands inherent in this contradiction? And what kinds of concessions must craftspeople make to their ideals if they want to sustain their business? Much of this book revolves around negotiating these terms, particularly between an old and new generation of craftsperson as they debate the tension between the need to innovate to stay economically viable and the desire to preserve, a desire that can so easily become reduced to the ideology of sustainability. I ask whether traditional crafting communities are equipped to translate their low-impact products and processes for contemporary commodity markets, meeting the quality, quantity, costs, and product longevity demanded by the market while maintaining their commitment to the integrity of their work and without being detrimental to the health of local ecologies. At the core of the dynamics that underpin *Dyeing with the Earth* is a tension between the promotion of resources such as craft traditions and local ecosystems for prosperity, their ability to be sustained for perpetuity, and the ways in which related uncertainties about their future function as productive and sustaining forces. In the context of my field site these dynamics combine to generate my core research questions: Can local craft processes and ecologies of production sustain a community socially, economically, and environmentally? And if so, what can we learn from such communities, and how might positive action be scaled up?

When I arrived in Amami in 2017, I had been drawn by dorozome and the specificity of this esoteric textile-dyeing process unique in Japan and developed only here because of local ecology, geology, and, as I will go on to describe, the sociopolitical history of the Ryūkyūs. But what I didn't imagine was how

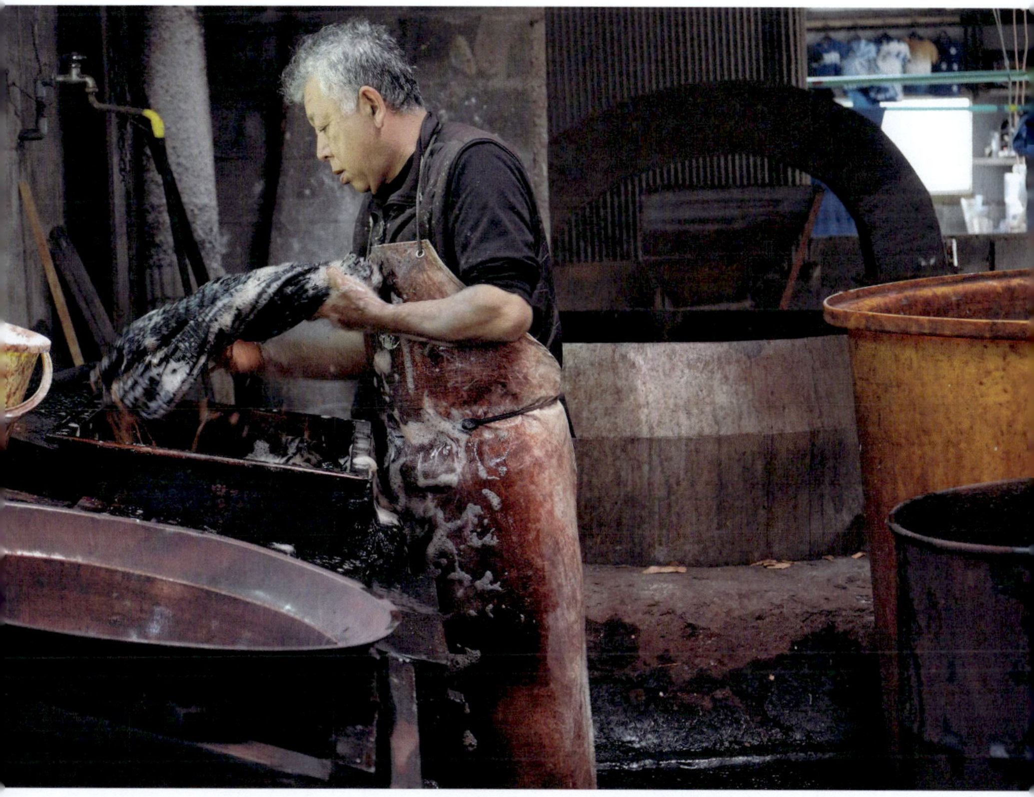

Figure 1.5 *The Shachō dyeing cloth using the dorozome technique.*

the research would develop with an aim to understand the craftsperson's wider relationship with nature, as imagined through the body, local discourse, craft materials, and resources. This research therefore moves beyond a study of people who dye and their dyeing materials to show the diversity of species interacting with the craft process. This specificity is crucial for understanding how local ecologies subject to resource extraction are informally subsumed into the island's economy and are then abstracted to join larger economic systems. My friend and colleague Kazuko told me on my first day working at Kanai Kougei that "in Amami, nothing is without nature." Local fruits and vegetables grown on village allotments, endangered frogs and newts living in the workshop's drains, domesticated cats and birds, aging technologies, weather and water systems, and the kami (gods) who watch over the workshop's furnace all contribute to a holistic sense of community, replete with its own harmonies and conflicts. The Shachō (figure I.5), too, highlighted the importance of nature, and I am indebted to him for the title of this book: "Nature (*shizen*) is at the heart of Oshima tsumugi and dorozome. The dyeing materials come from the trees, the mordant comes from the soil—we used to have a slogan at Kanai Kougei that was '*chikyū de someru*' (dyeing with the earth). This work is about dyeing with ingredients from the trees and the soil, natural things, so nature is important."

The Japanese word for nature, *shizen*, that the Shachō used, has been much discussed in Japanese studies (Asquith and Kalland 1997b, 8–10) because it was originally thought to reflect the more spiritual, inner nature of humanity, or "unconsciousness" (Moeran 1997, 86). In the Shachō's use of *shizen* I believe he was referencing the importance of the practical aspect of natural materials as being key to the dyeing process, as would be conceptualized along Western values of resource management. But it is important to note that the Shachō's slogan "dyeing with the earth" is referencing not only the soil but Earth (*chikyū*)—our planet—as being part of a dyeing cosmology. This is a specific worldview encompassing history, economics, science, nature, sociality, time, materiality, cultural practice, and aesthetics. The aim of highlighting this is not to engage in preindustrial nostalgia, to deny the existence or importance of synthetic materials and their use by craftspeople, including at Kanai Kougei, but rather to stress that to talk about natural dyeing among natural dyers in Amami, one needs to look beyond textiles. To define our individual but also our collective worldview, it is important to consider matters such as food, birds, water, and trees and the unique set of relations among them. The chapters that follow are therefore extensive in their reach to reflect the way I conceptualize natural dyeing as a cosmology. I argue that if we are to take responsibility for our ecological impact on the planet, we have to think beyond the scope of individual manufacturing sectors and the commodities they sell, to the everyday lives of factory workers and their overseers. By expanding the boundaries of production and taking an ecological perspective, we can begin to see how the producers of commodities make sense of the world and how they gather and use resources, whether material or immaterial, in order to sustain their livelihoods.

From Sustainability to Sustaining Processes

I worked as an unpaid dyeing assistant for one year, during which I spent between two and four days per week dyeing yarns, clothing, accessories, and home wares for Kanai Kougei's apparel business. This is a method I call participant apprenticeship, following in the footsteps of Michael Coy, who first surveyed apprenticeship as a research technique in 1989, and architect turned anthropologist Trevor Marchand (2010, 2022), whose research with craftspeople has demonstrated how apprenticeship allows for insight into pedagogy, expertise, and knowledge transmission but also unparalleled engagement with materials, process, and environment. Having trained in fashion and textiles and worked in the industry, I had the skills necessary to quickly learn kusakizome, although the process was unfamiliar enough that I came to it with a fresh pair of eyes. Given my creative background, I was drawn to produce sketches, photographs, and prints during my time in Amami (except where otherwise noted, all artwork and photographs in this book are my own). As a member of the extended textile community—an "insider-outsider" (Burke 1989)—I was thus able to offer my own professional proficiencies in design and practice in exchange for the acquisition of insider knowledge.

A number of anthropologists have studied textiles by seeking a "making point of view" (Bunn 2011) and demonstrating how the localized production of textiles can reveal larger social, economic, political, and environmental happenings (see Ahmed 2002; Küchler and Miller 2005; Portisch 2010; Makovicky 2010; Nascimento 2023). Stephanie Bunn, who has worked with Kyrgyzstani felt makers (Bunn 2010) and Scottish basket weavers (Bunn and Mitchell 2020), describes this generative approach as an important intervention to the study of material culture because it uncovers forms of knowledge, skill, and sociality that are difficult to garner by engaging with finished artifacts alone. Being embedded at Kanai Kougei, I built strong relationships with my work colleagues, the Kanai family, and their business and friendship groups, many of whom I was able to interview. I engaged with the daily running of the workshop, observed who was coming and going, and tracked orders as they arrived and were shipped out. I became acquainted with dyeing materials, over time establishing their origins, understanding their application and how they were transformed. My ability to acquire and use practical skills took priority over verbal communication, and learning while doing improved my Japanese and formed a constructive methodological ground.[14] This method of immersion, which Marilyn Strathern (2023, 3) says facilitates "'finding' the unlooked-for," led to the diversity of chapters that follow.

The importance given in this book to addressing small-scale traditional craft environments does not lie in any romanticizing sense of their exceptionality or outsider status. Rather, I argue that such environments have become entwined in the sustainability policies of public entities and global corporations. *Sustainability* can be traced back to the term *sustained yields* used in seventeenth- and eighteenth-century German forestry, which suggests that resource extraction should account for natural regeneration to avoid resource depletion. The word was little used until it was adopted by environmentalists in the 1970s, when scientists became increasingly concerned about overpopulation and overconsumption exceeding the earth's capacity to regenerate (Purvis et al. 2019, 682). It was around the turn of the millennium, however, that intergovernmental organizations such as the United Nations and the International Union for Conservation of Nature developed the three "pillars" of sustainability—the interconnecting spheres of the environment, society, and the economy—also committing to sustainable development initiatives (685). Broadly thinking, sustainability raises the question of how to manage the health and resilience of resources so that economic growth can continue, while sustaining what we have and the circles of extraction that came before (Brightman and Lewis 2017). Its breadth and ambiguity have allowed it to be employed disingenuously for the purpose of greenwashing or by those genuinely misinformed, with anthropologists defining sustainability as a "malleable" (Yamada et al. 2022, 3), "mythical" (Checker et al. 2015), and even "utopian" (Greenberg 2013, 55) discourse.

Sustainability's slow rise in public awareness from academia to public policy and its eventual dissemination in the media accumulated in a social imaginary that by the early 2000s began to influence individual behaviors in both consumption practices and working environments. In the fashion industry, outdoor clothing brand Patagonia's sustainability initiatives via product recycling, materials innovation, landscape conservation, and even ownership model have become world-renowned. The Kering Group, owner of Gucci and Saint Laurent, meanwhile, became "luxury's activist" in 2015 by publishing its environmental impact, and in 2020 the company released a "biodiversity strategy" to restore and regenerate habitats while committing to halving its greenhouse gas emissions by 2025 (Friedman 2015). Companies such as Patagonia and Kering operate under an inherent paradox and are not without controversy, but in adopting whole-systems thinking—that is, trying to address sustainability across the complexity of their operations—they remain in the minority. More commonly, market approaches to sustainability are apparent in brands identifying problematic processes and materials and adopting "drop-in replacements" (Ginsberg and Chieza 2018), as demonstrated by the trend of switching from synthetic to natural dyes for coloring textiles. Materials are the most visible and tangible aspects of production and can define how a consumer might gauge a product's sustainability.

At the industry level, recycled textiles made from used cloth or the waste of other industries have become commonplace, with polyester frequently made from used plastic bottles and fishing equipment, while other types of cloth and leather have been developed using orange peels, pineapple leaves, and cow's milk (Stenton et al. 2021). Anthropologist Lucy Norris (2010), who has researched secondhand clothing economies and textile recycling, brings a wealth of experience to contemporary discussions on what are widely termed "circular economies." Norris describes a circular economy as a "utopian vision" and "sustainable solution" for a thriving industry that is "systemic by design, close-looped, restorative, waste-free, based on effectiveness and runs on renewable energy" (2019, 205). While Norris appreciates the potential of circular economies, she questions the closed-loop system by suggesting that resources and technological innovations are held within the grasp of global corporations that favor recycling over reusing and may let producers and consumers off the hook for overconsumption by establishing a guilt-free, moral economy. The introduction of new materials on a global scale can also impact society in unexpected but often quite radical ways (see Küchler 2018). Plastic pollution, for example, is routinely in the headlines, and microplastics, including those shed from synthetic textiles, are said to be doing unimaginable harm in the most pristine environments, from Antarctica (Aves et al. 2022) to the human placenta, entering our bodies and those of other organisms via environmental exposure (Prata et al. 2020; Carrington 2024).

For commissioning designers and consumers, an alternative to circular economies is to switch the scale of production and adopt traditional craft. Traditional craft suits sustainability narratives because practices have been developed over long periods of time within the environmental, social, and economic limits of a given geography. To be sustainable—to have lasted as long as they have—notions of care and regeneration have been essential, whether securing the continuous supply and health of natural resources, transferring knowledge to a new generation, or adapting to consumer trends to maintain a market. Using "craft" in the abstract, promotional literature references slow production, biodegradable materials, handmade quality, and associations with localism, community, and sustainability. By extracting this value, outside businesses frame themselves as preservers of culture and custodians of the natural environment, encouraging consumers to "care at a distance" (Trentmann 2007).

However, anthropologists have shown that this form of ethical consumption is not without its problems, and sustainable fashion can be seen within this lineage. "Emotional branding" (Trentmann 2007, 1083) promoting reciprocity and solidarity has been used to "mobilise political traditions and value systems that favor certain identities and relationships" for decades (1086). Shaila Seshia Galvin (2018) has demonstrated this inequality with her study of organic rice cultivation in India, where she shows how the Global North set criteria for producers that are not always suited to local realities. Her participant farmers struggled to adhere to the global bureaucracy that organic certification required, straining local social and economic relations. This demonstrates the difficulty of translating small-scale, responsible production to global commercial markets with long supply chains embedded in the market economy. Despite often being established in good faith, ethical consumption is based on an ideal that "performs morality" (Galvin 2018), offsetting anxiety about the conditions of production. However, this action does not necessarily lead consumers to educate themselves on the social, political, or economic inequalities faced by producers or to grasp the extent of environmental pollution that might lead to their own behavioral changes. Rather, it might be said to replicate the same capitalist systems responsible for social and ecological damage in the first place.

While I appreciate that work carried out by governments, NGOs, academics, and corporate giants around the three pillars of sustainability is important and necessary, this book follows a different path, driven by a contrasting logic of scale. Existing at a universalizing scale, sustainability rhetoric has developed into a "catchall" to communicate a complexity of practices, materials, indexes, and goals that offer "solutions" compatible with economic growth while sustaining the status quo. This ideology has become widespread among the public, yet its rhetorical influence is all too often focused on ends-oriented change. While the impact of sustainability discourse can be seen on both individual and systemic behaviors, such shifts are often at the level of taking singular actions with definitive goals rather than promoting ongoing, adaptive change. The fashion and textile sector is a prime example, because despite best efforts to improve material components, labor conditions, environmental impacts, and carbon outputs, the mission is always flawed because commerce cannot function without the expectation of profit, which is difficult to achieve within such confines.

Problems lie between discourse and practice but also with what is realistic within the limits of existing frameworks, demonstrating that sustainability is just another ideology detached from lived experience. Anthropologist Kedron Thomas (2020) demonstrates this in her study with designers and business managers in small- to large-scale fashion companies in the United States and UK. While the individuals she interviewed were passionate about sustainability, she identifies implicit contradictions between sustainability, growth, and extractive tendencies of the industry (Thomas 2020, 733). She highlights, for instance, how sustainability requires long-term vision, but individuals are constrained by short-term profit and performance goals (727). In line with calls within anthropology to prioritize diverse and local understandings of sustainability (Brightman and Lewis 2017), the aim of this book is to place a more nuanced dynamic between the natural environment and cultural, material, and economic resource extraction at the heart of a discourse around textile production. This ethnography instead explores *sustaining processes*—those small actions my participants carry out on the ground in order to maintain resources, whether cultural, economic, or environmental, while being subject to pressure from local hierarchies, municipal bureaucrats, or commissioning designers.

How Amami sustains its local economy and community via craft is certainly a concern for my participants. But opinions surrounding the environmental impact of craft production were not always so clearly voiced. This is not to say that concerns and resolutions did not exist, but rather they might be said to have been conceptualized differently from those of designers and makers who voice moral claims in their sales pitch that might be reflected in their product's mode of production. Instead, the sustaining processes that care for the local economy, community, and environment are embedded in everyday practices of Amami's craftspeople and are imagined through their work as dyers, responsibilities toward friends and family, respect for local customs, and education about the environment. Because limitations exist, concerns are played against one another, meaning that contradictions and complicities are certainly at work—as will be addressed throughout this book.

As such, my decision to research small-scale traditional craft processes is driven by the argument that such sites are not hangovers from a preindustrial era but important registers of contemporary developments around how natural resources are valued, used, and sustained by communities. On the surface, these sites do not appear so prone to the profit-driven standardizations of global textile commerce, but at the ground level they offer an entrance for the ethnographer to understand these evolving forces, as they tangibly impact people, processes, and ecosystems. This research aligns with more recent industry developments that see local textile producers as a part of "bioregional fashion ecosystems" (Branwell et al. 2020), where producers of fibers, materials, dyestuffs, and garments are engaged in short, local supply chains that encourage regenerative agriculture, waste reduction, soil restoration, and "soil-to-soil" circularity. This is well recognized in the US-based nonprofit organization Fibershed (Burgess 2019), which brought together networks of producers in California and spread across the United States and into affiliate networks in countries such as the UK (Norris 2019), Denmark, India, and Australia. Rather than only *sustaining* resources, these producers seek to go further and *regenerate* the health of local ecosystems and communities (Wahl 2020). Regenerative-systems thinking therefore seeks to be net positive, with businesses expected to contribute more than they extract.

Scholarship in fashion and textiles has advocated for "slow," "local," "circular," and "regenerative" cloth and clothing that replicates these values, while increasing the social significance of the item and stretching its lifespan (Fletcher and Tham 2019; Klepp and Tobiasson 2022; McHattie and Stewart Sherrod 2023). These approaches align with the movement of degrowth that promotes the reduction of energy and resource consumption (Hickel 2021), a concept even being picked up by designer brands (Paton 2022). Yet as Thomas's (2020, 736) study highlights, significant gaps in knowledge and awareness persist among design professionals and consumers about the conditions under which clothing is made and the challenges producers face. The question also arises of how one contributes more than one extracts when craftspeople are struggling to sustain themselves. Whether the discourse centers on sustainability or regeneration, I suggest that the same complexity of issues arises, and, as this book demonstrates, the best intentions often have unintended consequences and compromises to ideals must be struck. Ethnography therefore allows one to ask what a study at the mesoscale of an ecology of textile production might contribute to larger discussions about resource extraction and sustainability as opposed to the reverse.

Sustaining Tradition and the Environment in Contemporary Japan

Industrialization arrived relatively late in Japan, meaning the micro and macro effects of industrial capitalism and globalization on local communities and ecosystems can still be located geographically or drawn from the memories of fieldwork participants. This is the case in Amami, where residents lived a subsistence lifestyle until the 1960s and development and modernization arrived rapidly with an influx of government funding; Japan was the world's second largest economy by 1968 (Kuwahara 2001).[15] Oshima tsumugi (figure I.6) played a major role in developing the economic and social infrastructure of Amami—where between the 1950s and 1980s many residents' mothers and grandmothers were the main breadwinners, weaving on home looms, which can today be found discarded in backyards. Although tsumugi is not the focus of this study, the remnants of this boom-and-bust industry are the foundation on which *Dyeing with the Earth* is built. In the context of Amami, where nature and culture are intimately linked and tied to the social, economic, and material fabric of the island, it is essential to consider the preservation strategies implemented at the national level in response to rapid development and how these contrast with local approaches such as those taken by craftspeople at Kanai Kougei.

Japan is world-renowned for its government-led Intangible Cultural Property (ICP) scheme (*mukei bunkazai),* with policy first enacted in 1868 but expanded and formalized in 1950 to protect cultural properties—that is, performing arts and craft techniques—that were feared to be disappearing under the pressure of industrialization (Goto 2013, 572). The ICP program provides infrastructural

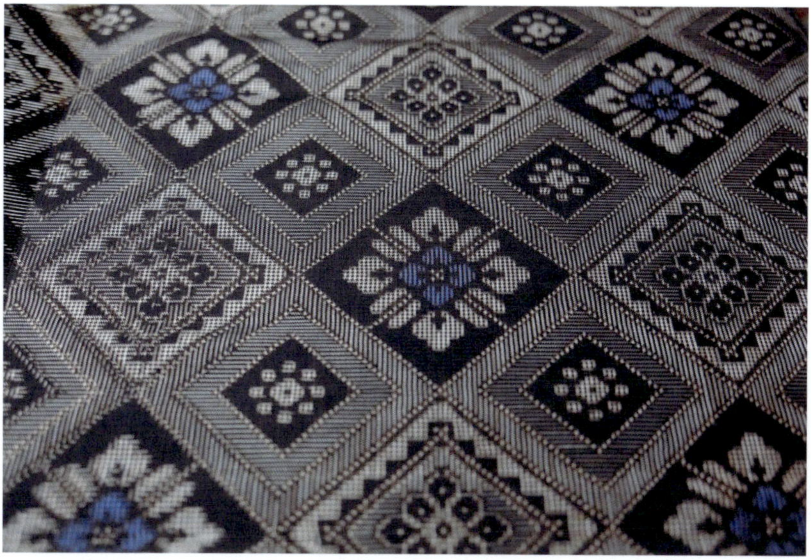

Figure 1.6 *Oshima tsumugi woven in the Tatsugo pattern on the loom.*

and financial support to protect the skills of Japanese arts and crafts of outstanding artistic value, and its most infamous feature is its Living National Treasure recognition, which provides holders with the prestige, finance, and support to continue their work and pass on the techniques. The Japanese scheme preceded the global initiative of UNESCO by more than fifty years, which adopted its own intangible culture heritage policy in 2003 to further sustainable development goals (567). Yet there is a common misconception that because Japan continues to invest heavily in culture, the livelihoods of craftspeople are secure. While the reputation of this scheme is good for Japan, promoting a strong national identity deployed as a form of soft power globally, it is not without problems and has in some ways proved unpopular with craftspeople, as will be discussed in chapter 1.

In contrast to the investment poured into cultural properties, it wasn't until the 1990s that the government turned its attention to its natural properties, which have experienced widespread and destructive environmental change resulting from industrialization. This damage has been far-reaching, with little land left untouched by industrial or infrastructural projects; 50 percent of Japan's coastline, for example, has been altered by concrete. Throughout this book I seek to understand how natural resources have historically been treated in Amami and across Japan for economic gain. I show how the Japanese government has consistently prioritized its economy above the life of its subjects, a habit that has also filtered down to practices performed by ordinary citizens who may choose economic efficiency over environmental responsibility. This counters the popular argument that the Japanese people are fundamentally "close to nature" through the traditions of animism embedded in Shinto, Buddhism, and Amami's own religious culture. Nevertheless, because of its geography and relative isolation, Amami's environment has fared better than that in other parts of Japan.

In 2003 UNESCO announced that Amami's virgin rainforests, mangrove forests, and coral reefs, home to thousands of rare and endemic species of flora and fauna, were of "outstanding universal value," making them a "major focus" for conservation (UNESCO, n.d.) In 2016 the Japanese government registered Amami's forests as a tentative UNESCO World Natural Heritage site, and together with neighboring Tokunoshima and northern Okinawa it was awarded this recognition in 2021. Although organizations such as UNESCO claim their primary aim is conservation, the Japanese government has been open about how World Natural Heritage can boost tourism (Brasor 2019)—and from my observations in Amami, businesses' and local authorities' desire to produce revenue appeared to be the motivating force behind the application, while wildlife protection was seen as a bonus. By demarking the intangible—unique skills, natural landscapes, and endangered species—as forms of property, the government is able to impose a level of control and appropriate and repackage these entities to increase their economic potential using the rhetoric of preservation as draws for domestic and international tourism.

This has been particularly relevant for Japan's depopulated, economically depressed rural regions that have for decades been propped up by the state but play host to "traditional" Japan through crafts, landscapes, nature, foodstuffs, and festivals. These rural regions are areas where land has little value as property, with its value in decline across Japan since 1992. Although urban land prices recently began to recover in response to the rise in international tourism, they have continued to decline in rural locales where depopulation has led to the closure of local facilities such as schools and hospitals while the uptake of farming remains low (Kyodo News 2018a). The role the ICP scheme plays in rural areas is perhaps an ultimate outgrowth of Japan's adoption of a Western capitalist economic model after the Meiji Restoration (around 1868)—a period of political and social change impacted by the United States forcing the country to open to trade—and its simultaneous strengthening of national cultural identity as a resistance to Western colonizing forces. Within this logic, state intervention to preserve cultural identity, located for example in a textile or an environment, is based on the cultural "property's" ability to cohere value and, by extension, to be economically productive locally while also performing in international commodity markets. Both ICP and World Natural Heritage are schemes that make global appeals to protect the unique properties of nation-states to *sustain* the "local" for perpetuity but also *promote* it for prosperity.

Amami's cultural and natural properties continue to be exploited by an "ideology of improvement" (Bhandar 2018, 8), making them subject to appropriation by the government and the market as assets. This ideology, whose origins can be found in the agricultural land improvement of the European Enlightenment, justifies the ownership and adaptation of the natural environment so it may be "put to profit" (Drayton 2000, 52). Legal scholar Brenna Bhandar's work in exploring the role of this ideology in settler colonial narratives shows how existing communities living on the land become bound up within the logic of improvement: "Communities who lived as rational, productive economic actors, evidenced by particular forms of cultivation, were deemed to be proper subjects of law and history; those who did not were deemed to be in need of improvement as much as their waste lands were" (2018, 8). Human and cultural capital is here intertwined with both the use and exchange value of land—outside of this framework, there is just waste. If imperial Japan's nineteenth-century resistance to Western colonialism led to the adoption of capitalism's imperative to improve and make profitable both land and its occupants, the tendency for the state to internally claim both the natural environment and the cultural production of its citizens "for the nation" is deeply tied to such an economic logic. With the World Natural Heritage recognition, I asked Yukihito-san whether the local authorities had considered investing in local businesses to make their operations more sustainable, whole-systems thinking that would boost the island's environmental credentials. Yukihito-san said not at all, but the local government had asked whether he would accept tour groups focused on Amamian nature and culture. Bringing tourists to Kanai Kougei would emphasize how Amamian culture is linked with nature and how its outputs are therefore sustainable (figure I.7). Yukihito-san refused, saying the local authorities were simply following government instructions and organized such activities with "no heart." One therefore needs to ask, How can economic thinking and the preservation of natural and cultural properties coexist without such extractive (and therefore ultimately corrosive) conditions?

In opposition to the motives behind these "globally hegemonic concepts of sustainability" (Brightman and Lewis 2017, 6), I consider how the desire to control both traditions and resources via the global circulation of ideas has both positively and negatively influenced government rhetoric and legislation to impact local communities and ecosystems. These global movements are what anthropologist Michael Hathaway calls "environmental winds," a metaphor coined by scientists

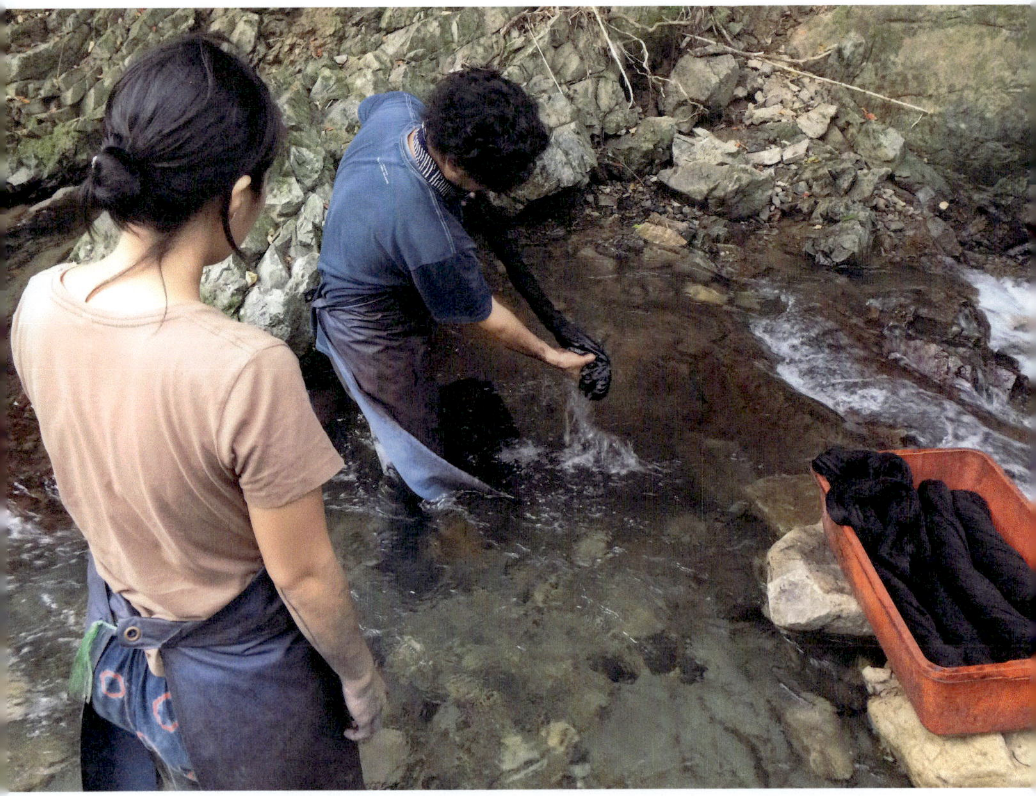

Figure I.7 *Yukihito Kanai and Kazuko washing yarns at the river. Note the rocks stained red by techigi dye.*

and conservationists based in Yunnan Province, China, which "describe times when political movements brought life-changing consequences." Hathaway's fieldwork with conservationists shows how the adoption of Western environmentalism brings global ideas "into being," but locally they may transform "into something quite different from their origins" (2013, 3). This demonstrates a two-way knowledge exchange showing how global ideas, if they are to take root, must be adapted to local contexts. For residents in Amami, there is little public engagement with ICP or World Natural Heritage, which are considered money-making schemes for the prefecture lacking "heart" rather than movements that will positively impact their lives. I suggest instead that the sustaining processes carried out by ordinary people in Amami are more flexible and responsive than those instituted from above and might be framed as an unintended consequence of anxiety about the unknown.

Uncertainty as a Catalyst for Change

Feelings of uncertainty hover precariously throughout this ethnography, but I argue that they are also present at a level that transcends the individual or the community, tied to the sense of a universalizing drive to *sustain* various aspects of nature, society, and culture through their harnessing as generators of capital. Bhandar after Cedric. J Robinson writes that "racial representations of preexisting cultural forms . . . and capitalist infrastructure" are produced in times of "uncertainty and flux" (2018, 15). Although this statement relates to the fact that violent racial regimes become more entrenched in times of uncertainty—through the rise of nationalism, the dispossession of Indigenous peoples, and the strengthening of borders, for example—governments and communities also draw on difference and appropriate it for identity-building in periods of economic, social, political, and environmental flux. Craft historian Tanya Harrod writes, in relation to the exhibition of traditional crafts in 1930s Britain, when the nation experienced a time of global economic and political volatility, that "craftsmanship in the broadest sense was invariably invoked to reassure" (2001, 37). Scholars of Japan have also shown how historical culture—from landscapes to rituals and crafts—have been monetized in periods of uncertainty (see Robertson 1991; Brandt 2007; Aso 2014). I engage with this literature throughout this book, especially as I explicate the rise and fall of the Oshima tsumugi industry after World War II. But what I am also able to show is that culturally valuable kusakizome is being promoted as a sustainable fix to damaging mass production at a time when environmental uncertainty permeates our lives. In this new configuration, the resourcefulness of rural societies, those left behind by economic progress, is now being turned to for answers in times of uncertainty.

Uncertainty is often seen socially as a negative phenomenon that has increased with the rapid and mutable nature of modernity. But if it is understood as part of everyday lived encounters, as it is for my participants in Amami, it may provide opportunities for reflection and positive action. My fieldwork consistently demonstrates how uncertainty about the future can be seen as a catalyst for change, since it allows one to become aware of and confront dominant structural systems that may have previously seemed monolithic. Over the centuries, Amami has been subject to the "ideology of improvement" with its land, people, nature, and traditions exploited for capitalist gain. Yet Amamians have consistently shown they are both literally and metaphorically able to weather a storm. The function of uncertainty as a productive and sustaining force can be traced back through Amamian history, particularly in the way it has been embedded in nature and spirituality. As American anthropologist Douglas G. Haring puts it: "Educated Amamians often asked me . . . 'How does science explain the obvious facts of witchcraft and death by magical cursing?' 'How does one explain the frequent disappearances of villagers seduced by tree-spirits?' Personally I invoked the *habu* (vipers) and other poisonous snakes to explain disappearances, but this reasoning left hearers cold. . . . No one could believe that I took no stock in witches and black magic; they reasoned that my ignorance required protection" (1952, 70). Haring was dispatched to Amami to carry out an ethnographic study for six months between 1951 and 1952 at the behest of the occupying US Allied forces. His report (Haring 1952) and archive of visual materials kept at the University of Syracuse holds invaluable data that capture a moment in Amamian history that I reference frequently. The excerpt above is especially poignant because it captures a feeling of doubt that is difficult to locate, one that can be found throughout this book. Although Haring "invoked the *habu*" to explain disappearances, doubt is also embedded in his answer—after all, how would he know?

Amami's Indigenous religion has been compared to Japanese folk Shinto, which centers around spirits or kami (gods) residing in nature. It was led by a powerful theocracy of female priestesses called the noro and yuta, who followed orders from Okinawa's Ryūkyū kingdom. Although Amami was claimed by the Satsuma clan (modern-day Kagoshima Prefecture) in 1609, the spiritual authority of the noro and yuta remained. This meant that wantonly logging trees in Amami's sacred mountains was prohibited, with the population fearing retribution from forest-dwelling kami or interactions with local *yōkai* (supernatural beings). Today the wrath of the spiritual world has been largely replaced by the threat of retribution from local environmental authorities. Yet the anxieties of the past and of the present collide in the forest, meaning many residents avoid leisure in the mountains. In addition, the forests continue to be home to those same deadly habu that elevate the threat level of safe entry. Uncertainty, whether caused by kami, authorities, or snakes, has therefore acted to sustain Amami's forests (figure I.8).

While historical threats to life and livelihood have been natural or supernatural, concerned with snake bites, typhoons, fires, wars, or even black magic, since the postwar period Japan has increasingly been subject to man-made threats resulting from industrial capitalism—those that are somehow more unpredictable. These threats initially seemed place specific, but advanced telecommunications and media networks have created an impression that emerging themes might be shared globally. Anxieties about one's career, the availability of work, the future of local crafts, one's standing in the community, national security, the health of ecosystems, consequences of chemical use, the quality of the drinking water, polluted seas, threat to property by damaging weather, dangerous particulate

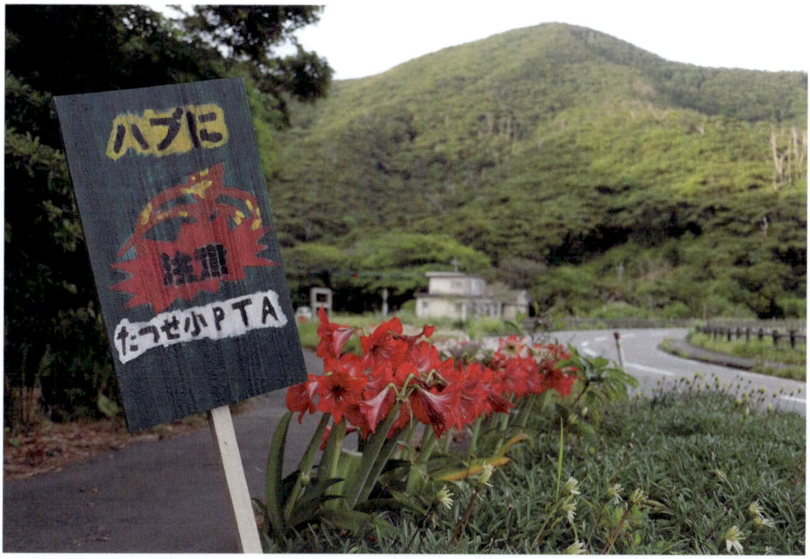

Figure 1.8 *A sign depicting red snakes reads, "Beware of habu! Elementary School PTA."*

matter 2.5 blowing in from China, access to sufficient childcare, the safety of foodstuffs—these *many* and *varied* concerns seemed all too familiar.

As members of what sociologist Ulrich Beck (1999) calls the "World-risk society"—a state encapsulating risk that goes beyond geographic boundaries—(cited in Yoneyama 2012) Japan's citizens have been subject to economic instability, the breakdown of social norms, and environmental destruction in the pursuit of economic growth. What became apparent through an analysis of my ethnographic data was that the spirits of the past, who I argue continue to grace everyday life in Amami, have been joined by what anthropologist Nils Bubandt (2017, G137) calls the "secular spirits of the Anthropocene": those unknowns that "ask us to notice the magic of the forces, human and nonhuman, that shape the atmosphere, biosphere, and lithosphere." Bubandt uses the example of a vast mud volcano that erupted in East Java swallowing twelve villages and displacing almost forty thousand people (G121). The volcano's eruption is thought to have been triggered by nearby oil drilling, although it was also attributed in some quarters to an earthquake. Bubandt explains that it is becoming increasingly difficult to "[distinguish] human from nonhuman forces" (G122) because human impact on geology can have as great an impact as a natural earthquake. This was the case in Japan during the triple disaster that began on March 11, 2011 (known hereafter as 3.11), when a 9.0 magnitude earthquake struck the Pacific coast off

Tohoku in northeast Japan, causing a tsunami with waves over forty meters high, which led to a radioactive spill at the Daiichi Nuclear Power Plant in Fukushima. Disasters of this kind are instances "where the forces of nature and human politics act to exacerbate each other," combining to become uncontrollable "secular spirits" (G124).

Before taking on the Anthropocene, Bubandt (2014, 35) examined the idea of "aporia" as an "analytical entrance point" to discuss the uncertainties and doubts that arose within his study of witchcraft in Indonesia, where witches called *gua* cause "social terror." *Aporia* is a complex term, with a history stretching back to Aristotle but rising again with poststructuralist philosophy and the work of Jacques Derrida in the 1970s. Peter Geschiere (2016, 244) helpfully summarizes an aporia as "a phenomenon that undermines all fixing parameters of knowledge," with witchcraft being "aporetic" and "so unsettling because it brings a confrontation with what is unknowable" (254). Bubandt explains that aporias are "those concerns that chafe the heels of the central dilemmas of how self, sociality, and time are made and unmade." They are invisible forces, "blind spots" of doubt, uncertainty, and anxiety that "grow out of and feed upon particular conceptions and practices of being" that are "embedded in particular historical, political, and cultural conditions" (Bubandt 2014, 38).

Bubandt's participants in Indonesia are particular because their belief in witchcraft fuses with modernity, exemplified by the mud volcano. But the "aporetic" is an interesting concept because it can be applied to those instances where nature collides with modernity through politics, economics, science, and technology. Satellites can predict the path of a typhoon, but the typhoon can change direction or gather strength, impacting an area in ways residents can only imagine. Measures can be implemented to limit the damage caused by earthquakes, but one cannot control the bureaucratic failings of states that provide essential infrastructure. The world is still recovering from the social, physical, environmental, and economic uncertainty and suffering of the COVID-19 pandemic, a coronavirus thought to have originated in bats captured for bushmeat. These collisions, or "secular spirits" (Bubandt 2017, G124), "[undermine] all fixing parameters of knowledge" (Geschiere 2016, 244), swerving our attempts to control or explain them through science, technology, or politics. But what comes to light in moments of crisis is that the institutions we trust also construct their own realities that include an embedded element of doubt.

In sociologist John Law's *After Method: Mess in Social Science Research* (2004), Law states that "ethnography lets us see the relative messiness of practice. It looks behind the official accounts of method (which are often clean and reassuring) to try to understand the often ragged ways in which knowledge is produced in research" (18–19). Law's work comes from science and technology studies, so many of his examples stem from laboratories and hospitals, where "science *produces* its realities as well as describing them" (13). He references Bruno Latour and Steve Woolgar (1986), who claim that "the tribe of scientists . . . are not very different from any other tribe": "Scientists have a culture. They have beliefs. They have practices. They work, they gossip, and they worry about the future. And, somehow or other, out of their work, their practices and their beliefs, they produce knowledge, scientific knowledge, accounts of reality" (Law 2004, 19). Problems arise when different "tribes" of scientists, but also societies with distinct cultural practices, produce "multiplicity"—different accounts of reality—as was exemplified in Douglas Haring's account of habu and tree spirits among Amamians in the 1950s. Law turns to anthropologist Annemarie Mol, whose ethnographic work draws attention to multiplicity in medical research. Law, after Mol, asks: "If there are different realities, then lots of new questions arise. How do they relate? How do we choose between them? How should we choose between them? . . . If truth by itself is not a gold standard, then perhaps there may be additional *political* reasons for preferring and enacting one kind of reality rather than another" (2004, 13).

What my ethnography was able to show are the methods by which societies seek "resolutions" (Pelkmans 2013, 3) in order to come to terms with their own doubts. But it also shows their "*political* reasons" for trusting one version of reality above another that "energizes" (4) them into taking a particular action. This is a point that connects uncertainty with sustainability, because sustainable commodities rely on the social imaginary of uncertainty, or the "fix" that allows uncertainty about the future to dissipate and consumption to continue as normal. The fashion industry uses its own version of reality, in what might be seen as an ideology of improvement, by identifying a threat to its economic foundation and "putting it to profit" (Drayton 2000, 52). A non-Japanese menswear designer based in Tokyo, for example, who dyed his garments with Kanai Kougei, had built his brand of luxury workwear by appropriating, to quote from his website, the "primitive techniques" of natural dyeing that "used as ingredients" the "natural biology of . . . plants and minerals" and the slow, skilled, hand labor of the craftspeople of Amami.[16] These references supported the designer's aims to "not further add to the unnecessary waste and stress already produced by this industry" and construct an imagined ideal that appealed to his customers. Yet despite these claims, he was well known at Kanai Kougei (and much gossiped about) for sending garments that were difficult and extremely heavy to dye, resource dense, and sent with short turnaround demands and for not paying his invoices and then asking for discounts.

Rather than only bringing to light these contradictions, which question the ideals of those commissioning natural dyeing, ethnography teases out the "messiness of practice" to show that fixes are not simple and, importantly, explicate the reasons why. Ethnography can also demonstrate instances in which societies deal with uncertainty on their own terms without engaging in consumption practices, as ethnography can "[catch] doubt in midair" because it "tends to vanish with articulation" (Pelkmans 2013, 4). Although some anthropologists have focused on the negativity of "precarity," documenting those who have become paralyzed by the sense of prevailing uncertainty (see Allison 2013 for Japan), anthropologist Mathijs Pelkmans in his *Ethnographies of Doubt* (2013) states that "even in the direst situations people will find new points of orientation and aspiration" (3). While aporia doesn't dissipate, resolutions are a way to keep anxiety at bay through an attitude, action or reformulation, catalyst for change, or way of seeing the opportunity that emerges from threat.

Habu snakes (figure I.9), called "the gods of the forest" by Amamians, are a recurring motif of risk in Amami, highlighting the paradox that from threat emerges opportunity. It is widely thought that Amami's forests would have been cleared and their land developed more widely if the number of habu was kept under control—evident by the many failed schemes to eradicate their numbers over the decades. But habu have emerged as staunch protectors of their habitat through the anxiety they induce in humans. Habu have therefore inadvertently protected other species that today are deemed worthy of World Natural Heritage recognition. In this reformulation, sustainability becomes an unintended consequence of anxiety about the unknown. If uncertainty forces resolutions, it also has the potential to prompt sustaining processes.

This optimistic outlook was seen again when Kanai Kougei's buildings seemed to be destroyed by a strong typhoon that tore through the island in September 2018. Half of the roofs had been ripped off the dyeing workshops, while the doors of the sales gallery had been blown in, causing flooding. A team of friends and relatives arrived to help with the cleanup. The buildings were turned inside out, the contents washed and spread in the sun to dry. I sat with Kazuko, who had moved to Amami with her family from Tokyo in 2015 to escape the threat of radiation in the wake of 3.11. We were depressed by the extent of the damage, but the Shachō was unfazed. He explained that this had happened many times before, it was part of life in Amami, and when the damage is bad people gather to help him for free. It was a chance to clean and tidy the workshop and fix anything in need of repair.

All around Toguchi village, where the workshop was based, insurance assessors wandered with clipboards. After a few days, when the electricity supply lines

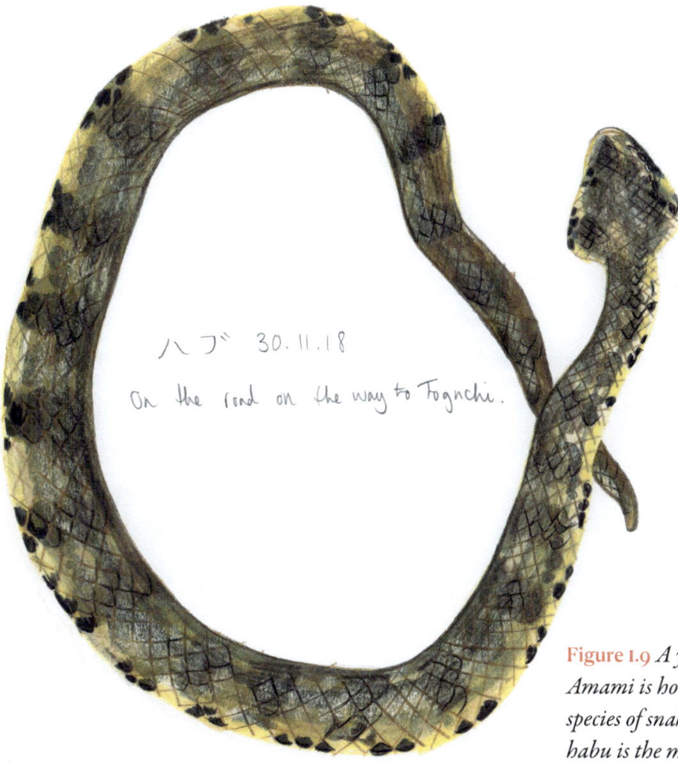

Figure 1.9 *A young habu. Amami is home to eight species of snake, but the habu is the most poisonous.*

had been restored, the workshop was back up and running, cleaner and tidier than before. Yukihito-san explained, "It's really hard to fix everything and go back to normal after typhoons. But on the other hand, all it is is a matter of time. . . . In times like natural disasters, I can rest. It's a chance to stop, to look at your feet [*ashimotomiru*, have time for reflection]." Kanai Kougei rarely stops production, with only a few days during the New Year holidays that the workshop is officially closed. Rather than seeing the destruction caused by typhoons as negative and uncertainty as a barrier, instead they are absorbed into the everyday and used productively. The Shachō and Yukihito-san are future thinkers, always considering better ways of doing things or cooking up new plans. The disruption caused by uncertainty is reformulated as time for reflection, to allow them to better consider how they might continue to sustain their business. What might be learned from this permeable attitude to uncertainty? How might this creative thinking generate sustaining processes for the local economy, the health of the community, and ecologies of production? Is it even possible to address the concerns that impact them all, or will some be prioritized over others?

The Dyeing Cosmology

This book might be conceptualized as being structured in halves. The first three chapters are concerned with the lives of the dyers who work at Kanai Kougei—both the older craftspeople and the younger ones who have returned or migrated to Amami. The second half of the book focuses on how nature is conceptualized in Japan and locally in Amami. It uses particular species and landscape elements to tease out the complexity of relationships with the land and with nature to put textile processes within a larger context and temporal period. One of the first questions I had when I arrived at Kanai Kougei was the last question I answered: Where does the *techigi* (yeddo hawthorn) wood, which provides the color constituent of dorozome, come from? The book structure reflects this, as I start by getting to know the wider context of Amamian textile infrastructure and end with establishing how dye materials used for dorozome are obtained.

In chapter 1, "The Mud Dyers of Amami Ōshima," I describe the geopolitical background responsible for Oshima tsumugi's economic rise and fall and present the challenges experienced by craftspeople who must sustain their industry through preservation or innovation. Oshima tsumugi is likely to become an ICP, but I document an alternative route pursued by a younger generation—that of making craft relevant to contemporary lifestyles and concerns. I suggest this latter response is a grassroots approach to preservation that advocates for an exchange of ideas, materials, technologies, and people, both locally and globally, allowing traditions to thrive.

Chapter 2, "The Alchemy of Producing Color," begins with this grassroots approach and focuses on the younger generation of dyers, many of whom have migrated from mainland Japan. They have left behind conditions of precarity, and I explore the appeal for them of acquiring skills in color-making and how this connects the craftspeople with a community of practitioners and ecosystems. This chapter argues that in order to be a successful craftsperson today, one also has to be an entrepreneur. Yet negotiating the balance between craft and business is challenging, because the process of natural dyeing conflicts with the demands of contemporary commodity production. Kanai Kougei must compromise to satisfy the market. But, I ask, at what cost does this come?

Chapter 3, "'*Mottainai*!' What a Waste!" explores how my participants who have dropped their income to pursue craft labor creatively reformulate waste and repurpose excess resources by drawing on skills and networks that revolve around the dyeing workshop. I conceptualize this using *mottainai* (what a waste), a Japanese term that reflects a tradition of frugality practiced during times of hardship. I argue that the adoption of mottainai is a consequence of postmaterialism driven by instability in the labor market but also a result of recent natural and environmental disasters. Focusing on the uncertainty around food security, I question whether the adoption of food activism, where the repurposing of waste, good nutrition, and environmental responsibility are built into production, might be seen as a precursor to more considered regimes of care surrounding textile production, use, and consumption.

While the first three chapters focus on human sociality, chapter 4, "The *Mejiro* Bird," is a starting point for examining multispecies engagements more closely. I delve into the history of Japanese bird conservation by engaging with the mejiro, a wild songbird kept as a caged pet at Kanai Kougei. Drawing on the photographs and writings of American ornithologist Oliver L. Austin, I show how the movement to protect birdlife was begun by Japanese elites but established by the Americans during the post–World War II occupation. I class the mejiro as a "totem" to understand how generational shifts in economics, politics, and international relations have influenced the ways nature has been considered a resource or companion. This historic case study demonstrates how attitudes to nature are influenced by the global circulation of ideas, but if lasting change is to occur, these ideas must adapt to local contexts. The chapter allows one to imagine how environmental responsibility and the sustainability of textile production might increase in the future, impacting the issues explored in the following chapter.

Chapter 5, "'The Industrious Way of Doing Things,'" aims to understand practices of wastewater and chemical disposal at Kanai Kougei, an issue of contention proving difficult to resolve. I argue that the "industrious way" resources are used has been influenced by historical and cultural practices and hybrid belief systems, with Amamian spirituality at the core. But I also suggest that modern attitudes are the result of an approach to government-supported industrialization that has favored economic growth and innovation at the expense of people and the environment.

Chapter 6, "Dyeing with the Earth," brings the book full circle and documents the source of trees that are essential for dyeing textiles in Amami. I use post–World War II forestry reports produced by the occupying US Allied forces as an entrance point for examining forest management and land access in Japan today. I ask how the dispossession of residents from their land and the desire for control of resources by the state and privatized entities has degraded local ecological knowledge and the creative, industrious, and sustainable ways residents use resources. I argue this dispossession has made access to trees difficult in the present, threatening the future of craft traditions and dyeing processes that have the potential to sustain the island's economy. I conclude the book by summarizing the main findings and questioning what impact the desire to control both traditions and resources has had. As the opposition of an epistemics of uncertainty, I consider how this might inform future narratives around sustainability.

1

The Mud Dyers of Amami Ōshima

As I arrived to work at Kanai Kougei one morning, Eriko Kanai beckoned me to the indigo workshop. I'd lived in New York working in the fashion industry myself, so she thought I might enjoy speaking with Hatsuko-san, a Japanese pattern cutter who worked at the New York–based brand Alexander Wang. The Japanese have a reputation in the design industry for being highly accomplished pattern cutters, and Hatsuko-san and I quickly discovered that some of my ex-colleagues were her friends. Like meeting Koki in similar circumstances, I was still surprised to make this acquaintance in Amami, far from the international cities that draw fashion industry workers. Chatting with Hatsuko-san, I learned that she had visited Amami two or three times a year since 2016, attracted by the qualities and traditions of *Oshima tsumugi*. She showed me the undergarments she had constructed using *tsumugi* cloth and *organic* cotton versions colored via *aizome* (indigo dyeing) and *dorozome*. She had dyed these design samples while participating in a public workshop at Kanai Kougei and had returned to interview

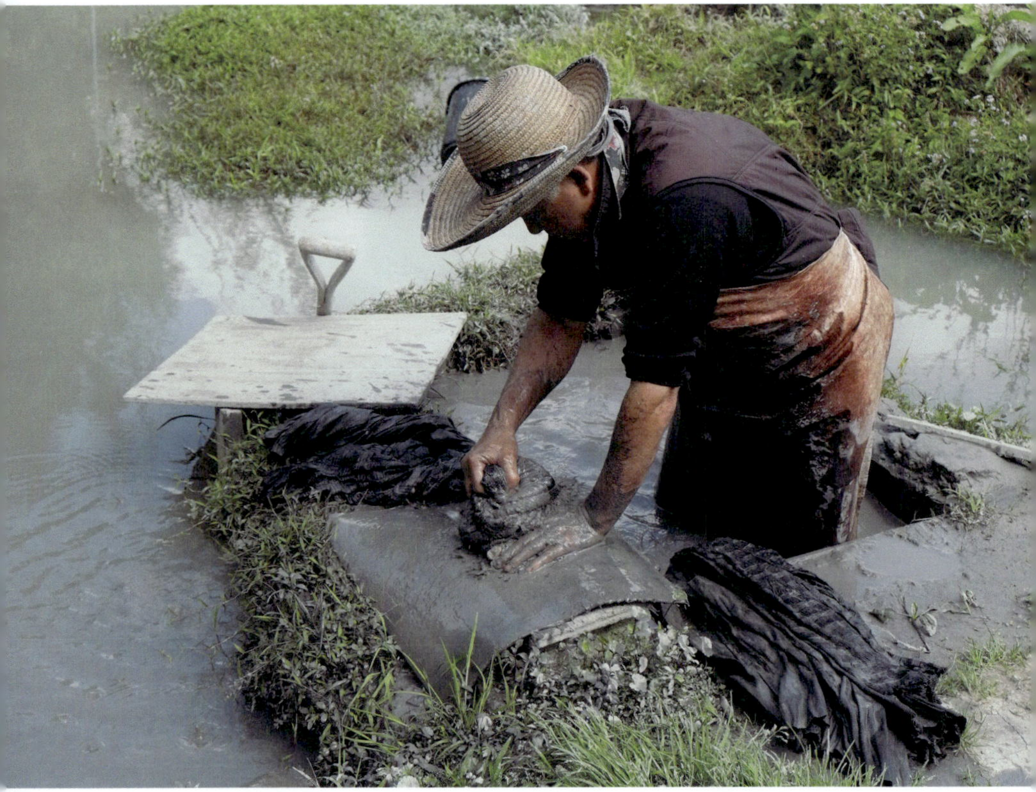

Figure 1.1 *The Shachō mordanting yarn in the dorota (mud field).*

the Shachō (figure 1.1) about Amamian traditional dyeing. Convinced that the "tight construction and unbreathable material" of brassieres might be "one of the underlying causes for breast cancer," Hatsuko-san has patented her smart design and was planning the launch of her brand. She later told me: "I want to create something gentle to the body using a natural product from the earth," thereby avoiding "transdermal toxicity"—the transferal of chemicals into the body through the surface of the skin. She is also mindful to "preserve the original tradition [of tsumugi] with an open mind towards new and innovative uses."

Hatsuko-san is representative of the kinds of clients who are attracted to Kanai Kougei, who can appreciate the technical sophistication of Oshima tsumugi—a cloth that passes through many hands across approximately twenty-eight unique production processes—but also its potential for "new and innovative uses." During the nostalgia boom that swept across Japan in the 1970s, the traditions of tsumugi were recognized by a nation of textile lovers who had material expertise equivalent to that of Hatsuko-san and the disposable wealth of a rapidly recovering economy. Tsumugi's silk yarn is space-dyed by dorozome to create contrasts of black and white and then handwoven into a complex series of patterns derived from Amamian flora, fauna, and material culture. A new *tanmono* (roll of cloth for one kimono) costs around ¥300,000–¥700,000 ($2,000–$4,600), which reflects its labor-intensive and complex construction that takes one year to complete from start to finish. Because of these "qualities and traditions," at peak production in 1972 the tsumugi industry provided the island's main source of income, becoming Amami's most significant cultural export.

The successes of the twentieth century, however, contrast significantly with the situation today. With shrinking demand, the workforce has dropped from twenty thousand people in the 1970s to only around 150 people, with many production processes carried out by aging craftspeople without apprentices in waiting. The enduring place of craft objects and processes in social, cultural, economic, and political life in Japan, at both the local and national levels, has stimulated much debate on how, as traditions, they are defined and the most appropriate way to sustain them. Bureaucrats and politicians, influential cultural elites, the various craftspeople involved in production, and the general public all have conflicting opinions regarding the future direction of traditional crafts. The growth of interest in sustainable commodities has in recent years given renewed fire to these debates, highlighting a paradox between the necessity to *preserve* and the need to *innovate*.

The route of preservation would see Oshima tsumugi become a *mukei bunkazai* (Intangible Cultural Property, or ICP). This celebrated Japanese government scheme recognizes historically or culturally valuable arts and crafts, prioritizing the skills held by individuals or groups rather than the objects they produce. While this recognition may grant status, providing financial and infrastructural support for craftspeople and preserving a craft for future generations, it often strips an industry of any real money-making capacity. The alternative path of innovation requires updating a craft to give it contemporary purpose either by modernizing the form or by singling out and developing an aspect of its production—as was captured by Hatsuko-san's brassieres that will eventually be sold to fashionable consumers in New York.

In this chapter, I first expand on the situation faced by Amami's craftspeople and consider how the debate between preservation and innovation is expressed across different Japanese craft sectors. I ask whether traditions should be deindustrialized to preserve their historical and cultural integrity under the instruction of external policy makers and consider what such an approach means for ordinary craftspeople on the ground. I then pose an alternative vision of the future that encompasses both the preservation of craft and a route to innovation via diversification as it has developed at Kanai Kougei. Rather than being static, I propose that across its history traditional practice in Amami has embraced innovation to respond to market demands, a process that has bolstered the industry in the short term, resulting in longer-term sustainability. By adapting the dyeing processes used in the manufacture of Oshima tsumugi, Kanai Kougei has helped sustain the wider textile economy. I argue that this adaptation is not simply a matter of practical, material transfer of process but is the result of a gradual evolution of tradition arising from social, economic, political, and environmental circumstances, too.

"Making It for Your Country"

As a form of soft power, Japan's preservation strategies are world-renowned partly due to the Ministry of Foreign Affairs (2016) "concentrating its efforts on international cooperation for Cultural Heritage as one of the pillars of its diplomatic policy," to quote the ministry's website. Since the Meiji era (1868–1912), Japan has protected a multitude of traditional crafts as important vessels of national identity, threatened as they were by rapid industrialization and urbanization, by writing acts of preservation into legislation. Before World War II, strategies focused on the preservation of tangible things such as "antiques" and "old properties" (Kakiuchi 2014, 2). But after the war, with the creation of the 1950 Law for the Protection of Cultural Properties, the revival of classical arts and crafts reminiscent of a preimperial time joined folk traditions under the ICP banner (Kaneko 2007, 10–11). Initially, the scheme supported high-value or "endangered" skills but later also included any crafts with "historical or artistic value" (Milhaupt 2014, 99). The scheme first took the form of a physical record of transmitted skills—written documents, samples, and films—but expanded to include financial assistance for craftworkers and efforts to incorporate crafts into contemporary life. The remit expanded in 1954 to include drama and music, folk cultural properties such as "ways of life" and "religious beliefs," and tangible properties such as architectural heritage, landscapes, plants, and animals, including Amami's black rabbit (Kaneko 2007, 11).

Despite the positive reputation and reach of ICP, my research has shown that the scheme has its problems, and the high opinion it garners globally is not necessarily shared by ordinary Japanese craftspeople. Oshima tsumugi is designated a Cultural Asset, a lower designation than an ICP with less finance and prestige, but the likelihood of an upgrade looms large. Nagata-san (age seventy), one of Kanai Kougei's oldest and most talented dyeing craftsmen, explained why he took issue with a potential ICP designation: "We will be able to keep making tsumugi, but if it becomes an official cultural heritage the craftsmen doing it will stop; we won't be able to make an industry from it—everything will stop. It will just become about 'making it for your country.'"[1]

This opinion, widely shared in Amami, is corroborated by the research of anthropologist Brian Moeran (1984, 1997), whose classic ethnography of *onta-yaki* (Onta pottery) in 1980s Kyūshū revealed how ontayaki is constrained by its *mingei* (folkcraft) categorization. Coined by combining the words *minshū* (common people) and *kōgei* (craft) (Moeran 1984, 12), mingei is both a style and *philosophy* defined by philosopher and art critic Yanagi Soetsu in the 1930s. Soetsu was heavily influenced by the Arts and Crafts movement of nineteenth-century Britain and its champions, including art critic John Ruskin and designer and activist William Morris. By establishing a similar movement in Japan, Soetsu joined a global intellectual elite who took what historian Kim Brandt calls "an anti-modernist reaction against urban industrialization" (2007, 1). Mingei realized itself through the handcrafted material culture of the "common people" such as pottery, farming utensils, textiles, and woodwork from across Japan's empire. Its philosophy was based on a romanticized ideal of "rural communalism," where nostalgia for the past saw "the countryside . . . as a repository of 'true' values [such] as frugality, altruism, harmony and cooperation" (Moeran 1984, 12). The sociocultural impact of the mingei movement was perhaps most notable in the aftermath of World War II, when craft was considered key to the "material and ideological reconstruction of a 'healthy' national life as well as manufacturing and exports" by the government and occupying Allied forces (Brandt 2007, 224). Mingei therefore defined both the aesthetics and philosophy of craft preservation in the postwar period, becoming the foundation on which ICP was built.

Moeran's ethnography as an apprentice potter in the Onta valley revealed the frustrations craftspeople had with mingei's legacy. Whereas Moeran (1997, 122) was free to create his own designs, his participant potters were said to be "bound by tradition"; they could not divert from "traditional Koishiwara ware," because Japanese customers would say it wasn't "proper" and they wouldn't "sell a thing." In 2018, Moeran's research was updated by anthropologist Alyssa Paredes, who studied how modernization via contemporary manufacturing technologies is still considered a threat to tradition. She outlined the "problem of mechanization" of 1971, in which potters debated with the Prefectural Cultural Property Preservation Board, the Ministry for Commerce and Industry, the Tourist Association, and the Mingei Association, which all defined ontayaki's Cultural

Asset designation and the promotion and funding accompanying it. The debate focused on the huge clay crushers (*karausu*) built into the village's ancient social and ecological infrastructure. Because they were operated by waterpower provided by the river, the karausu promoted egalitarianism that dictated the number of potting households and even the number of potters working at any time. In the 1970s, the potters wished to introduce electric-powered clay crushers to support commercial production. However, their plans were opposed by mingei ideology that resisted mechanization and saw the karausu as central to village communalism. Mingei ideology also advises that everyday objects must be affordable, but this did not account for inflation, rising business taxes, or the fact that potters struggled to meet demand for their products (Paredes 2018, 140). Paredes references local newspapers from the time, which suggest that the decision would be based on whether in the future ontayaki would be defined as a "commodity" or a "cultural property." While the potters argued that "clay is clay," the authorities denied the potters' request, reasoning that new machinery would damage the pots' handmade quality and be detrimental to social cohesion in this tight-knit community (141). In effect, the authorities actively supported craft labor in order to make ontayaki distinct from industrial production. Local knowledge and production processes were fixed in Onta's landscape, demonstrating how the politics and economics of preservation cuts through to the everyday working practices of craftworkers.

In 1995, ontayaki was upgraded to an ICP, meaning that it is now subject to even stricter regulations regarding make, materials, and design. As Nagata-san suggests, producing ontayaki today is "making it for your country." Paredes writes: "The guidelines streamline the understanding of an unfixed culture into its most legible form. Through the regulations, cultural life in Onta begins to make sense as a form of 'property' belonging less to the potters than to the state" (2018, 146).

These debates around preservation have existed for decades, affecting a multitude of traditional practices. In textiles, this is well illustrated by the cultivation of Tokushima's Awa indigo, preserved in 1978 as a Cultural Asset. Rowland Ricketts (2006, 9), an American artist who apprenticed with Tokushima's growers and dyers, has stated that because craftsmen receive government funding, producers "cannot deviate far from what is considered 'traditional.' This greatly limits the degree of mechanization in the farming and processing of indigo, raising the price of the dyestuff they produce and making it difficult to attract younger farmers to this extremely labor-intensive work."

In personal communication with Ricketts (Dec. 2016), I learned that it is the composting of indigo leaves, making a dyestuff called *sukumo* (see chapter 5), that is protected as unique to Japan, whereas cultivation is open to technological advances, such as the use of mechanized leaf cutters, chemical pesticides, and fertilizers. Yet even if farmers were able to increase their yield, they'd struggle to compost large quantities, as they wouldn't be able to use modern tools. Instead, they rely on wooden variants as specified by the Organization for the Preservation of Awa Indigo, which acts on behalf of the Department of Culture. As a Cultural Asset, Oshima tsumugi is already subject to a variety of rules to maintain its "authenticity," as I will discuss below, but Kanai Kougei's Shachō highlighted the current predicament of tsumugi as follows: "As a part of Japanese traditional culture, kimono culture will not disappear. However—I think [tsumugi] will cease being an industry as it has been. Perhaps it will become a mukei bunkazai [ICP]. If that happens . . . there will be a lot of new regulations around it. In that case, we won't be able to pursue profit from it as a business in the future."

Dye It Yourself

The Shachō (age sixty) and his wife, Eriko-san (age fifty-eight), established Kanai Kougei in 1982. The workshop is of particular interest because there were sixty dorozome workshops in Amami in the 1950s. Today four remain and only two of these, including Kanai Kougei, are prospering. Dorozome is a labor-intensive process, in which pre-prepared silk yarns are dyed in a liquor produced from the boiled wood chips of local *sharinbai* (yeddo hawthorn) trees, known as *techigi* in Amami dialect.[2] Tannins in the liquor, which are naturally occurring molecules existing in all manner of plant stuffs, bind with the textile fibers and then with iron (ferric oxide), which occurs in high quantities in Amami's mud, darkening the color. This diluted mud is applied in an outdoor space called a *dorota* (mud field). The dyeing process takes about a week from start to finish, changing a textile from white to pink to red to brown, and with up to seventy applications, to black. During the tsumugi boom period, the Shachō learned dorozome at one of several workshops in his village of Toguchi, training during the day and attending high school in the evenings. Although he had talent, the Shachō and Eriko-san moved to Osaka in the late 1970s, where Eriko-san trained in the knit industry and, in response to the real estate boom, the Shachō started a concrete carpentry business. After this business went bankrupt and Eriko-san became pregnant with their son Yukihito-san, at the age of twenty-three the Shachō returned to Amami to start Kanai Kougei. He constructed the workshop on family land, while Eriko-san secured a million yen from a state-funded Amamian business association to furnish it with equipment. From here they built the workshop's reputation and at peak production employed eight full-time dyers.

Being a first-generation craftsman, without the constraint of family obligation, the Shachō has always been a future thinker. Although Kanai Kougei has experienced ups and downs that parallel those of the wider industry, early on he sought out alternative streams of income. He attributes the workshop's ongoing success to its ability to innovate: "Apart from me most of the others [dye craftsmen] had never physically left Amami. Back when everyone was making good profits, I traveled around all over Japan—and it was then I realized we needed to do public workshops and so on. But the vast majority of the others were just doing their main tsumugi work, never leaving their workshops. I guess in the past maybe that was the *shokunin* (craftsman) mentality. . . . I don't know."

Opening the business at the start of tsumugi's financial downturn, the Shachō was careful not to rely on the success that the industry had experienced thus far. He made efforts to network, improving local and national connections, cementing his reputation as a craftsman but also as an innovator. Seeing how craft processes were being commercialized across Japan via a public workshop model, he recognized dorozome might have a life beyond tsumugi, blurring the boundaries of production and consumption. Since tsumugi was still profitable, this angered his contemporaries, who saw such deviations as "an interruption to [their] work." Working alongside the professional craftspeople for as little as an hour to a whole day, the Shachō organized dyeing workshops for tourists and locals (figure 1.2), who could (and still do) pay only ¥3,000 (about twenty dollars) to "dye it yourself."[3] While some participants want to engage with their cultural history and better understand unfamiliar craft techniques, others are simply looking for activities to occupy free time, much needed on an island where the beach is the main draw and the weather can be unpredictable.

Holding these dyeing workshops offered a window for Kanai Kougei to diversify, with the Shachō welcoming the flow of ideas, materials, technologies, and people from outside Amami, even in the face of significant criticism from his own community. Concerned that the extraction of the dorozome process for other purposes would undermine the cloth's complex manufacture, Amami's tsumugi community instead made efforts to diversify its product range (to include neckties, handbags, and so on) and reach new markets. But these attempts—which producers, the Oshima tsumugi union (which oversees production), and the local prefectural authorities have been carrying out since the 1980s—have mostly been unsuccessful in sustaining the industry.

With the bursting of Japan's financial bubble in the 1990s seeing kimono sales plummet, the Kanais encouraged their children to seek employment elsewhere. Yukihito-san (age thirty-eight), the eldest child, left for Tokyo in his twenties to

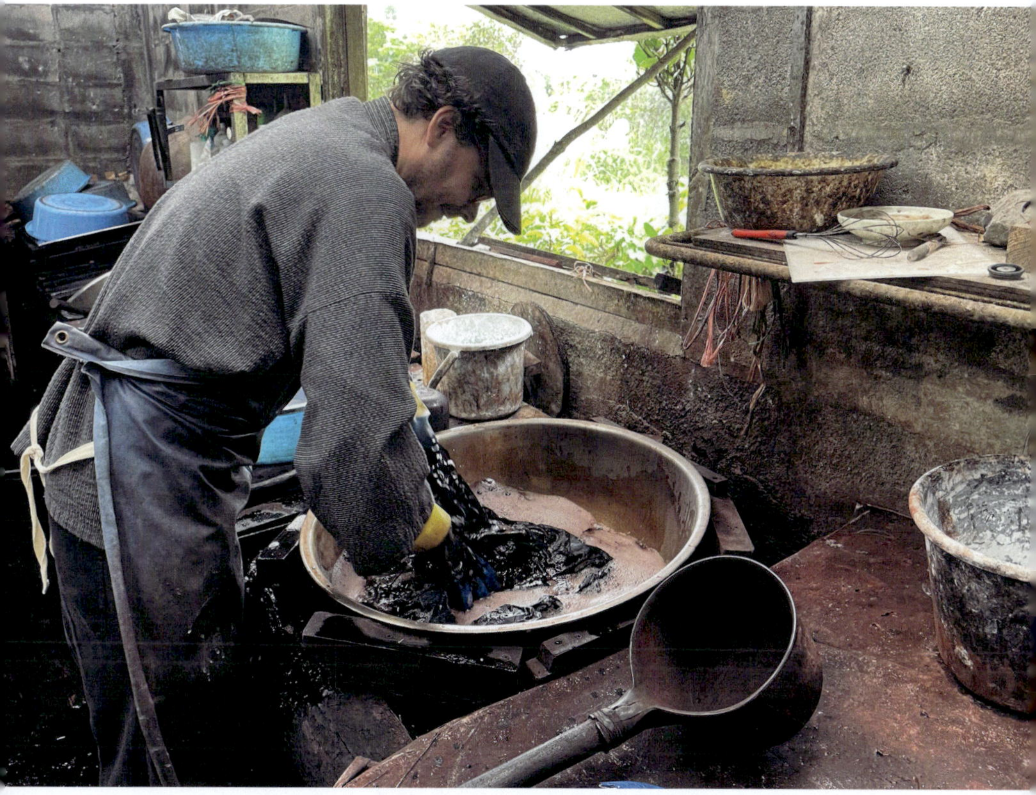

Figure 1.2 *A workshop participant practicing dorozome.*

pursue a career in music, and the Shachō and Eriko-san's three daughters also followed alternative career paths. Ai-san is a fashion stylist in Tokyo, Yuka-san is an employee of the Yakult Corporation in Amami, and Maiko-san became a hairdresser before returning to assist her mother at Kanai Kougei in the mid-2000s, when the public workshops for tourists took off. By now the workshop was employing just three full-time tsumugi dyers, and in 2004 Yukihito-san returned to Amami from Tokyo. He was concerned by the precariousness of work in the music industry, but he also missed the island. Not being trained in tsumugi dyeing, or encouraged to learn by his family (his father believes he lacks the temperament![4]), Yukihito-san recognized there was a demand for apparel-related work and created a job for himself, explaining: "Until I returned to Amami, the Shachō dealt with apparel just a little—he was turning down most of the jobs. Why? Because [artisans] cannot be bothered to deal with people from outside. It was then when I noticed there was no one here who is capable of handling communication. . . . I thought it would turn into work if I returned with colors, because apparel takes orders by colors."

Although the Shachō had been developing business networks beyond Amami, he was not always able to follow through with "special" orders. As social media and email became the dominant forms of communication between client and manufacturer, Yukihito-san stepped in. It was also around this time that sustainability discourse began to creep into fashion (see Fletcher 1998). On first impression, natural dyeing seems more environmentally friendly, and with Japan possessing a wealth of traditional dye techniques, fashion brands in Tokyo begun to pursue these alternative methods of coloring textiles. Yukihito-san had been experimenting with *kusakizome* (plant and tree dyeing) to develop a color palette, teaching himself using the skills he had absorbed from a lifetime around the workshop. Dorozome was the foundation, using wood from local sharinbai trees (creating black, brown, and pink). He supplemented these with other local or brought-in materials: Amamian *fukugi*, or common garcinia (yellow); Indian indigo and German synthetic indigo (blue); and *akane*, or madder (red). Without any promotion, only through word of mouth of his city contacts, the business grew. This, Yukihito-san claims, is reflective of the horizontal (heterarchical) relationships existing in the design industry (e.g., "I saw the dyeing work a friend of mine had done at your place. Could you do mine as well?") rather than the strictly vertical (hierarchical) nature of the tsumugi industry.

As a result of this policy of inclusiveness, Kanai Kougei dyes individual garments sent by non–design professionals but also textiles for Japanese design giants Issey Miyake and Yoji Yamamoto. This democratizing of process, giving access to anyone who wants something dyed (or indeed to dye it themselves), is significant, because little profit can be gathered through this approach to manufacturing—that is why factories typically have minimum orders. But taking this approach, small profits can be made, and a heterarchical attitude might foster further social, economic, or marketing opportunities. As such, a symbiotic relationship has formed between Kanai Kougei's tsumugi dyeing and its apparel work, with income from the latter supporting the dyeing of 70 percent of all of Amami's tsumugi yarns annually.

Since Kanai Kougei has developed strong relationships with the kimono cloth makers, many of the owners being friends or peers of the Shachō and Eriko-san, at present the volume of orders for tsumugi yarn is high and consistent. Payment is made on delivery of goods, usually face-to-face, meaning there is always cash flow to keep the company functioning. In contrast, apparel has a higher unit price, meaning more profit can be pursued. But invoices are typically paid two to three months later, with some companies defaulting on payment, protected by the safety of distance and the difficulty of pursuing legal action. Apparel is also changeable between seasons, and production is challenging because the textiles being dyed are varied and inconsistent, leading to mistakes. While this parallel model seems to work, demonstrating that innovation and diversification can sustain tradition, it exists in a delicate, precarious balance.

In order to understand how the innovative approaches of the craftspeople at Kanai Kougei have been able to succeed, due focus must be given to the industry from a historical perspective. I suggest that the reconfiguration of Japanese kusakizome into a contemporary production method relies on the authenticity, institutions, and social networks surrounding tsumugi. This is what anthropologist Lucy Norris (2019, 7) calls "embedded infrastructure," or the tangible and intangible connections between technology, people, and materials that exist in "traditional textile towns." Norris's (2011, 304) fieldwork in India has shown how textile heritage in postindustrial regions can be deployed as a meaningful marker of identity but also how craft traditions can be commodified by local authorities to represent state ideologies that "embody the principles of fairness, social accountability, and sustainability through their production values." But beyond these symbolic markers, Norris demonstrates how material infrastructures—such as decaying, dormant workshops containing supplies and equipment—are kept in a state of disrepair "waiting for another upturn" (292), because "maintaining their visibility and potential viability is crucial to success" (286). Kanai Kougei's reputation is built on the heritage of Oshima tsumugi, and accordingly the marketing of the dorozome technique draws heavily upon this heritage. By considering the long *durée*, one can begin to understand how tsumugi is valued locally, and how it is viewed from afar, but also how it has been possible to extract the dyeing process from the cloth's complex manufacture.

The Tumultuous History of Oshima Tsumugi

Around 1868, Japan underwent a period of transformation known as the Meiji Restoration, which marked the end of feudal rule by the military government of the Tokugawa Shogunate and reinstated the emperor. Widespread political, social, economic, and environmental change occurred, and industrialization was driven both financially and technologically by the textile industry (Clark 1979, 38). With the end of Edo era (1603–1868) and the abolishment of sumptuary laws that dictated the colors and fibers that members of society could wear, Oshima tsumugi was commercialized and from 1877 was prized throughout Japan's major cities (Milhaupt 2014, 94). Opening Japan to international trade

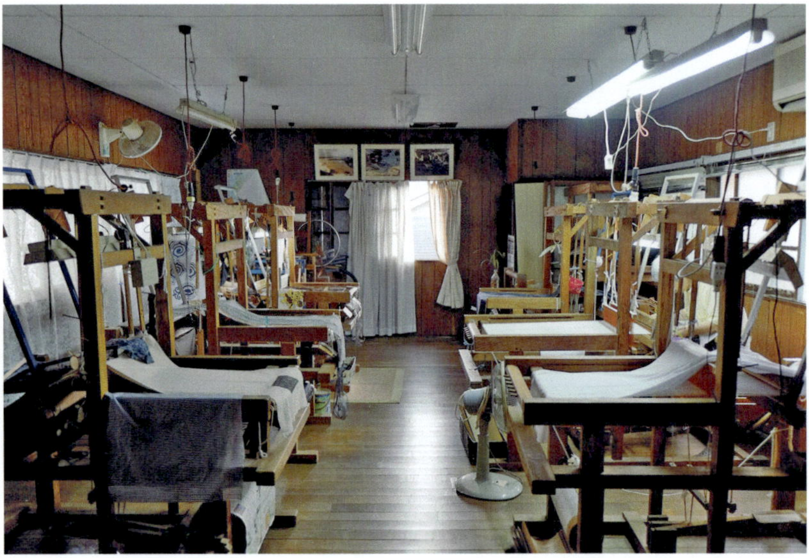

Figure 1.3 *Most of the weaving workshops I visited reflected Lucy Norris's (2011) idea of "dormancy," with multiple looms awaiting a return to productivity.*

disrupted internal commodity markets including that of Amami's main export crop, black sugar (*kokutō*). This necessitated that the labor force shift away from kokutō, which was devalued by imported sugar, and toward tsumugi.

Records from the Todaiji temple in Nara suggest that tsumugi, or "dark brown pongees," were given as tributes to the emperor by the Ryūkyū kingdom starting in the eighth century and used as tax payments to the Satsuma government during the Edo era (Tanaka et al. 2005, 99). As borders opened to trade after the Meiji Restoration, chemical dyestuffs were imported into Japan from Europe, bringing ease of application and a bright color palette to centuries-old dyeing techniques. A letter published in the *Miyazaki Shinbun* (a Kyūshū-based newspaper) in 1900 claimed that "'artificially dyed' Oshima Tsumugi should be better regulated because it would encourage over production of an inferior quality textile" (Yuge 2005, 126). This suggests that early in its commercialization, "historic" and "natural" methods of dyeing were being linked with quality, differentiating them from machine-era products produced in the rest of Japan. A year later, the Kagoshima Prefecture Oshima Tsumugi Cooperative was established to maintain quality and promote sales (Tanaka et al. 2005, 192). By 1929, Amami had established its own independent branch (referred to in this book going forward as the tsumugi union), charged with overseeing production and developing new techniques and products while drawing on local material and labor resources to protect "authenticity."

The expansion and development of tsumugi saw the introduction of a resist-dyeing technique called *kasuri*, borrowed from textile producers of *Kurume gasuri* in nearby Kyūshū (Milhaupt 2014, 94).[5] Kasuri is more commonly known as an ikat weave outside of Japan and is found throughout Asia. It is constructed via a complex process of space dyeing across the length of the yarns of the warp and weft, the pattern securely tied off to resist the dye using a coated cotton (figure 1.4). This allows an offset, "brushed" pattern to reemerge during weaving, as the space-resist areas are realigned (figure 1.5). Design historians Tomonuki Yamanobe and Kenzō Fujii (1996, 95) suggest that the introduction of graph paper into Japanese weaving communities meant more pictorial patterns could be developed and shared between weavers, standardizing patterns locally. This was a method a number of Kyoto weavers learned when they were sent to France in 1872 to study the Jacquard technique and acquire equipment (4). The invention of the Amamian *shimebata* loom in 1907 sped up this aspect of production (Tanaka et al. 2005, 183). Hand-binding kasuri is labor-intensive, and the shimebata loom instead weaves the resist areas into a "tsumugi mat." The complexity of the cloth's pattern is woven into an abstract grid system, increasing the scope for more detailed designs. This allowed Oshima tsumugi to compete with similar cloth being machine woven and sold in Tokyo, which imitated the small abstract patterns that had won tsumugi its reputation.

In the Meiji era, textile patterning across Japan became increasingly ostentatious, as detail on kimono moved from the legs and up the body to across the neck and shoulders—a trend thought to coincide with more people sitting at Western-style tables (Yamanobe and Fujii 1996, 12). Distinguishing itself with the originality the shimebata loom afforded, Amami responded with patterns inspired by its wildlife, cultural identity, and unique designs that reflected many of the weaving areas. For instance, the pattern of a *zanbara*, an Amamian bamboo rice basket, symbolizes the northern village of Akina, one of the only regions still growing rice today. The Tatsugo pattern includes graphic representations of *sotetsu* (cycad) fronds, habu skin, and hibiscus flowers and has been subject to hundreds of redesigns, but the most recent is said to have been influenced by a cloth from China (figure 1.6). Like the use of foreign chemical dyestuffs absorbed within existing Japanese techniques, the introduction of technology from near and far led to innovative approaches that advanced the craft and reduced labor costs, meeting market demand in quality, quantity, and aesthetics.

In 1940 "lavish textile production" was halted when the government issued a sumptuary law to pause the production of luxury items and prioritize munitions

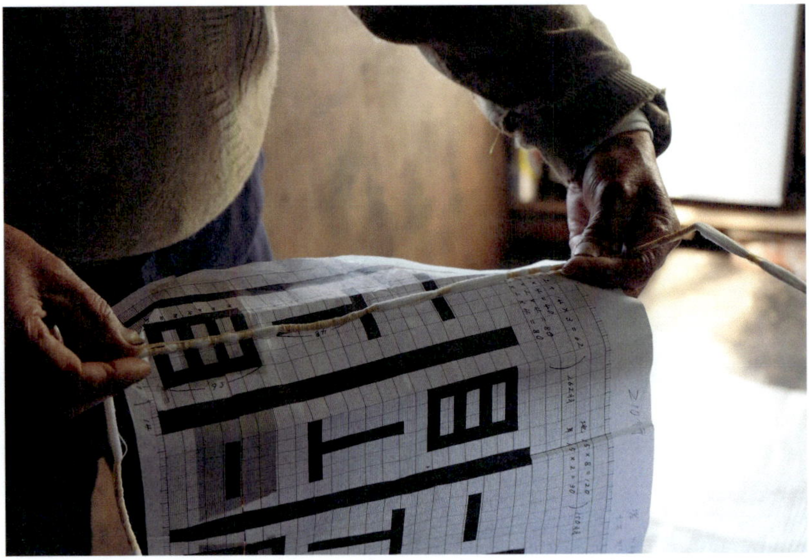

Figure 1.4 *Kurume gasuri binding.*

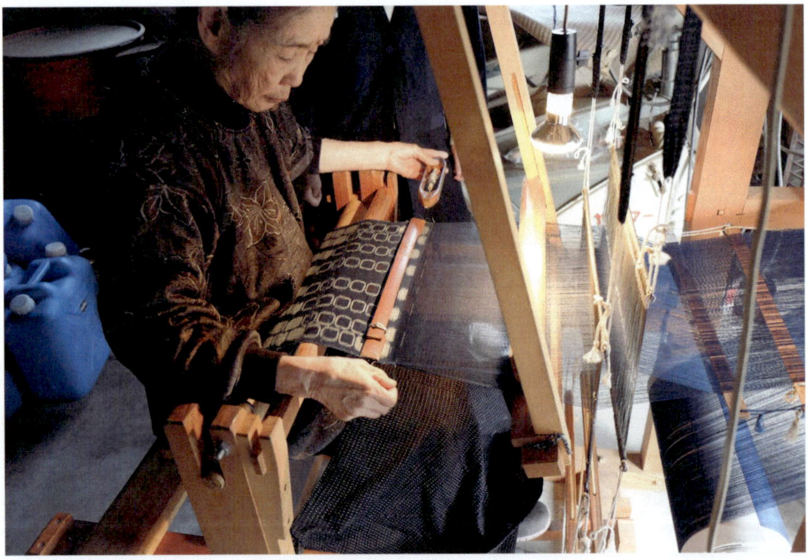

Figure 1.5 *Kurume gasuri weaving.*

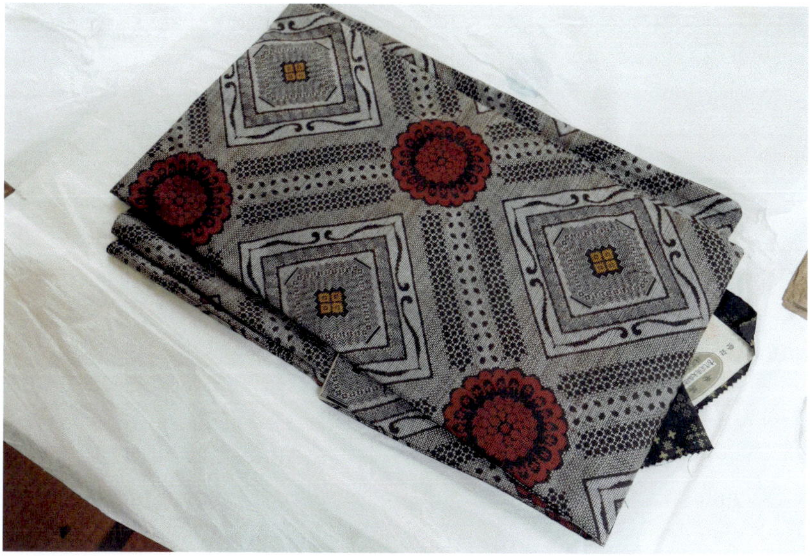

Figure 1.6 *A kimono from the 1950s featuring an early version of the Tatsugo pattern produced using red and yellow chemical dyes.*

manufacture after joining World War II (Yamanobe and Fujii 1996, 4). Amami was spared, because tsumugi was argued to be the islanders' "lifeline" and disrupting production would be detrimental to the maintenance of intangible local knowledge (Tanaka et al. 2005, 101). Preserving "unique" craft knowledge aligned with the government's approach to culture that, in the buildup to World War II, supported an increasingly nationalist agenda. Anthropologist Marilyn Ivy has described how Japanese traditional practices and commodities have been preserved as emblems of cultural continuity to counter the encroachment of Westernization. She suggests a "double movement whereby that which was marginalized by the advent of nationalist modernity in the Meiji Period—peasant practices, superstitions, the folkloric—was in the same movement objectified as most essentially traditional" (Ivy 1995, 25). Items such as kimono and their skills of production were mobilized as tools for "nation-building" and emblems of Japaneseness (Milhaupt 2014, 195). A traditional textile with a biography as ancient as tsumugi's and the intangible knowledge of its artisans gave it its exceptional status during the war for fear that "national-cultural identity, continuity, and community" (Ivy 1995, 26) would be lost.

Tsumugi production thus continued but its output was severely restricted, and by 1945 the economic postwar destruction of Japan and the dire consequences for the nation's material wealth left Amami's industry in a precarious position. This decline was documented in 1951 by American anthropologist Douglas Haring, who was commissioned by the occupying US Army to produce an ethnographic report on Amami. Over six months, Haring collected data on topics such as lifestyle, customs, and industry to ascertain sentiments toward the mainland, gauge the extent of communist infiltration, and ask how the US authorities might support social and economic development. Ironically Haring's words, which reflect the postwar recovery, mirror the situation being experienced today: "Exports of tsumugi are falling off because of failure to adapt to changes in Japanese taste, and new ideas in design, perhaps new weaving techniques might revive, and expand the industry. There is a strong probability that numerous Amami handicraft products might compete in the export market, if skilled industrial designers were to concentrate upon improved quality and aesthetic appeal" (1952, 39).

Despite this assessment, the industry regained its prewar output in line with Japan's "miraculous" economic recovery. The Allied forces saw the potential of the industry for economic development, supplying US investment grants, support for which continued upon revision of Amami's sovereignty to Japan in 1953 (Haring 1952, 38). From a position of economic weakness, traditional craft industries invested in technology to shore up their future. This allowed the tsumugi union to introduce more chemical colors to contrast with dorozome, appeasing changing consumer tastes on the mainland (Tanaka et al. 2005, 103). In addition, the tsumugi industry in Kagoshima (begun by Amamian migrants) recovered quickly. As such, local competition improved the quality of the cloth in both producing regions, prompting more willingness to break from traditional forms and patterns (Tanaka et al. 2005, 183).

The complexity of tsumugi's construction accounts for the high price it has always commanded, but despite its cost, a production peak of 290,000 *tan* (rolls) a year was reached in 1972 (Tanaka et al. 2005, 103).[6] Tanaka et al. suggest that tsumugi's popularity came about because, after the war, the public had "a strong nostalgia for the good old days again"; handwoven kasuri patterns were suitably "retro," so tsumugi sales skyrocketed (184). This peak coincided with Amami's tourism boom, as the Amami Islands were the southernmost Japanese territory with desirable sun and sea pull prior to Okinawa's 1972 reversion from the United States to Japan (Song and Kuwahara 2016). The people of Amami speak wistfully of this period, telling stories of hordes of tourists arriving by ferry and creating local revenue through the purchase of tsumugi and the frequenting of *izakaya* (restaurant-bars).

Jennifer Robertson has documented nostalgia and its monetization in Japan via the phenomenon of the *furusato* movement. Translating as "old village," but in sentiment meaning "closer to 'home' or 'native-place,'" furusato are ideal villages set within traditional rural landscapes (Robertson 1991, 13). Robertson explains how furusato tourism symbolized "motherly love" and pacified the societal anxiety caused by rural depopulation, environmental destruction, and urban development that occurred in the postwar period (20–28). The movement arose out of the 1970s oil shocks, which destabilized the economy when global gasoline prices rocketed, reminding the Japanese of their dependence on imported raw materials. As such, there was a desire to attain self-sufficiency based on the "harmonious tranquility" that existed in the "old villages" before "the onset of westernization, industrialization, and urbanization" (28–29). Marilyn Ivy (1995, 65) similarly describes the surge of postwar interest in tradition and folklore, suggesting that "a nostalgia for a Japan that is kept on the verge of vanishing, stable yet endangered (and thus open for commodifiable desire)," meant that a market for "vintage Japan" was maximized in the advanced capitalist context of a country with sudden disposable income. "Vintage Japan" was sold through various internal and international tourism campaigns, from the promotion of Japan Railways in 1936 to the "Cool Japan" of the 2000s, frequently accompanied by the "cultural icons" of women in kimono (Milhaupt 2014, 239). Oshima tsumugi was the quintessential Amamian commodity from a remote island with many "intact" cultural traditions. The combination of the textile's ancient past, superior handmade quality, and color palette of browns, blacks, and beiges perfectly matched the aesthetics of the Shōwa era (1926–89).

The social and economic reality of the postwar period that drove the kimono industry was explained by Koki, who first came to Amami when working for a Tokyo-based design firm specializing in the development of traditionally crafted products. Born and raised in Tokyo in an affluent family, he moved to Amami in 2017 wanting to use his hands again, having become disenchanted with commercial design. When I first met him, he had been learning tsumugi techniques for six months. He explained: "During the '60s to '80s when [tsumugi] was booming, the kimono was selling a lot because, my grandparents' generation, they could never afford to buy anything luxury before. They went through the war, then after the war *luxury* was not in their dictionary; it was about putting rice on the table.... But in the 1970s and 1980s those people who always wanted to wear silk and kimono, they could finally afford to buy those things because the country became rich. [But if] that generation becomes older, then that means the industry also sinks."

Kimono scholar Terry Satsuki Milhaupt explains how during the war and throughout the US occupation, kimono were bartered for food and basic material goods as Western-style clothing became increasingly domesticated. She suggests this was a time of "revolutionary change in the symbolic and material value of the kimono [marking] the moment when its meaning was transformed from an everyday garment into a largely ceremonial costume" (Milhaupt 2014, 190). Milhaupt even suggests the kimono's negative connotation with luxury during the war, "inadvertently laid a path for the garment's resurrection as the country's national form of dress" in the postwar period (239). As Koki described, when fortunes changed, many families spared no expense in acquiring luxuries, meaning the purchase of formal kimono for ceremonial occasions became a marker of the country's rising wealth.

During its peak, tsumugi developed into a highly lucrative industry, bringing wealth to many ordinary islanders. The tsumugi weavers were typically women, and good weavers could earn around ¥400,000–¥500,000 per month (around $2,600–$3,300), making more money than their husbands and affording the opportunity to send their children to university. Eriko Kanai's mother and grandmother were skilled tsumugi weavers, and Eriko-san herself has gained a reputation for her proficiency in dressing others in tsumugi kimono. As she explains:

> In the Shōwa '30s [1955–65], there used to be a saying, "Three daughters can bring a fortune." Because it is an isolated island, people used to send a male child to the mainland for study. Female children who stayed on the island weaved and earned a lot of money to fund the education of the male child. That's why there's a lot of hairdressers and delicatessens in the town of Naze. "You don't have to cook, just weave!" they were told. . . . As for the hairdressers, the weavers treated themselves and went out to have fun once they finally finished weaving a tanmono and received the money.

Weaving tsumugi was principally the reserve of women simply because of the traditional divisions of labor. With most households owning a loom, weaving could be done around child-rearing and housework, while heavy-duty jobs—dyeing or shimebata weaving—were left to men. The importance of women's labor to the tsumugi industry reflects the wider position of women in Amamian society. Because Amamian female priestesses (the *noro* and *yuta*) had, for centuries, authority over aspects of both spiritual life and governance, women have held relatively equal social standing to men and continue to do so today (see chapter 5). While this observation is based on the experiences of those Amamians I spoke with, women being the main household earners did not appear to cause substantial rifts. As Eriko-san says: "The Shachō acts as if he is powerful, but at the end of the day, he is in the hands of women!" It is important to note that tsumugi was rarely worn by ordinary islanders before the boom period; tsumugi was for earning money, not wearing. Nevertheless, increased financial mobility

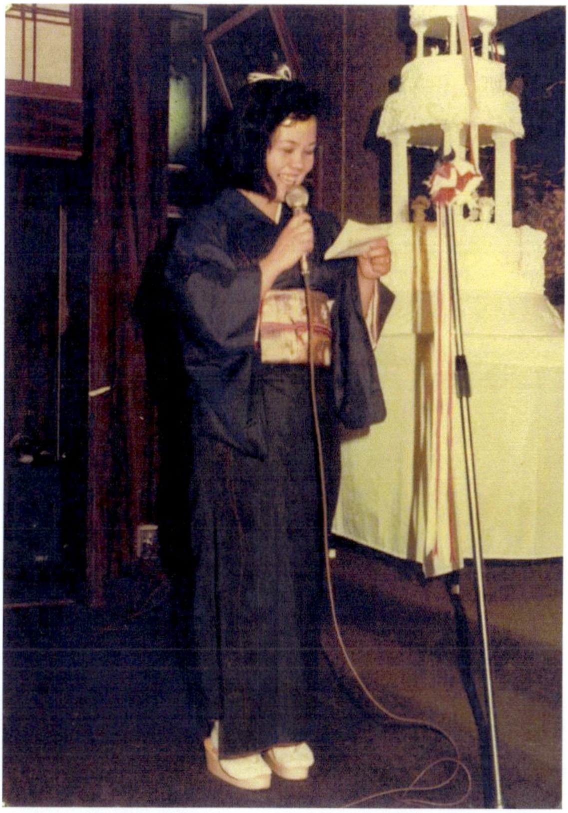

Figure 1.7 *Eriko Kanai wearing tsumugi at her friend's wedding in the 1970s. Photo courtesy of Eriko Kanai.*

meant islanders, too, were able to afford the products of their labor, allowing them to participate in regional nostalgia and identity formation (figure 1.7).

In the postwar period, Oshima tsumugi established its reputation as one of Japan's most luxurious textiles to the extent that *Oshima* developed into a generic name. By the 1960s, it was in such demand that Korean factories began copying and selling a cheaper variant on the Japanese market, using industrial production and low-wage labor (Tanaka et al. 2005, 193). This poor-quality cloth threatened to flood the market, damaging the reputation of Amami's output. Even today, there are whispers about individuals who sold Korean cloth during the boom period, trying to pass it off as the *honmono* (real thing). They were subsequently discovered and punished by gossip that lives on, fifty years later. As a result of this scandal, in 1974 tsumugi was designated a *dentō kōgei* (traditional craftwork) by the government (185), renamed "authentic Oshima tsumugi," and given an official seal (figure 1.8) distinguishing it from "Oshima" produced elsewhere (73). This seal is only applied after a tanmono has undergone inspection at Amami's tsumugi union, where the inspector checks for faults and consistencies to ensure he is satisfied with its quality and authenticity (figure 1.9).

By visually examining the cloth by running its length through his fingers, an inspector's authentication thereby differentiates a cloth that has the look and feel of something produced by a machine off the island, from that which has been made by hand in Amami. The inspector can often tell by eye or touch the identity of the weaver or dyer, "mooring" the cloth's production in the local community. Anthropologist Jean Pierre Warnier, with his discussion on *produits de terroir* (the products of a given locality) in France, suggests after Arjun Appadurai (1990) that "unmoored things" such as "commodities" or "cultural items have to be domesticated and locally moored." As Warnier explains, processes of globalization have "gone hand in hand with the politics of heritage on a worldwide scale." But assigning commodities to a region is "a means to produce locality . . . to create an inside and an outside with clear criteria of belonging or not belonging" (Warnier 2012, 85).

I observed the skill of identifying individuals in the make of cloth in inspectors of the Scottish heritage textile Harris Tweed on the Isle of Lewis, where I did fieldwork in 2015 (Linton 2016). The Lewis inspectors could recognize patterns in the cloth's tension that reflected a particular weaver, how energized the weaver was during production, or moments where the weaver took a break or stopped to greet the postman. But, as Lucy Norris (2011, 291) also observed of handloom weavers of khadi cloth in India, Harris Tweed manufacturers also must "remove all traces of the body and mind of the weaver," because "every inch of cloth can reveal the weaver's mood, [whether] they are tired, distracted or careless," which can lead to a decrease in the cloth's value. In contrast, Oshima tsumugi rarely fails inspection because the consistency of the production technique has reached a level of near perfection. Rather than inconsistences marking inferior quality, recognizable signs of perfection achieved by the craftsperson were qualities that made the cloth outstanding. The name of the weaver (but not the dyer) is attached to the final label alongside the authentication seal. This reflects the hierarchy of labor, where the weaver's skills are highly regarded while the dyer's manual labor is barely recognized. This demonstrates a key feature of Japanese craft preservation, where value is located in the skills of individual or collective groups of artisans in geographically defined areas rather than in the physical object itself.

Beginning in the 1960s, the Japanese state proactively created regional boundaries to bolster domestic tourism and investment in national heritage (neatly shown by a poster of traditional commodities produced in south Japan stuck to the wall of a weaving school) (figure 1.10). The postwar era of modern-

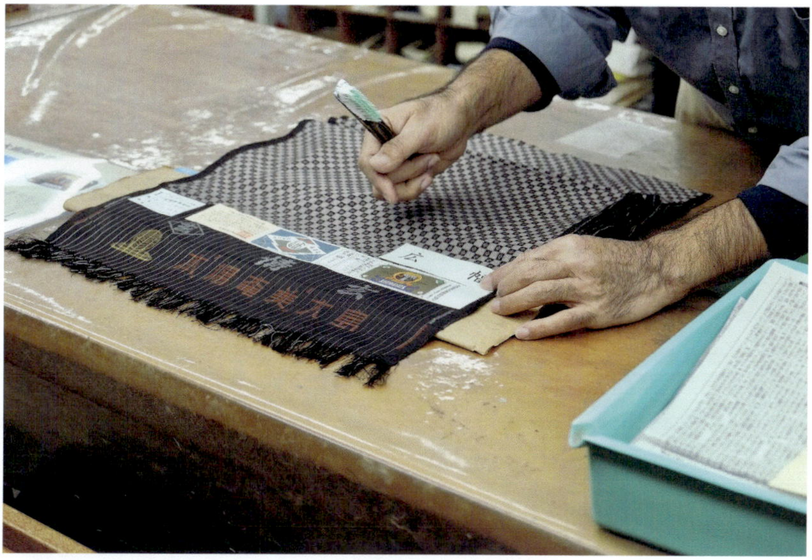

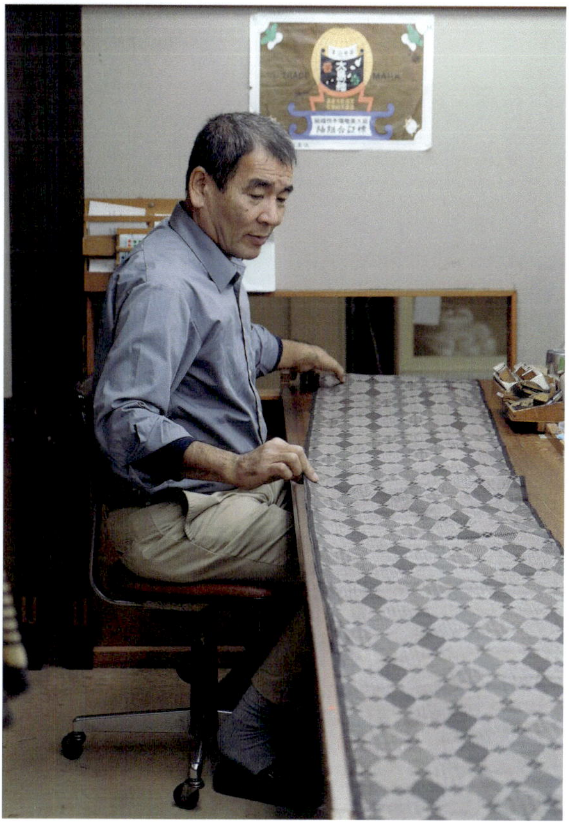

Figure 1.8 *An inspector applies official Oshima tsumugi seals.*

Figure 1.9 *The inspector examines a finished tanmono of tsumugi.*

ization saw Japan become the first industrialized nation in East Asia, bringing rapid social, economic, and environmental change. Anthropologist William Kelly (1986), through his research with rice farmers in Japan's Tohoku region, demonstrates the impact of the Green Revolution in Japan, whose aim was to decrease price while increasing yield. This meant updating infrastructure, reducing labor via mechanization, and encouraging the use of monoculture varieties and commercial chemicals. This extensive modernization stands in stark contrast to the argument to mechanize craft, as was played out regarding the karausu (clay crushers) of the Onta valley in the early 1970s and the rejection of machine-woven tsumugi imported from Korea. Reducing the costs of essential commodities (such as rice) created disposable income that the public could spend on luxury items, in effect stimulating the national economy. But by slowing the rate of change in the craft sector, prohibiting new technology, and regulating make, the government was able to fix high labor costs in different geographic regions to maintain what Marxist geographer David Harvey (2001) calls "structured coherence." This concept can be loosely defined as the social, cultural, economic, and geographic infrastructures supporting capitalist systems locally (Jessop 2006). Rather than allowing competing technological advancement to lower the price of craft, innovation in the craft sector was frozen and quality and authenticity were tied to hand labor and intangible skills that were geographically fixed.

In order to keep the price of craft affordable, it was increasingly subsidized by various government preservation schemes, because the state recognized that the abstract value of craft exceeded its commercial value. This suggests the government was speculating on the future value of craft, that is, the role it plays in strengthening national identity, bolstering tourism, and even being valued for its low environmental impact. Although environmental factors are unlikely to have been taken into consideration in the mid-twentieth century, it is certainly the case now that the government can use sustainability as a selling point when marketing Japanese craft internationally. The maintenance of Oshima tsumugi's status as a luxury product through high labor costs benefited local communities while the country had wealth; however, problems for the industry and for the sale of tsumugi began when the economy slowed and eventually crashed.

Finding New Purpose in Tsumugi's Techniques

The burst of Japan's financial bubble in the 1990s, alongside changes in fashion as Western clothing began to dominate, led to a loss of interest in wearing and buying kimono. The tsumugi market has declined year over year since

1972, and mirroring Douglas Haring's (1952) comments from the 1950s about the industry's "failure to adapt to changes in Japanese taste, and new ideas in design," Oshima tsumugi has developed a reputation for having a dated Shōwa era aesthetic. In secondhand kimono shops on the mainland tsumugi kimono that cost a small fortune when new can today be found piled high, selling for about ¥10,000 (sixty-six dollars) (see Valk 2020). Koki's judgment of tsumugi illustrates an opinion shared by many people I spoke with in Japan, including those in training: "If Oshima tsumugi was representing my generation, I would participate, but [the previous generation's makers] were doing it for the money, right? And they were selling it to older generations, and that's their taste. . . . I don't find that so exciting. . . . I want to make something that excites me, but what excites me about Oshima tsumugi is just its techniques."

Given its substantial economic impact and success in bringing notoriety to the culture and history of Amami, it is little wonder that there is still a strong feeling of loss for the industry's apex. This is most keenly experienced by families who were once prosperous, mainly the *orimoto-san* (weaving companies)—the manufacturers of tsumugi responsible for organizing and preparing each stage of production, then selling tanmono to mainland dealers.[7] One orimoto-san explained during peak production that the company sold around eight hundred tanmono a year, employing one hundred weavers working exclusively for them. Today, the same orimoto-san produces only one hundred tanmono a year, employing just fourteen weavers, with most of these women over seventy years old. Beyond weaving and dyeing, there are many specialized procedures in between. For example, there are only five men (also over seventy) working on the shimebata loom (figure 1.11), with no Amamian apprentices in waiting. The orimoto-san predicted that it will have to close its business within the next decade due to decreasing orders, but more significantly because of the lack of skilled craftspeople.

As a consequence, there is a general resolve among craftspeople that prospects for recovery are not good. This is evident in the fact that many craftspeople have not maintained the family line in knowledge transmission, aware that the craft is not financially viable and is subject to fluctuation. Instead, many craftworking families look to secure better futures for their children through higher education or by advising them to seek alternative employment. This was the case at Kanai Kougei, where the Shachō and Eriko-san discouraged their own children from pursuing a career in tsumugi. In this regard, the textile has been a victim of its own success. As Eriko-san explains: "Most places are planning to close when the artisans disappear. A number of them have already shut down their businesses. That's why the jobs these factories used to handle come to

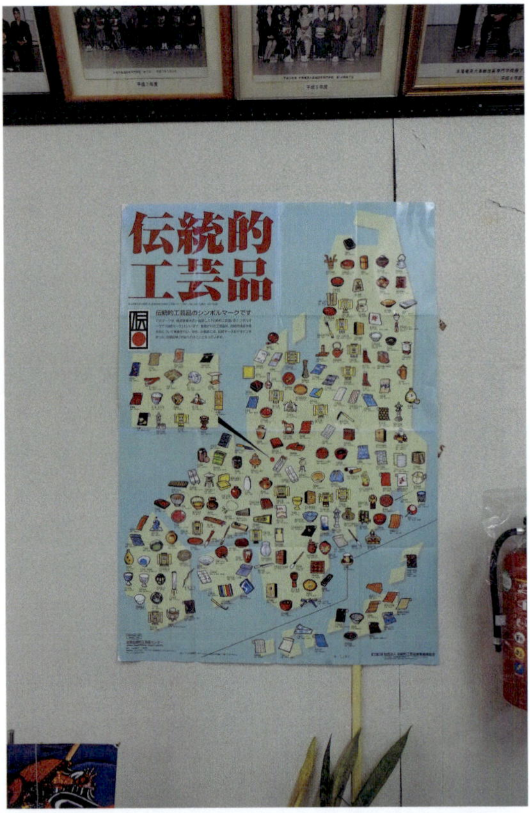

Figure 1.10 *A poster map of southern Japan's regional crafts. Oshima tsumugi are depicted in the poster's bottom right-hand corner, just to the left of the fire extinguisher.*

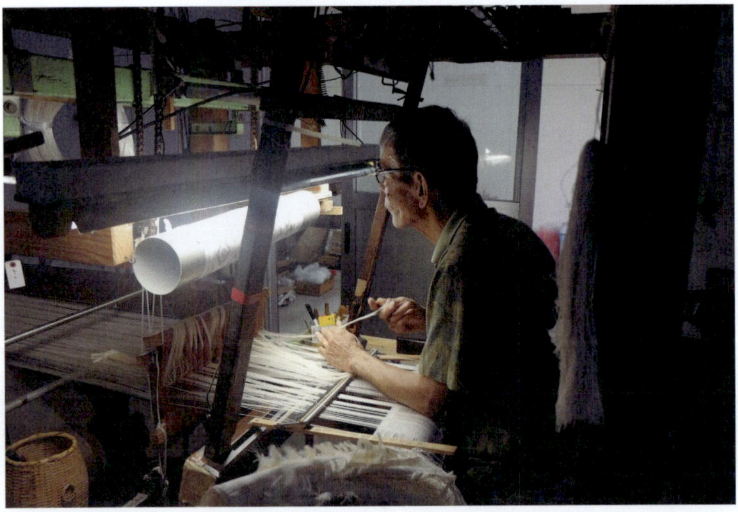

Figure 1.11 *A shimebata weaver creating the resist pattern. During my fieldwork there were no apprentices for this work.*

us. We are getting busier the past couple of years. Factories cannot avoid closing when they have no successor and the artisans are too old to handle the amount of dyeing work."

Before moving on to discuss the flow of people I propose are bringing a new purpose to dorozome and revitalizing kusakizome, I will reflect on my argument thus far. I have traced the recent history of the tsumugi industry to highlight that traditions are subject to influences outside of their geographies that might lead to innovations that sustain local industry. I have demonstrated how new ideas, technologies, and materials have been integrated into existing Japanese textile practices since at least the Meiji era, throughout Japan but also specifically with Oshima tsumugi. These developments did not dilute the ways in which textiles are used and valued but instead strengthened their economic potential. In the 1970s, technological innovation was put on hold, but when the craft was increasingly threatened by industrial manufacture, the adoption of new materials such as chemical dyes and nontraditional patterns was instituted industry wide. This line of argument supports the thesis that by incorporating innovation, "living traditions" do not remain static but are able to "traverse history" (Sahlins 1999, 408–9), questioning the meaning of "authenticity."

Throughout the 1980s and 1990s, a debate took hold in the social sciences that looked to "debunk" traditions that claimed unchanged heritage, with scholars such as Eric Hobsbawm and Terence Ranger (1983) and Stephen Vlastos (1998) arguing that many traditions are invented and done so with nationalist sentiments or money-making ambitions. Anthropologist Marshall Sahlins (1999) instead considers what traditions mean to those who live them and hypothesizes that the "inventiveness" of tradition is often constructed from manifestations of older practices, evolving alongside social, economic, and environmental change, beyond the control of makers. If one wanted to debunk Oshima tsumugi, a cloth claiming a heritage of 1,300 years, it could easily be done, because technological advances, new trade in materials, and global fashions have impacted its form and aesthetics since commercialization. The authenticity of a tradition should therefore not be based solely on historicity but be flexible to innovation to guarantee its continuity. Sahlins (1999, 410) proposes that traditions are the ways people "indigenize modernity," making them socially valuable. He calls these "visible signs of an invisible constituting presence. And, as sacred, they give a people commitment as well as definition . . . a sense of shared existence as well as determinate boundaries" (413).

This "sense of shared existence" is perhaps what has drawn a new generation of dyers to Kanai Kougei, because as a source of income it is far from profitable. Although Yukihito-san returned to Amami and gave the business a contemporary partner, he did so against the advice of his family, who had experienced the low wages and poor labor conditions prevalent in Amami (see chapter 2). Part-time dyers earn approximately ¥7,000 per day (about forty-six dollars), while a full-time tsumugi dyer will earn around ¥35,000–¥40,000 (about $230–$260) per six-day week. Because they are considered "freelancers," dyers lack the security of regular income, the benefits of lifetime employment, and sick leave and holiday pay. Moreover, their freelance status means it has been difficult for them to organize government support, because skills and hours across the various processes are diverse (see chapter 2). The work is also physically demanding and repetitive and requires good health, whether this is strength and stamina for dyeing or good eyesight and dexterous hands for weaving. In addition, it takes a significant investment of time and money to train, and when wages (or government stipends) are low it is difficult for apprentices to sustain themselves for the minimum five years required to master a foundation. Consequently, many quit before their training is complete. Nevertheless, weaving remains the most desirable tsumugi technique to learn (figure 1.12), as Eriko-san explained: "That's why Japan and Kagoshima Prefecture want to create a training school for residents of the island to acquire weaving skills. But the keen people who come to learn are typically from the mainland—art school graduates who love textile work."

In certain respects, this reflects the situation as it exists at Kanai Kougei. It is difficult to attract young local employees when they can earn better wages for less physically demanding work at somewhere like the ubiquitous convenience store chain Family Mart. However, Kanai Kougei is exemplary in that it is both a family business and one that readily employs staff from outside of the local community who are in pursuit of a labor of love—evidenced by the ease by which I gained access as a British anthropologist, with no formal introduction. This openness to "outsiders" is quite unusual in traditional Japanese crafting businesses, which have historically been structured around the *iemoto*, or household system.

Although over thirty years old, Dorinne Kondo's ethnography *Crafting Selves* (1990), which explored gender relations in a Tokyo sweetshop, can be drawn upon to consider the circumstances in Amami in regard to iemoto. Kondo explains that while the word *ie* can designate both a physical house and the household line, in the Japanese context "*ie* are best understood as *corporate groups* that hold property (for example, land, a reputation, an art, or 'cultural capital') in perpetuity" (1990, 122). She argues that despite the iemoto system being dismantled during the postwar constitution, it is far from "defunct" and

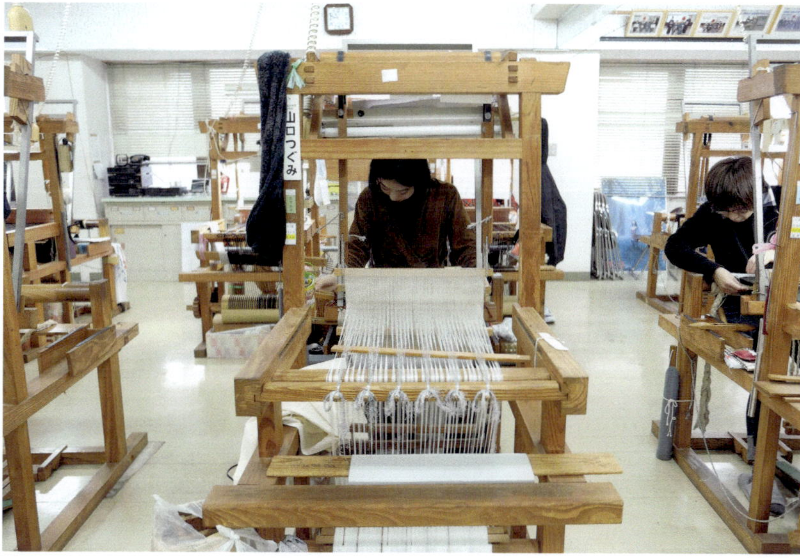

Figure 1.12 *Tsugumi-san* (center), *an apprentice weaver at the weaving school.*

the concept of "company as family" continues to operate either literally or symbolically (121).

Although I was told that Amami has historically followed a *shima* (island) system, where the islanders worked together to represent a large household (a mentality that has been retained), it could be argued that on a smaller scale the ie system has been absorbed from mainland Japan.[8] Kondo (1990, 121) says that the "core" of such a group may consist of kin—a mother and father who are responsible for the success of the business, who will pass it on to their heir, who historically has been the eldest son or an adopted "son" gained through marriage or law. Although Yukihito-san did eventually return to the family business, the Shachō's continued acceptance of outsiders across his tenure has seen Kanai Kougei's ie grow, providing access to social and business networks outside of Amami. This stands in contrast to many of the other tsumugi businesses that have struggled to maintain the line of traditional knowledge. As the Shachō described: "I think, *kuru mono kobamazu* ('accept one who comes to you'). So I accept anyone who comes, and *saru mono owazu* ('don't chase one who leaves'). I'm connected to many different people—including Kazuko-chan or Akiyo-chan [two Kanai Kougei dyers, from Tokyo and south Amami, respectively]—and that sort of thing expands and continues, right?"

This openness to new people and business has no doubt been aided by Kanai Kougei's significant media presence, the company's popularity stemming from the Shachō's attitude. The workshop has built a reputation that has seen TV networks such as NHK, the BBC, and CNN visit, with their global distribution helping to promote both tsumugi and dorozome. During the time of my fieldwork, Japan Airlines filmed a TV commercial at the workshop that draws heavily upon Japan's nostalgia for traditional craft: A young girl dyes a handkerchief with her father, who is a tsumugi craftsman. She returns home (on a Japan Airlines flight) as an adult with the same handkerchief, which she holds dear. During the filming the Shachō showed the actor how to dye "authentically," giving direction by demonstrating how to stir the mud in the dorota with his boots and distribute mud across the yarns. Asking Maiko-san—the Shachō's daughter and company's bookkeeper—about these visits, I was surprised to hear Kanai Kougei did not receive a location fee from Japan Airlines. Although this relationship might be read as commercial exploitation, it echoes Kelly's (1986, 612) research, whose farmer participants were renowned *nō* actors, in that the Shachō was "willing to risk the dangers of fetishization for the edge that their notoriety gives them."

Consequently, the Kanai family has used its notoriety to extend its ie by picking up craftsmen as dyeing houses closed and attracting new employees who are similar to Yukihito-san in their keenness to learn the craft. Kondo says entry into the ie "means belonging to an institution that links one to the past and projects one into the future" (1990, 122–23). Kanai Kougei sits very much at this meeting point, as the Shachō takes cares of tsumugi while Yukihito-san leads the apparel division. During the time of my fieldwork, they employed three full-time and one part-time tsumugi dyers, all Amamian men over the age of fifty. In addition, three men and three women between twenty-four and forty-one years of age worked on apparel, while Eriko-san and Maiko-san oversaw public workshops and administration.

This structure and mix of employees are significant, as the apparel dyers are all U-turners (those who have "U-turned" back to the countryside like Yukihito-san) or I-turners (meaning *inaka*-turn, from the Japanese word for countryside). *U-turn* and *I-turn* are existing economic terms used in Japan to describe individuals and families who have typically rejected more prosperous urban living, hoping for a more fulfilled and safer existence in the countryside. Anthropologist Susanne Klien (2016, 2020) suggests that this reverse migration movement, which bucks the rural-urban trend that has gone hand in hand with industrialization, has been prompted by negative economic growth, twenty years of deflation, and the triple disaster of 3.11. Prompted by job insecurity, Klien (2016, 40) suggests, there are those among Japan's youth who are rejecting the "orthodox *Sarariiman* (salaryman) mode of work and life" and turning their backs on the previous generation's inclination to overwork and the resulting material affluence. Instead, many young people are embracing more precarious forms of subsistence that value "self-expression" and "quality of life" (Inglehart 1995, 57). I-turners and U-turners are able to maintain city relationships assisted by the internet and social media, but they also foster local social networks leading to a richer engagement with an individual's community and environment (see chapters 2 and 3). As Koki explained: "One thing that was huge for me was when the earthquake and the nuclear disaster happened, that changed my way of thinking completely. That really destroyed everything, all those superficial things, they disappeared really easily. And then [I thought] maybe I should focus on something that is more a core part of things, that doesn't just get washed away."

The new-generation dyers find they value the work and the skills they are obtaining more than high earnings. Yet they manage to survive on minimal resources only because the cost of living in Amami is low. In addition, people tend to foster close relationships with their coworkers and neighbors, leading to the exchange of material supplies such as food, clothes, and even childcare. Functioning like an ie, the Kanai family extends access to its Amamian networks of knowledge to those migrating from the mainland. Access to this knowledge is often cited as a problem by I-turners in other areas of Japan, who find it difficult to connect with the local community. Whether it is finding an employee an affordable car, recommending the best place to collect seaweed, or dressing one's family in kimono, there will be a member of staff at Kanai Kougei willing to assist those new to the island.

Two of Kanai Kougei's dyers are working mothers, Satoko-san (forty-one) from Kyoto and Kazuko (thirty-seven) from Tokyo, who value this support network highly. The third female dyer working at Kanai Kougei, Akiyo, is a twenty-four-year-old Tokyo-trained fashion graduate from south Amami. The employment of Satoko-san, Kazuko, and Akiyo reveals a further evolution of tradition in that gendered labor roles, entrenched in the mid-twentieth century, are also becoming outdated. As I can testify, dorozome is physically demanding, and for full-time employees working a six-day week, it is not for the fainthearted. The new-generation dyers are strong women in body and mind, following an older Amamian tradition of women whose rights are equal to men's. This reversal of gender roles is working both ways, however, as Koki has been training at the weaving school in an activity historically the reserve of Amamian women.

Takahito-san, thirty (figure 1.13), who U-turned back to Amami after a string of failed job prospects on the mainland, told me his primary motivation in joining

Kanai Kougei was to sustain Amamian tradition. He described that when he lived in the city of Fukuoka, his friends were confused why he was there, because "Amami was so great"; it had its own culture and unique nature, but he was embarrassed to admit he knew little about it. One of his friends was working to preserve the Hakata Gion Yamakasa *matsuri*, a carnival-style event that involves carrying a huge float through the streets of Fukuoka. Takahito-san was so impressed by his friend's commitment to his own hometown's traditions that he decided to return to Amami and similarly dedicate himself. In his hometown of Yamato-son, a school friend had already been working on a matsuri for the old people of the village, and he felt ashamed that this person, who was younger than him, had achieved so much, while he had selfishly wasted time on a string of part-time jobs on the mainland. He decided to set up a nonprofit organization to support the village's *hachi gatsu odori* (August dance). This he felt would sustain Amamian culture and generate community solidarity. But realizing that it would be difficult to sustain himself economically, he instead took a job at Kanai Kougei. He knew nothing about dyeing and had no prior interest; he simply saw it as a means to sustain Amamian tradition. I asked him why tradition was so important to him. He answered: "It's the way tsumugi is so particular to this area—it's something that can only be found here. Even for someone from outside, when you see this kind of thing [the dorozome with tsumugi] there's a feeling of a kind of chain—like a sense of lively energy attached to it."

When I first met Takahito-san, I was told he was learning kusakizome so he could open his own dyeing workshop in his village, which was over an hour's commute from Kanai Kougei. I had assumed this was a business pursuit, but he said it was "for the people from Yamato-son." If he opened his own studio, "there would be more chances for them to come into contact with this tradition." But later the plan changed, he explained:

> Since both Nagata-san and Shachō are quite old, we don't know when they might not be able to keep going any more. So that's our current situation, and within that context—if there were craftsmen who could do the work spot on, then even if I'm not here it wouldn't matter—but that's not the situation. I'm working as a dyer [in Amami] but, make no mistake, there'll come a time when things at Kanai Kougei won't be able to go on any longer. And here at Kanai Kougei, people who can do tsumugi dyeing are necessary, and yet there isn't really any talk of bringing in more new ones. [If you want to get into the craft of tsumugi dyeing] they have to teach you here, and then if you think, "Actually this place isn't for me," and you leave, then there's no one.

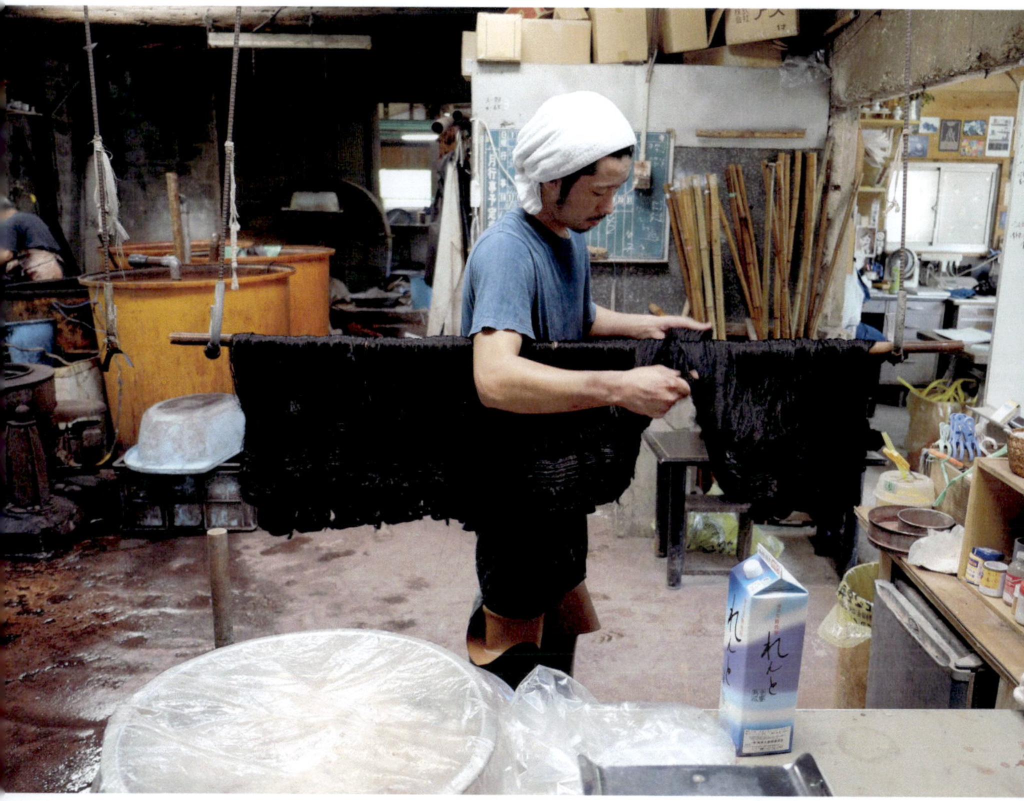

Figure 1.13 *Takahito-san drying tsumugi yarns.*

The point Takahito-san was making is that he is learning the skills now while there are people to teach him, and when the time comes for the older craftsmen to retire, he will be the only holder of this knowledge because he is the only apprentice. In a sense, he is binding himself to both the history and the future of the craft. As it turned out, Nagata-san (introduced at the beginning of the chapter), who was still working into his seventies, died suddenly from lung cancer in May 2019, never reaching retirement. What can be learned from the younger craftspeople at Kanai Kougei is that while the past generations of the boom era bought into tradition through the purchase of commodities to divert uncertainty, younger generations are more interested in pursuing a career in craft and making the commodities themselves. Eriko-san told me Takahito-san's apprenticeship is a draw for the orimoto-sans; they are sending more work to Kanai Kougei because they see a future for tsumugi at the workshop.

"The Nail That Sticks Out"

When the Shachō started public dorozome workshops in Amami in the late 1980s, in his words, "it actually angered the other dyeing companies." Today, all Amami's dyeing companies offer public workshops that financially support their business. Similarly, in the 2000s, Yukihito-san faced significant resistance from the tsumugi union, which was concerned that dyeing "cheap T-shirts" would devalue dorozome and subsequently Oshima tsumugi. As he describes it, "Our generation does not wear kimono so often. I was doing it thinking it would be nice if there were tsumugi for the everyday—it is a thing to wear—the same as kimono.[9] But from the point of view of the [tsumugi] industry, the entire opposite opinion bounced back to me. I was quite surprised."

In Yukihito-san's words, apparel became "the nail that sticks out." This refers to the Japanese saying "A nail that sticks out must be banged down"—a metaphor for the Japanese social tendency to favor and preserve collective harmony over individual uniqueness.[10] Nevertheless, he persevered:

> The side of apparel works as a job and I thought it would be better for dorozome to have the connection with young people. I just had to continue doing it and gain their trust. Did I gain their trust then? Well, I wonder. . . . I don't quite know if they approved of me or not, because how it works is different from the side of the [tsumugi] industry [being hierarchical]. . . . But now, the tsumugi union understands Kanai Kougei is a place that does this sort of work. So if there is a request, they would say: "Right, please go and speak to them." It wasn't always like that at the beginning.

In the case of Oshima tsumugi, Yukihito-san highlights that resistance to change in more recent years has been top-down, while innovation has been bottom-up. Historically, the tsumugi industry has been based on a strict hierarchy, with the dyers at the bottom. But by creating a more hybridized business that welcomes people, trade, and ideas from outside of the community, this hierarchy has been disrupted. Yet as I have argued throughout this chapter, traditions have always been pushed forward by external forces that can assist in the maintenance of tradition and which should not necessarily be considered threatening. Japanese craft continues to combine superior hand skills with innovative technologies, evident by the number of historic textile processes still carried out across the country today, even if output has dramatically declined.

On days when Kanai Kougei was overrun with tourists participating in dyeing workshops, they would inevitably disrupt workflow. This was often frustrating—

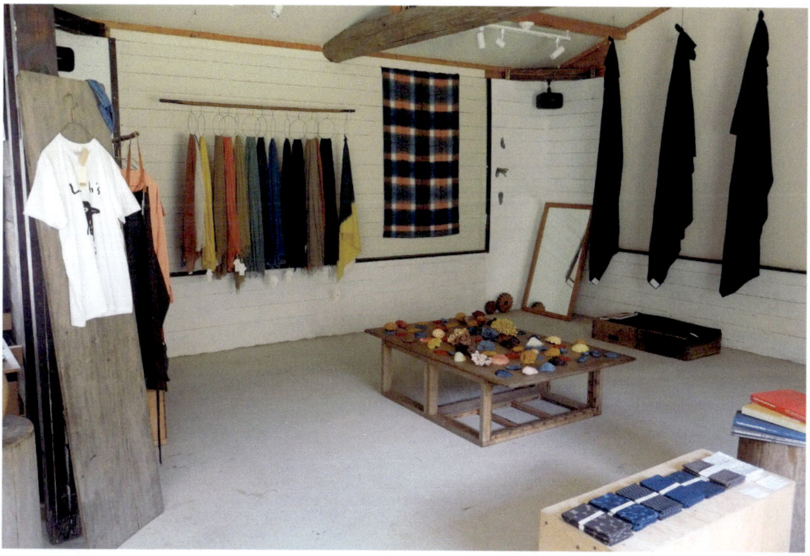

Figure 1.14 *The sales gallery at Kanai Kougei.*

and a point of contention between the Shachō and Yukihito-san. But, as I was told, tourists liked being in an environment where "things to wear," whether kimono or T-shirts, were undergoing production. Kanai Kougei is an exemplary case study as "an institution that links one to the past and projects one into the future" (Kondo 1990, 122–23). This is through its intimate connection with Oshima tsumugi, a cloth likely to become an ICP, but also as a place where workers, visitors, and clients can imagine a future for the craft. This case study demonstrates that the economic and cultural importance of tsumugi can be detached from the kimono as a cultural object and commodity, providing alternative streams of income through a process such as dorozome (figure 1.14). Innovation has been embraced in the face of local resistance, and the Kanai family has pioneered the democratization of a luxury craft process.

By establishing a symbiotic relationship among tsumugi, apparel, and public workshops, the family has created a precarious but functioning business that at present is prospering. Rather than choosing between preserving traditional practice and innovating to ensure long-term sustainability, Kanai Kougei shows that it may be possible to pursue both. As Yukihito-san says, "With the case of Oshima tsumugi . . . what is important is not the fabric—it is the background, Amami's nature and the wisdom of the people who made it. That is what should actually be endorsed." By mobilizing uncertainty about the future, Kanai Kougei has used it as both a productive and a sustaining force. In the following chapters, I will consider in more detail the global environmental, economic, and political conditions of uncertainty that have prompted a renewed interest in consuming but also making traditional craft objects. Chapter 2 focuses on the new generation of craftspeople in Japan who have been seduced by "the alchemy of producing color." They have used their passion for craft and pursuit of the "good life" to establish relationships between people and place locally, nationally, and globally. Using entrepreneurial acumen, they market the aesthetics and stories of labor to generate capital, but I ask, At what cost does this come?

2

The Alchemy of Producing Color

In 2004, Yukihito Kanai, head of apparel at Kanai Kougei, U-turned back to Amami from Tokyo with a desire to "think." Thirty-eight years old at the time of my fieldwork, he was born on the island but left after graduating from high school to pursue a career as a sound engineer in the music industry. His first passion is music, having extensive knowledge of Amamian *shima-uta* (island music) but also an eclectic collection of global music that provides a soundtrack to the workshop. After training at college, Yukihito-san struggled financially, supplementing freelance work with a job at an *izakaya* (a Japanese restaurant-bar)—a common occurrence, I was told, in this line of work. His return to Amami was prompted by job insecurity, but he stumbled into the family profession by accident. He had never intended to quit music, but passing time in the workshop he discovered a skill (and love) for making color and realized there was a demand for his dyeing services. By following up on inquiries that had gone unanswered and spreading the word among designer friends in Tokyo, by his own admission

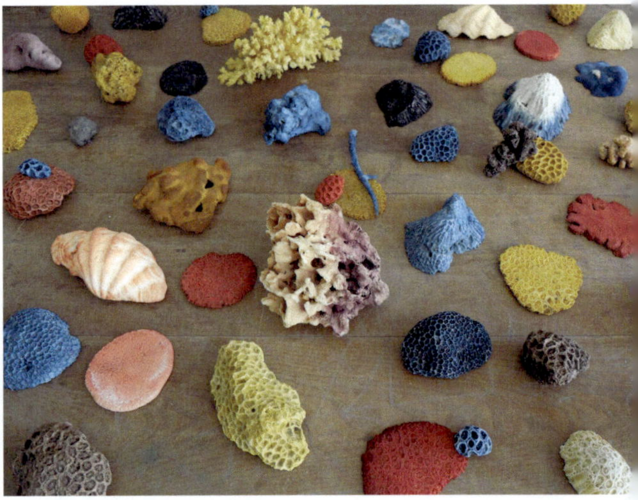

Figure 2.1 *Sea coral collected from Amami's beaches, naturally dyed, is sold in Kanai Kougei's gallery.*

he created a job for himself. Cultural theorist Angela McRobbie (1998, 184) describes this form of "job creation" in the creative industries as being "both planned through 'enterprise culture,'" cultivated by neoliberal governments in Europe and North America since the 1980s, "and completely unplanned in its cultural outcomes, the signs of which stretch across urban landscape, bringing color and vitality to run down, deindustrialized sites and spaces." In the 2020s, we would recognize this as urban gentrification, but in Japan in the early 2000s it was rural regions with their wealth of traditional practices that were primed for regeneration.

Beginning in the eighteenth century, industrialization across the developed world has encouraged a flow of labor from the countryside to work in cities. In Japan, this process began relatively late with a period of modernization ignited by the Meiji Restoration around 1868. By the 1960s and as a consequence of the post–World War II recovery, out-migration from the countryside affected around 60 percent of Japan (Manzenreiter et al. 2020, 1). Leaving behind an aging demographic, the flight of youth caused a crisis of rural depopulation, and lacking in taxpayers, local infrastructure in depopulated regions was financially supported by the state. When the bubble economy burst in the 1990s, causing significant instability in the labor market, increasing numbers of city dwellers began to reverse this flow by acting on state-sponsored rural repopulation initiatives. These ranged from the opening of employment and housing advice centers to local prefectures providing resettlement assistance and monthly stipends to individuals. Some, known as U-turners (like Yukihito-san), returned to the prefectures in which they were born or where their families traditionally lived, while I-turners—*I* standing for *inaka* (countryside)—moved to places with which they had no previous connection to pursue more "fulfilling" lifestyles through craft, agriculture, or rural regeneration projects (Hani 2001). These projects did not reverse rural-to-urban migration enough to solve the depopulation problem, however, and by 2000 the central government began to move away from a tax distribution system that used income from metropolitan centers to shore up depopulated regions and instead moved toward an emphasis on self-reliance (Love 2013, 116). This has led to the further degradation of services in rural areas—closures of schools, libraries, and transportation networks—but also to increasingly inventive plans by local authorities to draw people back to the countryside, giving individuals but also whole regions the opportunity to reinvent themselves.

The urban-to-rural movement gained pace after the 2008 global financial crisis and with urgency after 3.11, the triple disaster of earthquake, tsunami, and nuclear spill that unleashed widespread anxiety across the whole of the greater Tokyo area. The unfolding crisis was a catalyst for change that led many of my participants to move to rural areas either by themselves or with their families. Yukihito-san's friends Kitta-san and Sawano-san, whom I first met at MONO JAPAN in the Netherlands (see introduction), moved to rural Okinawa from Chiba Prefecture after 3.11, which gave them time and space to expand their naturally dyed clothing label, KITTA. In a magazine interview Kitta-san describes how she was "so heartbroken over the fact that humans had contaminated beautiful nature" (Kitta 2017). She was pregnant, and uncertainty, particularly around food safety, was causing her significant anxiety (see chapter 3). Seeking resolutions, Kitta-san and Sawano-san moved their family and business to find value, as Kitta-san describes, in the "joy of living" *(ikiru yorokobi)*. This term comes from the ambiguous Japanese word *ikigai* that has been translated into English as finding "that which most makes one's life seem worth living" (Mathews 1996, 718). Kitta-san and Sawano-san say they channel this sense of purpose through the objects they make and their processes of work but also recognize it through their appreciation of folk music, organic food, nature, and sociality (Kitta 2017).

In chapter 1 I situated my research in Amami's *tsumugi* community, the "embedded infrastructure" (Norris 2019, 211) guiding the lives of craftworkers on this traditional textile island. In chapters 2 and 3, I focus on the new generation of dyers, both U-turn and I-turn residents in Amami but also Okinawa, and the motivating factors that brought them to the Ryūkyūs. I consider the history of

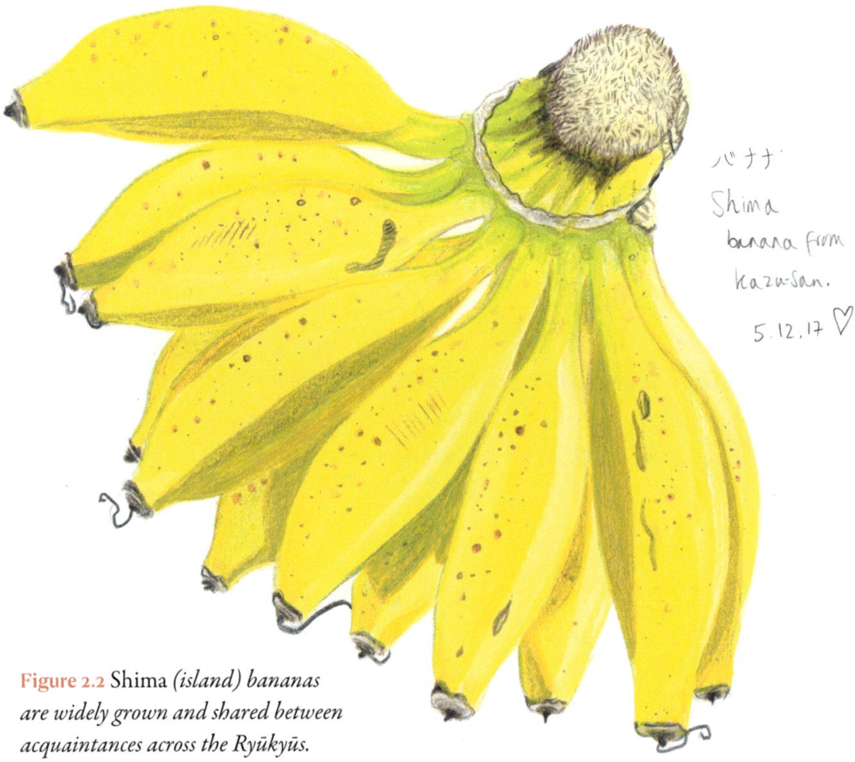

Figure 2.2 Shima *(island) bananas are widely grown and shared between acquaintances across the Ryūkyūs.*

twentieth-century migration into rural regions and explore the reasons why reverse migration has increased since the turn of the century. In this chapter I ask how craftspeople are regenerating traditional practices in the countryside and aim to establish the sustaining processes, but also the unintended consequences, that allow them to make previously failing industries economically viable. I am interested in how they facilitate a two-way flow of capital between the islands and the mainland using knowledge, ideas, experience, and connections that bridge two worlds. This, I argue, is driven not by an aspiration to accumulate capital but by a desire to develop skills and identity as craftspeople, engage in place-making, develop strong communities, establish a "connectedness to nature" (Yoneyama 2019), and experience the "joy of living." I suggest that the practice of natural dyeing and the alchemy of producing color allows these aspirations to be realized and generates a form of self-reliance that reverberates throughout creative communities both locally and farther afield. In chapter 3 I will look more closely at the ethical values driving these aspirations. But in this chapter, I consider how the "joy of living" is proceeded by an economic imperative that necessitates a form of entrepreneurism that reevaluates craft, its ideals, and the aesthetics of labor but also requires an element of self-exploitation. With this in mind, I question what skills are needed, networks established, and sacrifices made in order to sustain the "good life" when relocating to rural Japan.

Urban-to-Rural Migration in the Era of Neoliberalism

Urban-to-rural migration is often framed as a relatively recent phenomenon, but even in 1952 anthropologist Douglas Haring documented its occurrence in Amami. With visible bias he writes: "A minor reservoir of talent now unused occurs in the occasional highly-educated individuals who live the simple life of Amami peasants. Some have chosen this island and such a way of living to escape from 'civilization.' . . . A tactful approach might discover ways of utilizing the scholarly, scientific, and artistic talents of such individuals to raise Amami standards of living" (Haring 1952, 39).

In the UK, Diana Forsythe's (1980, 290) ethnography from the 1960s and 1970s was one of the earliest in the developed world to describe middle-class, "disaffected city dwellers," who were resettling in Orkney, Scotland, to pursue a "peaceful, quiet, friendly, safe, and natural" rural life "in contrast to the noise, dirt, anonymity, danger, and pressure" of the city.[1] In Japan, John Knight's (1997, 241) 1980s fieldwork documented the "salary-rejectionists" *(datsusara)* of the "back-to-the-land movement" on the Kii peninsula, where local youth had migrated to cities in the Kansai region, resulting in rural populations declining by half between 1955 and 1995 (239). With the help of the local authorities, city dwellers relocated to pursue a "'peasant' (*hyakushō*) lifestyle" and "natural farming" (238), an approach to land management that rejects the use of chemicals, promotes soil health, and is considered to have mental and physical healing power (see Fukuoka [1978] 2010). Michaela Benson and Karen O'Reilly (2009, 608–10) term this "lifestyle migration," which describes "the relocation of people within the developed world searching for a better way of life," including slow living, improved work-life equilibrium, access to affordable housing, community, and health benefits of climate and nature. The people they interviewed in Europe followed "a narrative of escape" yet tended to be "relatively affluent migrants who do not fit the stereotypical idea of a migrant . . . do not compete for jobs, and tend not to be racialized as other immigrants" (609).

In the context of huge levels of forced migration happening today at a global scale, historian Lorenzo Veracini (2010, 3) explains that, both in transit and upon arrival at their destination, migrants do not "enjoy inherent rights and are characterized by a defining lack of sovereign entitlement." In contrast, when considering patterns of internal migration, the term *settler* has been offered up as more appropriate (Addie and Fraser 2019, 1377). This term can account for both the presence of urban gentrification—in which wealthier outsiders move into city areas typically home to lower-income communities, leading to rises in house prices, new businesses, and ultimately the displacement of those existing communities—and the impact of urban-to-rural migration. Echoing the historical character of settler colonialism, *settler* contemporaneously invokes those moving into a community who bring their own politics, ideas, and tastes to hybridize a "new" settlement (Veracini 2010; Blatman-Thomas and Porter 2019). In contrast to the migrant, these individuals carry their "sovereignty" with them and, as such, the ability to assert their own experience of a political and social order. What many of the studies on lifestyle migration have in common are the incomers who seek nature, tradition, and community but often find it difficult to align their politics, ideas, and tastes with those of their hosts. Their high expectations are often dashed by the social, political, and economic realities experienced for generations by rural residents, those that prompted out-migration in the first place.

This growing body of anthropological literature, spanning more than fifty years, explores migration in terms of choice—internal migrants search for better lifestyles in rural idylls, often from a position of privilege; they typically have economic advantage over locals (savings, credit, wealthy city-based relatives), higher education and professional skills, and access to opportunities offered by local authorities.[2] Yet in the era of neoliberalism, it is important to question the idea of choice. The failings of neoliberalism have often stimulated crisis at the national, local, or personal scale, meaning citizens feel they have little choice but to take action to improve their living conditions. As with the ebb and flow between suburban areas and inner cities across the twentieth century, both social mobility and the sense of entitlement to act to improve one's quality of life, perceptions of safety, and cultural richness mediate patterns of movement. Rather than going "backward" to escape "civilization," as Haring suggested, an accusation that hasn't weakened over time (Parkins and Craig 2006, 78), today newly arrived residents see a future in the countryside, in its community, customs, and environments, more conducive to their own health and that of their families. Sociologist Menelaos Gkartzios documented what he termed "crisis counterurbanization" in Athens, for example, in the wake of the 2007–08 financial crisis. As a result of Greece's severe economic depression, mass unemployment, breakdown of social care, and infrastructural neglect by local authorities, he explains how people used circumstances beyond their control to "re-examine life, values and to prioritize needs accordingly" (Gkartzios 2013, 164). Gkartzios's interviewees relocated to areas where they might have family support networks to provide the care neglected by the state—a profile synonymous with Japanese U-turners. Anthropologists who have written more recently about internal migration in Japan (Allison 2013; Klien 2016, 2019, 2020; Rosenberger 2017; Manzenreiter et al. 2020) similarly foreground the sense of uncertainty or "precarity" that exists in contemporary urban life as a motivating force.

Precarity, a word whose origins can be traced to the labor movement of 1970s France (Allison 2013, 5), has become an increasingly popular condition of study in academic literature (Allison 2013; Muehlebach 2013; Tsing 2015). Anthropologist Claudio Sopranzetti says that "analysis of precarity has mostly emerged in the context of advanced economies and retreating welfare states," but it also describes "global trends in contemporary capitalism." He defines precarity as the experience of unstable, temporary, and informal labor, but the feeling of precarity created by these labor conditions goes "beyond the sphere of employment," extending "their characteristics of instability, flexibility, and individualization to subjectivities, social relations, or imaginaries of the future" (Sopranzetti 2018, 134). Experiences associated with precarious labor have been documented in Japan, where the burst of the bubble economy in the 1990s—the beginning of the end for "lifetime employment" (*shushin koyō*)—produced instability in the labor market, ushering in a range of neoliberal economic reforms.[3] While conducting his ethnography with financial traders in Tokyo, anthropologist Hirokazu Miyazaki (2010, 239) observed how deregulation and competition were increasingly prioritized in business by the government and media, "who promoted the rise of 'strong individuals' (*tsuyoi kojin*) ready to take risks (*risuku*) while taking responsibilities for their own risk-taking action (*jiko sekinin*)."

While driven by the experience of precarity, those who move to rural locations from urban centers are in many cases, but not exclusively, bringing with them an experience of income generation and living synonymous with the middle class. They are conscious that resettling in the countryside means a narrowing of access to amenities and job opportunities and perhaps a less liberal social and cultural context. Nevertheless, Susanne Klien (2020, 175) references a 2014 survey that concluded that 40 percent of Japanese would be interested in moving from Tokyo to rural regions. Such a migration has been facilitated through participation in local government schemes such as the Regional Revitalization Cooperation Officer Program (*chiiki okoshi kyōrokutai*) (Klien 2019, 75), which places individuals in agriculture, tourism, and even craft regeneration projects. Outside of these schemes, jobs in local industries are hard to come by or do not provide opportunities for personal growth. Consequently, migrants often commute to work in large cities, as was the case in Amami, where residents took advantage of frequent cheap flights provided by budget airlines. Alternatively, people make jobs for themselves through entrepreneurial activities—opening restaurants, working remotely in IT or finance, engaging in farming, or running Airbnbs. The impact of such settlement has begun to be visible, where local traditions and landscapes are "improved" for outside consumption, and coffee shops, hotels, and restaurants have been opened to appeal to other I-turners and tourists (Klien 2020; Traphagan 2020). While instances of conflict between rural residents and I-turn "settlers" certainly occur (Linton forthcoming), rural Japan presents a paradox because repopulation is actively desired. When I drove my elderly neighbor to her favorite beach, she pointed to new beachside houses, dismayed that their owners would probably be from Tokyo. Yet local residents also want to have local services restored, see children playing in the streets, and visit the new amenities arriving with newcomers.

While it remains unanswered whether the current tourism boom in Amami will significantly impact the cost of living as has occurred in urban regions, my experience in Amami was of a lack of concern around the potential for displacement or cultural erasure if the arrival of outsiders and the tourist industry gathered pace.[4] One explanation for this might be that such movement is not understood in terms of class conflict as it might be elsewhere, a sign of the general sense of middle-class homogeny existing in Japan. Anthropologist William Kelly (1986, 604) quotes the Japanese government's public opinion surveys that claim that 90 percent of the country's population is middle class, suggesting a common level of social and physical mobility across the populace. The Japanese pay a graded income tax, the education system is robust, health insurance is income gradable, one can draw unemployment insurance, and the country has one of the lowest pay differentials in the world. But as Kelly explores, there exist too many "contradictions and paradoxes" in education, in the home, and in the workplace, suggesting that the "90 percent" figure might underestimate instances of struggle or deprivation. Kelly instead labels the "loose pattern of expectations" contained within the 90 percent figure as "New Middle Class folk sociology" (605). The contradictions within such a folk sociology were apparent among my participants in Amami: They all finished high school, with some going on to college in Japan or abroad, yet in many instances they came from blue-collar families with little disposable income. For those individuals from white-collar families, the financial crises of recent years had eroded any possibility of inherited wealth. This idea is further complicated by a 2022 survey that suggested that Japan's middle class was in "crisis," with only 38 percent of respondents believing they lived a middle-class lifestyle, while 56 percent said they did not enjoy this level of comfort (Japan International Labour Foundation 2022).[5] With wages freezing despite inflation, it is little wonder that people wish to take their chances on what craft researchers Susan Luckman and Nicola Thomas call "DIY entrepreneurial career paths" (2018, 127).[6]

Other anthropologists working in Japan recall a similar situation as the one I observed in Amami, where migrants take significant risks by setting up a home or business in a new environment. Working with I-turn organic farmers, Nancy Rosenberger (2017, 16) called this "occupational edgework"—work that "takes on risk and uncertainty as a way of life" in order to "cope with the uncertainties of environment, food, family, and self-making in neoliberal Japan." This "edgework" brings together the rural and urban, blending "flexible, hybrid approaches" to gain access to regionally fixed land, traditions, and infrastructure, while metropolitan mobility allows them to "crisscross" social, geographic, and economic boundaries (15). Unlike the organic pioneers Knight (1997) references in his work from the 1990s, who in going "back to the land" were considered "resisters" of the capitalist system, the new generation follows a "politics of engagement rather than contestation" (Rosenberger 2017, 18). This is exemplified by Klien's (2020, 146) "social entrepreneurs" who move to rural regions and tackle social issues through business activities. Klien's research includes a furniture factory providing skills and employment for local people in Ishinomaki, a tsunami-devastated fishing town, and in depopulated Tokushima an enterprise selling wooden tableware turned by local carpenters to restore value to neglected Japanese cedar forests (145–73). Across this literature there is a genuine sense that professionals who relocate to the countryside have become disillusioned with the conditions defining urban life and possess a desire to work toward an improved society and environment. Yet my research shows this is not entirely altruistic, because Klien's participants, like my own, often relocate carrying with them a sense of sovereignty that allows them to follow their own creativity and find value in work not defined or confined by income. I met many people in Amami who had moved to combine commerce with creativity or health-related benefits: There was the herbalist who had trained in Edinburgh, UK, and moved from mainland Japan to grow and dispense her own plants in Amami's warm climate. There was a couple who moved to become commercial organic farmers in the hope that the sun, nutritious food, and a change of pace would cure the husband's skin complaint, yet who later lost a whole season's crop in a typhoon, pushing them instead to earn an income in tourism. I picked up a hitchhiker who had moved to Amami to pursue a career as a stained-glass artisan but whose lack of business acumen led them instead to become a "mongoose hunter," part

Figure 2.3 *An endemic Barbour's blue-tailed skink.*

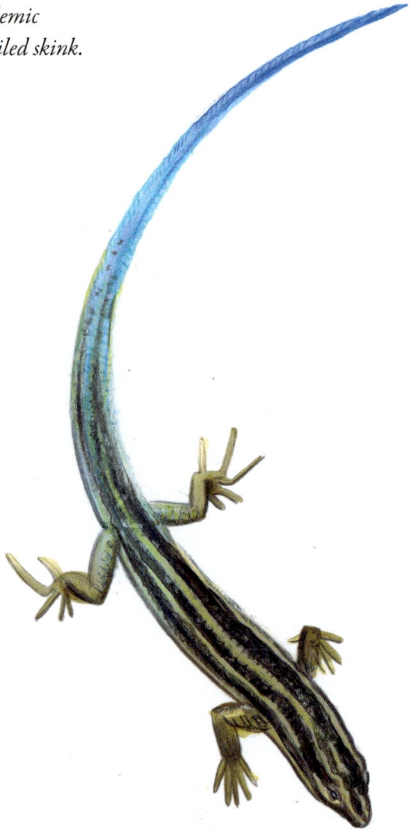

of a team employed to eradicate the introduced Indian mongoose that were decimating indigenous wildlife.

The apparel staff at Kanai Kougei provided a rich field site for examining the mechanics of combining creative labor with nature, community, and business. Like many of the Japanese craftspeople I came to know, Yukihito-san readily adopted the role of the craftsman who labors with focused intensity, but the apparel side of the business necessitates risk, innovation, investment, identification of new markets and opportunities, and implementation of useful ideas. His example highlights that in order to be a successful craftsman today, one needs to also be an entrepreneur. Yet rather than corresponding with the framing of the entrepreneur within business literature—one who acts at the frontier of new markets and financial risk with a view to ultimately reap the profit—entreprencurialism as I experienced it at Kanai Kougei could not be understood through the pursuit of personal wealth, because small-scale, traditional craft can rarely be financially rewarding. Instead, value is located in the development of craft skills that inform one's identity and in the pursuit of an improved quality of life for oneself and one's family within a craft community.

Rather than following in the footsteps of his father by training in tsumugi dyeing, Yukihito-san sought to bring an element of Tokyo back with him to Amami and to develop an aesthetic that chimed with his own personal understanding of taste. This taste was encapsulated in his bookshelves, where contemporary design and lifestyle magazines that have featured his work are stacked alongside the *Mingei*, a publication begun by the Japanese folkcraft movement founder Yanagi Soetsu in 1939, and books on Yukihito-san's favorite *mingei* textile artisans Keisuke Serizawa (1895–1984) and his apprentice Samiro Yunoki (1922–2024). Inspiring Yukihito-san's own craftwork, the work of these artisans is embedded in traditional Japanese craft techniques but also displays a creative freedom, playfulness with color, and love of global ethnology. Yukihito-san has begun to make huge *noren* (sign curtains) using graphic block colors that, when they're not on display in galleries, stores, or trade shows, he hangs in the workshop's sales gallery. These complement a beautiful glossy guitar treated with *techigi* dye, a traditional Amamian back-strapped *teru* basket, and objects for sale including local beach coral dyed in a rainbow of colors and *tenugui* (multiuse hand towels) arranged in tasteful palettes. These are positioned beside some of the clothes, textiles, and objects Kanai Kougei dyes for clients that resonate with Yukihito-san's own aesthetic judgment.

Despite his creative ambition, as Yukihito-san became more involved with the family business he began to care more about the future of the tsumugi industry and the aging craftsmen he had known since childhood. Rather than supporting only himself and his growing family, he wondered about the possibility of expanding the workforce and employing younger people. The drive behind these goals encompassed the upholding of responsibility toward his community, revitalizing local craft for the benefit of the island, and taking pride in the ability to make natural dyeing economically sustainable. Economic sustainability was a point of contention discussed among the older craftsmen in chapter 1, who lament the inevitability of tsumugi becoming a *mukei bunkazai* (Intangible Cultural Property) and the corresponding loss of *dorozome* as a business pursuit. In the context of Kanai Kougei, pursuing the "joy of living" is not therefore a selfish endeavor but can be understood to have wider implications.

For example, despite initially seeking men for the traditionally male work of dyeing, Yukihito-san found that the part-time labor of Kazuko (age thirty-seven), who had moved with her young family from Tokyo after 3.11, and Satoko-san (forty-one), who had come from Kyoto to escape the "temptations" of the city, provided a flexibility that suited Kanai Kougei when the apparel business was starting out. But he also found that he valued the creative discussions he shared with the female workers, who were interested in problem-solving and making things together. Takahito-san (thirty) was drawn to Kanai Kougei by his sense of responsibility for tradition (see chapter 1). Yuske-san (twenty-six) had I-turned from Fukushima Prefecture. Akiyo, a twenty-four-year-old Amamian fashion graduate, came to Kanai Kougei after a year working in Ireland, where she had realized the value of Amamian nature and culture. Beyond the staff, Kanai Kougei functioned as a creative hub attracting those involved in the tsumugi industry, both young and old, and also the extended friendship networks of creative people who lived on the island. There was the potter and carpenter who both sold their wares in the workshop's gallery, an art curator who commuted to work in Tokyo, and his wife, who was a textile designer. In addition, designers, artists, musicians, journalists, and photographers would pass through the workshop on an assignment or simply to overdye their Comme des Garçons sneakers.

Aside from government initiatives to preserve Japanese craft and the post–World War II interest in "tradition," how has it come to pass that traditional dyeing is drawing people in such numbers, despite the fact that its materials and techniques have been surpassed by synthetic colorants? In the introduction to this book, I suggested that this interest has been driven by the current environmental crisis and the rise of ethical consumption practices, but I believe the reasons are broader, as I will go on to explain. I suggest that these reasons encompass (1) an attraction to the magic of color-making; (2) the appeal to a younger generation in the development of skills and a subsequent identity as a craftsperson; (3) the pleasure dyers find in building communities that share skills, aesthetics, and values; and (4) the resourcefulness found within the image of manual labor itself in an increasingly mechanized and synthesized world.

Making Connections Through Color

YUKIHITO: Rather than taking up the job out of pure interest, I was concerned the work my parents were doing might disappear. I thought I wanted to try it out even if it was a little bit [risky]—but when I realized, I became *entirely* into the color-making.

KAZUKO: So it was like magic?

YUKIHITO: Alchemy.

Kazuko confirms—

KAZUKO: Alchemy, a little different.

CHARLOTTE: But also magic!

YUKIHITO: But *magic is* the right word. Boiling in pots—it looked like something a witch would do.

In my career as a designer, I found the chemistry of synthetic dyeing satisfying in its ability to produce quick, precise, stable, and vibrant color suited to the fast-changing palettes of the fashion seasons. But for natural dyers, including myself, making color from raw, natural materials is "magic" in comparison, "like something a witch would do." In July 2018 Yukihito-san, Kazuko, Akiyo, and I took a long-planned and much-talked-about trip to Okinawa to experience the colorful potential of plants in their most awe-inspiring concentration. Kitta-san and Sawano-san of the label KITTA, from whom I borrow the term the *joy of living*, had grown, harvested, and processed Ryūkyū *ai* (indigo) since relocating to the island and gaining access to their dyeing facility in 2011. The owner of the site, who passed on his knowledge and took rent from the pair, was growing old and unwell, and his son had little interest (for the time being) in producing ai. Sawano-san dyes garments designed by Kitta-san using local and imported dyestuffs, but indigo forms the core of their collection, grounding their work in the traditions and ecosystems of Okinawa. Farming ai is a cyclical pursuit involving preparing the soil, sowing seed, tending plants to ready them for multiple harvestings, and processing across the summer (figures 2.4 and 2.5). Attendance to help is by invitation only and the processes' increasing rarity and ability to enchant attracts dye experts from around the world.

On the morning we arrived to help, around twenty volunteers took two hours to handpick six hundred kilograms of ai that were bunched and weighed prior to processing. At a site backed by mountains resounding with birdsong and set among plots of characteristic Ryūkyū fruits and vegetables, the indigo leaves were washed of *mushi* (bugs) and mud, untied, and submerged in a huge steeping pool. When we returned to the site two days later, the leaves had leached their indican (indigo molecules) and had been removed from the water. What remained was an opaque, foaming turquoise accompanied by an herbal scent that Yukihito-san said reminded him of *kampō* (Japanese traditional medicine). The next stage was to oxidize the indigo. The pH of the pool was checked and some industrial lime (an alkali) was pumped into the pool to extract the molecules.[7] Oxidization renders the indican water insoluble, allowing the molecules to sink and the remaining water to be siphoned off. Using long wooden paddles, the

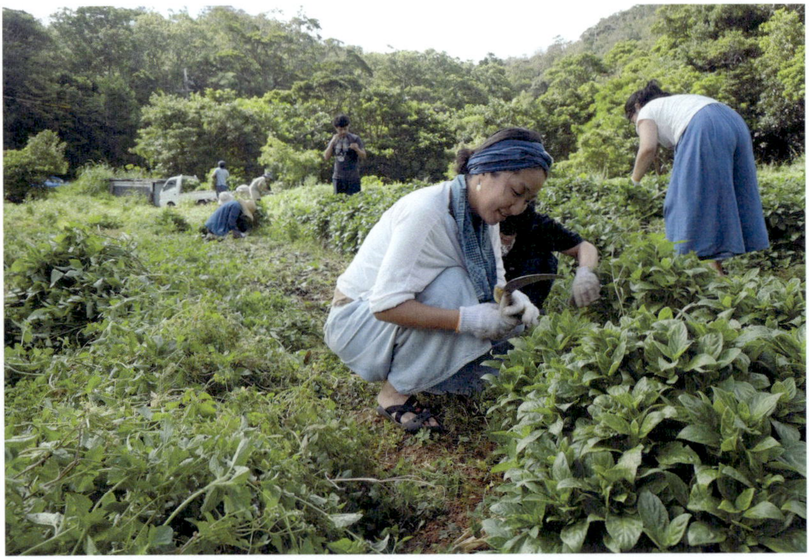

Figure 2.4 *Harvesting Ryūkyū ai in Okinawa.*

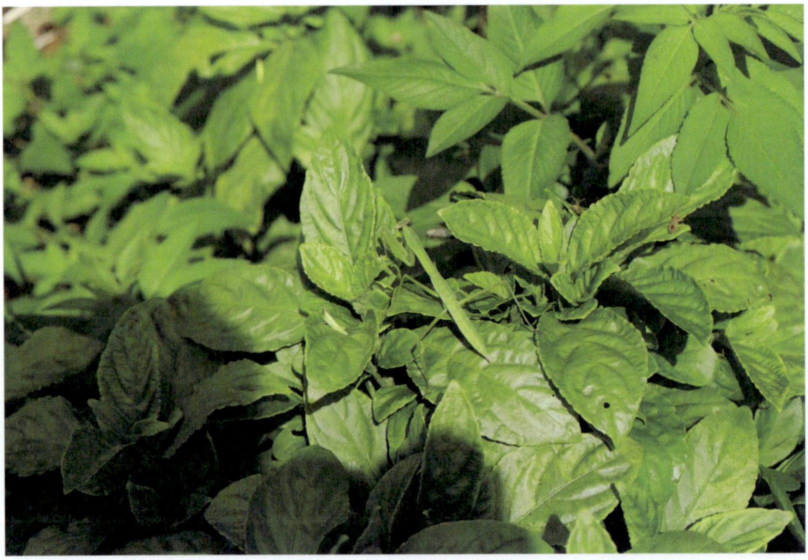

Figure 2.5 *A* kamakiri *(praying mantis) in the indigo field among at least six other types of insect.*

volunteers beat the ai liquid to encourage the indican to mechanically bind with oxygen in the air (figure 2.6). After a feverish forty minutes, the pool resembled a stormy ocean as the color changed incrementally from turquoise to deep navy with candy-cobalt foam frothing at the edges. As the paddles changed hands, the foam slowly hardened and darkened, gaining the characteristic iridescent sheen of oxidized *ai hana* (indigo flowers).[8] The now settled surface took on a brown stagnancy as the blue pigment sank. The pool was then left to *nekaseru* (sleep) for a week before the contents were transferred to a smaller pool where they would ferment. Once the water was removed, a high-quality pigment would remain that could be used for dyeing the KITTA collection, with any surplus sold to friends and acquaintances.

Although small-scale indigo production is breathtaking to witness, its romanticization risks masking the reality of its cultivation and processing. Indigo requires significant natural resources—land and water—and extensive knowledge, investment, and labor to gain good yields. In the Ryūkyūs, one must also consider typhoons that can destroy whole fields of ai in a day. These difficulties are exposed by the fact that indigo could be commercially produced prior to synthetization only by using extractive and exploitative land and labor practices that carry a "hideous and extreme" legacy (Taussig 2009, 158). The eighteenth-century global trade in indigo both relied upon and fed the growth of the European slave colonies of the West Indies and Central America (Phipps 2013, 128). On account of its unique properties—its antibacterial, anti-odor, and fiber-strengthening qualities and its partiality to being overdyed—indigo blue was used to dress the industrial workers and servicemen of Europe, making its export value exceed even sugar's (Taussig 2009, 136). After the abolition of slavery in the British colonies, indigo was manufactured through coerced labor and forced cultivation in the colony of Bengal, first by the English East India Company (until 1857) and later the British Empire. These landscapes of monoculture led to famine, resulting in violent and deadly labor revolts (Ray 2022). In Japan, too, commercial indigo production on Shikoku Island was said to be "the cornerstone of economic modernization in Meiji Tokushima" (Amano 1999, 225). Indigo created huge wealth for manufacturers and merchants, who established the island's trade and transportation networks and were intimately involved with the founding of the local banking system (235). This history prompts one to ask, Where is the value in producing indigo in Japan today when it is more efficient to buy pigment from India (strong color, natural, and affordable—but with unknown labor and environmental standards) or Germany (even stronger color, synthetic, and cheap)? Anthropologist Michael Taussig, in *What Color Is the Sacred?* (2009), quotes the 1850 account of an Englishman in Bengal writing

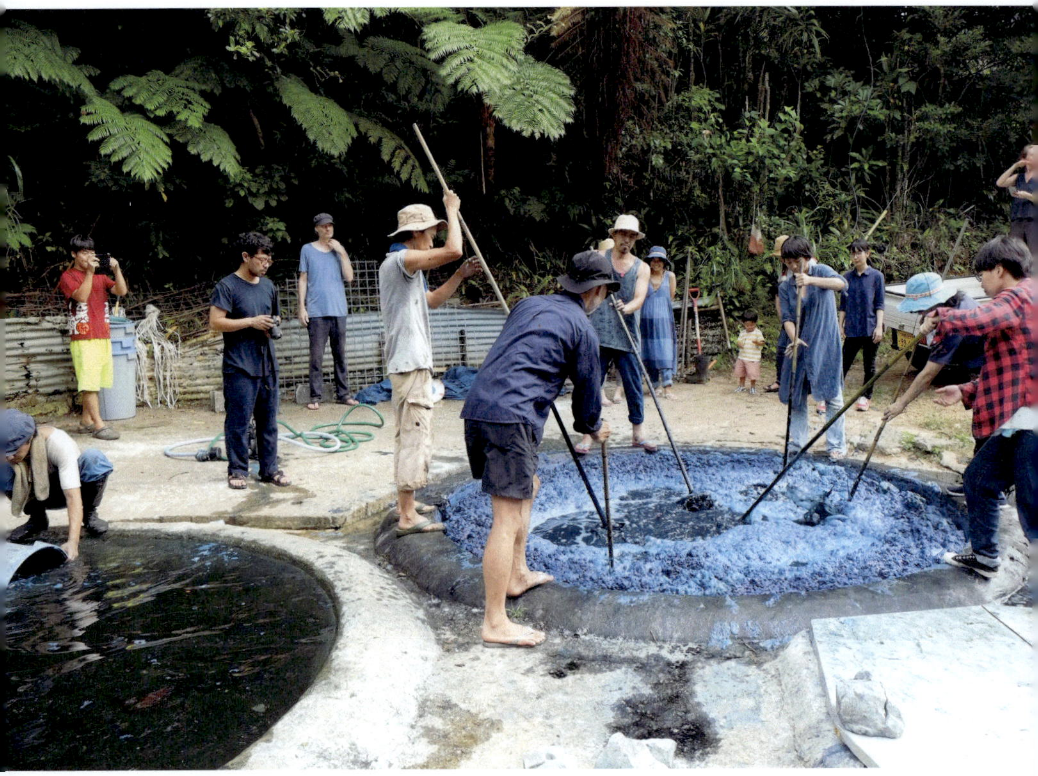

Figure 2.6 *Oxidizing indigo in Okinawa.*

home to his sisters, who described much the same process I encountered in Okinawa. Taussig concludes: "The view [of the indigo pools of Bengal] brings to the fore the art of nature, the recognition of which has been occluded by modern chemistry. It is as if the feel for materials, for the delicacy of physical changes in substances, and the questions those pose to ourselves and relationships to nature, have been cast into oblivion. The more scientists know about nature, the less we have a connection" (153).

Historian of science Agustí Nieto-Galan goes some way in describing how "the art of nature" was "occluded by modern chemistry" in the natural dyeing industry between the seventeenth and twentieth centuries in Europe. Dyeing was subject to the European Enlightenment agenda of improvement both in terms of agricultural productivity of dyestuffs at home and in the colonies, but chemists also sought to improve and standardize recipes and techniques for expanded production (Nieto-Galan 2001, 89). What is particular about Nieto-Galan's research are the "tensions and misunderstandings" he lists between dye craftsmen and chemists, with the latter failing to understand that to achieve a desired shade the dyer drew on a tool kit of intangible, flexible, sensory, perception-based skills that were impossible to translate into words and numbers (181). This knowledge was difficult to write down because it was context-specific and passed secretly between craftsmen. While early interventions into the dyeing trade by chemists were unsuccessful, by the nineteenth century chemists applied their own language and techniques to develop dyestuffs from coal tar, a waste product of the Industrial Revolution, leading to the founding of the modern chemical-dye industry. Artificial dyestuffs coexisted with older materials, methods, and technologies in Europe until around 1856, after which synthetic aniline dyes dominated (182). This history suggests it was difficult for natural dyeing to exist in Europe in its earlier form after chemists became involved, because natural dyeing resisted upscaling and cost-cutting as labor laws were introduced, science advanced, and industrial capitalism developed. Dyers were not scientifically trained, meaning they were unable to account for the chemistry happening before their eyes. Instead, experience taught them to adapt methods to replicate results as achieved by chemists.

In Amami, *daitai*, meaning "approximate" or "rough," a word I frequently used and heard, might describe such intangible knowledge, because measurements are often estimated, based on feelings gained through experience. *Daitai* can also be used to describe a person, one who completes tasks without precision, while not necessarily suggesting a person does not have skill or is neglectful. Some natural dyers have expanded their knowledge to better understand the science behind their practice, yet natural dyeing contains so many geographically embedded variables that the flexible, intangible skills are relied upon to accurately replicate processes. Producing indigo pigment and then dyeing with it oneself could therefore be understood as an attempt to reestablish local connections with nature, the land, the atmosphere, and regional cultural and industrial histories.

Anthropologist Diana Young (2018, 2), who specializes in the study of color, explains that color perception is subjective in science, "a product of individual brains and eyes," but in lived experience "color is about practical engagement in the world, not just a set of finalized theories." This was demonstrated when processing Ryūkyū ai, where environment, materials, technology, history, and action coalesced, becoming a focal point for those who exchanged knowledge and experience of color-making. Young quotes the work of psychologists who claim that rather than being internal, color is externally understood as a quality that "composes" something. As such, "getting to know color is relative to the situation one is in—ecologically and environmentally" (2–3). Growing, foraging, or harvesting dyestuffs situates a dyer in time and place within a broad conception of community. One must have an awareness of seasonality and availability of materials, needing to know the best time of year (or even day) to harvest and which species will provide the best colorant. Consequently, the dyer better understands their ecosystem by watching the seasons, the changing weather, and even other species with whom one is in competition for resources.[9] Taussig (2009, 153) states that expanded knowledge of the science of color has obliterated one's connection to natural materials and processes, but natural dyeing has the potential to counteract this effect, because the more dyers know about nature, the more they can establish a connection through color.

Incoming craftspeople, seeking to establish a grounded knowledge of their adopted geography, can familiarize themselves through the manipulation of local materials. But even when materials are imported from India or South America, the colors one can achieve still depend on local environmental conditions. This sensitivity is extended during the dyeing process, where skills combining botany, chemistry, aesthetic judgment, and bodily and environmental awareness are required to achieve flat, even, and consistent color fixed to a specific spot. The atmospheric humidity, strength of the sun, or the pH, minerals, and chemicals in the water supply can all affect the consistency of dyestuffs, which will in turn affect the final dyed result (see also chapter 5). This means that natural dyeing requires geographic fixity and knowledge so the craftsperson can control the many locally specific variables to an extent that matches the results that can be achieved with scientific accuracy. Dyeing is therefore a hugely challenging, gratifying, even magical pursuit located in an entanglement of the senses of the craftsperson who intertwines nature, cultural practice, and economy in time and place. As the Shachō explained: "Dorozome is the most difficult of the dyeing techniques, because you have to rely on your experience and intuition. Normally, you can write a recipe and teach it—how many grams of water, how many grams of dye material—but this isn't something you can write a recipe for, it's up to the sense of the individual."

Natural dyeing is a lifelong pursuit of knowledge accumulation. Nagata-san, the oldest and most skilled tsumugi dyeing craftsman at Kanai Kougei, told me that after fifty years he was still finding ways to improve his technique. While I have established that this knowledge is adapted depending on physical and environmental context, it also changes with social interaction within a "community of practice" (Lave and Wenger 1991). It is a good example of Jean Lave and Etienne Wenger's (1991) "situated learning," or "learning [that] is always a political project, a collective endeavor, situated in everyday practice and a key to future transformative change" (Lave 2019, 8). The transmission of traditional, embodied, context-specific knowledge has been widely discussed in regard to the traditional arts and crafts of Japan, where "mastery of form" is established through a master/apprentice relationship (Moeran 1984; Singleton 1998). This is widely understood to be based on a pedagogy of "stealing" intangible knowledge from the master through observation and repetition (Singleton 1998, 10). Although this style of education is not specific to Japan, anthropologist John Singleton points out that there does exist a "historical appreciation for these practices" (10), meaning craftworkers gain a level of respect in public discourse in Japan that is not necessarily observed elsewhere. Lifelong learning means craftworkers develop their own sense of identity within a community of practice that shares "knowledge, identities, values, techniques" (4). As Lave writes: "Crafting identities in practice becomes the fundamental project subjects engage in—it is a *social* process. Becoming more knowledgeably skilled is an aspect of participation in social practice. By such reasoning, who you are becoming shapes crucially and fundamentally what you 'know'" (2019, 95).

What is interesting about the younger generation of dyers in Amami is that they fall both within and outside of this area of discussion in regard to learning in Japan. Yukihito-san, for example, has certainly "stolen" knowledge and techniques from the craftspeople around him, but for the most part he is self-taught because his interpersonal relationship with the Shachō meant that he never apprenticed in dyeing *Oshima tsumugi* at Kanai Kougei or elsewhere. As his mother, Eriko-san, told me, when Yukihito-san started the apparel business, he did it on his own with little help from his family. One could argue he is the ideal entrepreneur, one who has pursued his own learning and creativity using "broader networks of collaborative socialized production" and cultural and economic resource extraction. Having identified the commercial potential of Amamian textile techniques, he has provided the market access to local cultural heritage, transforming it "into tradable property rights, attributable to individual genius and inner 'talent'" (Arvidsson and Niessen 2015, 111–12). Yet rather than foregrounding the individual creative entrepreneur, the work of Lave and Wenger suggests, for instance, that the pursuit of craft knowledge and the development of identity contributes to a sense of local belonging and strengthening of community that is multiregional, cross-generational, and also cross-species. This allows the craftsperson to assert their own place among a wider network of craftworkers that, if not based on friendship, is established out of professional respect.

This is not exclusive to traditional Japanese craft; many of those writing about the creative industries in art, fashion, and design globally have pushed back against the stereotype of "individual genius" because creative success is nearly impossible without the help of others (see Luckman and Thomas 2024).

Since the late 1990s, McRobbie has observed workers in the creative industries who take on risk and financial insecurity to pursue individual "artistic integrity." She explains that deindustrialization led to a "wholesale shift in working practices," emphasizing flexibility and innovation (McRobbie 1998, 177). This meant that the fashion designers McRobbie studied had to be "multi-skilled in hand work, design work, publicity and promotions, management and business and having some idea of manufacture, as well as being in possession of creative vision, imagination and all the other qualities associated with fashion design. These new workers are posed midway between labour and capital, doing the job of both at the same time" (188).

But McRobbie (1998, 180) also stresses the "informal relations of dependency and reciprocity" that emerge across creative networks. Business success is therefore based on "social interaction . . . and a more subtle reputation economy" (Arvidsson and Niessen 2015, 123), where skills, favors, contacts, materials, time, and space are exchanged—as was the case when we visited Okinawa. While Yukihito-san has a physical base and biography in traditional craft, much of his knowledge has been gathered via local "communities of practice." But he is also participating in the global circulation of ideas when international visitors participate in dyeing workshops or during the times he brings the workshops to Tokyo or Europe. This is not to say that competition between similar practitioners does not exist and communities are conflict-free, as local competition has indeed created a culture of secrecy in the dye industry in Japan. But when one's local conditions are so geographically specific and the pool of practitioners has shrunk to such an extent, the sharing of knowledge across boundaries, nationally or even internationally, does not necessarily impede one's own business prospects; instead it could be said to enhance them. The alchemy of natural dyeing, then, not only results in color but generates identity within a community of practice.

The Reevaluation of Craft

> This isn't something you can make by machine, so more than a regular factory we have many . . . potentially harmful influences on our work—the influence of the weather, for example. . . . So we always say: "This is how we're making the work, please understand when looking at the pieces." . . . When companies do make the effort to contact a place like us with prices that are high for them, I want to ensure I explain clearly. If we are going to do good work together, it has to be a situation where both sides have found a way to be in balance—otherwise the work won't be any good.

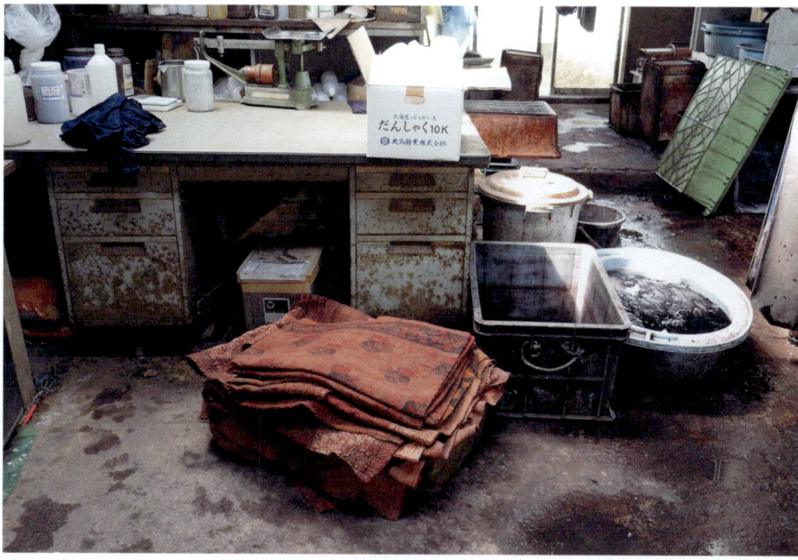

Figure 2.7 *Kiruto (quilts) dyed with techigi ready for mordanting with iron.*

> So, I think the discussion aspect is really important. Even more than the product you make.
>
> We can try our best to accommodate the client, but in the end because we're working with nature, we can only compromise as far as we can compromise. . . . Otherwise it just becomes a burden on the person doing the dyeing.—Yukihito-san

I have suggested that developing knowledge of one's local environment is key to becoming an established dye craftsperson. I have also claimed that communities of practice, both local and wider afield, foster respect and reciprocity that influence business success. The following sections develop the argument further to consider at the macroscale the reasons why craftwork and the aesthetics of labor have been revalued. I will then explore the compromises used at the microscale to translate the ideals of craftwork and natural dyeing, as explored in the previous section and as imagined by the market, to make commercially viable products using the regulation of time. The case study of *kiruto* (quilts) that Kanai Kougei overdyes in significant numbers for a design shop in Fukuoka will be used to illustrate these points (figure 2.7). On the surface, kiruto seem sustainable, as they are made in India using recycled garments and overdyed using "natural" materials in Japan by master craftspeople. But scratch the surface and this product reveals complex tensions between nature and economy that disrupt the narrative of ethical craft.

Originating in Bengal where they are known as *kantha*, kiruto are a style of quilt made from old saris that are layered, patched, and hand-sewn together in a labor-intensive process (figure 2.8). Lucy Norris (2004, 63), who has researched Indian recycled-textile economies, notes that kantha were historically made by mothers using treasured or well-worn saris. Their popularity outside of South Asia has in recent years made them a commercial product now being shipped abroad in significant numbers. Their popularity has likely been assisted by low material and labor costs, meaning a large kantha can be obtained in a tourist shop in Delhi for around twenty dollars. When they are shipped from India to the shop in Fukuoka, the shop's owners select those in the best condition for immediate resale; the remainder are sent to Kanai Kougei. When Kanai Kougei has a lull in workflow or excess techigi, kantha are fetched from storage to be overdyed. Overdyeing these quilts using ai, dorozome, or *ai-doro* (a blend of both techniques that makes a quick black) uses significant amounts of dyestuff because they are large and their layers of cloth render them absorbent. As products that demand time, space, and resources, they inevitably raise tensions between the tsumugi and apparel craftspeople. Their absorbency also makes them challenging to dye. When German synthetic indigo is used, which produces the quickest, cheapest, deepest shade of blue, it takes two people to squeeze the liquid from the textile. When techigi is used, the quilts are dyed in *tarai* (tubs) that require use of the whole body, using the feet as anchors to wring out the liquid. This was a task I was banned from doing because it was deemed too exerting, especially in the summer heat.

While I was there, the kantha arrived in multiple color and pattern combinations that we would informally judge on their level of *kawaii* (cute). Once dyed, they took on a completely different but distinctly Japanese aesthetic evocative of *boro* (rag) textiles, a popular style of antique Japanese peasant textile made from repaired and recycled cloth. The kantha emerged from storage smelling musty, with light stains and wear marks made by the garments' previous owners. After being dyed, they underwent a transformation, wiping the biography of both the saris and the kantha clean. They emerged as expensive Japanese kiruto, evoking a worker's aesthetic (figure 2.9) and dyed with "natural" materials, that when shipped back to the mainland retailed for ¥41,000–¥46,000 (approximately $265–$300).

The fashion appeal of the worker's aesthetic, including jeans, dungarees, and overalls that historically would have been dyed using processes such as *aizome*

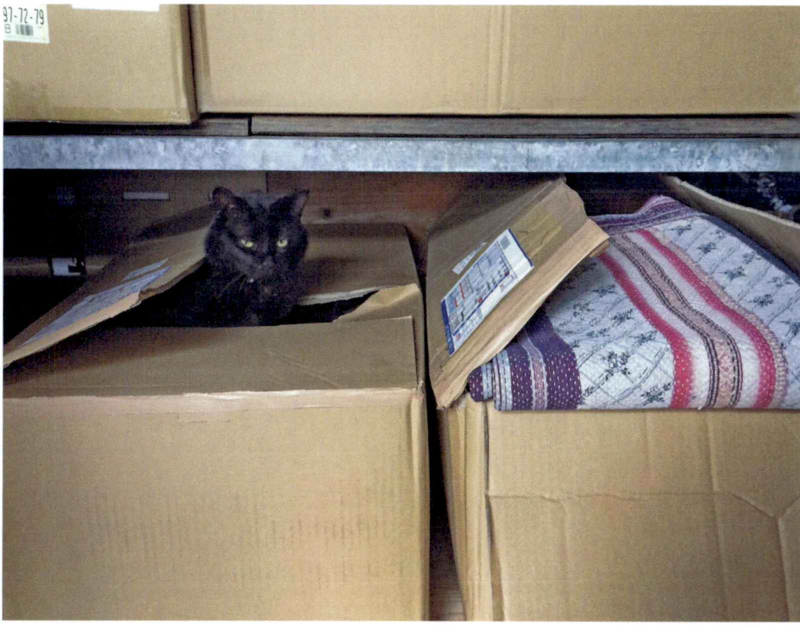

Figure 2.8 *The workshop's cat, Paru-chan, resting in the stored boxes of kantha.*

and dorozome, has been increasing since at least the 2000s. While jeans as workwear have a history stretching back to Levi Strauss's patenting of rivets in the 1870s, Daniel Miller and Sophie Woodward (2007, 338) explain that denim became an icon of rebellion in the 1950s and 1960s as a way for youth cultures to assert themselves "against a suffocating parental and national ideology of normative order." Although jeans have become ubiquitous, almost a uniform of ordinariness (338), the extension of workwear into the professional sphere in recent years reflects changing aspirations in middle-class youth cultures, exemplified by the "uniform" of Apple founder Steve Jobs. Whereas formally a suit was a marker of success, the popularity of workwear might reflect what anthropologist Richard Ocejo (2017, 3) calls a "reconfigured understanding of taste." The comfort and practicality of working-class garments reflect an uptick in middle-class interest in "traditional" and "artisanal" professions. Baking, butchery, and carpentry, for example, have become intimately connected with the ideals of craftsmanship, authenticity, and heritage. Workwear might be said to identify those with the agency to blur the boundary between work and leisure or to highlight those with the privilege to trade a university degree for life as a butcher—as has occurred in hipster communities worldwide.

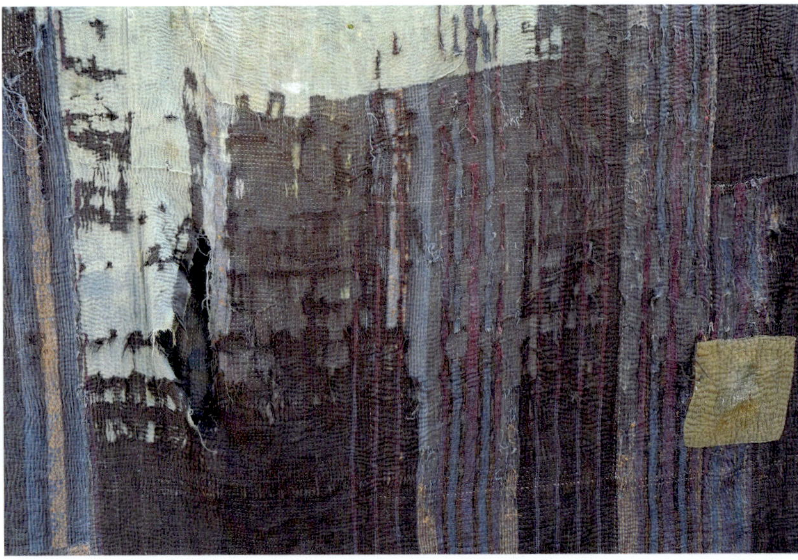

Figure 2.9 *Kiruto overdyed with indigo and reminiscent of Japanese boro textiles.*

Although there are signs that the appeal of the craft aesthetic is waning (D. Walker 2015), the term having been overused or inappropriately adopted by branding and marketing executives, the commercial potential of the aesthetics of labor should not be underestimated in Japan, where designer workwear has reached new conceptual and financial heights.[10] Kanai Kougei was able to cater its services and products to this market, most keenly demonstrated by the development of a dyer's apron, produced by the Japanese high-end workwear brand Johnbull. The company has designed an Aprons for Artisans series, making aprons for the chef, bookseller, arborist, wine connoisseur, gardener, shoemaker, and beyond and selling them to nonprofessional consumers for ¥10,000–¥30,000 ($65–$195). Kanai Kougei's dyeing apron was developed on-site and was planned to be worn by dyers to attract color stains before being returned to the company and sold online. The identity of the craftworker were therefore embedded in the fibers, giving the garment a value exceeding the faux distress implemented on mass-produced denim. As Miller and Woodward (2007, 345) claim, jeans are one of the "most global" but "personal and intimate of all items of clothing," reflected in the wear marks that ingrain themselves in the textile. But they are also a "secure base" (345) for those with fashion anxiety, and workwear similarly might be seen as a comfortable uniform reflecting a particular taste but also the location of one's ideals.

The rise in fortunes of the worker's aesthetic represents a fascinating shift in the disconnect between object and image perpetuated in the field of clothing design. McRobbie's (1998, 177–78) research into the fashion industry of the 1990s highlights how garments made by young designers and the glamorous aspirations they contained were wholly disconnected from the reality of the labor conditions behind their production. Designers sought to distance themselves and their products from the "skills associated with the more menial side of fashion, manufacture and production," wanting to "believe that they are above manual labour" (186). McRobbie's ongoing research, conducted for over twenty years, is significant in how it predicts and traces a shift in which designers would retrieve the value and visibility of hand skills. This shift is perhaps the result of the expansion of university arts education, where the overaccumulation of highly trained workers and small designer brands worldwide has forced designers to seek skills that differentiate them from their peers (Arvidsson and Niessen 2015, 125). But designers are also increasingly seeking labor with meaning, inserting them within a historical lineage of makers and traditions that are geographically and socially grounded. In 2013, McRobbie (2013, 994) described how designers moved out of backrooms with their sewing machines and onto the shop floors to share their "making stories," which Luckman and Thomas (2018, 9) say place "attention on the skilled work and hours of labour that go into making an item." The aesthetic of the product is therefore intimately connected to the identity of the craftsperson, with the commodity's value lying in the labor, lineage, and communities of craft. McRobbie writes: "The old is associated with high quality craft skills no longer found in this sector and so it accumulates value on the basis of past exclusiveness in comparison to contemporary mass produced and especially 'fast fashion.' This re-birth of craft . . . is in fact grounded and founded in the spaces of new social media, in blogs, on Instagram, and in the editorial brief of the online style magazine. . . . In this context craft becomes a major site of innovation" (2015, 167).

Since it has opened a previously closed world, social media has indeed played a huge part in the rise of craft's status allowing customers to engage in cross-cultural interaction, while the skills involved in styling and photography can be essential to the marketing of a product (Luckman and Thomas 2018, 122). It was through Instagram, for example, that I first learned about Buaisou, a company begun by two I-turners from Tokyo who relocated to Tokushima to grow, process, and use natural indigo. They had used social media to create a buzz around their practice, attracting international media and corporate partnerships. After Buaisou opened a satellite studio in New York City, where I was living and working as a designer at the time, I participated in a dyeing workshop and subsequently learned about dorozome and Kanai Kougei from the director of the space. Yet the irony of the "rebirth of craft" is that despite makers aspiring to the slowness it promises, disrupting the rhythm of commodity production is always an aspiration, because makers must compromise to conditions as they are dictated by the market—conditions that demand speed.

The Regulation of Time

On the Kanai Kougei workshop noticeboard (figure 2.10), the list on the left describes the current work under production. The text in red and in black to its right is a recipe for one of these products. On the far right (partially hidden) is the recipe for kiruto dyed via dorozome, translated by Kazuko and difficult to understand for the uninitiated (figure 2.11). Also on the board is a note of chemical quantities for making ai and the weights of certain products so that the ratios of the chemical hypren NFS (ハイプレンNFS), a "friction fastness enhancer," can be mixed accordingly (Tanaka Nao, n.d.). What is significant about the contents of this board is that the recipes in the center conclude with the direction *nekaseru* (put to sleep), whereas the instructions for the kiruto reference only the use of hypren. *Nekaseru* means that freshly dyed textiles get rested from a few hours to a few days between dye layers—a concept new to me in the production of textiles, as I had been trained in the immediacy of chemical dyeing. A little like a stain, the longer a dye substance sits on the fabric the more impregnated it will become. This increases the bonds between dye and fiber, improving fastness to washing, wearing, and light. Indigo garments represent the best example of this, as historically they were kept in the dark for one to two years to let the indigo "mature" before they were worn. In addition, the cloth is sometimes mordanted and rested prior to dyeing with a mineral such as alum or soy milk, making the textile more susceptible to plant tannins. Kanai Kougei rarely has time to premordant fibers, but KITTA can premordant textiles because the company works according to its own time frames by selling its collections at one-off sales events. Slowness in production therefore leads to a longer life for the color but also for the garment, increasing its sustainability. Yukihito-san explained that since the customer dictates the speed of production, he was only able to rest garments from a few days to a week, and in the case of kiruto rarely at all. Because of the fickle nature of the fashion and textile industry, whose orders are inconsistent from one fashion season to the next, he rarely refused jobs, meaning he wasn't afforded the luxury of time to create the best product he could.

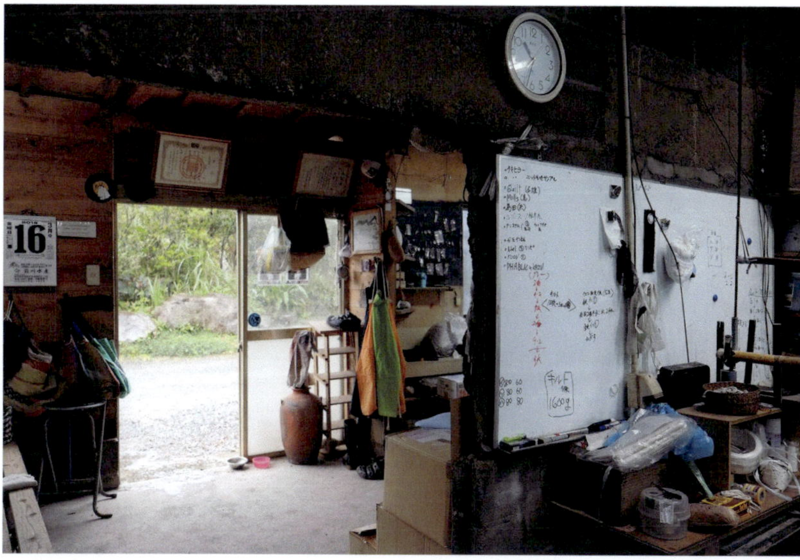

Figure 2.10 *The Kanai Kougei noticeboard showing recipes and guidelines for dyeing kiruto.*

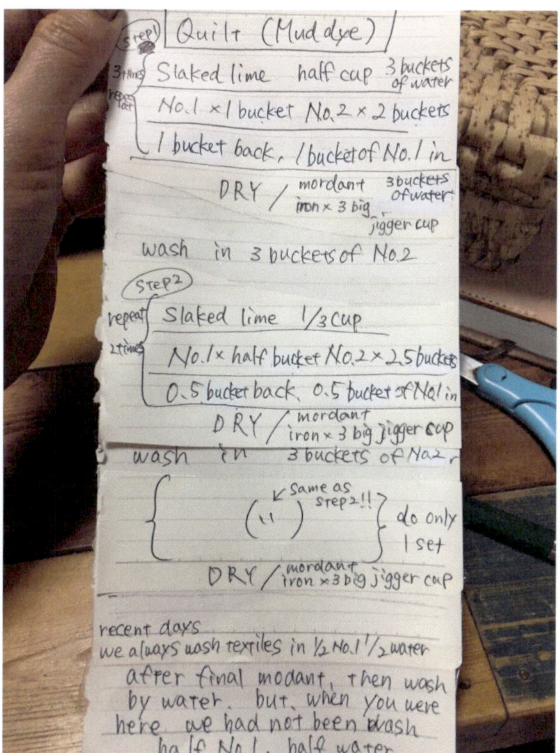

Figure 2.11 *The recipe for kiruto dyed via dorozome, translated by Kazuko.*

Instead of relying on time, Kanai Kougei fixed colors on textiles by using the aftertreatment agent hypren. Bought from a well-known print and dye supplier in Kyoto, it is a silicone emulsion used by the textile industry that wraps itself around fibers, preventing the direct friction of color. Rather than allowing time to let dye materials embed themselves in fibers, hypren acts as a barrier to stop "crocking"—the transference of color to a paler object or to one's skin (think new blue jeans after a day's wear). The application process involves soaking the textile in a diluted solution overnight, then drying it in the sun or in cupboards heated by kerosene furnaces and/or electric dehumidifiers. The process is then repeated, but on the second cycle the textile must be parched with heat. Left with the scent of gasoline, hypren's effectiveness is debatable and rather hard to measure, as is its effect on waterways when the spent solution is washed down the drain (see chapter 5).[11]

While finishing the product revolves around hypren, what was not as visible was the amount of energy necessary to heat the textile to fix the chemical. This came to light when Maiko-san told me what the workshop's highest overheads were: "Manpower [labor] and also fuel costs. Fuel costs much more than the dyes. I realized last year after we'd calculated our income and expenditures just how expensive it is. For the kerosene oil . . . so I said to Yukihito we should stop making kiruto in the winter! They never dry so always end up in the dehumidifier for ages. Just fuel costs are maybe ¥130,000 or ¥140,000 a month. Last December was the most expensive month for fuel: around ¥180,000 [approximately $1,165]."

Beyond kerosene, electricity is required for general building usage, including power for the air conditioner, dehumidifiers, *dasuki* (spinning machines), and groundwater pump. Kanai Kougei is served by the Tatsugo power station, a diesel-fueled plant located in Sedome, the village where I lived. Located in a deep fjord, the site was presumably chosen for water access but also for protection from typhoon winds, because it's also home to a gas storage facility and concrete-mixing plant. When the power was cut in bad weather, production at Kanai Kougei would stop, because groundwater (the main water supply) could not be pumped, sometimes for days at a stretch. While Sedome would be the first village to have its power restored, the payoff was diesel particulate matter from the chimneys coating the outside of buildings. Its position added to my own sense of anxiety about the health consequences of air pollution and the risks posed by a small oil tanker entering sensitive waters (figure 2.12). Despite my anxiety about future risks, my landlady told me the waters were already polluted—no longer clean enough to swim in or eat fish caught from the bay.

The kiruto reveal just some of the materials and infrastructure used to reduce production time and speed up the everyday in Amami, but this comes at a cost

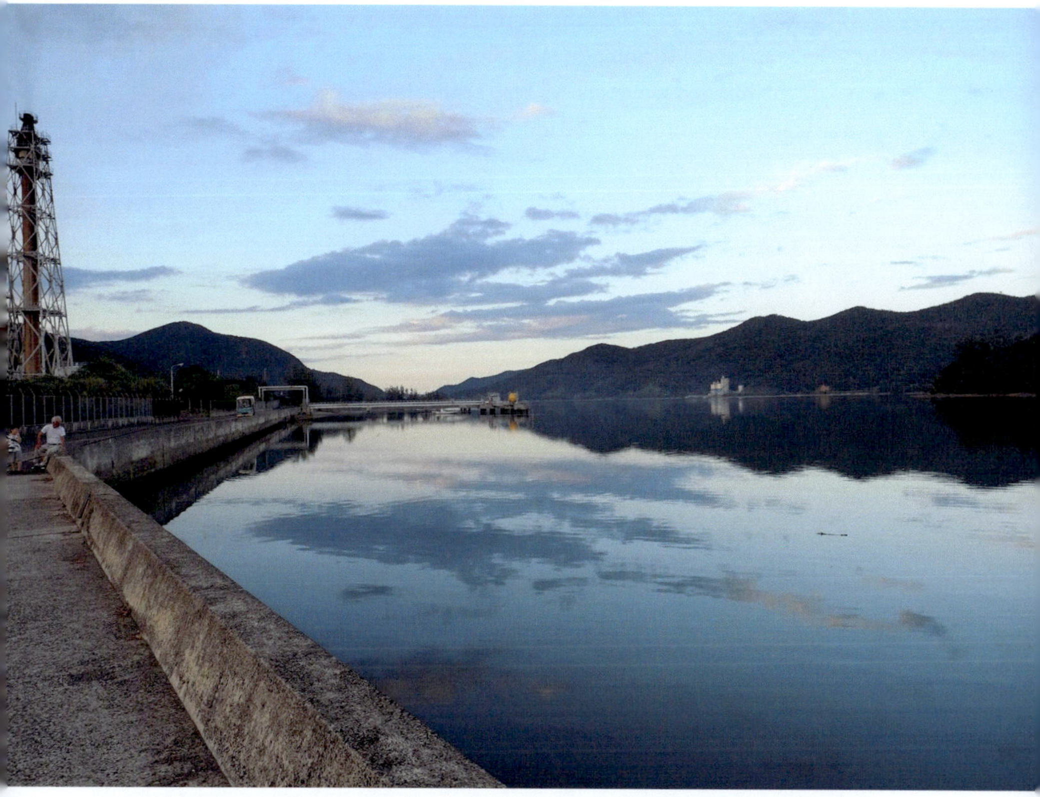

Figure 2.12 *My neighbor and his grandson fishing in Sedome Bay with the power station to the left, boat dock and diesel lines in the center distance, cement silos across the bay, and a gas storage unit farther in the distance.*

to the environment and at a financial cost to Kanai Kougei. Profits on items such as kiruto are small, forcing the workshop to replicate models of mass production to make the work worthwhile. This is counter to the image sought by the shop commissioning the products, but as Yukihito-san said, they have to find "a way to be in balance." In order to improve the situation, Kazuko asked Maiko-san, "Wouldn't it be better if we could charge a bit more?" This could cover additional material, energy, and labor costs. But Maiko-san explained that the shop in Fukuoka keeps ordering, and the number of kiruto is increasing or constant. This means Kanai Kougei has to offer a reduced unit price if it wants to keep this company as a customer. Maiko-san and Yukihito-san sought a seasonal solution to this issue, yet Maiko-san explained that the summers are too hot to carry out this very physical labor, even though the heat of the sun could be better used to reduce energy bills. Instead, she proposed: "We thought of doing kiruto only in spring and autumn. But then there's no chance in spring here either because of the rainy season! . . . Kiruto are really tough. . . . The work takes up lots of space; there are big fuel and dye costs. It's really difficult."

Maiko-san's solution is embedded in better use of seasonal time, an element that is free. But Amamian seasons are not favorable to the labor, time-saving processes, or atmospheric conditions required to produce a large number of kiruto. Solutions were therefore sought through labor, evident in the constant tension about working hours present throughout the year I spent at Kanai Kougei. This was particularly a problem for the flexible female labor that had benefited Kanai Kougei as the apparel business was established. Although Yukihito-san seemed to understand the conditions under which the female staff wished to work, even supporting their family obligations when he could, shortly after I arrived in December 2017 the Shachō insisted that he wanted all workers to become full-time. This meant 9:00 a.m.–5:00 p.m. six days a week, a schedule that did not always respect public holidays. Full-time work was seen as necessary to both increase the number of workers and limit disruptions in production, because an absentee worker led to communication breakdowns, often resulting in mistakes. As I have demonstrated, dyeing is a complex process, so with textiles passing among many hands, information can be lost, such as how many times a garment has been dyed; whether it requires finishing; the length of time it has been sleeping, and so on. Across several weeks, Kazuko and Satoko-san tried to make full-time employment work, all the while looking exhausted, leaving me concerned for their health. Not able to get involved, I felt angry about the pressure they had been put under, which was loosely framed as "work full-time or quit." Yet every time I complained to Kazuko that the Japanese worked too hard, she would correct me, saying this was not the case in the whole of Japan, "only in Amami." The insistence on a six-day workweek was indeed "old-fashioned," conflicting with the modern working standards that Yukihito-san had tried to implement to establish a sustainable source of casual labor. But it even appeared to act as a barrier to attracting full-time labor, as Yukihito-san had struggled to secure staff willing to do this demanding job for low wages. Akiyo, for example, who was young and strong and had little responsibility aside from helping her parents run the house, managed full-time employment better and enjoyed the work. But she, too, would complain of a lack of energy, too tired or distracted by housework on Sundays to do hobbies. Eventually Kazuko and Satoko-san slipped back into part-time work, realizing that working full-time was physically and mentally unsustainable, and the Shachō, too, gave ground. Akiyo, however, has since left Kanai Kougei and Amami to pursue personal projects, and it's unclear whether she will return to the island or to the dyeing profession anytime soon.

Because Kanai Kougei has struggled to expand the workforce, Yukihito-san appears to make projects happen by devaluing his own time. He works long hours for low wages and can be found at the workshop most days. This is because he tries to plug gaps in labor, but also because he holds all the knowledge, supervising overlapping commissions. McRobbie's (1998, 2013, 2015) work with fashion designers in London and Berlin and anthropologist Laura Bear's (2015) research with river pilots in India shows how love of one's profession can be used to solve financial deficit and fix the problem of industrial time. Instead of overwork being a condition specific only to Japan, a country with a bad reputation for *karōshi* (overwork death), exploiting love of one's profession might be said to be a method recognized globally. Bear's (2015, 138) ethnography with river pilots who steer container ships along India's Hooghly River shows how responsibility is pushed onto the individual in order to overcome failing infrastructure, the result of austerity measures because of huge state debt. The acquisition of skill, "heroic agency," camaraderie, and love for the river combines experience, knowledge, and sensory capacities but also old and new technologies. Bear explains that central to these skills is the ability to "overcome the problems of timing by achieving fusion with the ship and the forces of wind, waves, current and tide on the river" (140). A pilot's "sense of workmanship" (178) is measured by one's ability to manage time. As Bear writes, "Timespaces of labor are now full of incommensurable forms of social and nonhuman time that are in increasingly in conflict. As a result all of us, like river pilots, are frequently faced with the challenge of trying to bring into relation through our labor divergent rhythms and temporal representations. . . . Circulation will continue as long as we continue to see these difficulties only as a problem of time" (149).

If it is not possible to reduce costs and time using free natural resources or material manipulation, then exploitative labor, even self-exploitation, is often the only remaining option. This reveals the friction between "real subsumption," Karl Marx's term that explains "the ability of capitalism to progress . . . to encompass all" (La Berge 2019, 22), and an individual's willingness to work more hours for less money, which might conflict with the pursuit of the "joy of living." In a study of academic and artistic vocations, Leigh Claire La Berge explains, "In a regime with a goal of extracting absolute surplus value, the working day can be extended to increase profit. But that increase has an end, obviously, and after it's [*sic*] limit has been reached, a regime to extract relative surplus value takes over" (22). This situation is reflective of labor becoming increasingly individualized around the world, where in the realms of neoliberal capitalism workers take on more responsibility for their own labor as workloads have increased and new technologies accommodate increased flexibility. This includes the expansion of work into areas of time and space not typically considered the domain of work, such as taking clients to dinner or replying to emails and text messages from colleagues in the evening. This sprawling of the working day sees people continue to work not because they necessarily want to but because they feel pressure to perform expected roles, an obligation to their superiors and colleagues, or a need to provide a basic level of income for their families. They may also take pride in the integrity of their work or feel placed under strain to maintain their reputation as a hard worker.

Claudio Sopranzetti (2018, 110) shows how his study participants—self-employed motorcycle taxi drivers in Bangkok—use the narrative of "freedom" as a way to "make sense of and make do with the political, economic, social, and conceptual shifts" that similarly infiltrate their daily lives. He describes how taxi drivers celebrate being their own boss, who, besides working longer hours than they did on a factory floor, are happier with their sense of freedom and the pride and personal dignity of being able to pursue entrepreneurial activity. This form of "self-exploitation" was a "sacrifice" that allowed his participants to make their own decisions and benefit from their own profits, despite the risks and uncertainty their work generated (128–29). In the Japanese context, Klien also notes the "freedom" narrative among her participants who left jobs as a *sararīman* (salaryman) in Japanese companies where they'd been subject to overwork or confined by hierarchy or lacked the agency to pursue "creative dynamism." By relocating to the countryside, her participants lived and worked "in the moment" without long-term trajectories, providing them the time to plan their next career move. Yet she notes that "freedom" coexists with "ephemerality," creating a "grey zone" where "individuals attempt to create something new and find themselves entrapped in existing systemic constraints" (Klien 2019, xxvii). Sopranzetti (2018, 130–31) neatly concludes after Marx that "freedom becomes the hook that drags people into a false sense of empowerment while carrying them into accepting and participating in contemporary capitalism or similarly oppressive projects." He shows that emancipation via entrepreneurialism can be as oppressive as working for a company, because the "hardest boss" is often oneself (130).

Despite my participants being subject to the pressures of the market, an outside force beyond their control, my ethnography demonstrates the compromises, contradictions, and complicities they must accept to make their life and business economically sustainable. Compromises are made in order to pursue the acquisition of craft skill, to build "communities of practice" (Lave and Wenger 1991) and establish a "connectedness to nature" (Yoneyama 2019). These skills, communities, and connections accumulate to repatriate a sensory autonomy from the disempowerment of the market, an autonomy reflected in the vibrancy, shade, and taste they can achieve when making color. Finding value in the "joy of living," an ever-evolving endeavor, subsequently serves a double purpose. It works to improve one's quality of life, but the objects my participants make and the images of their lifestyle capture at least an ideal of ethical, joyful, rural living. This is visually communicated via social media and in high-end lifestyle magazines, creating added value that can be traded upon to sustain that very lifestyle. This added value strengthens local industry and traditional practice, which offers a broader conception of affluence—even if it comes at a personal cost.

It is important to recognize that improving one's own quality of life can result in a grassroots approach to craft preservation that often evolves into a political project. Despite critiques of gentrification surrounding lifestyle migration, those who move to rural locations often become more politically engaged than they were in the city, whether intentionally or not, as they are drawn into micro-issues of local politics in order to offset anxiety about things they care for. Quite early on in my research, I recognized that Yukihito-san was engaged in the future of tsumugi through his creative reformulation of tradition, but he was also variously visited by high-ranking officials from Kagoshima Prefecture, or companies who wanted to inject money into tsumugi to reboot the industry. Without asking for it, Yukihito-san had become a spokesperson for what tsumugi could become. This resulted in meetings with local bureaucrats in an attempt to raise the wages of all tsumugi craftspeople—from dyers to spinners and weavers—through a government-supported stipend scheme. Yet the problem of working hours recurred during these discussions. In September 2019, the local authorities announced that tsumugi craftworkers would be paid an additional ¥100,000 (approximately $650) a month by the government—a substantial amount, given that dyers were either making minimum wage (at this time ¥1,000 per hour, or about $6.50) or working on a piecework basis that resulted in wages inequivalent to the quality of their craftsmanship. However, support offered would only be available to those who worked full-time—in effect directly discriminating against those with caring commitments, who tended to be female. This was not surprising, given that female voices were not included in the negotiations, which continued in fits and starts for over three years.

While Yukihito-san was directly involved in initiating these early discussions, as of October 2020 negotiations had been handed over to the *orimoto-san*s, the tsumugi weaving companies that orchestrate the production of tsumugi cloth (see chapter 1). Dyers have typically been at the bottom of the tsumugi hierarchy because, although highly skilled, their work is hard, dirty, manual labor. The orimoto-sans, however, have historically sat at the top of this hierarchy, meaning they have latterly redefined the conditions under which one could apply for the

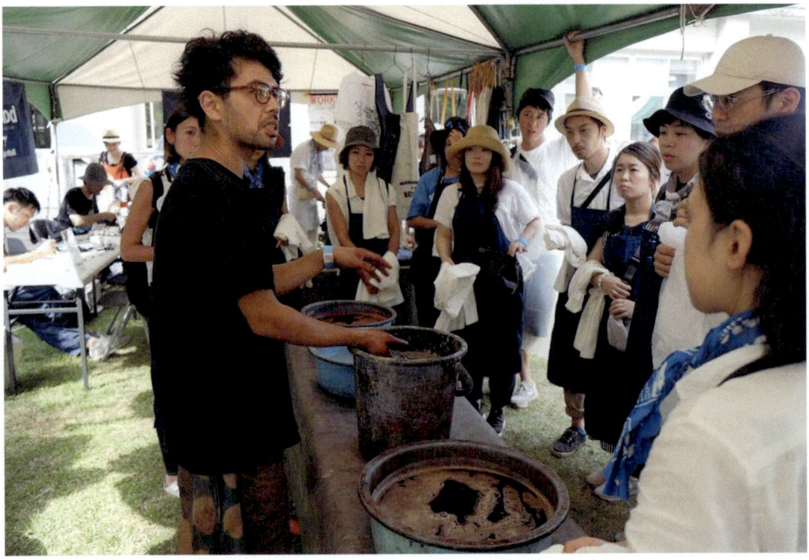

Figure 2.13 *Yukihito-san leading a dorozome workshop at the Good Neighbors Jamboree 2018, a music and lifestyle festival in Kagoshima.*

stipend program. Workers had to be full-time, but they were also required to be new apprentices working in the craft for less than two years to qualify. Akiyo and a second Kanai Kougei craftsperson (employed after my fieldwork ended) applied for the program, but neither was accepted. Instead, support had been given to those chosen by the orimoto-sans.

Although the increased cachet of manual labor has, in recent years, provided an aura exceeding any association with class, the example of these wage negotiations demonstrates that the value attached to labor power itself has not shifted, as old power hierarchies persist. Yukihito-san was nervous about upsetting this hierarchy and about taking an active responsibility for the negotiations, even though members higher up the chain seemed incapable of bringing about effective change. Yet he had learned which battles were worth fighting—whether with the Shachō or the tsumugi industry—knowing he had greater autonomy among influential creative networks located elsewhere. Yukihito-san was being forced to negotiate the "multiple temporalities" (Shove et al. 2009, 3) that dictate the social norms established in a place—a navigation between understandings of history and its ties to specific geographies. He stood in the unique position of being able to bring together Tokyo and Amami via his family's craft pedigree and his own metropolitan mobility and to present a future sitting somewhere between traditional craftmanship and modern entrepreneurialism. Doreen Massey (1995, 186) argues that rethinking "the relationship between past, present and future can help us reinvigorate the way in which we conceptualise geographical places. . . . It helps us to think of them as temporal and not just spatial: as set in time as well as space." This conceptualization of place as both geographic but also temporal disrupts the narrative that rural places are slow and traditional while the city is fast and modern, a debate continued in chapter 3.

I suggested to Yukihito-san that although he initially faced resistance, the work he was doing now was helping to solve a broader issue: the island's precarious economy. He was bringing work, finance, and labor from the mainland that was promoting and sustaining Oshima tsumugi—whether those at the top of hierarchy wished to admit it or not. Yet he told me: "Back then [in the early 2000s], I hoped it would be like that one day. But I am not the kind of person who could do something with such a sense of responsibility. So, relatively speaking, [pursuing craftwork] was truly something personal. But I am quite surprised and find it interesting that how I hoped for it to evolve is actually turning into a reality." By being attentive to a practice he had taken for granted, Yukihito-san discovered something he cared for. Dorozome stretches back across the cultural, geographic, and economic history of Amami and holds a prominent position in his family's own story. But as a process, it has also provided him with new skills and resources and access to communities and opportunities to make his mark as a craftsman. The alchemy involved in creating color produces physical, material, and visual results but also generates knowledge, finance, and social networks that stimulate discourse around craft, sustaining them for the future. Although Yukihito-san and many of his peers migrated to the countryside as a result of precarity, uncertainty about the future acted as a productive and sustaining force. Yukihito-san doesn't believe the accumulated "wisdom" of Amamian craft has to end its journey with the kimono, and through persistence and patience his combined craft practice and entrepreneurial acumen has proved that the skills embedded in Oshima tsumugi have relevance for the here and now.

The Amamian example does highlight, however, that natural dyeing is not a sustainable "fix" for more damaging industrial processes, because natural dyeing is only financially viable if the craftspeople themselves manipulate time by using self-exploitation or by adopting chemicals. Nevertheless, the ways in which Yukihito-san and his employees are tied to cycles of self-exploiting labor, while problematic and contradictory, should perhaps be considered distinct from the self-exploitation occurring in the context of urban neoliberal creative industries, where the individual is foregrounded—whether that individual exists within a creative community or not. Amami's craftspeople experience the "joy of living" by having enriching interactions with a diverse understanding of community and environment. This is not only the result of spatial displacement but also due to the necessity of interacting daily with varying temporalities—for instance, in production processes designed to speed things up and those requiring extended time and care to achieve durability and aesthetic depth. In chapter 3 I shift the focus from dye materials to food as a conduit to better understand how these different temporalities function in building stronger connections locally, and I pick up as yet unaddressed questions surrounding the environmental ethics of commodity production.

3

"*Mottainai!*" What a Waste!

> I've never really lived in places other than big cities, like in Tokyo or London. I am finding a new me here, you know? Life is really different. You don't get dressed up every day . . . and don't get stressed about it. Once you are in Tokyo, shopping is like another form of sports. People work Monday to Friday then on the weekends do sports-slash-shopping . . . I think our generation started to realize something we value more than labels or materialistic purposes.—Koki

Koki had relocated to Amami from Tokyo to explore the processes of *Oshima tsumugi*, later learning to weave the kimono cloth himself. Although his postmaterialist attitude is not necessarily widespread, a lineage of financial instability and environmental disasters in Japan have led to a general decline in materialistic attitudes that peaked worldwide in the 1980s.[1] The moment of national reflection that followed 3.11 has been a significant factor in this growing disinterest in commodity culture. The disaster brought into focus not only economic instability but Japan's precarious food, energy, and infrastructural security, questioning the political foundations on which these had been built.

Historian Eiko Maruko Siniawer (2014, 2018) describes the shift that Koki hints at, in which a millennial generation (and those whose ages skirt it) has become increasingly concerned with the concept of "wastefulness"—or what the Japanese term *mottainai*. Described by my friends in English as a feeling of "what a waste," mottainai is generally discussed in relation to leftover food or waste materials that could be reused in other ways. In her study of kimono culture in Japan, anthropologist Julie Valk (2018, 68) translates the expression as "it's a shame," as it was spoken by women referring to kimono lying unworn in their *tansu* (kimono drawers). Mottainai is fascinating because the word is thought to have taken on different meanings across history, reflecting the wider sociopolitical landscape. Dictionary definitions date the word's origins to the thirteenth century, when it was used to describe "trouble, harm, and impropriety" (Siniawer 2014, 165), but mottainai's popularity swelled after World War II, when Siniawer (2018, 12) claims language from the turn of the century "about health, hygiene, efficiency, and rationalization" was resuscitated to "urge waste consciousness in the workplace and at home." Suffering was so widespread and resources so scarce that mottainai practices were a necessity for survival. People were taught "that material things have lives,"[2] while the wartime motto *Luxury is the enemy* became ingrained (Siniawer 2014, 170–71). One's possessions were cared for, maintained, repaired, or reused to sustain their useful lives, while resources such as food and energy were used frugally. Siniawer (2018, 8) argues there is a common misconception that the Japanese are more frugal than other societies, yet she suggests this myth resonates with the "impressions of Zen . . . with clean aesthetics and simplicity" that have come to define an idea of how the Japanese live, at least outside of Japan. But mottainai can be said to resonate with wartime scarcity in Europe too, where food waste was criminalized by the UK government in 1940 and rationing was extended into the 1950s.

While mottainai was embedded in the minds of those who had been debilitated by scarcity, consumption was encouraged in Japan after the war to kick-start the economy, meaning that the children of this generation grew up in a hugely different economic environment. Using a newly acquired disposable income, consumers in the postwar period bought into commodities of the future—electronics, designer clothes, imported foodstuffs—but also the nostalgia of tradition through *furusato* tourism or, in the case of Oshima tsumugi, purchasing expensive kimono. Jennifer Robertson (1991, 29) suggests this was a means to offset the anxiety caused by encroaching "westernization, industrialization, and urbanization." As the country become rich, waste reflected an undesirable "excess," but also "the desirability of a middle-class life had become so deeply fixed" that "its conveniences and comforts were not to be sacrificed but defended" (Siniawer 2018, 13). When waste management spiraled out of control in the 1970s, Tokyo's governor fought a "war on waste" by increasing landfill and incineration and calling on companies and government regulators to encourage recycling schemes. These responses saw existing infrastructure as the problem, not the act of overconsumption itself (93–94).

In line with its war-era usage, I heard mottainai mentioned in regard to fallen *tankan* (tangerines) that no one was collecting but also in regard to the clearing of trees for paper pulp on the mountains (see chapter 6) and the rebuilding of Amami's natural beaches in a tidier style preferred by tourists. These feelings expressed a sorrow about the "waste" of the natural environment—a direct result of economic intrusion. This newer formulation is supported by Siniawer, who claims that *waste*, by the twenty-first century, has expanded to include all that is wasteful in one's everyday life: time, money, work, food, resources, skills, nature. She quotes contrasting data from the Japanese Cabinet Office that show attitudes from 1975, when people felt that material wealth (*mono no yutakasa*) was more important than what anthropologist Shoko Yoneyama (2019) terms "spiritual wealth" (*kokoro no yutakasa)*. Yet by the 2000s, attitudes had reversed, resulting in "environmental commitments, a search for individual and national identities, and attempts to define anew relationships with things and with time in continued pursuit of an affluence of heart, mind, and spirit" (Siniawer 2018, 14). Although this outlook might be considered optimistic—with my ethnography demonstrating inconsistences between discourse and practice—the argument presented in the previous chapter supports at least the continuous attraction of this ideal, as my participants in the Ryūkyūs pursue the "joy of living." The triple disaster that occurred on 3.11 sparked a catalyst for change as people like Koki questioned their careers, living conditions, and lifestyle choices. For many, this prompted a move to the countryside that eased the way for a rejection of materialism, as one would need to accept a lower income than was achievable in the city. Koki also highlights that in the countryside one's lifestyle—and the commodities that support that lifestyle—become scaled back. In Amami a good pair of *bīchisandaru* (beach sandals) can be more essential than multiple pairs of shoes, and when working at a dye workshop one relies on a supply of old clothes, not smart new ones. Consequently, there is a natural tendency for people to become more resourceful and inventive and avoid wastefulness to satisfy material needs.

In this chapter I will unpack in more detail the reasons why mottainai has gained a renewed energy in the twenty-first century and attempt to understand what this might mean for the way people live their lives in Amami beyond the confines of Kanai Kougei's workshop. Through the example of my participants, I argue that a postmaterialist generation, those in their twenties through forties, attempts to reformulate a sense of "affluence" not in material or financial terms but by adopting caring practices toward their local community, culture, and natural environment. I should stress that none of my participants resemble radical, ethical citizens like John Knight's (1997) organic pioneers discussed in the previous chapter, whose "back-to-the-land" movement aimed to resist the capitalist state. Rather than being wholesale resisters, they are ordinary people trying to do their best within their own means. This sees them engage in a politics that is grounded in community action and participation with a growing respect for the natural environment that does not necessarily involve direct care.

Key to this discussion is the history of damage to the Japanese natural environment that I make legible through everyday engagements with food. My reasoning behind this focus stems from the dominant role food plays in Amamian social life, as I experienced it, but also food's importance in both contemporary and historical national debates in Japan. I look at why those moving to rural regions, particularly but not exclusively mothers, are driven by a need to better understand food production and control their own food security to offset uncertainty. I argue that seasonality and awareness of one's environment, as experienced through food, helps ground people in time and place when they have been uprooted or experienced trauma. I suggest that this sustaining process offers a path back to community and the environment that requires reengaging with the natural world and traditional practices, thus considering how one can live more attentively and thereby ethically. I begin to pose the question of whether these ethical values might be extended to textile production and argue that developments in food activism might be seen as a precursor to a consumption of commodities subject to more considered regimes of care.

Seeking Security

Since the beginning of the year in 2018, the female dyers at Kanai Kougei had been discussing collecting *aosa* (green laver) from the beach (figure 3.1). A common type of sea lettuce collected and eaten globally, aosa is rich in protein, fiber, amino acids, vitamins, and minerals. In Japan, where seaweed is said to make up 10–25 percent of the diet, aosa is added to miso soup or cooked tempura style (Yaich et al. 2011). Food was a popular topic of conversation among the staff at the workshop, as we discussed the contents of each other's *bento* (lunch boxes) or

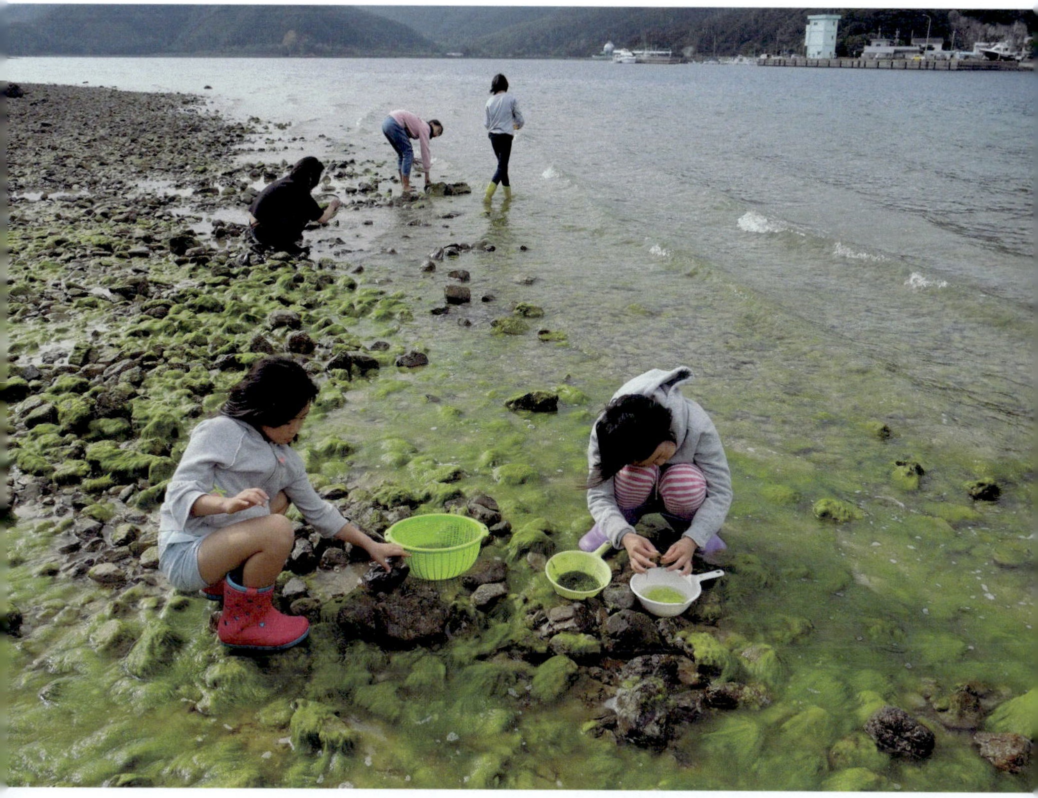

Figure 3.1 *Collecting seaweed on a spring tide.*

observed the foodstuffs that passed through the office during *kyūkei* (tea break). Beautifully wrapped snacks brought by visitors—*senbei* (rice crackers), mochi (sweet rice balls), and *dorayaki* (red-bean pancakes)—were omnipresent *omiyage* (souvenirs) from visitors' home prefectures on our communal office table. These snacks would vie for room with cucumbers, daikons, and bananas grown by the *tsumugi* dyer Kazu-san on his *hatake* (allotment). Huge jars of organic honey or sacks of organic brown rice Satoko-san or Kazuko ordered from contacts on the mainland were distributed to staff, who would collectively split the shipping costs. Eriko-san, the workshop's administrator and mother of the Kanai children, also took advantage of Japan Post's efficient system for shipping seasonal fruits and vegetables across the country.

Arriving at the office, hairy *nagaimo* (Chinese yams) from Hokkaido slept in sawdust-filled cardboard boxes, and perfect plastic-packaged strawberries from

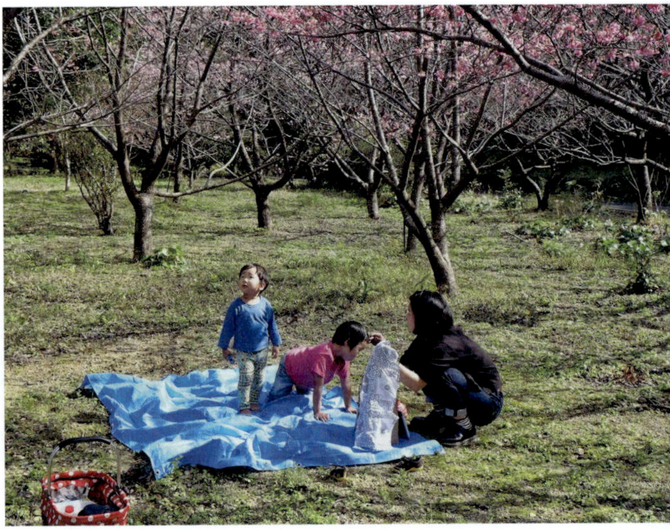

Figure 3.2 *Akiyo with Kazuko's sons, Nisa-kun and Chiraku-kun.*

Fukuoka were gifted to workers as treats by the Shachō. Stacked cartons of Amamian tankan and passionfruit would wait to be collected by the postman as return gifts to friends and relatives on the mainland.

Satoko-san would frequently glance up at the tide calendar pinned to the wall of the office identifying the low spring tides ideal for collecting aosa. An I-turn resident, Satoko-san (forty-one years old) had been living in Amami for fourteen years since removing herself from the "temptations" (her own words) of her hometown, Kyoto. Employed by Kanai Kougei part-time on and off for several years, Satoko-san began to train in tsumugi dyeing at another workshop but quit when she became pregnant with her second child. She is an accomplished home cook who has gained a reputation for her knowledge of Japanese but also Amamian local ingredients, dexterity with natural dyestuffs, love of *shōchū* (the local sugarcane rum), and warmness of heart. With the sunshine returning to Amami after the short winter, Satoko-san led a plan to collect aosa at the beach with a picnic, which we would eat beneath the newly blossomed sakura (cherry blossom) trees (figure 3.2).

Amami, alongside Okinawa and the surrounding Ryūkyū islands, is the first to enjoy this sign of spring just a few weeks after the New Year. Although sakura is adopted commercially year-round as a symbol of "Japaneseness" (Skov and Moeran 1995), it is during spring that sakura fever peaks. The activity of *hanami* (cherry-blossom viewing), often accompanied by a picnic, is just one of the ways nature is used to celebrate the beauty of the changing seasons and mark the passing of time.[3] Dorinne Kondo (1990, 242) suggests that the passage of the "four seasons" (*shiki*) has potency in Japan because each is climatically distinct and marked by "culturally constructed seasonality." This seasonality manifests itself through *matsuri* (festivals), food, dress, activities, and even commodities (Daniels 2009b) that become "part of everyday existence and cut across class and regional boundaries" (Kondo 1990, 241).

From January to May, crowds gather to enjoy the white-pink *somei yoshino* (Yoshino cherry), the most popular variety, so beloved because the petals flutter in the wind like snow (*hanafubuki*). In contrast, the *higanzakura* (Higan cherry) of Amami has robust magenta-pink flowers that resist the wind and rain, and because the forests mostly retain their leaves throughout the winter, for several weeks the sakura glow like beacons against green mountains. Planted in recreational areas and on the paths to Buddhist and Shinto shrines, they seem relatively young on account of their diminutive size, suggesting that they were planted in the postwar era when the nostalgia boom proliferated and Amami's fortunes swelled on the back of Oshima tsumugi (see chapter 1). The local economy at this time was boosted by mainland finance to raise the standards of living but also through compensation Japan paid out following the occupation of the islands until 1953.[4] In the archive of Douglas Haring, the American anthropologist who spent six months in Amami between 1951 and 1952, he notes that by 1962, $60 million (almost $5 billion in today's money) had been spent by the US and Japanese governments on construction in Amami alone. This paid for extensive tunnel boring through Amami's mountains that connected villages with newly built roads, power stations, schools, hospitals, and, one might imagine, recreational areas. From a historical perspective, it could be argued that importing and planting seasonal Japanese plants was a way to tie the long archipelago together as "one nation," as the country spans subarctic Hokkaido to subtropical Okinawa, each with its own distinct flora and fauna but also seasonal cultural traditions. Amami's seasons are not climatically distinct; it has a short winter (December–February), when the temperature drops to fifty to sixty degrees Fahrenheit. Spring is brief, giving way to a long summer (around April–November) peaking around eighty-six degrees Fahrenheit. The rainy season (May and June) and typhoon season (July–October) produce weather that is sporadically powerful rather than the daily norm.

Kazuko, a thirty-seven-year-old dyer who quickly became a great friend of mine but also a key research collaborator, told me that when she first moved to Amami she missed "traditional Japanese plants" and the sights and smells from the blossoms of the somei yoshino, *ume* (plum), and *momo* (peach) that marked the arrival of spring. She also missed the *kōyō* (red leaves) of the *momiji* maple—whose range didn't extend as far as Amami—as the turning of the leaves sweeps across the country from the north of the archipelago in autumn. Kazuko and I spoke often of how concerns around radiation had prompted her family's relocation; her first son, Chiraku-kun, had just been born, and if Tokyo had become "dangerous" she didn't want him growing up there. The circumstances of 3.11 demonstrate that this anxiety did not exist without reason. The earthquake had significantly damaged the buildings at the Daiichi Nuclear Power Plant, but the backup generators designed to cool the reactors in the event of an emergency had been destroyed by the huge tsunami that followed. Overheating led to explosions, leading to the release of radioactive materials from the reactors but also to spent fuel rods that were being stored in perpetuity. These materials contained dangerous cesium 137, a cancer-causing isotope that can exist in the environment for thirty years. Models created by a volcanologist show how radioactive particles were taken up and out with the wind across the Pacific Ocean on March 11, but on March 14 the wind changed direction, blowing dust-filled clouds over Tokyo (Brumfiel 2011). Radioactivity did not literally rain down on the city; instead, the clouds dropped their load farther inland, back toward the plant and Japan's northern mountainous areas, a key food-producing region. In May 2012 Tokyo Electric Power Company, responsible for running the power plant, released data suggesting that 900,000 terabecquerels of radioactive materials had been released into the air at the time of and the days following 3.11.[5] These huge numbers were reported to "correspond to 17% of the amount for [Ukraine's] Chernobyl plant, the site of the world's worst nuclear disaster" (Obe 2012). Meanwhile, 150,000 terabecquerels had been released into the sea, a number that continues to rise (Yoneyama 2012, 1). To add to the uncertainty of the aftermath, figures released by the government, Tokyo Electric Power Company, and independent scientists did not align, with news reports suggesting the government figures severely underestimated the extent of the fallout. Newer scientific papers instead argued that the radioactive damage could amount to closer to 43 percent of Chernobyl's spill (Yoneyama 2012).

As a result of the triple disaster, around twenty thousand people were reported missing or dead, 350,000 people were displaced (Allison 2013, 185), thousands of livestock and domestic pets were killed or abandoned, and wild plants and animals suffered genetic mutation and population decline (Mousseau and Møller 2014). Cleanup and compensation costs are running into trillions of yen, and the radiation problem is proving impossible to solve. Background radiation, but also contaminated food products, had cast a heavy anxiety over the country. One can easily understand why Kazuko felt Tokyo had become dangerous and

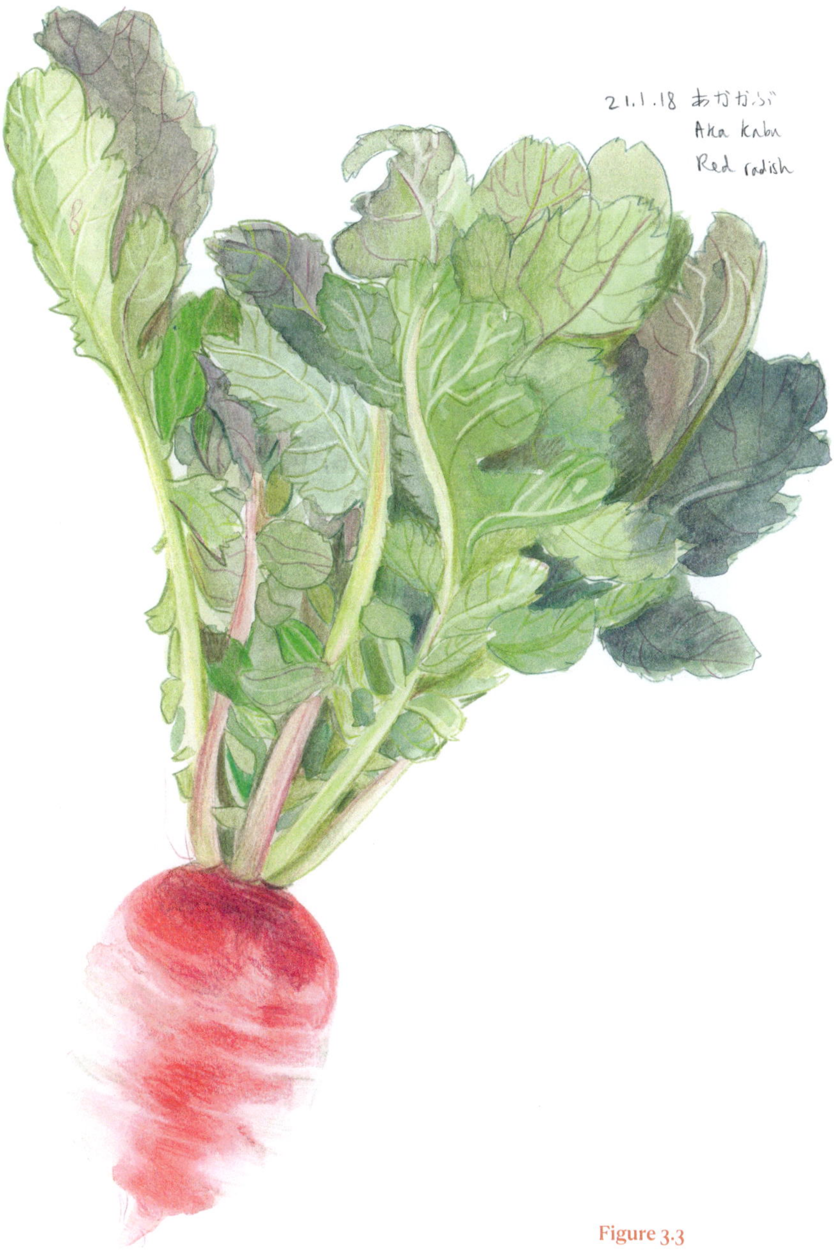

Figure 3.3
An akakabu *(red daikon) gifted to the author.*

why a drastic move to the southern reach of the archipelago—to Amami, where her husband had business contacts—was a risk worth taking.

National (In)securities

In the aftermath of 3.11, fresh concerns about food security surfaced from a history of food scandals that have troubled Japan since at least 1955, when arsenic-poisoned powdered milk produced by the Morinaga Milk company resulted in the death of over one hundred children. Sociologist Stephanie Assmann (2013, 8) says mislabeled food products, foods laced with illegal levels of additives and pesticides, and expired ingredients have routinely caused outbreaks of food poisoning. Assmann (2010, 243) has chronicled a range of food scares across her work on the rise of Japan's slow food movement, in which she concludes that consumers are increasingly turning to regional (often organic) produce for its nostalgic properties but also its health benefits and trustworthiness. Poor-quality domestic and imported ingredients have prompted anxiety about food security in Japan, where in 2022 self-sufficiency reached only 38 percent (Japan International Research Center for Agricultural Sciences 2024). This low number is the result of import deals with overseas producers such as the United States, which have flooded the market with Californian rice and catered to a shift in diet toward meat, dairy, and wheat.[6] But low self-sufficiency has also been blamed on the decline in number of domestic farmers, the consequence of long-standing out-migration depopulating agricultural regions and a lack of policy to protect farming livelihoods (Assmann 2016, 244; K. Yamashita 2019).

Food security in Japan, while also being under threat globally—brought to public consciousness by the recent war in Ukraine—has become an increasingly contentious topic. This was particularly apparent after 3.11, when the Japanese government came under criticism for its stance on food contaminated with radioactive materials. It was a prime example of how science is increasingly understood less as an objective reality but as a subject influenced by ideological bias (Latour 2004). To maintain social order and protect the economy, it was widely understood that the government presented scientific facts in a way that suited its objectives (Sternsdorff-Cisterna 2015, 456). In January 2012, an emergency standard allowing five hundred becquerels per kilogram of radioactive cesium was passed as safe for domestic vegetables, grains, meat, eggs, and fish (Fukushima Prefecture, n.d.). Four months later the limit was dropped to one hundred becquerels (Sternsdorff-Cisterna 2015, 456). While this seems considerably stricter than EU levels (1,250 becquerels per kilogram), the regulations state that a comparison cannot be made because these guidelines "[take] into account the estimated impact of the amount of food ingested" and "the proportion of food containing radioactive substances" (Fukushima Prefecture, n.d.). The lower limits in Japan suggest widespread radioactivity in food products but also in the water supply, and because Tohoku is a major food-producing region, consumers were advised to distribute their radioactive intake across their diet. Anthropologist Nicolas Sternsdorff-Cisterna (2015) states that the health impact of long-term, low-level radioactivity is difficult to measure, so the government's lack of transparency and safety guarantees led to widespread mistrust in the period following 3.11. This was against the backdrop of downplaying the nuclear fallout and of accusations that the government had colluded with the nuclear industry to prioritize protecting the economy above the health and safety of people and environment.

Accusations of environmental negligence have been made against the Japanese state since at least the 1950s. While most industrialized nations have faced—and continue to face—similar charges, the scale and consequence of environmental pollution in Japan drastically contrasts with the nation's image as one that lives in harmony with nature (Kagawa-Fox 2012, 3–8). The rush to industrialize after World War II meant that by the 1970s, Japan was the world's second largest economy but also one of the world's largest polluters. The Chisso chemical factory's dumping of mercury-rich wastewater in Minamata Bay, Kyūshū, from 1956 onward is perhaps the earliest, most widely recognized environmental disaster in Japan, which cemented the country's poor environmental reputation globally. Tens of thousands of locals were poisoned after consuming sea products that caused Minamata disease, a debilitating and deadly neurological illness; wild and domestic plants and animals also died. For over thirty years the government and the Chisso Corporation demonstrated "avoidance behavior" (Pharr 1992, 151) by denying the extent of the problem and were unwilling to take responsibility. It was only because of the work of American photojournalist W. Eugene Smith, who internationally exposed the Japanese malpractice, that action was eventually taken. Smith's images of Minamata and its sufferers were published in *LIFE* magazine in 1972. The *New York Times* reported that copies were "rushed off" in time for the United Nations Environment Conference in Stockholm, "where it created a sensation" (Thornton 1975). A range of legislation in the 1970s saw industry in Japan clean up its act, as the government recognized that environmental regulation was essential for international trading relations (Kanatsu 2013).

As this legislation came into place, Japan developed its nuclear power industry to maintain its industrial and economic standing, despite the severe harm that nuclear technology had inflicted on the country in 1945. Historian Kate Brown (2017, G38) explains that the drive to "celebrate" the potential "power of radiation" began in 1946, soon after the atom bombing of Hiroshima and Nagasaki, when US occupation officials distributed the MGM biopic of Marie Curie to cinemas across Japan. In the postwar era, this development was considered necessary because Japan was a "resource-poor country," having limited access to domestic oil and gas while coal was buried too deep to mine efficiently. After World War II the country used cheap Middle Eastern oil to help rebuild its economy. But the oil shocks that rocked the global economy in 1973, the result of an embargo implemented by Arab oil producers who raised the price of crude from three to twelve dollars per barrel, led Japan to seek energy self-sufficiency (Macalister 2011). "Belief in technology" meant that the government pursued the atomic option despite the suffering that atomic weaponry had caused the country (Kanatsu 2013, 289). In 1974, the government implemented the Three Power Source Development Laws, which were designed to enable the buy-off of opposition to the planned construction of power plants in depopulated regions from local fishermen, farmers, women, and victims of the atomic bombs. Historian Martin Dusinberre (2012, 153) explains that the laws allowed tax paid on energy bills "to be funneled back into power station host communities so as to fund major infrastructure projects (roads, schools, port development, and so on) over an initial five-year period." While this was made available to any community that hosted a power plant, nuclear power stations supplied the biggest bounty (Dusinberre 2012). By the 1980s Japan had subsequently become one of the world's biggest supporters and users of nuclear energy. This powered industry and the economy but also the supply of energy to the homes of those increasingly accustomed to middle-class convenience. "Nuclear villages" received financial benefits to ensure power supplies in megacities like Tokyo were maintained, "which resulted in hiding or not appropriately dealing with the potential dangers" (Kanatsu 2013, 306). The meltdown of the reactors in Fukushima and the extent of the devastation, although caused by a natural disaster, were ultimately blamed on human error for lack of preventive and emergency procedures overseen by government regulators. Political scientist Takashi Kanatsu states that Tokyo Electric Power Company and the government were warned that the plant needed repairs as early as 2000, but collusion among big industry, local bureaucrats, and government ministries meant these warnings were ignored (306–7). Kanatsu states the economy was prioritized at the local level in order to satisfy national targets.

This "evasion of responsibility," first demonstrated in Minamata and later by the bureaucratic ranks in Fukushima, highlights an issue with the concept of Japanese "groupism," in which individuals conform to hierarchical roles while working for the health of the group. Widely considered to be responsible for

Japan's postwar economic miracle, groupism has many benefits and is encouraged from an early age at home and school so it can later develop in the workplace (Kondo 1990, 301). Anthropologist Fiona Graham, in *Inside the Japanese Company* (2003), explains that most modern companies were built by those who had migrated directly from villages. Consequently, "the company is a kind of village" where workers demonstrate "mutual sympathy, comfort, mutual help, co-operation, and familiar cultural environment"—in effect, traits that work to distribute risk (Graham 2003, 154–55). Individual blame is avoided, unless an individual steps forward to sacrifice themselves for the health of the group. However, if an employee or community member does not fit in, they might be subject to "ostracism and bullying," revealing the tensions inherent in the dichotomy between the group and the individual (155). At an individual level, "avoidance behavior" (Pharr 1992, 151) is omnipresent in Japanese society, as Brian Moeran argues in his compelling book of ethnographic fiction, *Ōkubo Diary* (1985). Moeran attempted to identify who was at fault for a spinal injury his son obtained when diving in his elementary school's swimming pool while he was conducting fieldwork in the Oni valley, accompanied by his family. He found that each party—the teacher, school, Education Authority, and national bodies of the Japan Swimming Federation and the Ministry of Education—feared that if an individual took the blame, "the whole system would come under fire" (Moeran 1985, 144). Rather than make the incident public knowledge, Moeran was encouraged to stay quiet and take insurance money for his son. But in the face of rising medical costs, he was forced to sue the Education Authority, leaving him ostracized from the community and labeled a "foreigner" (246).

Understanding how groupism is deployed ethnographically, as in Moeran's case study, demonstrates how a nation can become paralyzed by inaction if responsibility is evaded over concerns that it will damage the reputation, finances, or social standing of a member of the group, breaking the myth of social harmony. This was seen on 3.11 with the exceptionally sad story of the Okawa elementary school in Ishinomaki, where seventy-four of seventy-eight pupils and ten of eleven teachers died in the tsunami. An independent inquiry confirmed that the deaths occurred because none of the staff broke rank to defy the headmaster, who followed poorly prepared emergency procedures overseen by the prefecture (Parry 2017). It is difficult to implement change if individuals feel that they are unable to speak up or that, if they do, their concerns will be ignored. Anthropologist Andrew Littlejohn has shown how in "old-fashioned" areas, such as those affected by 3.11, where his research is based, "conflicts between residents . . . intersected with familiar social hierarchies, notably of age and gender." As one of his female activist participants claimed, "Whatever the big-wigs say is gospel"

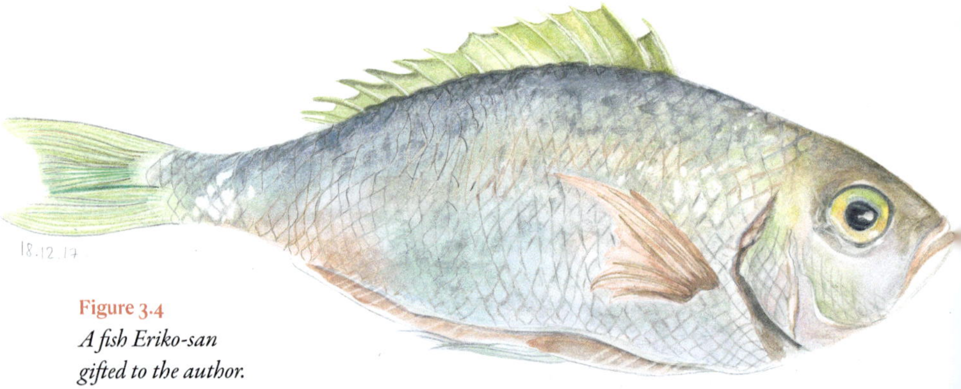

Figure 3.4
A fish Eriko-san gifted to the author.

(Littlejohn 2017, 63). These "big-wigs" tended to be older men, demonstrating the gender bias that plagues political life in Japan, where, as of 2023, only 10 percent of members of parliament were female (World Bank Group 2024). The political environment, locally and nationally, is dominated by the Liberal Democrat Party, which has been in almost continuous power since 1955, barring an eight-month period in 1993 (Kanatsu 2013, 285). Group mentality overseen by a powerful few has seen environmental disasters perpetuate, because change is slow and resistance too often unable to make itself heard.

After 3.11, consumers who could afford to shop at trusted grocery stores bought organic products or those from the west of Japan—those they considered free of radiation (Sternsdorff-Cisterna 2015). Yet Anne Allison (2013, 184, 203) demonstrates the potential social consequences of resistance by explaining that when citizens (mostly between the ages of twenty and forty) refused to eat or avoided eating produce from the Tohoku region, they faced accusations of being "*hikokumin* (non-citizenly)" by older Japanese (those over fifty). This generation insinuated that younger people were not supporting local farmers who desperately needed customers and were acting against the advice of the state. This politicized rhetoric of helping regional economies through public consumption practices has a history and was seen in the period following World War I in the UK. Frank Trentmann (2007, 1082) shows how government propaganda encouraged housewives to "Buy Empire Goods"—from farmers in New Zealand to Jamaica and Canada—to support the British Empire's economy as the world entered an economic depression. Eat Out to Help Out, a 2020 British government scheme rolled out across the UK following the country's strict COVID-19 lockdown, can be drawn upon as a more recent comparison to what Japan experienced after 3.11. The British government asked citizens to take risks (eating in restaurants with food prepared by, served, and eaten among strangers) in an atmosphere of high health anxiety to help the national economy and prevent further closures in the hospitality industry.

In an environment where food becomes an ideological and political issue, and science is reframed to produce different accounts of reality, how might one demonstrate resistance but also foster solidarity existing outside of state or corporate institutions? Sternsdorff-Cisterna describes alternative forms of less conformist solidarity that arose after 3.11, counteracting that encouraged by the state. He documents the rise in "scientific citizenship" that residents of Tokyo and affected areas in Tohoku used to educate themselves so they could effectively navigate the food system and evaluate risk. Local networks shared seminars, reading clubs, and Geiger counters, an action reflecting Mathijs Pelkmans's "Outline for an Ethnography of Doubt," where he claims doubt can be alleviated though processes of domestication. Pelkmans (2013, 23) claims doubt can be "debilitating" and "tempering," but it can also have an "energizing effect," "stimulating the quest for (academic) knowledge," pushing one to seek resolutions and to stabilize uncertainty through everyday actions. In so doing, doubt is transferred "to an area beyond the horizon of our immediate consciousness," despite it "resist[ing] disappearing entirely" (22). Radiation is troubling in its invisibility and in the irregularities of its impact on human health, from the "psychological stress" of exposure (K. Brown 2017, G44) to physiological extremes including cancer, cardiovascular disease, infertility, and premature death. By making it "visible" through education, the anxiety it produces can be temporally suspended.

The formation of these education networks following 3.11 was particularly promoted between mothers, because they were considered the "providers" of the family. Female-led activism around food in Japan can be traced back to the rice riots of 1918, when housewives started a protest movement to highlight the rising costs of rice. Robin LeBlanc's (1999) classic ethnography *Bicycle Citizens* describes how women have been locked out of the political world because they are overburdened with obligation for the house and home. But using the metaphor of the back streets and alleys women navigate on bicycles, she shows how they use local networks to operate in alternative spaces to ones dominated by a male political class. LeBlanc (1999, 198) suggests that although housewives might become engaged in local politics, they do not fully enter the political world because they have a general distrust of the political elite, whom they see as "murky, money-hungry, male, and over organized." Although published almost twenty years later, Lynne Nakano's (2018) paper on "housewife" activism reaches a similar conclusion, when Nakano writes that women will be able to enter politics professionally, at an equivalent scale to men, only if systematic gender and labor imbalances are addressed through the reforms of labor and tax laws that discriminate against women. It was by using the strength of Japanese maternal symbolism that mothers protested ineffective government policy and the favoring of "corporate interests" (Slater 2012, 4) in the aftermath of 3.11. There were street protests of a magnitude not "seen in Tokyo for decades," in which older antinuclear activists joined groups such as Women from Fukushima Against Nukes (22).

While concerns around food safety were documented by academics and popular media in the years following the disaster, over a decade later, issues persist. As of 2023, the buildup of contaminated groundwater at the Fukushima site exceeded one million tons, and with storage units full, the government said it had no choice but to release radioactive water into the sea and dilute it (Tsoi 2023). This prompted both international condemnation and protests by local fishermen, who claim they had only recently begun to win back public trust. Late in 2019, I received an outraged message from a Japanese friend who shared news of government plans to recycle tons of contaminated soil to grow vegetable crops in Fukushima. While initially it was proposed that this soil, with a reading of one thousand becquerels per kilogram, could be buried beneath newly constructed roads across Japan (in effect redistributing risk nationwide), the plan was now to sort, decontaminate, recycle and return it to farmland to solve the problem of long-term storage (Ministry of the Environment of Japan 2024; Otake 2023). Anthropologist Peter Wynn Kirby (2019, 3) calls this the "conceit of recycling," made to "imbue the effort to remove radioactive dirt and other abominated debris with flattering hues of eco-responsibility and resource efficiency." It is not inconceivable that it could be seen as a solution to the economic problems faced by Fukushima's farmers, who would be allowed to plant flowers or energy crops using this soil. But, Kirby argues, this prolongs the shadow of radiation that farmers here live under, who are desperate for Fukushima to regain its place as one of the country's largest food-producing regions (14–15). When viewed in this contentious environment, migrating to rural Japan begins to look less extreme.

I-Turning to Amami

Although Kazuko had studied psychology at a college in the United States, in Tokyo she had worked variously as a lighting technician for music events and as a leader of *aizome* workshops. In Amami she hoped to pursue more creative work yet initially struggled to adjust, wanting to return to Tokyo. She missed friends and family and the anonymity of the city. But when she and Satoko-san

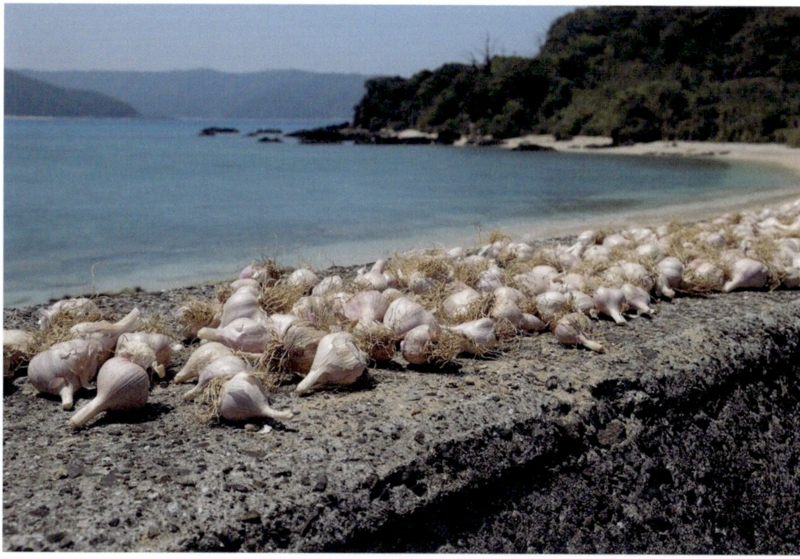

Figure 3.5 *On sunny days, fruits and vegetables can been found drying in the sun all over Amami, and this homegrown abundance is often shared with family and neighbors.*

chatted with me, they explained Amami was a good place "to grow kids"; there was "nature, there is the ocean in front of the house, and you can get watermelon from your neighbors!" I-turn residents relocating to the southern islands have access to cheap seasonal fruits, vegetables, and sea products, whereas in Tokyo these come at a premium (figure 3.5). Produce is also frequently shared or gifted, increasing accessibility for residents who have decreased their income to make the move. Amamians also have better access to alternative economic networks that expand beyond a conception of economy centered on wage labor and capitalist markets. Understanding how the island's diverse economy functions is essential for local people in Amami if they are to remain content and not move on or back to the city. As I was told by an emergency room doctor who had moved from Tokyo, Amami is an island where local people treat children as "treasure." He had four children of his own and explained, "In Amami, there is a strong relationship in the community. When parents are working, neighbors look after the children; therefore, it's easier to have a bigger family. People take care of each other; this is a good thing." Feminist geographer J. K. Gibson-Graham's (2014) Diverse Economy Iceberg diagrammatic method is a helpful way to visualize the objects, materials, skills, and knowledge that can be exchanged, bartered, or swapped and that exist outside of, while feeding into, capitalist systems, allowing communities to reclaim their local economies. Drawing an "iceberg" diagram based on my own experiences in Amami was exceptionally helpful for seeing how I was able to get by on a low income over the course of a year without feeling the need to live excessively frugally.[7]

Nevertheless, in communities that are made up of former city dwellers and rural residents who collectively wish to engage in community-making, tensions or frustrations certainly arise, because all members have different expectations of one another. Kazuko and Satoko-san explained that on a small island you must stay on friendly terms with *all* members of your community, negotiating social harmony. This was particularly important to ensure access to opportunities and the health and safety of their children and to avoid being ostracized or gossiped about. Such daily negotiation was *taihen* (hard work), with relationships requiring time and maintenance that Kazuko and Satoko-san didn't always want to provide. As Kazuko explained, "Living in the city area, there are many people. If we think 'I hate someone' [and we see them], then just run away, it's fine, but in Amami if we hate someone, we cannot run away. . . . We have to figure out the 'good point' of them and keep in touch—*we have to*. So, it's a bad point but it's also a good point—it's difficult for us from the mainland, [we are] city girls!"

Susanne Klien also documents the work that goes into conflict avoidance to maintain social harmony, requiring both settlers and established residents to enter compromise. For her participants this might mean allowing your I-turn neighbor to sleep in late if they have worked a night shift in a restaurant, even if you want to drop off vegetables and chat (Klien 2020, 181–82). But settlers also needed to give back by showing a willingness to engage in local customs and community-making. Kazuko told me that in those early months Amami seemed like "a foreign country"—she was a new member of the community so she stood out, meaning she couldn't move around freely without someone recognizing her. But the food, plants, and mountains were so different, and the monotony of Amami's seasons added to her homesickness.

Japanese studies scholar Peter Ackermann (1997, 40) says acknowledging the four seasons is "one way of *visualizing* order, harmony, 'the way things ought to be.'" Such "nature images," he explains, "express in a particularly tangible manner a sequence of changes and transformations, or steps, towards a specific *state*" that in turn moves one to a metaphysical "sphere" beyond the seasonal cycle (46). This can be related to the cycles of birth and renewal "at the base of East Asian thought," but distinct seasonality has also been used to "visualize universal principles of cosmic order that should be obeyed in order to avoid calamities" (Daniels 2009b, 175). Using this ideology to enforce structure and

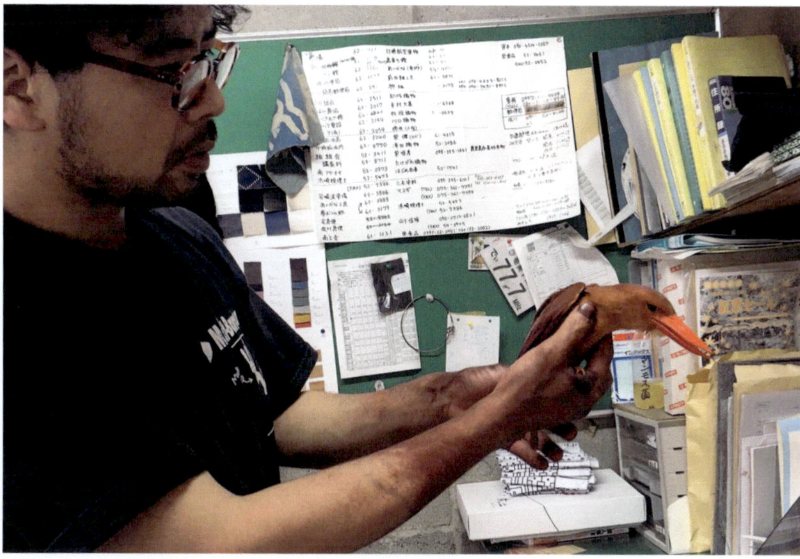

Figure 3.6 *Yukihito-san holds an akashōbin that had flown into a window of the Shachō and Eriko-san's house. Photo by Akiyo Shidama.*

authority (Ackermann 1997, 41) on everyday life may have a stabilizing, grounding effect when one's life is subject to upheaval.[8] Kondo (1990, 243) explains that "seasons and seasonal rituals locate you in a flow of time and link you to people who are part of your past, present, and future. In Japan, the rhythms of the changing seasons punctuate the rhythms of human life." Enacting Japanese seasonal activity such as engaging in hanami, eating a picnic, and foraging for seaweed maintains continuities with life on the mainland, particularly important for those residents brought up in different social, cultural, and physical environments. But at the same time "culturally constructed seasonality" (242), which feels most present in cities, runs the risk of masking local microprocesses that might go unnoticed but are important for demonstrating and maintaining a healthy ecology.

After several years of living on Amami, establishing a network of friends and securing her job at Kanai Kougei, Kazuko says she can now see the subtle changes in the flora across the year, the coming and going of seasonal foods—banana, papaya, tankan, aosa—that mark the passing of Amamian time. She has become more attuned to her surroundings, to local microprocesses, but also seeks information from locals. She asked me one day whether I knew that the *akashōbin* (ruddy kingfisher), an iconic bird in Amami, only migrates to the island in the summer (figure 3.6). I gave an affirmative, and she said, "I didn't know that! Chiraku's teacher just told me!"

Living Slowly and Consuming Ethically

Sitting beneath the cherry blossoms, we ate salad, *onigiri* (rice balls), fried *gohan* (rice), sweet tofu, and pickles, all prepared by me, Akiyo, Kazuko, Satoko-san, and their children and two of Satoko-san's friends who were new arrivals to Amami (figure 3.7). The children kept wandering off, so warnings of *hebi!* (snake!) were shouted, while *habu!* was directed to Satoko-san's determined three-year-old, Kaiyō-kun. Snakes at this time of year are particularly dangerous. While in the summer they are mostly nocturnal, in the spring they wake from hibernation and can be found hunting in the day. These snake warnings resonated as we climbed down to the beach along an uneven path overgrown with vegetation. The older children were already collecting aosa, holding sieves filled with what looked like a bright green slime. Satoko-san showed Akiyo and me how to distinguish seaweed from moss, which was lighter in color and stringier, while aosa is soft, flat, and silky with a delicious, salty taste (figure 3.8). I asked Akiyo whether her mother had picked the aosa we ate tempura style at the workshop during the week. She shook her head and said she'd bought it from the shops. Akiyo's mother produced the tastiest Amamian cuisine, and Akiyo, who was born on the mainland because her father was in the Japanese army, was slowly acquiring her mother's cooking skill and knowledge. Although she was schooled in Amami, Akiyo had recently U-turned back to her hometown after spending several years studying garment pattern cutting in Tokyo and living abroad. Now she was living with her parents in their ancestral home in south Amami, drawn back by the desire to learn Amamian traditional *kusakizome*. "This is great," she said. "Free, fresh food!" I asked whether aosa was specific to the island, but Akiyo said Kazuko used to pick it in Tokyo. After an hour we climbed back to the comfort of the picnic and ate vegan banana bread Satoko-san had baked with Kazu-san's homegrown *shima* bananas. Kazu-san was as adept with agriculture as he was with dyeing and generous with the plants and animals he foraged in the mountains. The sight of a rack of bananas in the back of his *keitora* (minitruck) was enough to generate a mild hysteria. Later that evening I prepared miso soup with aosa using stock from a fish Eriko-san had bought each member of staff from the fisherman Mitoshi-ni, who had a part-time job running jewelry classes at Kanai Kougei. While I dried the surplus seaweed on top of my space heater, Kazuko shared her aosa with Nagata-san, who took it home to his wife.

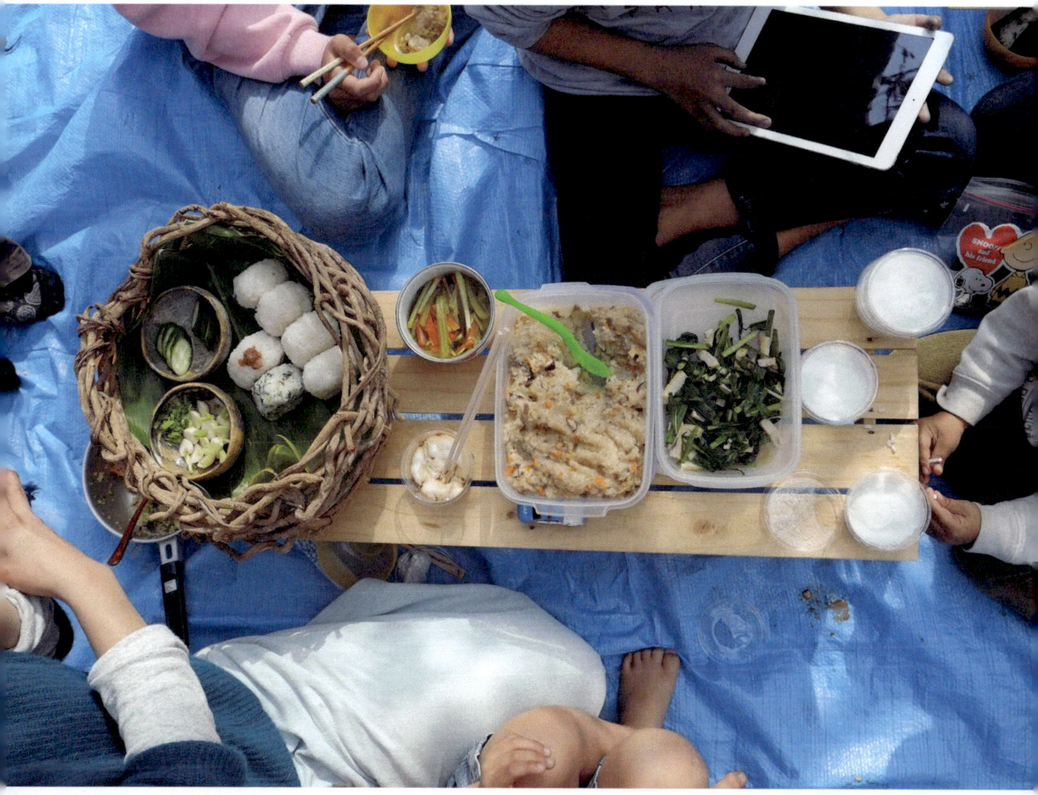

Figure 3.7 *A hanami picnic.*

Internal migration is often prompted by erosion of trust in the state, whether caused by precarious employment, the retreat of the welfare state, economic stagnation, industrial negligence, environmental pollution, or food security. Anthropologist of Japan Anne Allison (2013, 5) claims that in the midst of economic recession, poverty, and war, people around the world are dealing with the consequences of "neoliberal globalism run amok." Her book *Precarious Japan* (2013) specifically charts precarious employment but also the uncertainty unleashed by 3.11. The publication is unrelenting in its critique of neoliberalism and the failings of the state, which Allison argues have led to extreme alienation in many of her ethnographic examples. Her perspective offers a bleak picture of contemporary Japan, where precarity is equated with a sense of "pain and unease" (16), giving little room for what Frank Trentmann calls "the elasticity of everyday life." In contrast to Allison, Trentmann claims that "quotidian disruptions" caused by disasters but also blackouts or traffic jams "offer a snapshot of

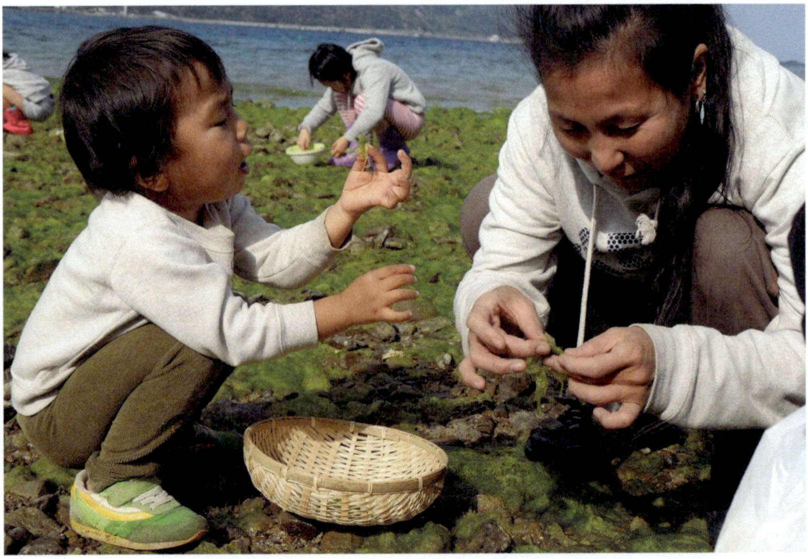

Figure 3.8 *Between picking aosa, the children dug for small crabs or poked at sea anemones, pointing them out to anyone who showed an interest.*

rhythms as they unravel and are braided back together again, capturing the work needed to keep them going." Disruptions, from this perspective, "are not freak accidents or aberrations but natural, constitutive features of lived normality" that provide opportunities to "open up" the politics of everyday life. He elaborates: "[Disruptions] raise questions about accountability (who is to blame), entitlement and social justice (who should get what) and, most profoundly, about 'normality' (how can or should members of a society live). Disruption therefore is a particularly useful way to explore connections between practices, politics and socio-technical systems" (Trentmann 2009, 69).

The events of 3.11 ruptured the everyday, causing a national trauma, but living precariously can also open up the politics of solidarity and identity—as communities around the world experienced throughout the COVID-19 pandemic. While being mindful not to dismiss the suffering many people experienced at the hands of such disruptions, such disruptions do indeed force Trentmann's (2009) question: "How can or should members of a society live?" Doreen Massey (1995, 184) states that "place-*based* struggles" do not necessarily need to be "place-*bound*," and this is even more apparent as technology has removed the barrier of distance. A sense of uncertainty about one's future prompted my participants to seek resolutions by moving to the countryside. However, I argue that those seeking a slower life and a career in craft relocate to rural regions but continue to engage with the larger struggles facing Japan, even if they are not based at the epicenter (see also chapter 2 of this book). This pushes back against the idea that rural living is a retreat "backward" to a place where "time goes slow" and counters common misconceptions about the countryside and city, the modern and the archaic, that fall into binary oppositions. This argument is supported by Elizabeth Shove et al. (2009, 3), who describe how society is perceived to have shifted from having a slow, "traditional," pastoral conception of time, dictated by seasonal rhythms influencing labor and festivities, to an urban, "'modern' regime" structured around "industrial time." This "speeding up of society" has seen a city-based proletariat squeezed by industrial capitalism and by the enabling of technologies and infrastructure that were supposed to save time but frequently see one work harder (Shove 2009, 26). Instead, Shove et al. argue that what occurs in reality is the coexistence of "multiple temporalities," varying rhythms and routines individuals use (wherever they reside) to navigate the everyday (2009, 3). As recent work in anthropology has shown, acknowledging the coexistence of temporalities "help[s] us think about spatiality in new and interesting ways" (Anand et al. 2018, 16; see also Bear 2015). In the previous chapter, I highlighted how such temporalities meet and intertwine in the use of chemicals shipped in to fix natural dyes made from fifty-year-old trees or in the ways local (rural) politics might challenge the supposedly advanced political urban elite. I also suggested that labor conditions might be considered "backward" for women working in the countryside, but I would equally argue that women continue to face similar gendered hierarchies in the city—as demonstrated most tellingly by Japanese politics. Memorializing seasonal time through hanami or the collection of aosa, meanwhile, reminds my participants of their hometowns, while using smartphones, microwaves, and rice cookers to prepare a picnic binds knowledge and friendships in the present.

This rethinking of time resonates with the philosophy of the slow food movement, which has in recent years gained traction in Japan (Assmann 2016). Wendy Parkins and Geoffrey Craig (2006, 3), who took a sabbatical from academic careers to investigate the movement in Italy, state that slow living is not a desire to go back in time but is "deriv[ed] from a commitment to occupy time more attentively." Slow living is not about performing acts more slowly or having more time; it is an engagement with the practice, materials, and/or people surrounding that action. Time is made for care and for taking pleasure in practice—as Shove argues, "Practices *make* time" (2009, 17).

Though my participants would buy food from the supermarket and occasionally a cheap and convenient lunch of prepackaged onigiri and instant coffee from Family Mart, we made frequent trips to the pharmacy in Naze city, the only store

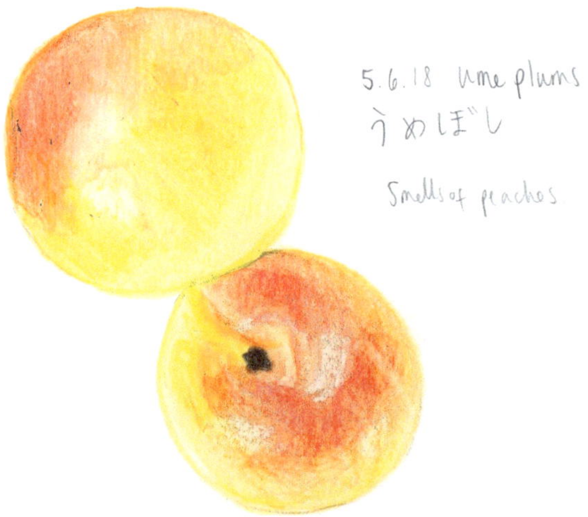

Figure 3.9
Ume plums.

in Amami that stocked a small but expensive selection of organic and macrobiotic foodstuffs. In an attempt to sidestep the expense, we made our own organic *umeboshi* (aged, pickled plums), after Satoko-san's contact shipped the fruits to us from Okayama, salting them with Amamian sea salt (figure 3.9). After they were ready, we ate them throughout the year, benefiting our gut microbiome and helping fend off colds. We made miso (fermented soy bean paste) using an ancient recipe Satoko-san read aloud, while the other I-turners with experience shared knowledge and techniques (figure 3.10). The soy beans came from Satoko-san's sister's organic farm in Kyoto and were boiled on a makeshift fire using wood from an old tsumugi loom gifted by the Shachō. We crushed and mixed the beans with *kōji* rice inoculated with a beneficial mold, before putting the paste to "sleep" (*nekaseru*) for around six months. While it took several weeks to buy and source materials, the task itself was carried out over a morning, yet the results could be enjoyed for years to come.

Political theorist Jane Bennett (2001, 8) might suggest that the pleasure taken in these annual culinary practices is an example of "the marvelous erupting amid the everyday." Bennett argues that by seeking out "magical sites already here" (8), paying care and attention to the mundane, we might overcome some of the issues faced by modern society. By allowing oneself to be "enchanted" by nature but also by the "literary, machinic, and electronic" (11), she suggests that "chronological time and bodily movement" can be suspended, creating "a momentary immobilizing encounter" (5). The experience of enchantment has been critiqued for its association with elitism: How does a single mother with three jobs and three children find the time and energy to be enchanted? It has also been sug-

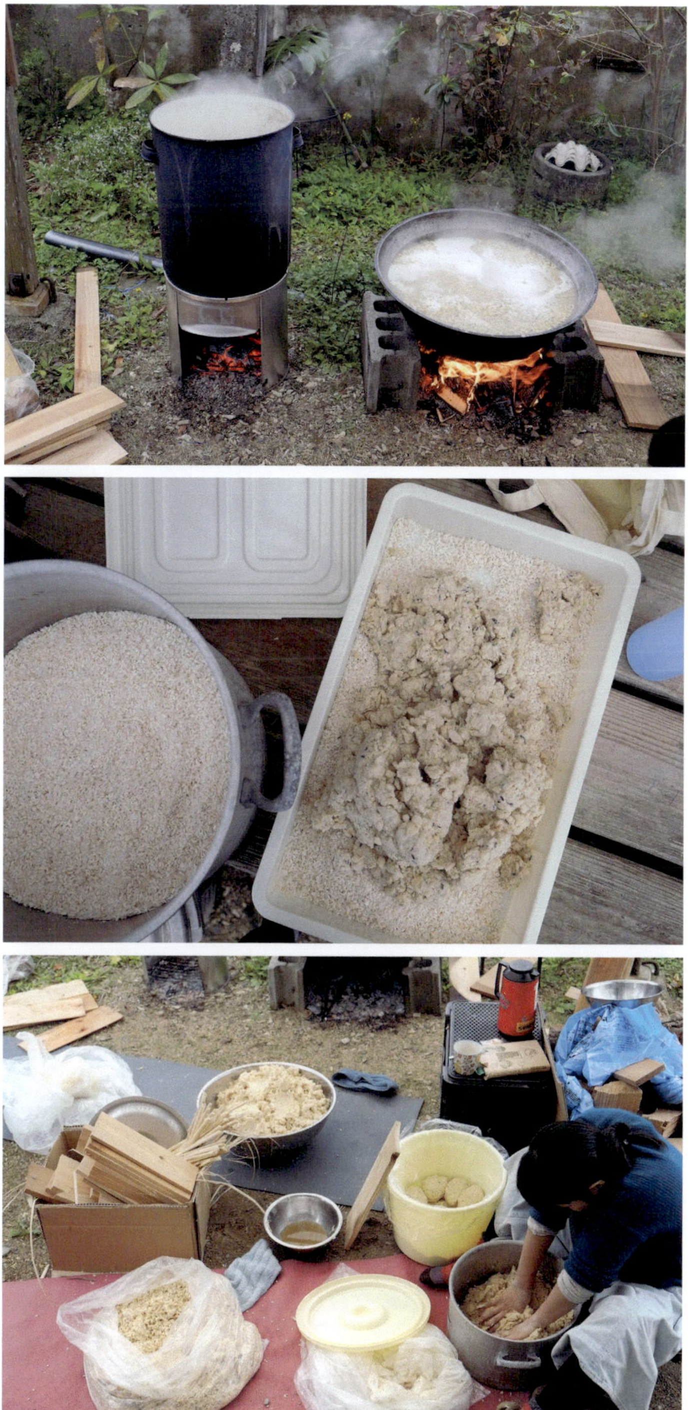

Figure 3.10 *Miso-making, attended by workshop staff and their I-turner friends.* Top to bottom*: Boiling the soy beans; mixing beans with* kōji *and salt; and Kazuko making miso balls.*

gested that those who seek enchantment want to "forget about injustice, sink into naïveté, and escape from politics" (10). But Bennett argues the opposite can occur. Being enchanted can motivate one to care about everyday practices and encounters within the community, resulting in a recalibration of affluence that "rehabilitates" more "ethical behavior" (5). Yet can enchantment alone promote meaningful action? Yukihito-san's engagement with color-making, discussed in chapter 2, could certainly be described in Bennett's terms as an "enchantment," but how is this transposed to more ethical behavior, or what one might understand as sustaining processes, those small actions that communities carry out to maintain and care for local cultural, social, and environmental resources?

In chapters 1 and 2, I claimed Kanai Kougei has prioritized what one might define as economic and social sustainability—providing jobs, sharing knowledge, and sustaining traditions by investing in the local textile economy. But natural dyeing also inspires an image of environmental sustainability. As I argue throughout this book, the reality of natural dyeing is more complex than its image. Its production processes create a friction that might variably be conducive or damaging to local ecologies. Those who commission dyeing with Kanai Kougei take advantage of this ambiguity, because it is almost impossible to create a commercial product using natural dyestuffs that can turn profit without compromise—as introduced in the previous chapter. These compromises might bring into question a product's authenticity (with authenticity being central to the appeal of natural dyeing) or the ability to dye textiles in a manner considered (at least in popular discourse) environmentally sustainable. Instead, commissioning companies leave consumers to make assumptions based on their own knowledge or trust in a company, ultimately putting environmental responsibility for ethical consumption in the hands of consumers. So how does one move beyond the *image* of sustainability to enacting something closer to a reality?

Gibson-Graham et al. offer a way forward that reframes manufacturing as a "matter of care." They explain that manufacturing has moved from being a "matter of fact" to a "matter of concern," evolved from an economic issue—that is, the decline of manufacturing in the Global North and its subsequent prominence in government policy in postindustrial economies—to an environmental issue. They examine how in recent years overconsumption and problematic manmade materials, resulting from "the Great Acceleration" of manufacturing in the 1950s, have transformed and damaged the surface of the planet (Gibson-Graham et al. 2019, 3–7). Referencing María Puig de la Bellacasa's 2017 book *Matters of Care*, in which she examines "more-than-human" relationships via permaculture practices, Gibson-Graham et al. suggest that manufacturing might be treated as a "matter of care" to embrace lifestyles that recognize our interdependence with, and maintenance and care for, other species. Puig de la Bellacasa references Joan Tronto's "much quoted generic definition of care" as "everything that we do to maintain, continue and repair 'our world' so that we can live in it as well as possible. That world includes our bodies, our selves, and our environment, all of which we seek to interweave in a complex, life-sustaining web" (Tronto 1993, 103).

Puig de la Bellacasa argues that care work activates a sense of ethics and politics because "concern" or "worry" drive one to take responsibility for others. As she explains, "A politics of care engages much more than a moral stance; it involves affective, ethical, and hands-on agencies of practical and material consequence" (Puig de la Bellacasa 2017, 4). Relevant to discussions on manufacturing, she highlights how corporate greenwashing has in recent years called upon companies to visually project "how much *they* care," asking those who consider buying their products to show how much "*we* care" (9). This raises the questions of where and how care might be enacted during manufacturing. And how might care be approached across different scales?

Gibson-Graham et al. state, "Care involves seeing with our fingers and a kind of acknowledgment that when we care about things—the layout of the manufacturing floor, microbiomes, babies—we touch and are touched by them. Care entails active experimental doings that involve negotiating interdependence and constraint in place, deciding, choosing, privileging and taking responsibility, and enacting an ethos" (2019, 10). Gibson-Graham et al. provide examples from their field sites of large-scale manufacturers who have embraced a caring ethos—for their environment, employees, communities, and customers. Yet this "ethos," which chimes with Bennett's "enchantment," might result in meaningful action at the local scale, but it does not necessarily address the wider issue. This is because "sustainability" is a broad and unwieldy ideology, meaning the ethical impact of a product's manufacture might not be immediately apparent to makers or consumers. Anthropologist Sarah Wilkes (2015, 213), working at the intersection of materials, design, and sustainability, claims her "participants [designers, suppliers, and brands] spoke about the difficulties involved in assessing the sustainability of a material in a generic way if you don't know the specific context of extraction, production, use and disposal." She also highlights that ideas about what constitutes "sustainable" are not universal by quoting a mining expert at a conference who explained, "'What's fashionable here in London may be very different in the rest of the world: here, carbon and environmental impact are very high on the agenda' but in India 'HIV, keeping staff in jobs, water and political problems' are more immediate concerns." Wilkes states her participants "found themselves confronted with extremely difficult trade-offs," explaining that "it is not the case that they don't care," but "in the dynamic of daily decision-making, they are constrained by finite limits, particularly time and money," meaning that "they inevitably have to prioritize some aspects of sustainability over others" (219). This perhaps mirrors the situation I observed at Kanai Kougei, but how does one make the leap toward environmentally sustaining processes when confined by the market, which pressures manufacturers to keep costs low, or when one's capacity to care is limited by the reach of one's knowledge?

Shove (2012) and Gibson-Graham et al. (2019, 7) have argued that for too long the drive toward sustainability has foregrounded the potential of innovation where hopes for the revitalization of manufacturing systems or infrastructures have been placed in "technoscientific solutions." However, Shove (2012, 369) argues that solutions to social and environmental issues might be sought in the "fragments of failed regimes." As she writes, "Those wanting to develop cycling (or lower carbon diets, or recycling, or organic food, etc.) in different countries and cities should begin by searching not for niches of innovation but for pockets of persistence. They should ask themselves what happened to the remains of past configurations, and how might these be activated and incorporated anew?" (372).

One might argue that revitalizing "pockets of persistence" promotes the values of mottainai. These values lead to questions about how past materials, practices, objects, knowledge, and time scales might be integrated with contemporary life and material worlds and "activated and incorporated anew" (Shove 2012, 372). My participants were interested in natural materials and ingredients and sustainable processes, and they tried their best to incorporate them into their lives and working practices. I had discussions with Kazuko and Koki about alternative laundry detergents; Kazuko gave me some soap nuts to try, while Koki had discovered a natural bleaching agent. Kazuko produced a small line of natural candles (using beeswax sent from Satoko-san's friend on the mainland), in which she had included powdered pigment that Yukihito-san had made with waste dye materials. If they had the income, my friends would wear organic cotton and hemp, and if they had the time and resources they would grow, process, and dye with natural indigo. Instead, with Yukihito-san's permission, all of Kanai Kougei's apparel staff actively engaged in revitalizing their wardrobe by overdyeing tired garments in their own time. When on maternity leave, Kazuko asked workmen clearing the bush near her house to save *adan* (pandanus) leaves so she could weave a hat. This idea was inspired by Koki, who had woven adan *zōri* (pandanus sandals) in Okinawa and who had also been weaving fabric for a jacket made from old, shredded cloth (*sakiori*) overdyed with cloves. The cloth had taken on a mauve shade of gray and a beautiful aromatic and antibacterial scent. Akiyo, meanwhile, had set about making new garments with recycled kimono fabrics donated by Eriko-san, recutting them into a casual coat and a dress for her friend's wedding. At the center of these practices were aims to creatively reformulate waste and enact mottainai, highlighting that the sharing of materials and things in reuse economies is often driven by social and economic benefits and responsibilities rather than purely environmental values. In contrast to the larger discussion about the economic potential of circular economies (Norris 2019), these are "small scale and mundane practices," in which materials and objects pass between hands in informal "diverse economies" (Lane and Watson 2012, 1262) existing outside of markets based on monetary exchange.

It might even be suggested that through creative practice my participants treat Amami as a form of commons, whether by foraging for materials or by using waste to make new things—such as burning a tsumugi loom to make miso or using cut pandanus leaves to weave a hat. A "common" good can be described as a resource that is "owned in common or shared within the community [that satisfies] needs that go unmet by either markets or institutions" (Vivero-Pol et al. 2019, 6). Although I will explore in more detail the history and ideas behind commoning in chapter 6, it is relevant to note here that the idea of a material commons and a knowledge commons suggests that these are resources governed locally and are "socially and environmentally relational" (10).

As I have argued elsewhere (Linton 2016), island cultures globally are known for their skills in recycling, repairing, and sharing materials and objects, most likely because of their historic isolation and the difficulty of obtaining materials quickly and cheaply. This is particularly apparent in the care and repair of tools and machinery and the creative adaptation of alternative parts. Such ingenuity was the case in Amami, where the extremities of wind, humidity, salt air, and torrential rain led to buildings frequently getting damaged and anything made of metal suffering from rust. For example, the workshop's thirty-year-old *dasuki* (spinning machines) had been variously repaired with car body filler or bicycle wheel inners, because the machines are hugely expensive to replace. But one might also argue that these old machines, "material things [with] lives" (Siniawer 2018, 170–71), have garnered a respect that recalls *tsukumogami* (tool kami, or tool gods); when they broke down, the essential role they played in the workshop would become apparent (see chapter 4). They also made themselves heard through their loud whirring as they spun yarns or their clunking and squealing if they had been incorrectly loaded or were "sick." The dyers enacted a kind of "product stewardship" over the dasuki, understood as the responsibilities we have toward a product from its conception, through its use, and up to its disposal, an idea that undermines the concept of singular property ownership.

Geographers Ruth Lane and Matt Watson explain that, across its biography, an object will pass among multiple individuals with "rights and responsibilities" toward it. By recalibrating conceptions of ownership toward stewardship, an expectation can be located toward care of an object for the wider, "public good" (Lane and Watson 2012). The dasuki were such key pieces of machinery at Kanai Kougei, meaning that workers would take care when using them and supervise visitors in case they mistreated them, while Kazu-san took almost sole responsibility for their maintenance.

Although rapid communication, online commerce, and delivery systems have made island living easier in their ability to slash time and costs in obtaining new materials, making do with what one has at hand (or can borrow from a neighbor) is a mentality that persists in Amami and is passed on to I-turners. For example, the emergency room doctor explained that in Tokyo he feels he has access to anything, he can leave his house, and if he has money can buy whatever he wants. But in Amami, he naturally feels more isolated with less access to commodities and consequently is less likely to engage in the trappings of a materialist lifestyle. This is not to suggest that it is necessary to self-inflict isolation and scarcity to prompt sustaining processes; rather, island cultures offer insight into the ways in which resourcefulness, innovation, and living seasonally resist the drive toward the production and consumption of new commodities. Lane and Watson explain that environmental policy work has tended to focus either on sustainable material economies at a large scale by encouraging manufacturers to reduce waste and pollution, to implement circular economies, or to focus on individual consumer behavior. But they suggest that what is missing is research at the "meso-scale," where there is a "diversity . . . of actors, their collective interests in goods and materials, and a shared identity in the form of language, norms and values that is to some extent grounded in a material setting" (Lane and Watson 2012, 1256). Referencing their own research, they highlight that citizens will follow instructions to recycle because they might care about the environment and it "makes them feel good," but a more likely reason is because recycling has become "a process of collective normalisation . . . partly because a household's participation is visible to their neighbours" (1261). Second, they use the example of people renting skips who actively hope their discarded materials will be scavenged by others and put to new use (1262). The skip acts like a holding bay of materials where questions of ownership become ambiguous. If skips are imagined as a type of commons, it might be considered more socially accepted to "skip-dive," because a collective responsibility for stewardship of the material that lies within the item is recognized. Sustainability, in this case, becomes an unintended consequence of anxiety about the unknown. The kimono that Eriko-san gave Akiyo to recut, for example, had belonged to the Shachō's mother. Rather than seeing them go to waste or sold to a secondhand kimono dealer for a few yen, her anxiety was appeased and she took pleasure in seeing new life emerge from the old garments.

Compromise or Paralysis?

When I returned to Amami a year after finishing my fieldwork, Koki had completed the first year of his tsumugi weaving apprenticeship but had left the program to work in public relations for a fashionable new hotel. He had become dispirited about the kimono cloth, and while he enjoyed weaving, he found tsumugi too repetitive, lacking the creativity he sought in his life. While he lived on minimal resources, Koki's metropolitan mobility and social ease meant he could take a job in PR despite never having worked in PR before—a privilege that gave him freedom to pursue "meaningful" work in his spare time. I asked whether he had finished the clove-dyed jacket, but he explained he had lost momentum because he hadn't made enough cloth to cut the jacket and would need to weave some more. He was also asking himself, What was the point? The question arose in conversation as we shared concerns as creative people around how we come to terms with the fact that the world doesn't need more "stuff." Is it enough that commodity production contributes to human well-being, to the "joy of living," to the rehabilitation of enchantment, if the item exceeds practical purpose and ultimately contributes to environmental degradation? My participants, those working in or around Kanai Kougei, were aware that current patterns of production and consumption are unsustainable. This was apparent in the discussions we would have about local construction projects and pollution, but it also brought about a disruption to the creative process itself. Koki, for example, was both debilitated by doubt and propelled to act. He was trying to establish how to treat waste as a resource or how to make things in such a way that they wouldn't do further harm. He told me he had been thinking about growing a garden and making botanical blends that could be used in beauty products. Or perhaps his time would be better spent promoting the traditions of the countryside (as a nonmaker) in a way that was tasteful and respectful toward the community. Koki's anxieties are familiar ones in an age of widespread awareness around the interlinked environmental and social crises—how might he make a positive difference, rather than contribute to the problem?[9]

Koki's quandary suggests that individual makers can contribute to discourses around environmental impact because they have the skills, knowledge, and ingenuity to problem solve but also tend to be geographically grounded and eth-

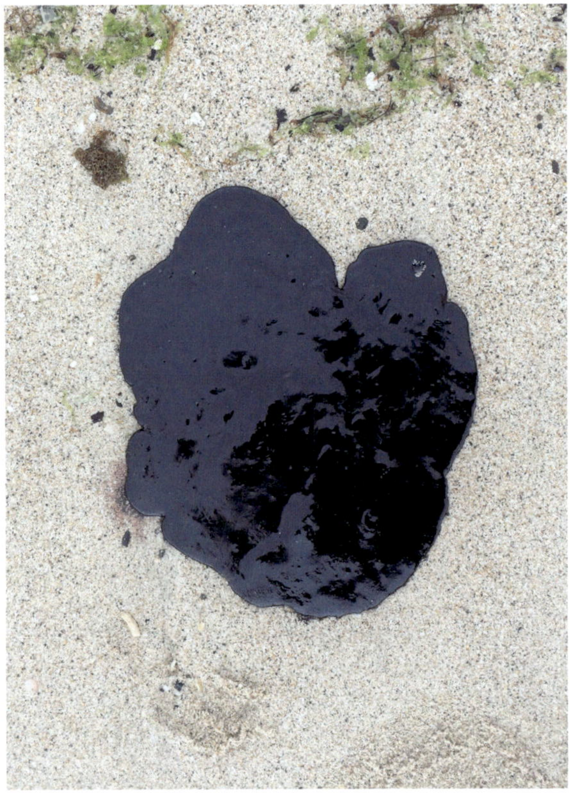

Figure 3.11 *Crude oil washed up on the beach from a sunken Iranian oil tanker.*

ically entangled. Although makers might be prone to contradictions, the fact that they tend to share skills, materials, resources, and opinions means ethical thinking can be infectious—even if it's based on an element of competition. In a paper titled "Geographies of Making," Chantel Carr and Chris Gibson (2016, 309) highlight the problem that makers are often absent from discussions on resource use, suggesting that "the task is to find the conduits and infrastructures that can be cobbled together so that the voices of makers are more audible, and that others listen." If one were to use the comparison of food, advanced capitalist societies have for decades ignored the farmer or the fisherman, who has been physically or metaphysically distanced from consumers. Governments have handed responsibility to supermarkets or put trust in trade partnerships to benefit international relations and provide food security. This has benefited big businesses, which have increased their profit share often to the detriment of producers and the environment. But with slow food systems that have arisen with ecological awareness, society has begun to learn how ethical, responsible production is beneficial for nature, soil health, and human health with access to fair, nutritious food being a right for all—even those on the margins of society. Although this is an ambition still to be realized, it is a step in the right direction.

If the textile industry were approached in the same manner as the food system, what might be learned and how might change be implemented? Bioregional textile systems are building potential (see this book's introduction and Burgess 2019), yet the work of local producers is a drop in the ocean of the global fashion system, and the value of local, natural materials remains largely obscure among the public. Yet what if we were to give materials the time to do their job, rather than focusing on the "tradable features" (Vivero-Pol et al. 2019, 2) of their utility, style, or aesthetic? Might we remember what made them popular in the first

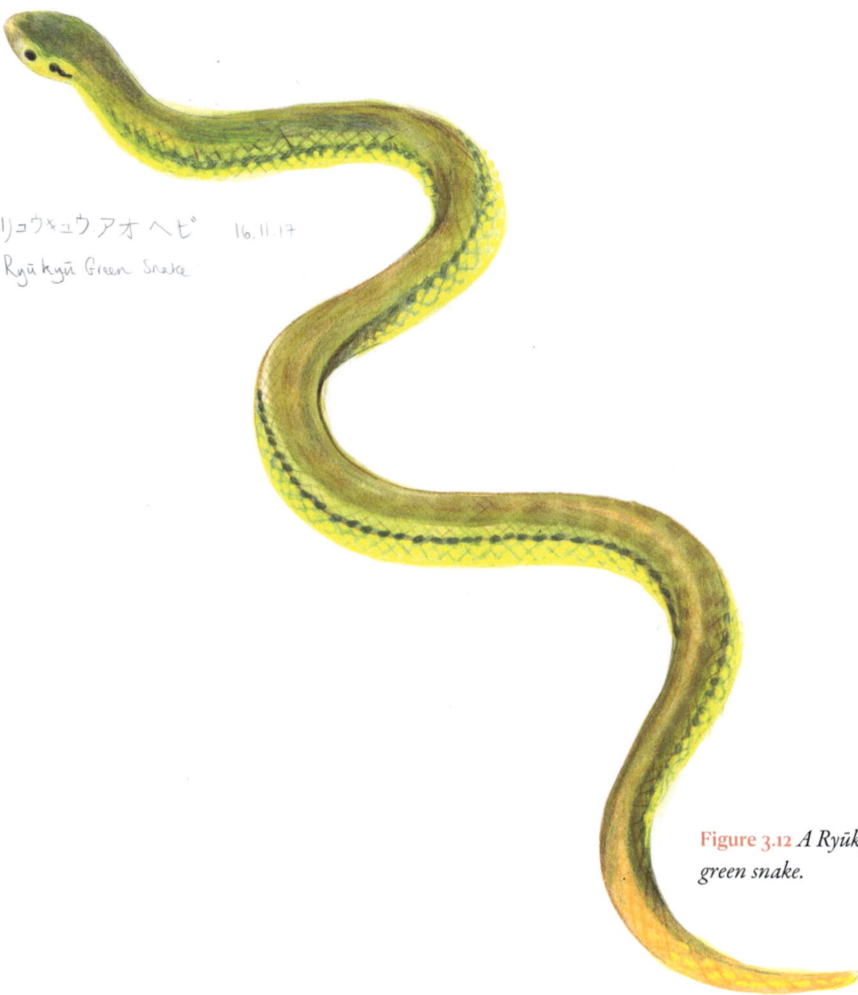

Figure 3.12 *A Ryūkyū green snake.*

place? If the antibacterial and strengthening properties of aizome or the showerproof quality of *dorozome* were better recognized, dyed garments wouldn't have to be laundered so frequently and would last longer. By denying society access to these inherent material qualities, society is also denied the opportunity to implement a co-constitutive notion of commodity stewardship.

Having enjoyed a productive day at the beach, we decided that we would return to collect more aosa at the next low tide. But these plans were shelved when news filtered through that an Iranian oil tanker had collided with another ship off the coast of Shanghai on its journey to South Korea and sunk 315 kilometers west of Amami in mid-January 2018 (Kyodo News 2018b). The *Japan Times* reported that an endangered sea turtle had washed up dead on the coast, oil clogging its mouth. When I first arrived in Amami, Kazuko told me that one day while she was swimming, a sea turtle surfaced from the reef and swam with her for a while. Kazuko had learned to tidal swim at school in Tokyo, and with Akiyo, we formed an after-work *suiei-bu* (swimming club) to wash off the sweat and smell of *techigi* during the humid months. After I swam with a turtle for the first time, my desire to repeat the "enchantment" meant I saw them often, having ascertained the locations where they, too, foraged for seaweed. By February and into March, cleaners in hazmat suits were spotted on the beach, and I was distraught to find a patch of oil when walking there myself (figure 3.11). In a classic example of mottainai, Kazuko warned that we shouldn't eat local fish, maybe we couldn't swim, I shouldn't touch the toxic oil, and we certainly couldn't collect aosa from the beach for a while. This interdependence on ecosystem resources is discussed further in chapter 4, as I explore wildlife conservation in Japan and how contemporary Amamians conceptualize nature.

4

The *Mejiro* Bird

Mejiro-san was kept in a cage that hung from the outer wall of the indigo workshop (figure 4.1). The Shachō would bring it out from his house in the morning, lifting the cage into place until evening, when it was brought inside overnight because of the threat of snakes. Acid green with a yellow neck, white belly, and a white-ringed eye (which provides the bird's Japanese name: *me* [eye] and *jiro*, a sound mutation of *shiro* [white]), *mejiro* are small but effervescent songbirds. They are resident throughout the warmer climes of Japan, but Amami is home to four subspecies, likely plentiful because of the annual abundance of fruits, flowers, and insects. *Kaki* (persimmons) are a favorite, but I also saw them feeding on *tankan* (tangerines) and *kuchinashi* (Cape jasmine). I recognized we were in direct competition for the kuchinashi's bright orange innards when four of us were in the gardens of Toguchi picking the fruits one lunchtime. Once dried, kuchinashi can be drunk as a health-supporting tea or used to dye a soft apricot color onto textiles. Many of the fruits were peppered with holes

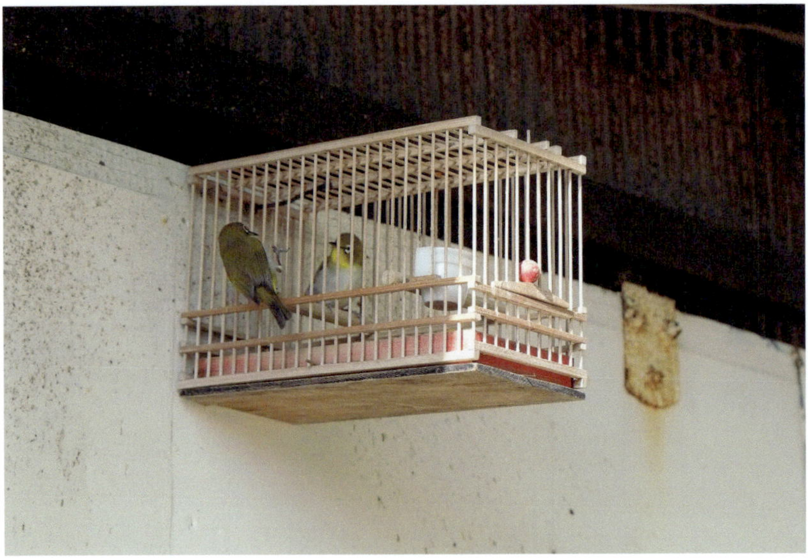

Figure 4.1 *An uncaged bird visiting Mejiro-san.*

from tiny beaks, and on returning to the workshop I balanced one on top of Mejiro-san's cage.

Given their appetite, mejiro are effective pollinators, fertilizing neighboring flowers as they move through the trees. Their love of nectar, particularly of camellia and cherry blossoms, has made them popular subjects in traditional Japanese arts (Brazil 1991, 242). They are sociable birds, feeding in family "troops" (Austin and Kuroda 1953, 578) and found "wander[ing] in parties, often with other species" (Brazil 1991, 242). This was evident when Mejiro-san was visited by uncaged birds who fluffed up their feathers and interacted through the bars of the cage, uttering *chē churu* (or *tsee tsee*), prompting Mejiro-san to puff up like a ball.

Ornithologists Oliver L. Austin and Nagahisa Kuroda (1953, 579) explain that "in captivity the birds frequently sit on a perch touching each other side by side, a habit seen occasionally in the wild and the source of the Japanese idiom '*mejirooshi*' (目白押し) or 'white-eye huddle.'" This festive term is used to express shelves brimming with a variety of goods or a full events program at a *matsuri*. The birds' infiltration of artistic and linguistic culture, alongside their song, said to be "sweet, melodious and quite varied" (579), made them popular among those who kept caged birds, a practice that has existed for over seven centuries in Japan (Koyama 2015). Before the 1950s, songbirds like the mejiro were caught indiscriminately using nets and sold either for food or to the pet trade. The ending of this practice, which this chapter recounts, was established by the passing of wildlife protection laws, meaning that many "wild" species underwent a change in status. Mejiro-san's presence at the workshop was therefore an anachronism that could be considered a lens through which to view generationally changing attitudes toward the natural environment in Japan.

When I broached the subject at the workshop, I discovered Mejiro-san was already a popular topic of conversation, because my colleagues had private opinions and stories to share. Satoko-san told me that the Shachō had rescued the bird after a snake attack, which I communicated to Kazuko, but she denied the story. Confirming with the Shachō, she said that in fact he had caught it with a net, and while he had saved it from a snake, it was because he had left it out one evening and saved it just in time. On another occasion, the Shachō was cleaning its cage when Mejiro-san escaped to a nearby bush. Yuske-san (one of the young male dyers) was watching, willing it to fly away, but as the workshop cat, Paru-chan, moved in, it became apparent that Mejiro-san had lost the ability to fly. The Shachō picked it up and returned it to its small cage, further cementing the Shachō's unforgiving nickname, of "mejiro killer," coined by a previous worker.

As a member of the Kanai Kougei family, Mejiro-san provides an entrance point to consider how Amamian nature intersects with the workshop community but also to think about how nature is conceptualized generationally. By *generationally*, I refer to those of the World War II generation, their postwar children, and their children's children, as these are the older *tsumugi* dyers and the younger generations who work in apparel at Kanai Kougei, in whom I encountered differing attitudes toward nature. While local attitudes toward the natural world are discussed in the proceeding chapters, this chapter considers how "environmental winds" brought Western environmentalism "into being" in Japan but also how these ideas in local contexts developed "into something quite different from their origins" (Hathaway 2013, 3). Anthropologist Michael Hathaway uses the metaphor of "winds" to "describe times when political movements brought life-changing consequences" (3) for the scientists and conservationists he works with in China. Hathaway suggests that "despite transnational winds" often bringing ethical movements into being, "most do not question how they got there" (187).

I therefore use discussions around Mejiro-san to document the largely forgotten history of Japanese bird conservation. I focus on the role that the American Allied forces played in Japanese ecology in the immediate postwar period and the period after, when Japan as a nation gained a position of economic strength. My purpose in centering this history in this chapter is to show how shifting attitudes to nature as a resource, conservation ideologies, and the conceptualization of nature as a companion are affected by both geopolitical and "environmental winds." Hathaway (2013, 188) demonstrates, and my research shows, how these winds "do not blow in a straight line and often push up against one another, which makes them unpredictable in their force and direction." How a society interacts with its environment has a culturally historic character, but it is also formed by the political and economic circumstances that a community is subject to in particular eras. Japan is a fascinating case study because as a nation that engaged in limited trade with the outside world before the nineteenth century, it developed both a practical and philosophical approach to environmental protection and resource management. This was influenced by religion, cultural values, folk traditions, individual thinkers, and government policies that have at times aligned and at others clashed. This became apparent when Western ideologies, imported into the country after the Meiji Restoration, fundamentally changed environmental relations at the local and national level, often with dire consequences, the inheritance of which was discussed in chapter 3.

Bird conservation, as a relatively recent phenomenon, offers a cultural framework for how ideas of conservation and sustainability become part of public discourse and lead to behavioral change. This chapter's aim is to demonstrate how the adoption of environmentalism at a national scale is not always a moral choice but a political, economic, or public health one—as is becoming apparent with the global climate emergency. Although a discussion around birdlife might seem like a stretch from natural dyeing, I argue that motivations to turn to natural dyeing—whether as a maker or as a consumer—are intimately linked to discourses around sustainability, nature conservation, and a morality that is inherent in practices of consumption. This highlights that the scope of "sustainability" as an ideology (at least within commodity production) is frequently too narrow in its ambitions. I argue that the *longue durée* of bird conservation in Japan might be used to show the complexity and time that it takes for movements to filter through global geographies and take on a locally specific character. Key to this argument is a recognition that, as users of natural resources, humans become engaged in a dynamic of use and extraction in which control of nature is seen as essential yet where such control ultimately impacts the environment in ways beyond the bounds of regulation. Conservation has emerged from these dynamics of logistical control (see chapter 6), seeking to contain, preserve, and rebuild habitats and wildlife populations, and has developed into a rights-based framework that conveys a human duty to act reciprocally toward nature in a manner more in line with notions of companionship. The period immediately after World War II, which I refer to often throughout *Dyeing with the Earth*, is crucial because it marked a moment of widespread modernization and industrialization in Japan that spread to the countryside with aims to improve standards of living. This time of change is therefore relevant when thinking about how sustaining processes might become normalized throughout craft communities and scaled up, if responsible stewardship toward other species, things, and materials was regained.

Nature as Resource: Harvesting Wildlife

When researching the mejiro, I came across *The Birds of Japan* (1953) a book authored by the American ornithologist Oliver L. Austin and Japanese ornithologist Nagahisa Kuroda, a member of a formerly influential samurai clan. Predominantly based on a manuscript Kuroda had prepared, Austin rewrote it for an English-speaking audience. The volume is insightful for its scientific content but also as a record of human-bird interaction around the time of the American occupation. Mainland Japan reverted to Japanese control in 1952, Amami in 1953, and Okinawa in 1972, but from 1945 the occupation provided the Allied forces with unprecedented access to all areas of Japanese life. Social scientists like Douglas Haring—the American anthropologist based in Amami in 1951 and 1952—were sent to study Japanese society (see chapter 1), and natural scientists were dispatched to study Japanese wildlife and resource management (see also chapter 6). The context in which their reports were produced was problematic, but the military detail makes for fascinating reading. As discussed in chapter 1, the work of these scholars resulted in policy decisions and economic investment that continue to influence Japanese life in the present. It is unlikely, for example, that the tsumugi industry could have recovered in the postwar period without significant American and Japanese investment. Personal testimonies from embedded field researchers give a more nuanced understanding of the political motivations and social dynamics that existed between the Allied forces and the Japanese and within their varying factions. This was the case among those with an interest in birds, where Japanese elite and peasant classes encountered high-ranking US military officials, scientists, and ordinary GIs.

Having served in the Pacific region under the US Navy, at the end of the war Oliver Austin was dispatched to Korea and then as a demobbed civilian to Japan, where he became the head of the Wildlife Branch of the Allied Powers' Natural Resources Section. He was asked to record war-induced ecological damage and charged with "surveying populations of birds and mammals throughout Japan with a view to assessing their economic value, particularly as a source of food" (Austin and Kuroda 1953, 123). Austin worked with elite Japanese counterparts who had been fighting for the rights of Japan's wildlife for a number of years and who had collectively founded the Japanese Ornithological Society in 1912.[1] Ornithology at this time was not an academic discipline in Japan but rather a pursuit of highly educated noblemen working under the charge of Prince Taka Tsukasa, the emperor's cousin. In Austin's words, "They were the only ones with the funds and time" to research, meet, and campaign on behalf of birds (Austin and Austin 1978, 32).

Through extensive field research, Austin and his team surmised that bird populations had been severely depleted nationwide. This was due to habitat destruction, a consequence of the "war machines'" need for timber, and the harvesting of 7.5 million songbirds per year (Tsutsui 2003, 302). This huge number had been achieved via mist-netting (*kasumi ami*), a highly efficient practice in which a black silk net was hung against a dark background to catch flying birds. Left unharmed but trapped, the birds were harvested for food while their feathers were said to fill the pillows of war veterans (Culver 2017, 158). While it provided food for a famished population, mist-netting was ultimately counterproductive, Austin deemed, as small birds are insectivorous and could naturally control pest populations in forests and crops.[2] Austin's reasoning followed the discipline of economic ornithology, a practice defined as "the study of birds from the standpoint of dollars and cents. It deals with birds in their relation to agriculture, horticulture, trade, and sport. . . . It is the practical application of the knowledge of birds to the affairs of everyday life" (Palmer [1900] 2020, 259, in Kronenberg 2014, 166). Economist Jakub Kronenberg (2014, 164) compares the golden era of the discipline (roughly between the 1830s and 1930s) with the current-day concept of ecosystem services that "appl[ies] economic reasoning to environmental management." The protection of birds was encouraged because of their essential role in agriculture, birds being "the farmers'" and "horticulturists' hired men" who work "365 days in a year" and ask for nothing in return (Howe 1915, 71, in Kronenberg 2014, 169). It was also acknowledged that birds benefited the economy by providing people with the leisure activities of hunting and bird watching and thus the production and sale of materials and equipment needed for those activities. The economic values of "voice, symbolism and inspiration," meanwhile, were more difficult to put a monetary or market value on (Kronenberg 2014, 169). Consequently, Kronenberg states, economic ornithologists were taken seriously by the authorities only because they stressed the economic benefits of conservation—a familiar rhetoric in the current era of climate financing—and distanced themselves from "sentimentalists" (172). Likewise, Austin foregrounded long-term sustainability and food security to argue for widespread reform of Japanese game and hunting laws and for the implementation of strict conservation measures to allow population recovery. With American military force and his aristocratic Japanese connections, he recommended and succeeded in outlawing mist-netting, with legislation passed in the late 1940s (Culver 2017, 162).

Without further investigation (if records even exist), it is difficult to prove how birdlife was affected by the war in Amami, which, compared to many other regions of Japan, escaped significant fighting and bombing. But drawing on writings from both Austin and Haring, one can speculate. Haring (1952, 2) writes that in some areas "deforestation approaches denudation," which caused flash flooding during typhoon season—"the consequence of over-cutting of timber." Given that a significant area of Amami's mountains were turned over to agroforestry during the Meiji era, one might assume that forests were heavily felled to assist the war effort (see chapter 6 for an in-depth discussion). In addition, Amami is a place where wildlife harvesting has endured for generations. During times of famine Amamians have relied on plantations of the ubiquitous *sotetsu* (cycad) nuts—the seeds of the plant that features on *Oshima tsumugi* patterns (figure 4.2). The nuts require extensive processing to rid them of a dangerous poison, with the resulting flesh used to produce a high-starch, flavorless porridge (*okayu*) (figure 4.3). As a result, periods of famine took the name "sotetsu hell" (*sotetsu jigoku*), referencing both the bland taste but also the dangers of eating a potentially deadly porridge (Hayward and Kuwahara 2012, 30).

In Haring's (1952, 48–53) field report, he provides forty-six main-meal menus recorded by a middle-class housewife. He notes that there is no mention of sotetsu on these menus—likely because of its (embarrassing) association with poverty (Hayward and Kuwahara 2012, 31). Yet Haring acknowledges that it did feature in the Amamian diet, with photographs supporting his notes. Aside from fish, the menus list wild pigs and black pork. They also include "lean meat," though Haring (1952, 51) did not specify a source, simply calling them "tiny bits of several kinds of meat." Viewing Haring's archival slides, I was surprised to find a pair of caged Lidth's jays (*rurikakesu*) on a slide sheet with other wild and farmed animals, including an endangered Amami black rabbit wearing a leash (figures 4.4 and 4.5). Since the jay's call is noisy and shrill (*gyā!*), one might assume these would have been trapped for meat rather than bird-keeping. In contrast to the mejiro, which Austin and Kuroda (1953, 579) state is "too small and difficult to net in large quantities to be used as food," the jay is "considered a game bird in Japan, and shot for food whenever opportunity offers. . . . Its habits do not make it easy to net in quantity, and only 50,000 to 75,000 are reported killed each year" (511).[3] Although Haring does not allude in his writings to why these birds are caged, one might assume mist-netting was still happening in Amami in 1951–52. One can speculate that wild meat, too, was absent from the housewife's menus, much in the way that sotetsu was concealed. Because

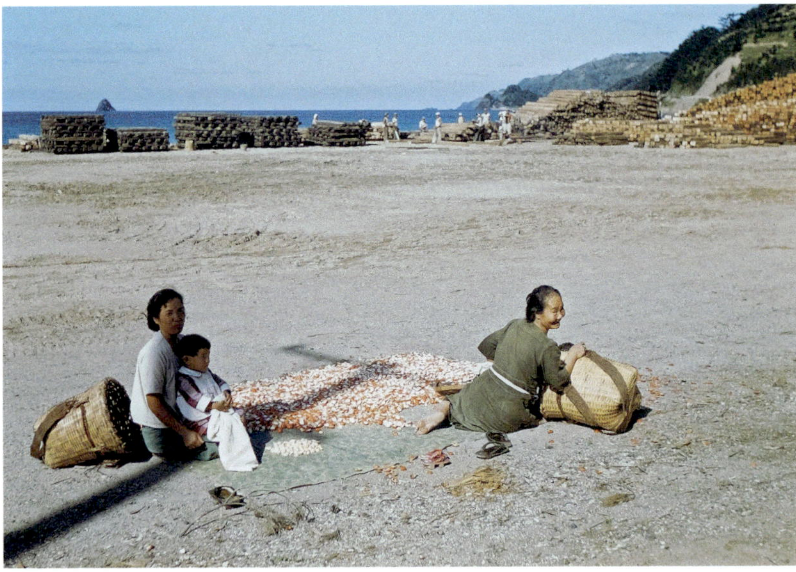

Figure 4.2 *Beach at Naze. Cycad nuts spread to dry in the sun, 1951–52. Douglas Haring Papers, University Archives, Special Collections Research Center, Syracuse University Libraries, Syracuse, New York.*

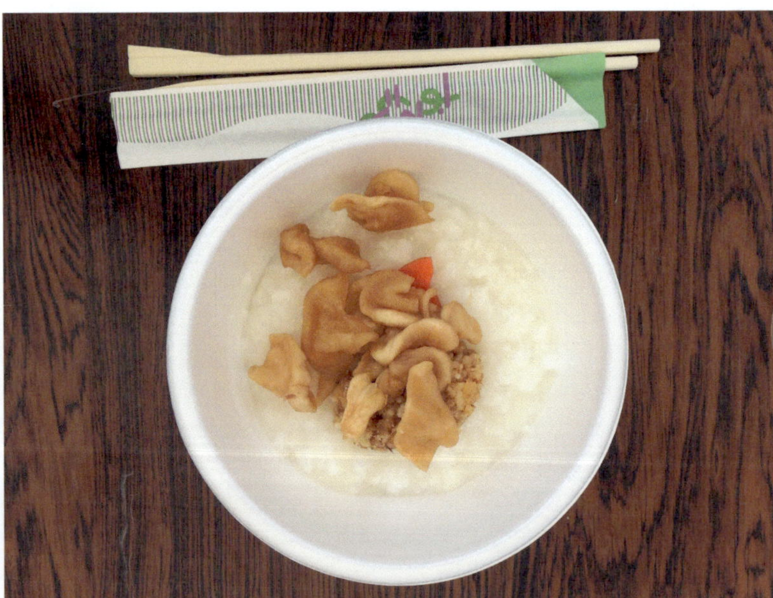

Figure 4.3 *Rice okayu with* nari-miso *made from sotetsu nuts served at an Amamian matsuri.*

mist-netting was outlawed in 1947 (Culver 2017, 162), admitting the consumption of wild birds to a proxy military official wouldn't have been wise. Haring (1952, 64) writes that Amamians were already suspicious about his identity, with many concerned he was secretly working for the Japanese police.

The caging of the Lidth's jay is poignant, because the bird, found only on the Amami Islands, has undergone two population troughs. The jay's feathers were highly prized in the nineteenth- to early twentieth-century European and North American millinery trade (Ishida 2014, 5), with overhunting leading to their designation as a National Natural Monument in 1921. This designation "protects" a species, meaning numbers began to recover. But the jay was listed as endangered in the 1970s and 1980s due to habitat loss and nest predation by the introduced Indian mongoose released in Amami in a failed attempt to control snake numbers.[4] After the pillage for the millinery trade, it is unclear whether Lidth's jay populations would have recovered by the 1950s for the bird to have reentered the Amamian diet, so I consulted my participants about whether they had any knowledge of these birds being eaten as food. Whereas Akiyo (twenty-four years old), the youngest dyer at Kanai Kougei, didn't imagine it possible, and her parents (in their early sixties) couldn't recall, she asked two members of the workshop staff, Eriko-san and Kazu-san (aged between fifty and sixty), with excellent knowledge of Amamian cuisine, who confirmed at that time, "People ate everything they can eat!"[5]

Historian Christopher Aldous (2015, 144) states that the authorities admitted the difficulty of enforcing the newly written legislation, quoting from a volume of the official history of the Allied occupation, which said, "As late as December 1950, bunches of songbirds were still available for purchase in the public markets of Tokyo." Austin's photographs of bird-meat shops on the mainland (figures 4.6 and 4.7) and the catch numbers William Tsutsui (2003, 302) quoted (7.5 million songbirds a year) suggest not only that wild birds were consumed by local hunters but that a substantial industry existed around their trade. How could it be that knowledge of eating a food embedded in the national diet could be forgotten only two generations later?

Bird Conservation in Japan

In a 1978 interview, Oliver Austin describes how Japan's 1947 constitution was rewritten to erase much of the American influence after 1952. Yet he shows how the internal adoption of external ideas, particularly promoted by elites, can bring about political and public change in opinion:

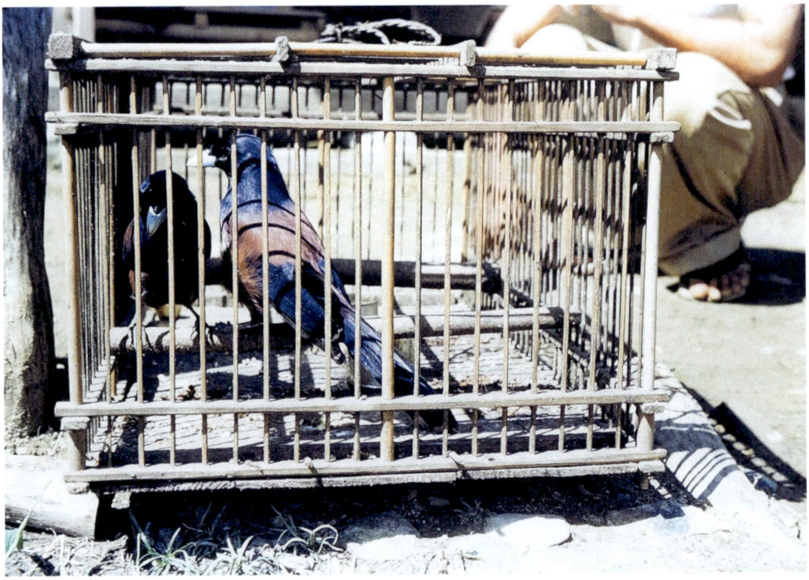

Figure 4.4 *Rurikakesu, 1951–52. Douglas Haring Papers, University Archives, Special Collections Research Center, Syracuse University Libraries, Syracuse, New York.*

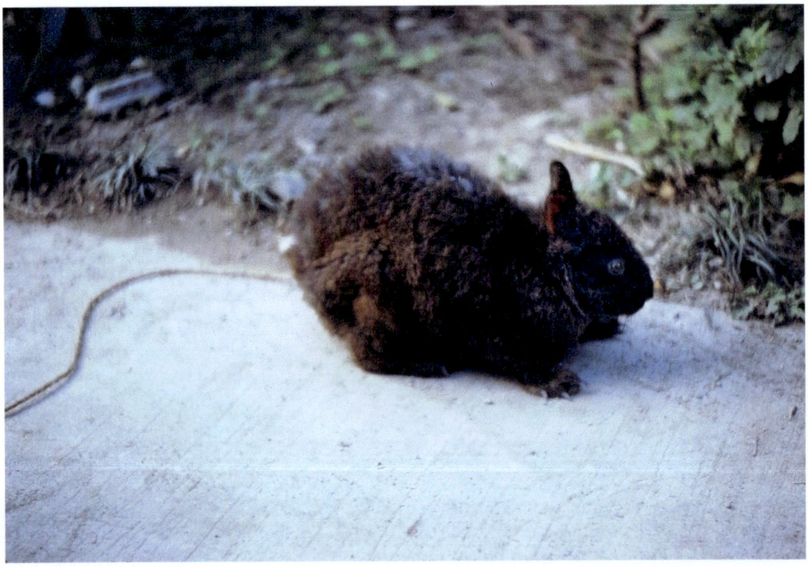

Figure 4.5 *Amami black rabbit, 1951–52. Douglas Haring Papers, University Archives, Special Collections Research Center, Syracuse University Libraries, Syracuse, New York.*

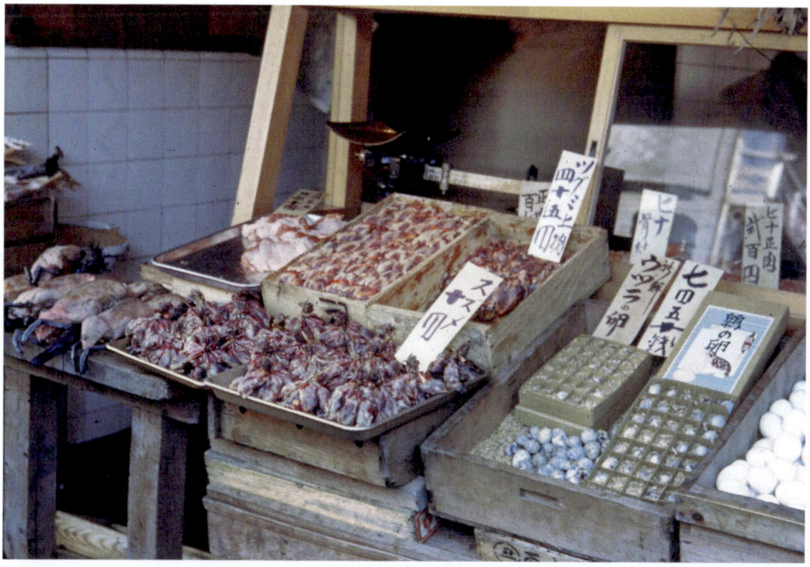

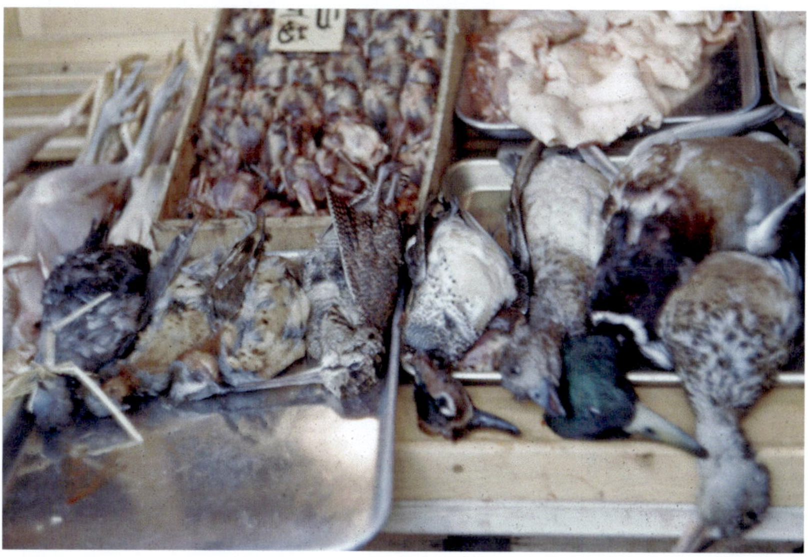

Figures 4.6 & 4.7 Bird Meat Shop, Sparrows, Quail Eggs *and* Bird Meat Shop, Ducks, *both 1946–50. The labeled birds and eggs for sale* (top), *labeled as* kamo *(duck)*, tsugumi *(thrush), and* suzume *(sparrow), are accompanied by quail eggs and what appear to be duck or chicken eggs. The unlabeled birds* (bottom) *are more difficult to identify but also appear to include duck and thrush and possibly a woodcock, a mallard, and a ring-necked duck. Oliver L. Austin Photographic Collection: Occupation of Japan, Special Collections and Archives, Florida State University Libraries, Tallahassee, Florida.*

> After the peace treaty was signed—one of the first things that the Japanese did was abrogate the new constitution and throw it out the window.... And my Japanese bird friends, Kuroda and Yamashina, and [Prince] Takatsukasa ... put up a great fight and an advertising and propaganda campaign telling the people how important it was that the small birds be saved, that they not be used for food. That they were important for part of the environment and by George, they put it through! ... And it's the only one of the occupation-enforced changes that I know of that the Japanese kept with them when they wrote the new constitution. (Austin and Austin 1978, 46)

Although Japan regained its sovereignty in the 1950s, it remained indebted to the United States, putting it in a position of political and economic weakness. Ignoring scientific advice regarding food security might have also been reckless during a period of social and political instability. But this was a time of national identity-building following a humiliating defeat and dismantlement of a colonial empire. The following sections examine the possible reasons the government decided to keep this "occupation-enforced change." I suggest, first, that the measures cohered with a wider public relations campaign to counter the "barbaric" reputation that had been fostered of the Japanese abroad; second, I suggest that they conformed to internal projects intended to restore the ideals of Japanese identity. Austin revealed the need to reframe Japan's reputation in his introduction to *The Birds of Japan*, which highlights a prejudice rife during this time: "The Occupation brought many innovations to Japan, and made many changes in the customs and practices of centuries. The new constitution, the various land, educational, and labor reforms were perhaps among the most important innovations, but nowhere was the contrast between the two ideologies more marked than in the field of wildlife conservation. Here, two radically different concepts of man's relation to wildlife were brought together, those of the very old world and those of the comparatively new, and two radically different methods of attaining more or less the same ends" (Austin and Kuroda 1953, 284). While Austin fails to elaborate on his understanding of the "two radically different concepts of man's relation to wildlife," scholarly work by historians of science can help read between the lines. While Austin aimed to conserve birdlife to improve food security, as Annika Culver (2017, 160) explains, the moral "winds" of "US-inspired modes of conservation"—with their "particular language and ideological rhetoric" that emphasized "American-style democracy and its favorable links to science"—also nodded toward progressing the civility of the occupied society.

Harriet Ritvo's *The Animal Estate* (1987) is helpful for considering how wildlife conservation was co-opted by Western societies as evidence of progress and, consequently, to justify colonial exploitation and conquest. Using the example of the British Empire in Africa during the 1800s, she explains that settler colonial expansionism encouraged the clearing of people and wildlife to make way for white settlement, a process of Lockean "improvement" that readied "wild" lands for cultivation (Bhandar 2018). Yet when whole populations of wild animals had been eliminated, the status of species changed, leading to a process of "individuation." Psychologist and animal rights advocate Kenneth Shapiro (1989, 185) explains that animals are often considered part of a group on a species scale, a form of "deindividuation" that means the "replacement of one with another has no ethical cost"—a point that makes them "vulnerable." Yet when populations crash, individuals are recognized and viewed as "a valuable resource requiring protection"—what Ritvo (1987, 284) calls in the colonial context "a special kind of property." Marxist geographer Noel Castree, reflecting on the works of contemporary Marxists writing on nature, suggests that this form of "individuation" is one of the core elements of commodification. He explains that "individuation" entails "the representational and physical act of separating a specific thing or entity from its supporting context. This involves putting legal and material boundaries around phenomena so that they can be bought, sold and used by equally 'bounded' individuals, groups or institutions." Castree elaborates that individuation entails a "discursive and practical 'cut' into the seamless complexity of the world in order to name discrete 'noun-chunks' of reality that are deemed to be socially useful" (2003, 280). Castree's definition of individuation highlights that protecting wildlife has an economic imperative (in terms of speculating on future financialization), but it also plays a role in social relations. Ritvo writes that in British Asian and African colonies, laws and restrictions on hunting were introduced in the late 1870s, "symboliz[ing] British stewardship of its colonies." For these campaigns to be successful, it was necessary to expand regulations into other European colonies to account for migration, which Ritvo states were agreed with reluctance given Britain's propensity to express "preeminence" (1987, 284). The purpose of this symbolism was twofold in that it signified both economic astuteness and compassion toward other species.

It is important to note the historical cross-fertilization of concepts of "conservation"—whose use in environmental spheres suggests the management of nature at a species scale to ensure long-term sustainability (often for profit)—with "animal welfare," which, in general, focuses on the abuse of individual animals. The "humane movement" preceded that of conservation and began in England in the early 1800s led by members of the church and upper-class "ladies" (including Princess Victoria) who saw brutality toward "lesser fellow creatures" as "sinful" and contrary to "Englishness" (Ritvo 1987, 126–30). The first law to prevent cruelty to cattle was passed in 1822, but it wasn't until 1854 that this was extended to other domestic animals. Wildlife protection laws in Europe came into being only when animal trapping for food, fashion, and sport, alongside the loss of habitat, resulted in population crashes of native species. Protestations by the female-led group Feather, Fin and Fur Folk (Greenoak 1997, 17) and the poet William Blake ([1862] 2000), who claimed that "A Robin Red breast in a Cage, Puts all Heaven in a Rage," established a Victorian sentimentalism that shifted public opinion, revealing an emotional attachment to nature that fell outside of utilitarianism. The first law to protect seabirds was passed in 1869, while the UK's Royal Society for the Protection of Birds was founded in 1889 and the Audubon Society of America in 1905. Conservationist Paul Jepson (2010, 325) suggests that "in Euro-American bird conservation frames" there are strong "associations between flying birds and freedom"—an attitude that still holds today. A new awareness of the vulnerability of wild bird populations reconceptualized songbirds in particular as creatures to be enjoyed by bird watchers, leading to their reevaluation. As Culver (2017, 157) writes, by the time of World War II, this perspective on wild birds was ingrained "in the American civilian imagination"—they were "not eaten as food, as they might by ordinary people starving for protein in post-war Japan."

Following the devastation of the war, attitudes toward nonhuman species in Japan were influenced by these projections of civility and barbarity. Culver (2017, 157–58) notes that the act of hunting waterfowl with a gun—quick, clean, and humane—by "'gentlemen of science' of whom many were aristocrats" was contrasted with the "old world" Japanese methods of the "bird harvester's workaday 'barbarity' in quickly processing his kill," which Culver describes as "pressing on their sterna, skulls, and back-bones [with the thumbs], or simply sitting on a full sack of them." While Austin succeeded in banning mist nets, he tolerated game hunting if newly implemented quotas and laws were obeyed (Aldous 2015, 146). While the hunting laws were changed with the aim to conserve resources, the perceived moral issue at stake was not the killing or commodification of birds but the method by which they were slaughtered. This can be evidenced by the actions of the American military, whom Austin called "to-the-victor-belong-the-spoils advocates," who frequently flouted regulations (Austin and Austin 1978, 49). These hunters felt that as the occupying force, it was their right to hunt as they pleased, creating tensions that spanned the hierarchy of the military (Aldous 2015, 139). Ritvo (1987, 287) notes that in colonial Africa, too, white hunters protested new restrictions by arguing that their "modern" technologies were not responsible for extermination of whole species; rather, it was the fault of "native" methods. This racist logic draws on an ideology of improvement to maintain post-Enlightenment racial and colonial hierarchies, which asserted Western "civilized" and Christian nations as evolutionarily advanced and eviscerated the lives, cultures, and lands of originating peoples. Consequently, by adopting Western ideals when managing natural resources, Japan would appear to be making itself anew, expelling the "barbaric" slur projected throughout the Allied nations because of Japanese war crimes and realigning itself with the liberal humanist tone of the 1947 constitution.

Regaining "Harmony" with Nature

Japan's commitment to wildlife protection laws externally projected a commitment to pacifism. At the same time, by embracing Western scientific and economic rationality, the country could alter its public image from a place (in Austin's words) of the "very old world" to one that was "comparatively new." After the war Japan underwent a rapid period of modernization and Westernization, but as occurred after the Meiji Restoration in 1868, it maintained and even exemplified the "uniqueness" of Japanese culture. While before the war, opposition to "the West" contributed to rising nationalism, in the postwar period the nation experienced a crisis of identity, and nostalgia arose for a time before Japanese imperialism. This crisis was soothed by the ideology and popular genre of literature known as *nihonjinron*, which has been described as "theories of Japaneseness" (Goodman 1992, 11). Although nihonjinron emerged during the Meiji period (1868–1912), anthropologist Harumi Befu argues that its popularity exploded after World War II. While nationalist symbols such at the anthem, flag, or public rituals caused discomfort, nihonjinron gave "explicit explanation as to what national identity consists of and why one should be proud of one's nation" (Befu 1992, 42). Nihonjinron was highly regarded for its take on the natural environment and its claim that prior to Western intervention Japanese people had lived in "harmony" with nature due to unique spiritual, material, climatic, and sociological parameters. Regaining "harmony" by protecting birdlife could therefore be considered part of an internal project that assisted the recovery of bird populations but also the self-esteem of the nation.

Much of this concept of harmony was rooted in East Asian thought, where principles shared between Chinese Daoism, Confucianism, and Japanese Buddhism are less anthropocentric and individualistic than Western philosophy and theology (Parkes 2017). Equally, Japan's indigenous belief system, Shinto, is perhaps the foundation of the country's ecocentric cosmology. Meaning "the way of the kami," Shinto is described by anthropologist John Clammer as nature "inhabited by a myriad of beings in which effectively the boundaries between the spiritual and material are dissolved" (2001, 219). Kami may be place-based spirits or natural forces like the wind or sea; animate beings such as birds and whales; or deified spirits of esteemed ancestors. As spiritual forces with power and energy, kami can be simultaneously benevolent and destructive, so any material or ephemeral entity considered kami was treated with respect and care. While similar to Shinto's animist worldview, it should be noted that Amami has its own spiritual belief system, which historically was led by a female theocracy of divine priestesses called the *noro* and *yuta* (see chapter 5). These priestesses presided over Amami's natural resources, the harvesting of timber and land cultivation, and they led the veneration of landscape features such as rivers, trees, and rocks, while butterflies, cats, and snakes were considered kami (Haring 1952, 5).

Writers of nihonjinron, such as Kitarō Nishida (1870–1945) and Tetsurō Watsuji (1889–1960), combined these Japanese religious and cultural values with Western philosophy, which favored moral ethics and scientific reasoning, to develop a Japanese environmental philosophy (Kagawa-Fox 2012). Clammer (1995) draws on Watsuji, despite acknowledging him as a writer of essentialism, to consider how this cosmology functioned in social life. Watsuji claimed the Japanese are unique because they are a monsoon people with a strong relationship to nature, attributed to the design of the traditional Japanese house—where the boundaries between inside and outside are blurred. He also claimed wet rice cultivation relied on harmonious cooperation between species and entities resulting in the concept of "groupism" (Clammer 1995, 72). Groupism is therefore an ecological state of being: "There are no 'individuals' at least in the sense that individuals do not exist except as a result of and in the context of relationships" (63). Following Pierre Bourdieu, Clammer justifies Watsuji's ideas in their ability to place the body in an environment and climate so that nature is considered part of the habitus—present in "social, economic, political, somatic and aesthetic arrangements" of a community (60–70). While it cannot be denied that Japan's and Amami's spiritual, material, and sociological parameters have led to a unique attitude toward the natural environment that, historically at least, foregrounded respect and a wide conception of community, Midori Kagawa-Fox (2012) claims that the cultural values that promoted an environmental ethic were not carried through by the Japanese government after the Meiji Restoration. Instead, economic growth and industrialization were prioritized, ignoring the ethical principles that, for centuries, had helped manage Japan's limited natural resources.

This idea is taken forward by Peter Oehlkers, a scholar of environmental communication, who claims that when Commodore Matthew Perry landed in Japan in 1854 (when the Japanese were forced into trading relations with America),

American officers engaged in a cruel slaughtering of Japanese wildfowl with rifles for sport, much to the disgust of their Japanese counterparts. He suggests that the "opening" of Japan led to the introduction of modern firearms, habitat loss, trade in exotic feathers, and breakdown of religious principles, creating a schism in human-wildlife relations (Oehlkers 2016). While these arguments appear to align with nihonjinron, in that they uncritically adopt the premise that prior to Western influence the Japanese lived in harmony with nature, Japanese studies historian Susan Hanley shows that the reasons for this schism are more complex. She argues that precisely because the Japanese could not import resources throughout the Tokugawa period (1600–1868), all residents had to "rely only on the plants and animals available in their islands" (Hanley 1997, 53). Although the major protein sources were seafood and soy beans, game meat—including bird, bear, and monkey—was consumed despite Buddhism's prohibition of the consumption of four-legged animals or any fear of retribution by kami (65–67). Food historian Eric Rath concurs by stating that the crane was a highly esteemed game meat subject to sumptuary regulation because of its symbolic association with the samurai. Rath, however, highlights a critical cultural difference between the Japanese and Europeans. He quotes a sixteenth-century Portuguese trader who claimed that the upper echelons of Japan only ate game meat because they considered eating domesticated animals reared in one's house to be "cruel" and "unclean" (Rath 2010, 107). Hanley states that as the human population increased, wild animal populations came under pressure from loss of habitat and overhunting; by the time Commodore Perry landed in 1854, consumption of wild birds might have decreased because, as occurred after World War II, the capacity of the land to provide nourishment had been stretched beyond sustainable means (1997, 67).

While these historical contradictions can undermine the nihonjinron ideology of pre-Meiji harmony, it is also clear that human-nonhuman relations did shift in Japan under the influence of the West and the social and economic upheavals that occurred with the Meiji Restoration. It could be argued that with the creation of the Japanese state, capitalist logics supplanted ecocentric ontologies when conserving or extracting natural resources. As was apparent from Western imperialism, economic strength gained from industrial capitalism resulted in great power and influence. Aaron Skabelund's *Empire of Dogs* (2011) argues that cultural assimilation was just one of the ways the Japanese avoided colonization by European or American imperial powers and became colonizers themselves. Skabelund's (2011, 60) book tracks the spread of "canine imperialism" to Japan—a fashion for keeping dogs both as companions and as working animals that was a highly symbolic act of assimilating the habits and commodity practices of Western elites, even to the extent of hunting wildfowl with European gundogs. Yet the Japanese assimilated "on their own terms" (6) by essentializing indigenous dog breeds that were praised for their loyalty and compliance. As occurred in Europe and America, animal welfare groups were formally established in Japan around the turn of the twentieth century, mainly by the government to protect military animals (Miller 2013) or, as has been discussed, by Japan's elite, who used their wealth and influence to fight on behalf of birds. But it was not until the postwar period—when scientific evidence pointed to improved food security and symbolic gestures of public atonement and national identity-building came to prominence—that the way was opened for social and governmental engagement with the principles of environmentalism, which, by this time, had coevolved with animal rights.

Improved standards of living also occurred with the postwar economic boom, resulting in evolving tastes, disposable income, and the expansion of global commodity markets. A newly "gentrified" diet influenced by military regimes of nutrition made rice and soy sauce the "centerpiece," which was combined with Chinese spicing to flavor bland or inferior-quality food and with the calorific and economic resourcefulness of Western cuisines (Cwiertka 2005, 417). Military ideas about health and the economy, alongside foodstuffs distributed by the Allies (including American wheat and dairy), spread across the country, taking pressure off indigenous wildlife and foraged foods whose consumption might have been afflicted by a stigma associated with the poverty and rationing of the war years. While I was surprised that the Lidth's jay and the Amami black rabbit were eaten within the last century, the fact that both Akiyo and her parents were also surprised indicates a lack of communication of this history across generations. These factors all contributed to the disruption of wild birds' status as a commodity, allowing for the possibility that they might be "resingularized" (Kopytoff 1986, 73) as companions.

Following Donna Haraway's (2004, 302) definition of "companion species," a "heterogeneous category . . . including such organic beings as rice, bees, tulips, and intestinal flora, all of whom make life for humans what it is—and vice versa," companion species are locked into relationships of dependence. They may be domesticated cats, dogs, and birds but also songbirds that assist agriculture. Haraway is careful to add, however, that "to be in a relation of use to each other is not the definition of unfreedom or violation. Such relations are almost never symmetrical ('equal' or calculable). Rather, relations of use are exactly what companion species are about" (2008, 74). Haraway's thesis is important because interdependent relationships between humans and other species or landscape elements have ceased to be recognized as such by many societies globally, leading to neglect, degradation, and exploitation of resources. But like with the example of songbirds, acknowledging the important work that other species do for humans can bring about a closeness and new meaning to companionship.

Hathaway's (2013, 188) point that environmental "winds do not blow in a straight line and often push up against one another" can be recognized in the protein source that replaced wild birds, and which some Japanese argue "saved them from a major famine" (Kalland 1998). During the war canned whale meat entered the military diet, and after the war the occupying Allies promoted and supported commercial whaling. By 1947, whale meat made up over 50 percent of Japanese meat consumption, at 76,000 tons annually. By 1962, 220,000 tons were entering the market, bolstered by the 1954 School Lunch Act that saw whale meat consumed in schools nationwide (Morikawa 2009, 29). By the 1960s, in line with diet gentrification, whale meat was displaced by more costly pork, chicken, and beef (30). International relations scholar Jun Morikawa (2009) argues that this coincided with increased international environmental activism that became a matter of growing national interest. As a result, whale meat fell out of favor, disappearing from the school lunch scheme by the 1980s.

What is of interest for my argument is that in the 1950s, while Japan was still economically dependent on the West, laws to maintain bird conservation remained in the 1947 constitution, despite the history of wild bird consumption and a substantial industry existing around their trade. Culver (2017, 158) claims, for example, that songbirds were historically preserved in bran-filled barrels and served yakitori (grilled-bird) style during New Year celebrations. But changes in the law and public opinion resulted in an almost blanket "social amnesia" (Jacoby 1977) in regard to their consumption within the last century. This was brought to the fore in 2001, when Tokyo's then governor Shintaro Ishihara suggested the city might solve its war on jungle crows, whose numbers had swelled because of the increase in food waste, by encouraging people to eat crow pie. International newspapers picked up this quirky comment, ignoring the fact that crows were considered game meat globally until relatively recently (Struck 2001). The case study of wild birds contrasts with the internationally contentious debate around the hunting and consumption of whales. Since the 1970s, from its position of economic strength, the Japanese government has assertively argued that the consumption of whales, dolphins, and porpoises is important to national identity and the maintenance of tradition, despite a large majority of the populace showing no interest in eating them.

Yet Morikawa explains that the history of whaling in Japan conflicts with the "tradition" argument. Although whaling has taken place in Japan since the Edo era (1603–1867), commercial whaling only began in the 1890s and local communities have mostly been in opposition, aside from in a handful of "whaling towns" (Morikawa 2009, 28). Morikawa quotes the example of Same village in Aomori Prefecture, where whales were venerated as *kamisama* (gods); the community believed that whales blessed them with their "important sardine harvest," leading fishermen to clash with the whale station, which was polluting the sea with blood and oil (22). In 1982, the International Whaling Committee, a scientific body, implemented a "zero catch limit" (Kalland 1998), but commercial whaling continued and even expanded in Japan under the guise of "scientific research." Although whale populations have recovered globally, anthropologist Arne Kalland explains that NGOs such as Greenpeace and the governments of New Zealand, Australia, and the UK have switched discourse from conservation to animal rights and welfare, arguing that whales are exceptional creatures "equivalent to humans" in the marine environment. As a result, international pressure applied to Japanese whalers has resulted in consumer boycotts and accusations of barbarism, with Kalland (1998) arguing that whaling is no longer an ecological issue but an intense international dispute about national identity. Kalland and Brian Moeran claim that in the postwar "vacuum . . . of national symbols whale meat has provided a particularly powerful image" that communicates Japanese pride (Kalland and Moeran 1992, 194). Those who remember eating whale at school might be affected by nostalgia, but a younger generation has a "deepening awareness of global environmental issues" (Morikawa 2009, 121).[6] However, what will likely bring about real change in these eating habits are the significant concerns over food safety (see chapter 3), as cetaceans harbor potentially dangerous levels of PCBs, dioxins, mercury, and heavy metals that have been released into the seas as industrial pollution (32). These compounds can be detrimental to human health, particularly fertility—a subject of intense debate in Japan due to the country's falling birth rate. This further demonstrates that "environmental winds" that arrive with moral purpose will take hold only if they align with local objectives. It therefore follows that interest in marine ecology—admiring dolphins and whales from a distance—will offer a new form of consumption; this is the case in Amami, where a growing economy exists for whale watching.

Nature Between Resource and Companion

During his fieldwork in Yamagata Prefecture in the late 1970s and early 1980s, William Kelly documented a critical point of change for agriculturalists in Japan. The Green Revolution bought into conflict the traditional farming practices of the war generation with the "rationalized" scientific agriculture embraced by their children. Kelly explains how members of local land improvement councils would meet at the shrine for the *mizugami* (water spirit) in the village where his fieldwork was based. The kami of this area have influence over "hydrology, rice growth, and spiritual energy," and he was told "the mountain spirit receives the winter snowfall and descends through the rivers in the spring as the water spirit" (Kelly 1986, 603). Kelly admits he initially dismissed this local lore as nostalgia, especially since the area had recently capitalized on the *furusato* tourism boom (see chapter 1). These traditional ideas were also difficult to align with the extensive land and labor improvement work implemented throughout the area between 1965 and 1980. This work included the "rationalization of water use" that saw "enormous state subsidies and technical direction" to dam rivers, implement straightened, concreted irrigation canals, and bulldoze existing paddies into regulated ones following a grid system (607). Electricity lines, sewage systems, and water supplies were laid and new roads constructed to improve access. Machinery was introduced to replace handwork, and chemicals were adopted to treat monocultural rice varieties. The motivations for these works were twofold: to improve food productivity but also to address state concern "that farmers were wasting water that was sorely needed for expanded municipal uses, hydroelectric generation, and industrial plants" (607–8).

With this paper, Kelly shows how the push toward rationalization has created both nostalgia for tradition and a nagging feeling that the traditional agricultural skill and knowledge that helped farmers work with the landscape and nature—with the kami—is out of reach. Environmental philosopher Toyoda Mitsuyo (2017, 188) explains that "if people do not feel connected with the land through their everyday experiences [the spontaneous power of nature] might remain merely abstract." By losing the connection with traditional agricultural knowledge, a knowledge understood and shared through "indigenous narratives" of kami and other spiritual beings (179), one loses the ability to manage the land in extreme weather events but also to profit from nature's abundance. Such narratives were not simply forms of entertainment but carried important practical knowledge about one's local environment across generations. Essentially, myriad spiritual beings helped a community make sense of the world and encouraged respect and care for natural phenomena. But if one loses their connection with the land, does this mean spirituality linked with the power of nature becomes distant or even irrelevant? And if so, is it possible to reestablish those connections?

When I arrived at Kanai Kougei I was perplexed as to why someone would cage a wild bird when hundreds move busily through the trees in one's yard. But I was never brave enough to ask the Shachō why he had trapped Mejiro-san; it seemed a taboo subject and I didn't want to offend him, given that my

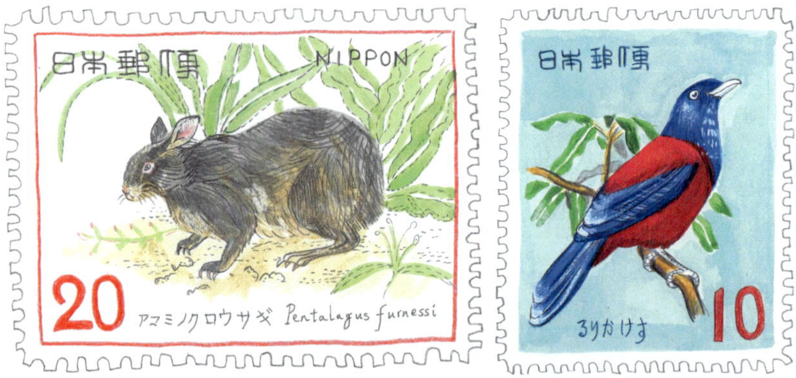

Figure 4.8 *Stamps from Kagoshima Prefecture featuring the Amami black rabbit and Lidth's jay.*

own feelings of anguish at the sight of domestically caged animals have been formed by late twentieth-century Anglo-American social norms. Mejiro-san appears an anachronism in the 2020s, because wild songbirds have been "publicly precluded from being [materially] commoditized" (Kopytoff 1986, 73) by the Japanese state, using legal restrictions but also social boundaries that define what is deemed acceptable among peers. As the Shachō perched a twig on Mejiro-san's cage with a desire to catch another, Eriko-san, the Shachō's wife and company administrator, whispered disapprovingly, "He's going to get arrested one day." Under Japan's Wildlife Protection and Hunting Law, enacted in 1918 but updated in 1998, all of Japan's wild species are protected, with only a handful of mammals, birds, and sea creatures permitted to be hunted as game or captured for scientific research after obtaining a license or permission (Ministry of the Environment of Japan 2017). It could be that the Shachō caged Mejiro-san along the lines of European collecting, where nature can be understood as a form of property (Ritvo 1987, 284). Yet one might also consider whether the Shachō's mejiro brings about a closeness with an individual—through a formal notion of pet ownership—but also a connectedness with the species as a whole, as he would be able to recognize characteristics among wild birds that he might not have otherwise noticed. Might Mejiro-san be a companion that links the Shachō with nature, creating closeness based on proximity and intimacy that may foster a better understanding of the workings of a shared ecosystem?

While it would be difficult to argue that drastic legislation regarding bird conservation was not a necessity in Japan, applying more nuance to the evidence is helpful for understanding how events unfold. Conservation is, in most cases, top-down

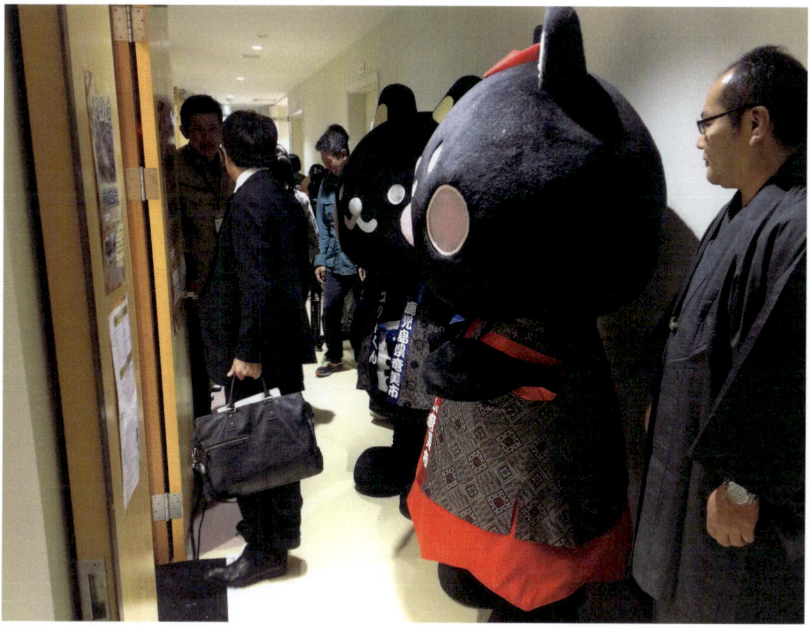

Figure 4.9 *Amami black rabbit mascots (called Kokutō, or "black sugar"). When not wearing Oshima tsumugi, these characters have a white bandage indicating an injury sustained from a car collision , a reminder of their vulnerability.*

and instituted by outside forces. Critics of conservation frequently highlight a lack of understanding of local context and cosmologies, although in recent years critical work has been done to address this problem. Companionship, meanwhile, could be conceptualized as a grassroots approach to environmental stewardship. But because the law no longer permits the trapping of wild birds as companions, what might companionship outside of pet ownership entail if nature, in some instances, has reverted from commodity to companion? I suggest that reconfiguring the boundaries of companionship and better understanding how different species "co-constitute each other" might offer a more conducive way forward.

Although nature literally permeates the walls in Amami, there is also an overwhelming sense that vibrant, living nature has become abstracted into material and portable forms of companionship. The rurikakesu (Lidth's jay), only found on Amami and the neighboring Kakeromajima and Ukejima Islands, is the prefectural bird of Kagoshima (registered in 1963) and can be found symbolically rendered across Amami. Together with the black rabbit, both species are Special National Monuments, joining Japan's unique crafts and culture (including textiles) under the Cultural Properties *(bunkazai)* umbrella. These species symbolize

Amamian identity nationally, and the island's official mascot, a black rabbit named Kokutō (meaning black sugar, the island's famous sweet export), is said to represent "the symbol of the nature of Amami" (figure 4.9) (Kuwahara 2011). The rabbit has a distinctively *kawaii* (cute) persona, found printed on conservation posters but also local vegetable packaging, tourist information sheets, *omiyage* (souvenirs), and Hello Kitty merchandise, and it even lends its name to a local car mechanic (figure 4.10). These rare species that are "remote" in daily life have been replaced by an excess of material forms. This phenomenon is similarly described by Kalland and Moeran in Japanese whaling towns where "cute" whales and dolphins, once hunted in significant numbers, adorn fire stations, bridges, manhole covers, and pachinko pinball parlors (Kalland and Moeran 1992, 24–30). Kalland and Moeran argue that whales have become ideological "totems" for environmentalists but also visual totems of "self-identification" (42), as they "foster a strong community identity—itself seen as an important strategy for survival" (194).

To consider this contemporary iteration of animism, it is productive to draw on Émile Durkheim's ([1915] 2008) theory of totemism, developed via an understanding of Aboriginal Australians' "system of social organization" and "mode of relating to nature" (Descola 2013, 145) through communities, names, objects, and geographies. Durkheim explains that "[behind] these figures and Metaphors . . . there is a concrete and living reality" whose "primary object is not to give men a representation of the physical world" but to exist as "a system of ideas with which the individuals represent to themselves the society of which they are members" ([1915] 2008, 284–85). This totemism uses representations of nature and/or spiritual beings to bring about closeness with local geographies but also fosters relations between members of a community who share ideals. Anthropologist Philippe Descola describes, for example, how Penobscot and Mistassini Cree of North America took as "totems" or "guardian spirits" the animals they hunted: "The Cree considered the animal species to be the legitimate proprietors of the hunting territories that they allowed humans to use," meaning species would have lent both their name to the group that hunted them (beaver, eel, wildcat, etc.) and their territory to the hunters for human survival. This relationship was not "arbitrary" but based on "an accepted material relationship of dependence reached between [species] . . . that had imprinted the mark of identity on the territory" (Descola 2013, 170–71).

One might argue that in the context of Amami, these totems have become "economic animals" (Kanatsu 2013) whose charisma is capitalized on to raise funds for conservation or to support local communities through the draw of tourism, a method exploited globally. Anthropologist Nayanika Mathur (2014), for example, questioned the symbolic use of "tigeraphernalia" at the Ranthambore

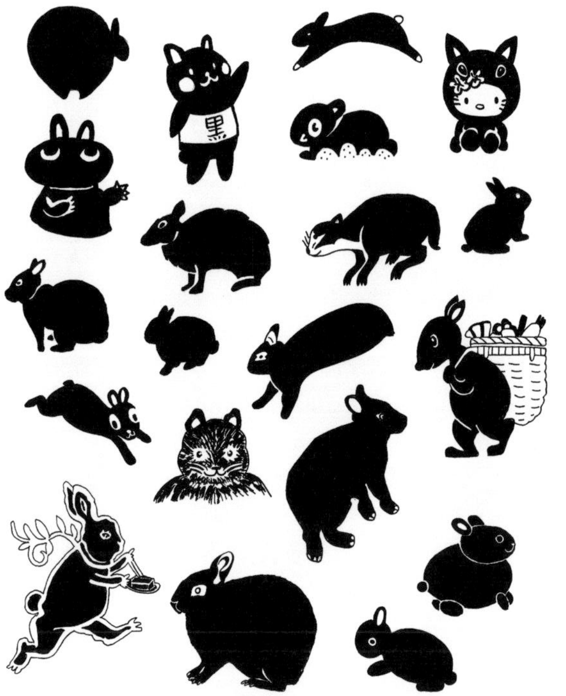

Figure 4.10 *Drawings of Amami black rabbit iconography collected across the island.*

tiger sanctuary in India, where images of friendly "talking" tigers are distributed through signs and merchandise. Mathur's research documents widely cited incidents in which residents have been killed by critically endangered big cats, leaving little evidence behind. She argues that filling the void created by this ghostly presence with positive visuals might counteract their negative or threatening reputation. Depicting them as "cute" and communicative instead strikes an emotive and relatable chord that promotes understanding and care, as much as it harnesses the tiger as a source of income. But like this case in India, one might ask whether symbolic representations of wildlife that remain largely absent from daily life in Amami can really promote feelings of closeness to nature and a sense of companionship? Or are these images of nature simply a form of commodification?

Anthropological work addressing commerce in religious spheres has suggested that mass distribution and consumption of religious forms can still generate meaningful experiences, and similarly the spiritual processes of companionship that adhere within cultural images of endangered species are not necessarily erased by their commercial imperatives.[7] Inge Daniels has argued that "material objects which mediate between the spiritual and the material worlds enable people [in Japan] to have a multitude of embodied interactions with deities."

Embodiments of spiritual beings have been consumed for centuries as lucky charms called *engimono*, "things that bring about good fortune" (Daniels 2003, 620), but also to ward off uncertainty or promote ethical behavior by linking the spiritual with domestic life. This means that spirituality can play an essential role in the economy, whether spiritual forms are sold at shrines or consumed through drama. Daniels explains that "*engimono* are not mere embodiments of luck," but their efficacy is grounded in the "homophonic association (*goroawase*)" linked with their physical properties. The power of the frog (*kaeru*) engimono, for example, lies in the fact that *kaeru* also means "to return," meaning they are used as charms to "help people to 'return' to their everyday routines" after travel, a stay in hospital, and other situations (624). The charms help people influence their luck but also necessitate that one take moral responsibility for one's actions as well as bestow the specific material forms with respect and care.

These ideas and practices became relevant during the COVID-19 pandemic, when a mermaid-like *yōkai* (supernatural being) called Amabié was resurrected as a talisman to ward off disease. Amabié was first sighted in 1846, when it was reported to have appeared offshore of Kyūshū Island. Telling a fisherman that six years of abundant harvests would be followed by a pandemic, it advised him to "draw me and show me to the people" (Furukawa and Kansaku 2020, 531). A yōkai artist shared a drawing of Amabié on X (formerly Twitter) on January 30, 2020, creating "a super-spreader event," prompting thousands of Japanese citizens and businesses to re-create Amabié's image in painting, sculpture, and even bowls of noodles. The Japanese Ministry of Health, Labour, and Welfare adopted it in its public information campaign as "cultural buy-in for sharing images as an alleged way to ward off disease" (533) (figure 4.11). Although, as Daniels (2003, 624) explains, the "sheer variety of forms and applications of engimono makes it difficult to attempt a comprehensive explanation of their independent efficacy," the repetition of Amabié allowed it to fulfill its own narrative by repeating a public health warning. Amabié's abundance made visible the invisible presence of COVID-19, encouraging individuals to take responsibility for their actions and look out for others. As medical doctors Yuki Furukawa and Rei Kansaku claim, "When people are feeling isolated and perhaps helpless, the cute 19th-century mercreature provides a comforting, playful, uniquely Japanese means of expression for connecting people with each other and claiming a small sense of protection and control for themselves" (2020, 533).

The community act of making visible revered environmental totems could be said to be occurring in Amami. But does an abundance of black rabbit or rurikakesu forms, even if they have joined myriad spiritual beings in connecting a community to nature, result in moral action? Although the impact of these practices

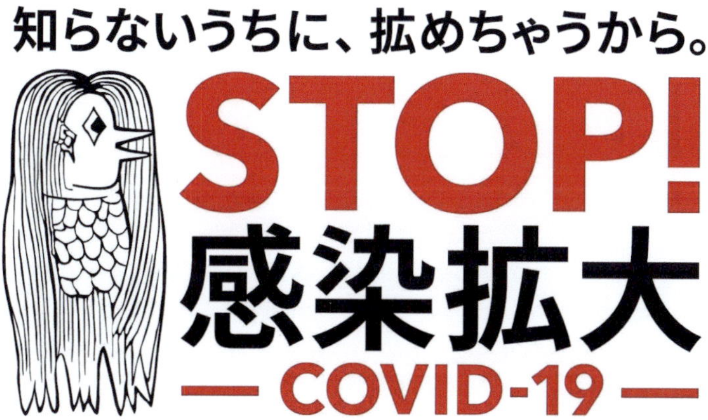

Figure 4.11 *The text of this poster reads, "Before you know it, it will spread. STOP! Spread of infection COVID-19." The poster's illustration depicts a yōkai, or supernatural being, called Amabié. Courtesy of The Japanese Ministry of Health, Labour, and Welfare.*

on environmental responsibility is individualized and ambiguous, there is some local evidence of their efficacy. In 1995 Amamians fought the construction of a golf course that had been granted planning permission in Akiyo's hometown of Sumiyo-son, where the mountains are inhabited by a range of endemic species including endangered black rabbits. The case gained attention in the national and international media because lawyers named the rabbit as a plaintiff, in effect regarding the animal as a legal person.[8] This form of environmental law, which originates in America and has had significant success in countries such as New Zealand (Sanders 2018), had never been used in Japan, and although it set a precedent, the case was lost. Since the lawsuit occurred during Japan's financial crash and the proceedings dragged on for years, the development was dropped for economic reasons (Kagohashi 2002). Participants have told me that during this time, many local people cared little for the rabbits, which were seen as vermin—damaging vegetable crops and valuable citrus trees—thereby favoring the construction of the golf course. Yet thirty years on, Amamians place bumper stickers featuring black rabbits like membership badges onto the rear of their vehicles. This externally identifies them as caring Amamians, while issuing a conservation message warning others to drive carefully to avoid rabbit causalities on the roads at night. The example of Amami demonstrates that conservation narratives "do not blow in a straight line and often push up against one another, which makes them unpredictable in their force and direction" (Hathaway 2013, 188).

This can be seen in the fate that eventually befell Mejiro-san. Toward the end of my fieldwork, the Shachō did eventually forget to bring the bird into the house one evening and it was tragically killed and eaten by a snake. In an unexpected twist akin to a fable, after eating Mejiro-san, the snake became too engorged to escape the cage and was later killed by one of the craftsmen. This fable demonstrates a speciesism innate in humans that denotes a lack of sympathy with the predator, the snake, and a benevolence toward those that are harmless or helpful toward humans, the bird. Given the great power they wield, snakes have been revered for centuries by Amamians, but they have also been persecuted by residents in exchange for cash by the authorities. This shows how totems—that can be at the same time destructive or benevolent—litter the social and material sphere, and behind each is a complex system of ideas and "obscure but intimate relations which [an individual or collective] have with it" (Durkheim [1915] 2008, 284–85).

In *Beyond Nature and Culture* (2013) Descola considers how anthropology as a discipline has moved from a distinct position of nature-culture dualism toward increasingly divided subdisciplines. Each of these, he says, seeks to understand how different societies interact with their natural environment. Yet he argues instead that "the multiple and tangled links that every individual is constantly weaving with his or her environment hardly sanction such a cut-and-dried distinction between practical knowledge and symbolic representations—at least not if one allows some credit to the meaning that the members of a collectivity attach to their actions" (Descola 2013, 83). This suggests that human-environment relations are both expansive and complex and generationally and geographically collectivized. As this chapter has shown, the adoption of environmental resistance at a societal level is dependent on a broad range of factors and might take decades to become widely accepted. For the Shachō, Mejiro-san might have brought about a closeness with a species, helping him to better understand his environment. But my younger colleagues who grew up in the 1980s and 1990s were subject to lively environmental activism and animal rights discourse. I propose that for them, Mejiro-san's caged presence evoked an impression of the past that did not sit comfortably with their ethical ideals. As a totem commanding respect, Mejiro-san was not only a symbol representing a system of ideas but a living being whose sentience made it more powerful.

Although the Americans were able to rapidly halt the unregulated harvesting of wild birds and address the sustainability of this form of resource extraction within about a decade in Japan, this would not have been possible without the "progressivism" voiced by elites, changes in economic fortunes that gentrified the population's diet, rigorous policy intervention, and the moral winds of Western conservation that aligned with a reappraisal of Japanese identity. But it should also be remembered that there was an economic and public health imperative to conserve wildlife, and it was only later that this was backed by a moral stance.

Kronenberg (2014, 174) notes that economic ornithology fell out of favor after World War II when chemical pesticides replaced the "services" of birds. This, however, did not result in the reversal of environmental gains, because the emotional attachment that humans have for wildlife took on a greater presence than that of economic reasoning.[9]

Recognizing the characteristics and habits of birdlife can lead one to understand how our lives converge and the roles birds play in "the affairs of everyday life"—in our diet, economic systems, spirituality, and material culture and in the ecological networks that sustain local traditions. Interacting with nonhuman species, in all their natural/cultural forms, can foster a connectedness, helping individuals and collectives establish links with their environment. This is demonstrated by the mejiro, which feed on the flower nectar, pests, and ripe fruit of Amami's fruit groves, spreading seeds and pollinating trees that will in turn produce a harvestable food or dye crop. Without pollination, the benefits of local citrus fruits—a significant part of the island's agricultural export and important for fostering sociality—would be lost, demonstrating that the mejiro really is true to the term *mejirooshi* in its ability to create a sense of abundance. The abundance of visual forms of nature, meanwhile, aligns with Austin's argument when outlawing mist-netting, that songbirds are more valuable to the food chain—to ecologies of production—when they assist humans rather than when they are food themselves. The narratives that surrounded Mejiro-san had a significant impact on those who observed them—initiating a form of unspoken allegiance—that might influence the way the observers interact with nature and their capacity to care in other areas of their lives. An ecological perspective that embraces companionship might offer a route back to a connectedness with nature that helps a community make sense of the world and take responsibility for their actions, a role historically performed by animism.

Using the historical arc of bird conservation in Japan, this chapter offered a cultural framework to demonstrate the time, work, and collaboration needed to address urgent environmental issues that can rarely be solved with quick fixes and moral discourse. It shows the level of public engagement required and locally adapted comprehension to better understand why evident everyday and mundane practices might have a wider environmental impact. This is the setting as I move on to chapter 5, where a paradox presents itself in the form of a veneration of nature that coexists with the polluting practices that occur during textile production. I consider the ways Amamian spirituality, embedded in a local form of animism, clashes with industrial capitalism in the use of the Toguchi River, where Kanai Kougei is based.

5

“The Industrious Way of Doing Things”

I had been at Kanai Kougei for around six weeks when Kazuko asked whether I’d like to help her prepare new *ai*. This task was performed at least once a week, especially during busy periods, because the strength of the dyebaths weaken through use and across time. In a metal jug, we combined two parts indigo pigment, one part hydro (sodium hydrosulfite), and two parts caustic soda (sodium hydroxide), with Kazuko warning me not to shake the chemicals to avoid them going airborne. Because indigo is insoluble in water, the blue pigment must be immersed in a bath including an alkali solution to raise the pH (caustic soda) and a reducing agent (hydro) to remove oxygen, making the indigo molecules available to the textile fibers. We headed outside to the boiling shed to heat some water. An electric motor was linked to an industrial furnace, with a kerosene bottle feeding the fire via a plastic tube. The setup was menacing, and Kazuko was clearly as nervous as me when she started up the motor. The boiling area had recently been relocated outside of the main buildings to make way for a

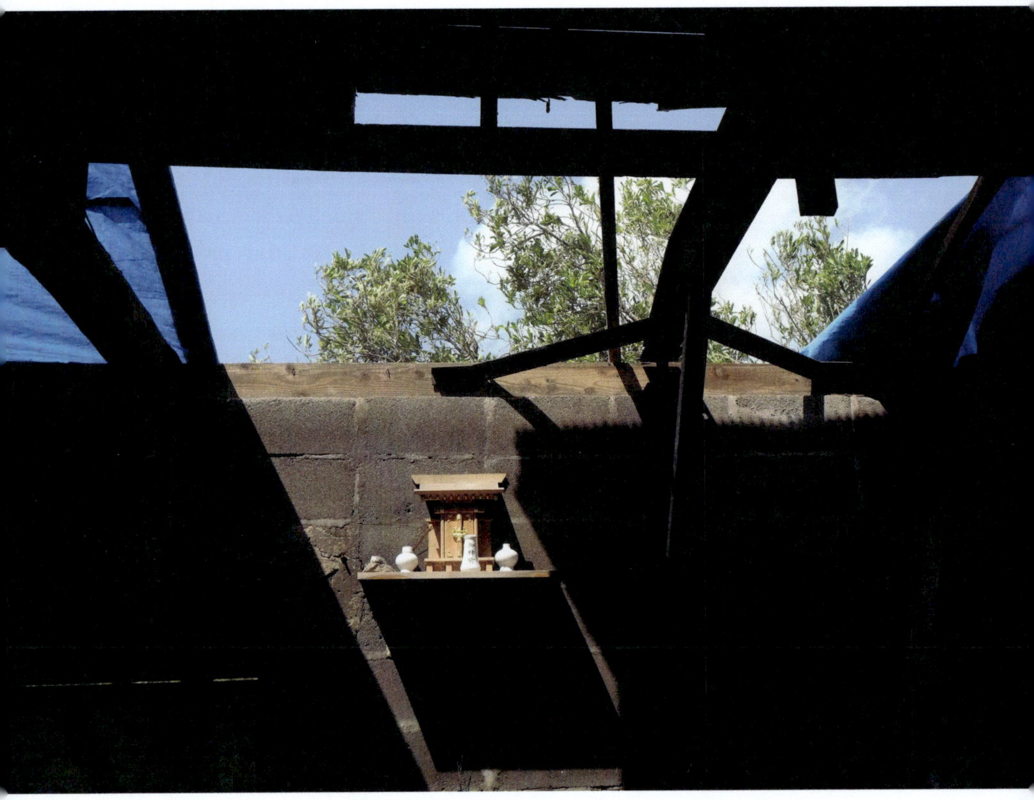

Figure 5.1 *After a strong typhoon the dorozome workshop lost its roof, but the kamidana was mostly untouched.*

new drying cupboard but also for safety reasons. Formerly, smoke and dye fumes would dirty the air, and the workshop had experienced fires in the past. Kanai Kougei had installed two small *kamidana* (god shelves) to protect the company from such misfortunes. One was located at the heart of the *dorozome* workshop above the huge boiling pot (*kama*) and wood-fired furnace used for making *techigi* liquid (figure 5.1). A second was found in the office over the computer where Eriko-san and Maiko-san, the workshop's administrators, communicated with clients. In historian Helen Hardacre's (2017, 1) book on the history of Japanese Shinto—the Japanese cosmology where spirits inhabit a range of animate and inanimate things from fire and water to tools and the wind—she says that when erecting buildings, "it is 'only proper' to begin by asking permission from the kami, with prayer, food, drink, gifts, and a place for them to receive these offerings. . . . Without a shrine, a place is 'unfit for human habitation,' because proper relations with Kami have not been established." Although Kanai Kougei's kamidana is a Shinto device, Yukihito-san clarified that he is not following Shinto; he follows Amamian religious culture, which bears similarities. The kamidana held a model shrine to house "territorial spirits" (Daniels 2011, 86), receptacles of water, *shōchū* (the local sugarcane rum), and sakaki (*Cleyera japonica*) leaves, sacred in Shinto, that Yukihito-san left as offerings to the Amamian fire and water kami. As he explained, "We use fire, we use water, we often work with the elements. So if we don't use them well—fire, for example—it's dangerous . . . because it could lead to fires in the workshop."

While Kazuko and I waited for the water to boil, we emptied the chemical mixture into a plastic bucket. Kazuko became distracted by some designer friends visiting from Tokyo, and I wandered off to look for wildlife in the neighboring *hatake* (allotments). I returned to find her hurriedly pouring water into the bucket, after smoke had started to rise from the burning plastic. In their dry but mixed state, the chemicals are so corrosive that a colleague once melted a hole through the bottom of a bucket. Natural dyeing relies largely on dyestuffs obtained from plant, tree, and animal materials and naturally occurring minerals. Yet prior to my arrival in Amami, I was aware that Kanai Kougei, like many other natural dyeing businesses, often combined natural dyestuffs with synthetic chemicals. Visitors who arrived to participate in indigo dyeing workshops, however, were generally unaware of the chemically stringent materials they were using, thinking their rubber gloves served as protection only from blue hands. From my perspective, the "authenticity" of the dyeing processes wasn't in question, because synthetic indigo compounds have been used in Japan and globally for decades—a knowledge Kanai Kougei shared openly. Yet the question of how the spent indigo, textile pretreatment, and finishing agents were disposed of concerned me. On a weekly basis, I watched these chemicals being poured into drains, which I would later discover led to the river, then out to sea. I found it difficult to understand this action on an island where UNESCO deems the biodiversity worthy of conservation and where the economic foundation and spiritual cosmologies of the community are based on a reverence for, and reliance on, the natural and supernatural world. By exploring how water is accessed, used, and disposed of during the production of contemporary textiles, this chapter aims to unpack this paradox within the confines of a traditional Japanese natural dyeing workshop. I argue that rather than being exclusive to Kanai Kougei or Amami, this paradox reveals the global frictions occurring between the desire to manufacture commodities sustainably and the social, economic, historical, and cosmological factors that resist the imperative to act against environmental pollution.

In the current era of amplified environmental crisis, citizens of industrialized societies, both producers and consumers, are under pressure to take environmental responsibility for the manufacture, use, and disposal of materials under their stewardship. Whether using synthetic or natural dyestuffs, manufacturers rely on large volumes of water to prepare dyebaths, while textiles must be thoroughly washed to ensure unproblematic aftercare, making the textile industry one of the world's largest polluters of water. Textile scientist Rita Kant suggests that "80% of the dyestuffs stay on the fabric, while the rest go down the drain" (2012, 22). The safe filtration and disposal of industrial wastewater is essential, but environmental and health and safety regulations implemented at the national level are not always enforced (Niinimäki et al. 2020, 194).

On account of its reliance on organic materials, the process of natural dyeing is assumed to be more "sustainable" than chemical dyeing. Yet rather than treat the industrial and traditional as binary, I show how the modes of production are more complex. Craft does not exist in a vacuum, and innovation—which goes hand in hand with industrial capitalism—rather than preservation has been central to sustaining textile traditions in Japan (see chapter 1). For natural dyeing to remain economically sustainable, new materials, technologies, and processes have been adopted to increase efficiency and performance qualities. However, through a detailed analysis of the field site using the prism of resource use and disposal, I show how postwar industrial capitalism clashes with the remnants of traditional practices, resulting in actions that might be detrimental to local ecosystems.

While in the previous chapters I examined the treatment of nature in Japan more widely, in chapters 5 and 6 I focus on Amami. In this chapter, I first take a micro view and examine four sites across Toguchi village, where Kanai Kougei is based. Congregating around water, these sites reveal a porosity between systems of production considered "craft" and "industrial." On account of the workshop's reliance on water, craftspeople garner respect for these ecologies of production. Yet there is also an absence of care, resulting in pollution, a factor that appears out of sync with local spirituality, explicated by rituals such as those surrounding the kamidana. I next take a macro view of practices of disposal within textile manufacture by comparing water management at Kanai Kougei and another dyeing workshop in Kyūshū. I try to account for the paradox that exists between local environmental discourse and daily practice, where people say one thing but, despite good intentions, do another. I argue that to remain competitive, and sustain its business and traditions, Kanai Kougei has taken an entrepreneurial path that embraces innovation and economic efficiency (see chapter 2). Within wider environmental discourse, the moralized concept of "good intentions" has emerged as a helpful shorthand for indicating the positive or neutral intent that individuals or governments have when they perform actions to limit their social or environmental impact. But my research shows that the complexity of commodity production means that conflicting relations and unintended consequences that cannot be reduced to individual morally qualified decisions sometimes have to be accepted in order to deal with external pressures. This perspective reveals how the decisions and actions that a community makes regarding the stewardship of materials and natural resource management is not only dependent on individual agency but can be defined by historical, spiritual, and economic practices particular to their social context. Finally, I consider how change might occur in the future as those with responsibility seek settlements to offset their own uncertainty.

The Dyeing Workshops and Their Ecologies of Production

Having a subtropical marine climate, Amami experiences high pressure systems that bring dry and humid heat and an annual average temperature of around seventy degrees Fahrenheit. But the Kuroshio Current in the sea, frequent typhoons, and a long rainy season produce around 3,000 millimeters of rain per year—comparable to that in Indonesia or Bangladesh. This means Amami is a "globally rare place where rainforests are found in the subtropical zone" (Government of Japan 2017, 18). This abundance of water supports biodiversity, but being so plentiful makes textile dyeing an economically sustainable process. Embedded in a valley, Toguchi village is surrounded by mountains (which provide their own microclimate) and is cut through by the Toguchi River, which draws one to the mouth at an inlet on the coast. The importance of freshwater sources for Kanai Kougei should not be underestimated, and their centrality to the functioning of the workshop was revealed in the aftermath of a strong typhoon that caused significant damage to the village. Yukihito-san explained that typhoons are part of Amami, so residents of the island have to follow "nature's course." But conversely, he stressed, "there's lots of stuff [the island] enables us to do. . . . We can get materials. . . . We have easy access to water. . . . So—in a good sense—I think it can't be helped because that's just the way Amami is. It's no good saying 'the typhoon is coming,' because it's not like we can do anything about that. And we can't change our location; if we did than we couldn't get any water." Yet the disposal of wastewater was far more complex, which on both a social and infrastructural basis requires further analysis. In the following section I highlight four sites in the village (figure 5.2) where, I suggest, water is a central binding

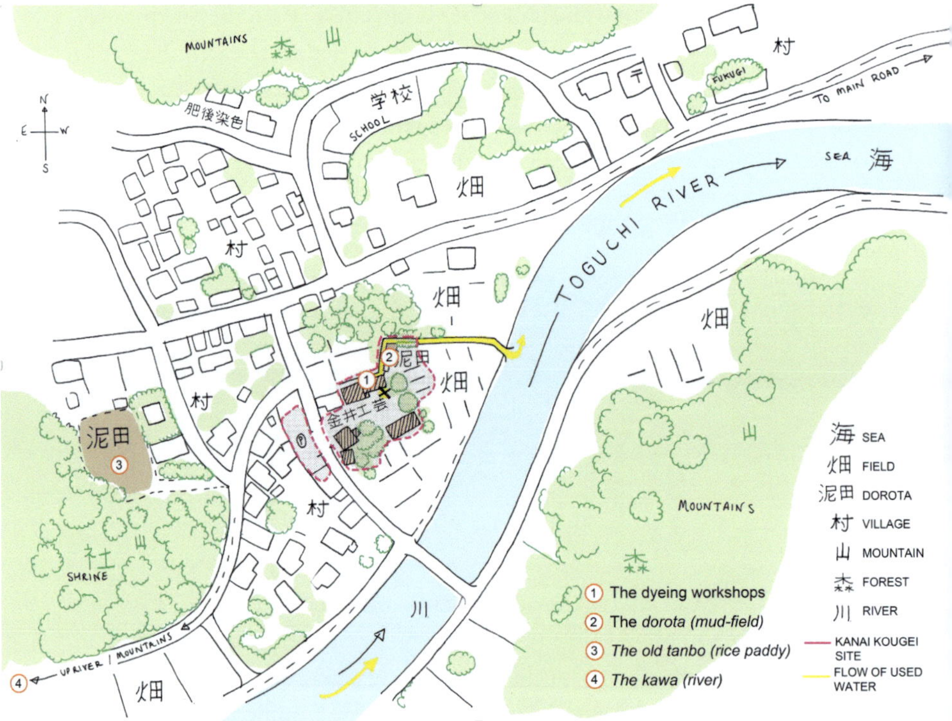

Figure 5.2 *Toguchi village and its water sites.*

force that enmeshes history, ecology, utility, and capital. These are (1) the dyeing workshops; (2) the *dorota* (mud field); (3) the old *tanbo* (rice paddy); and (4) the *kawa* (river). These are all essential water sources that allow Kanai Kougei to function as a "traditional" dyeing company.

To describe these sites, I borrow the term *ecotope* from ecology, defined as "the smallest spatial object or component of a geographical landscape" (Troll 1950), such as a pond, tree, or copse, which gather to create different but related "ecosystem patches" (Klink et al. 2002, 7). While ecotopes are bound by their physical characteristics (geology, hydrology, soil chemistry, etc.) and/or biota (the plant and animal life of a region), "the flows of energy and material that sustain them" are also studied (Johnson and Davidson-Hunt 2011, 269). Boundaries can be blurred, as in my example, because water flows laterally and vertically. Taking this focused, geographic approach, I follow landscape ethnoecologists such as Johnson and Hunn (2009c, 279), who explain how the discipline "ties pragmatic knowledge of how to make a living on the land to self-definition, cosmology, meaning, and morality. . . . Landscape ethnoecology . . . is the sum of what one needs to know to live in a place." Johnson and Hunn have expanded the definition of *ecotope* to incorporate "folk or cultural ecotopes," areas that may include "human technologies, cosmologies and living systems." They suggest that "it is not useful to create a category binary contrast between 'natural' and 'anthropogenic' landscapes because in fact this varies between cultures" (2009a, 3).

These terms are helpful because they demonstrate instances where nature, culture, and economy converge. They are evidence of a connectedness with one's environment and of sites of mediation between human needs and desires and those of other beings or landscape elements. Yet I borrow these terms from the specialized discipline of landscape ethnoecology lightly, without being bound by classification. My aim instead is to use them heuristically to highlight the importance of each site, because to the unobservant, they may appear to be nothing out of the ordinary.

Neighboring the Kanai family home, the dyeing workshops are divided into two. The first is used for dorozome and *kusakizome* and the second exclusively for *aizome*, because indigo is potent and tends to contaminate other textiles. At the location of an old well (marked with a cross, between points 1 and 2, in figure 5.2), an electric pump draws clean groundwater, which feeds taps inside the buildings. This water is said to be pure and stable with low iron and calcium content, meaning it does not affect the preparation of the techigi (yeddo hawthorn) liquid used for dorozome. Natural dyeing is sensitive to environmental conditions, so the stability of this water source is paramount to achieving consistency in color, rendering the site unique.[1] Groundwater fills the butts in the dorozome workshop and a clever three-tank water system in the aizome workshop (figure 5.3). The first tank, used for washing undyed textiles, fills up before overfilling into the second (for dorozome), then into the third (for aizome), the last of which routinely turns bright blue. Being the "dirtiest," since the water has now been used three times, it overflows into the drains. In the dorozome workshop, waste dye and water are poured directly onto the floor, as are the petrochemical agents used to improve a textile's performance and stability. These industrial chemicals used for apparel are applied as a pretreatment to improve color absorbency or after dyeing to soften, prevent fading, or prevent the transference of color from the cloth onto other surfaces. Wastewater from both workshops congregates in concrete drains that flow to the river, then out to sea. Amphibians frequent these damp environments, often laying their eggs here; the drains presumably provide safety from predators that reside in Kanai Kougei's dorota (figure 5.4).

At the end of the working day, after the wastewaters have drained, a pipe connected to the third tank routes clean water to the dorota to maintain the water level and prevent stagnation. The dorota is a unique space, where high levels of iron (ferrous sulfate) occurring naturally in Amamian mud are used to

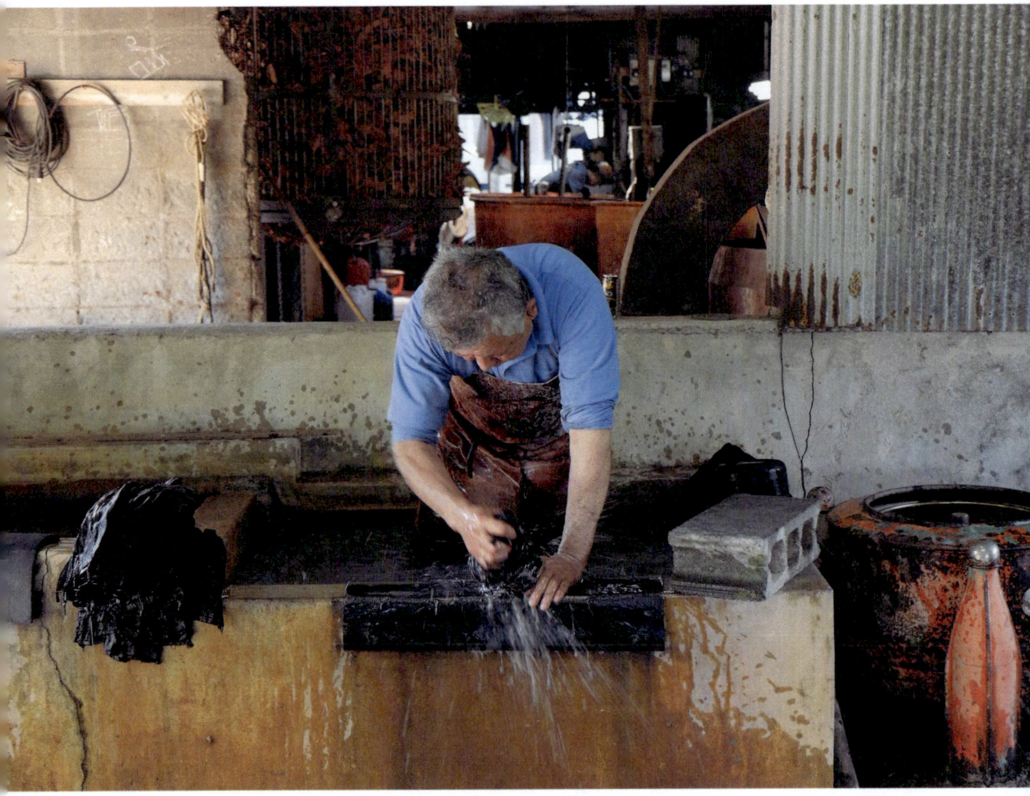

Figure 5.3 *The Shachō washes yarn in the third water tank located in the aizome workshop.*

mordant—fix and darken the color—the brown techigi-dyed textiles. Mud is unsettled from the bottom of the dorota by the dyer, who pounds it into the fibers to fix the iron to the tannins, resulting in a deeper shade. By allowing water to sit on top of the mud, oxidization is prevented, making the iron available to the tannin. If during the working day someone forgets to disconnect the pipe, wastewater will enter the pool and the workers will have to deal with the wrath of the *tsumugi* dyers because the contaminating indigo can affect the shade of tsumugi yarns.

Before they were used for dyeing, dorota originated as tanbo (rice paddies) (figure 5.5). Kazu-san, a tsumugi dyer who had extensive knowledge of Amamian natural history, explained that the deep mud and spring water all over Toguchi and into the valley make it a suitable area for rice cultivation. This makes the area prime agricultural land because the soils are shallow on Amami's steep slopes. Amami's landscape follows the *satoyama* (mountain-village) model (Sugimura 2021, 48), a Japanese system of micromanaging woodlands alongside the wet environment of tanbo and the dry environment of hatake (allotments), which supports a variety of wild and domestic flora and fauna, creating "dynamic bio-interrelationships" mutually beneficial for humans and nature (Washitani 2003). After World War II, urban migration and imports meant satoyama ecologies broke down across Japan as landscapes lay unmanaged and native trees were replaced by monoculture forestry. Given Toguchi's location cocooned among the river, mountains, forest, sea, and a mosaic of agricultural and craft ecotopes, it could be argued that the village still functions as a satoyama, yet without the working rice paddies that make this landscape visually distinctive. To my knowledge, the dorota's ecosystem remains unstudied by ecologists. This point is significant because it is an ecology of production—a space shaped by both human and other species collectively working in a productive capacity both within and outside of capitalist systems—that provides a suitable habitat for rare wildlife.

Kazu-san and the Shachō informed me that at least five resident species of frog and various lizards, crabs, newts, nymphs, beetles, and snakes inhabit the dorota grounds alongside a multitude of plants. I also identified an endangered damselfly (*Coeliccia ryukyuensis amamii*) (figure 5.6) and vulnerable sword-tail newts (*Cynops ensicauda*) (figure 5.7). Oriental storks fished in the river and gray-faced buzzards hunted amphibians, snakes, lizards, and rodents, the latter of which we knew lived in the workshop's stores. I asked Kazu-san whether he was concerned about life in the pool when indigo or any other substances did accidentally enter. He said that, although he was no professor, he had never seen any dead creatures, so he didn't think it detrimental and, "actually, by mixing up the mud we're adding oxygen to it, right? So maybe we're making it easier for them to live there!" The importance of human disturbance was apparent when I visited an old tanbo with Kazuko and Kazu-san. Since at least the 1970s, it functioned as the village dorota but today it is used only by Toguchi's one other remaining workshop, led by Higo-san, and is mostly overgrown, because Kanai Kougei built its own dorota next to its workshop approximately ten to twenty years ago. The fact that Kanai Kougei's dorota is so young is a village "secret," as they have led people to believe the space was always there, because provenance matters in the heritage industry (see chapter 1). To construct Kanai Kougei's dorota, mud was dug from its section of the communal dorota and moved to the site next to the workshop, where it is found today. Although promotional materials (TV, magazines, books, etc.) often state that *sotetsu* (*Cycas revoluta*) fronds are placed in a dorota to restore its iron and copper content, Kazu-san explained that it is quicker to come to the communal dorota and dig more mud because the iron content beneath the mountain that towers above is so concentrated.[2] Kazu-san said that because the dorota is waist deep, medaka (Japanese rice fish)

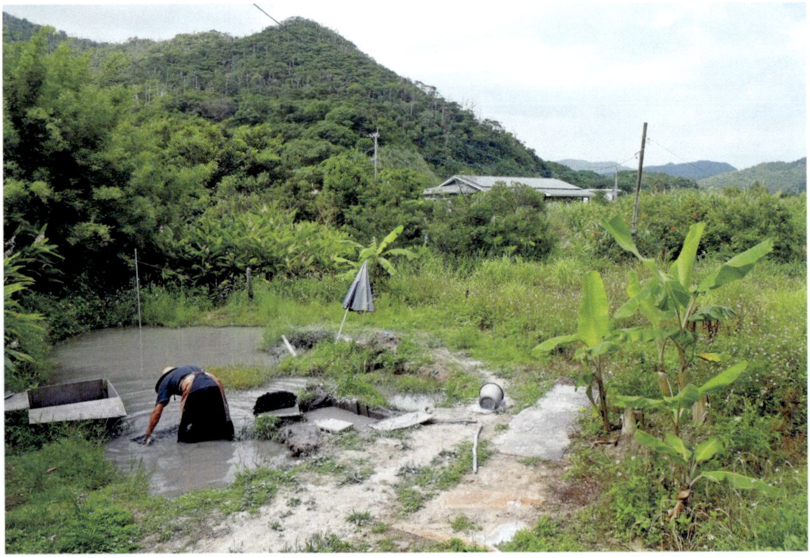

Figure 5.4 *Kanai Kougei's dorota.*

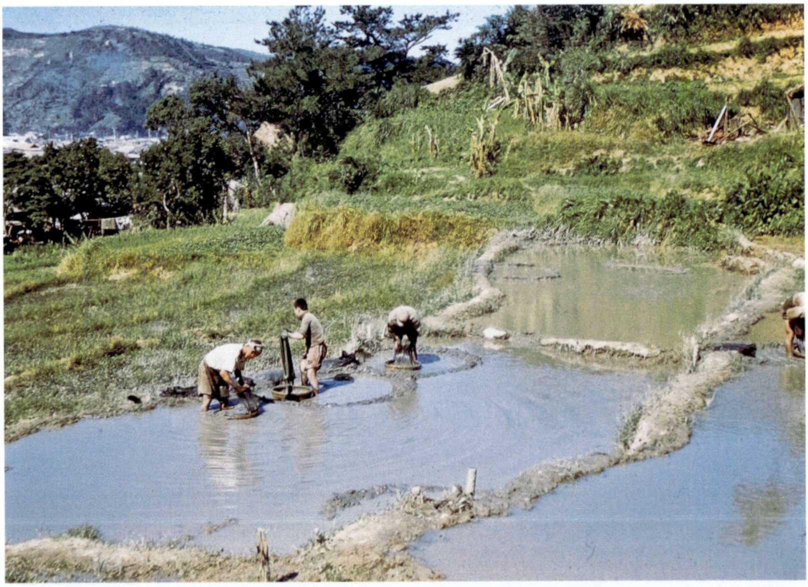

Figure 5.5 *Rinsing dyed tsumugi yarn in mud to set dye, 1951–52. Douglas Haring Papers, University Archives, Special Collections Research Center, Syracuse University Libraries, Syracuse, New York.*

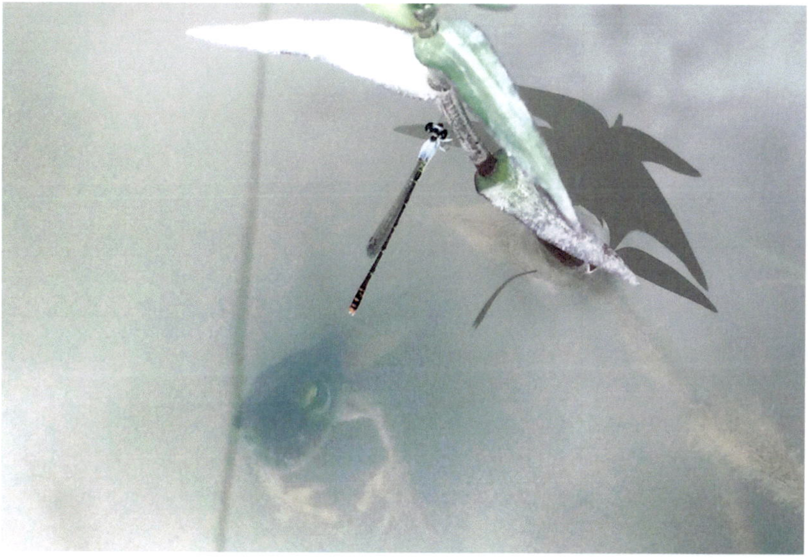

Figure 5.6 *A submerged Amami tip-nosed frog with a damselfly (*Coeliccia ryukyuensis amamii*) in the dorota.*

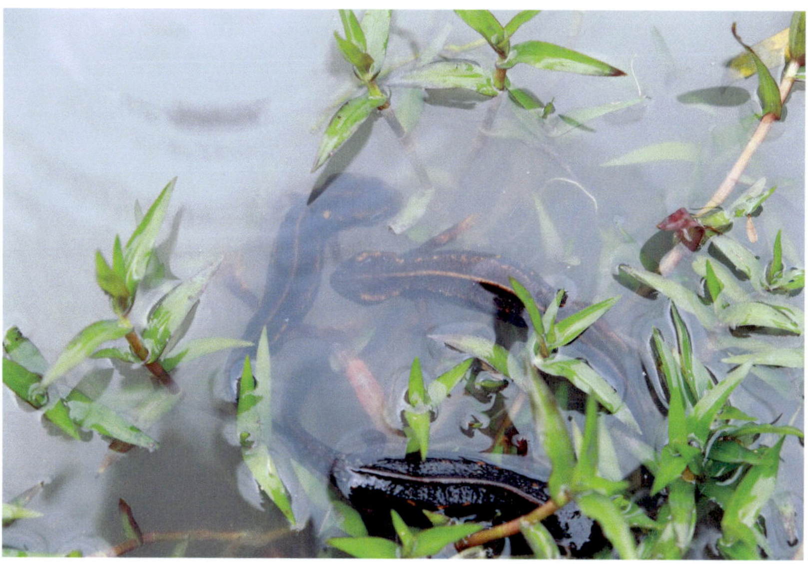

Figure 5.7 *Sword-tail newts* (Cynops ensicauda) *in the dorota.*

and *funa* (crucian carp) live here. One might assume the mismanagement of the old tanbo has been a mixed blessing—while species like *makomo* (wild rice) were thriving, the lack of human maintenance may have had a detrimental effect on less aggressive species. Increasingly in short supply, dorota clearly provide the perfect "anthropogenic ecotope" for a diverse array of species.

Around ten minutes' drive into the mountains from the workshop, the craftspeople stop at a spot on the river (kawa) (figure 5.8), home to the endangered fish the Ryūkyū ayu (*Plecoglossus altivelis ryukyuensis*). After fifty years of the fish's absence there, the Toguchi River was recognized as a habitat for this rare species, but it's unknown whether dyeing, nearby mining, agricultural runoff, or public works have impacted its numbers (figure 5.9). Since the stone quarry farther up the mountain relocated to the neighboring mountain thirty or forty years ago, the spot is remarkably quiet aside from birdcall, the bubbling river, or overhead *kaminari* (thunder). Tsumugi dyers have washed yarn at this spot for over forty years (figure 5.10). The water is clear of mud and debris, shallow enough to stand in, but deep enough to submerge textiles. Kazu-san explained the nook he uses has the perfect streamflow because it removes the dregs without causing the fine yarns to knot. Yukihito-san also uses this exact location, indicating the transferal of knowledge and identifying it as a "folk ecotope" (Johnson and Hunn 2009c), because one wouldn't know it existed without visiting with a dyeing craftsperson. The work conducted at the river is physically demanding—washing yarns means plunging them in the water, adopting a bent stance, and moving the yarns back and forth between the legs with a fast stroke, requiring strength in the arms but also in the back and core. Most of the older craftsmen wear support belts to reduce back pain and hernias, conditions that plague the dyer. Despite such effort and pain, the beautiful spot on the river is a special place for the craftspeople, and there is a consensus that working in these spaces is essential for well-being. Yet Kazu-san joked that Yukihito-san does not like it here, explaining that he once tried to grow Ryūkyū indigo (*Strobilanthes cusia*) on nearby family land but failed. The *yutagamisama* (Amamian priestess) told Yukihito-san "the place was not good," so he quit. Kazu-san laughed, saying, "Yukihito-san *really* likes yutagamisama and spiritual things!" Yukihito-san contested the influence of the *yuta*'s advice to a certain extent; while he did seek consultation, he also recognized he had chosen the wrong season and environment to grow indigo.

Yukihito-san and many others in Amami continue to follow the local religious culture based on the *unari-gami* (sister-deity) faith, stemming from Okinawa's Ryūkyū kingdom. In Japanese folklore, Unari was said to be the protector of her brother Ihiri, but while she was benevolent, she also had the power to curse—a contradictory trait found in many Shinto gods (Igeta 1983, 249–50).

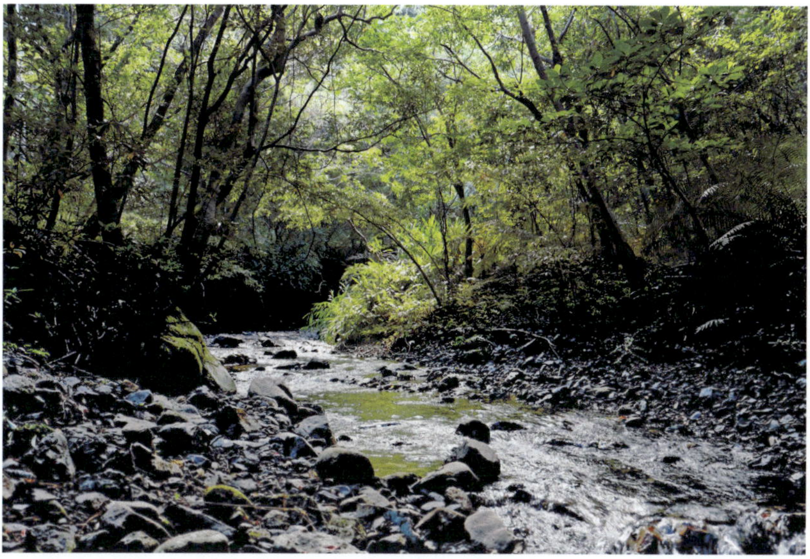

Figure 5.8 *The folk ecotope on the Toguchi River.*

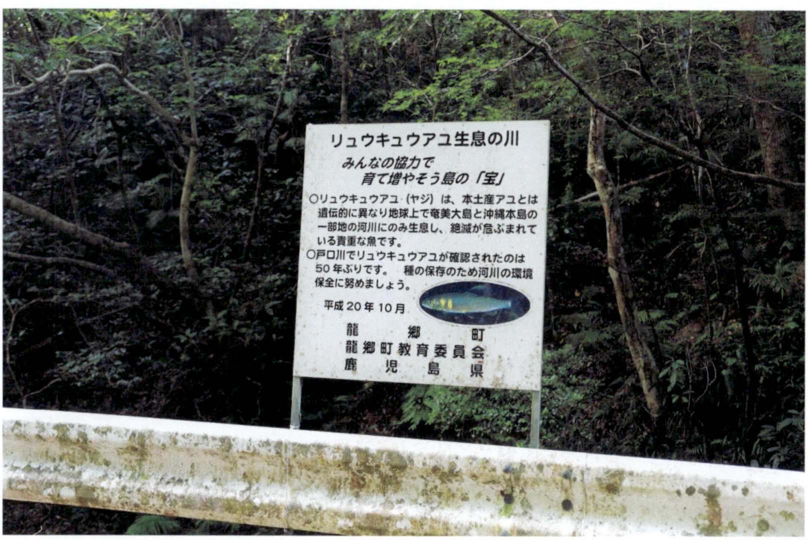

Figure 5.9 *Signs such as this one are posted along the river, mostly in areas uninhabited by humans. They read: "Rivers inhabited by the Ryūkyū ayu. With everyone's participation we can nurture and increase the island's treasure. The Ryūkyū ayu [*yaji *in local dialect] is biologically different from the mainland ayu and only exists in certain rivers on Okinawa's main island and Amami Ōshima. It is a precious fish threatened with extinction. For the first time in fifty years, the Ryūkyū ayu has been seen in the Toguchi River. Let's make an effort to protect the river's environment! October 2008, Tatsugo, Tatsugo Town Board of Education, Kagoshima Prefecture."*

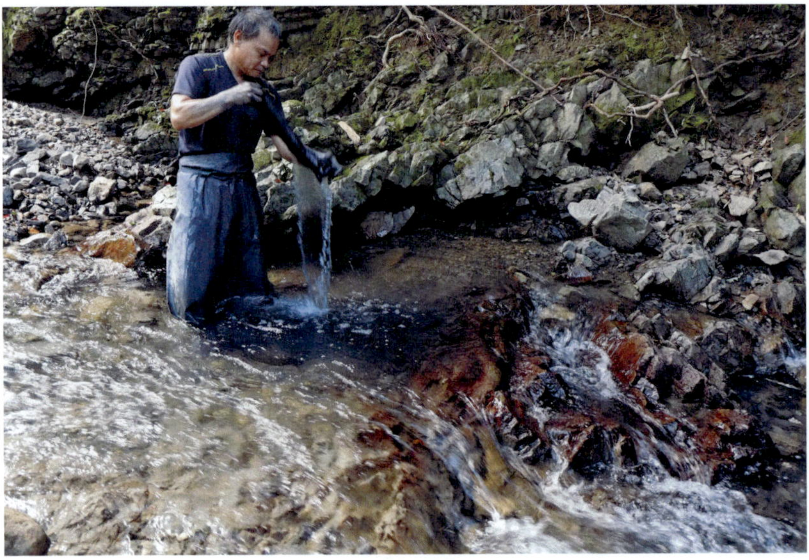

Figure 5.10 *Kazu-san washing indigo yarns in the Toguchi River. Note the red techigi-stained rocks.*

Douglas Haring (1952, 56–57) said this religion was similar to an archaic form of Japanese Shinto, because at its base were spirits residing in a range of animate and inanimate things such as butterflies, rocks, trees, and rivers. It was led by a female theocracy of *noro*, who officiated rituals and decreed laws, and yuta, priestesses who possessed the ability to contact divine beings and practiced "black magic" and "death-by-cursing" (Haring 1953, 109–11) (figures 5.11 and 5.12). From my observations in Amami, Shinto, Buddhism, and Catholicism are all present, as are Mormons and Jehovah's Witnesses, who have gained a footing through a stream of young American missionaries to the island. But these introduced religions are "pick and mixed" (Reader 2005, 440) with indigenous religious thought, and Amamian spirituality emerges as a hybrid.

Tim Ingold (2011, 21) suggests that "a specific cultural worldview or cosmology" can be embedded in the landscape where everything from "plants and fungi" to "waterholes and hills" act as "carriers" for meaning. Referencing Aboriginal Australia, where ancestors are remembered through landscape features, Ingold claims, "Through conception, birth or long-term residence a person incorporates the essence of a locality into his or her own being, even to the extent of substantial identity" (141). Similarly in Amami, cultural knowledge is embedded and embodied at the river and is passed down through generations and on to newly settled residents, those outside of local ancestral lineage. My ethnography therefore demonstrates how taken-for-granted natural elements such as water contribute to economic production, ecological health, well-being, spirituality, and a sense of history and ancestry that might encourage respect and prompt a community to care for the environments under their stewardship. Yet by highlighting Kanai Kougei's ecologies of production, it is evident that the barriers that should promote care are permeable. It is therefore essential to establish the conditions that have allowed for this permeability to be socially accepted.

Amamian Spirituality and Patterns of Land and Resource Use

Amami's geography has physically structured its religious practice—the mountains are centrally located, covering 80 percent of the island's landmass, sloping down through the forest into settlements that look out to sea. At the *kamiyama* (celestial mountains) the noro and yuta would welcome the god of the mountains (*teruko no kami*), and at the beach the god of seas (*naruko no kami*). They would then escort them along the *kaminichi* (celestial path) to the *miya*—a worshipping area historically found at the center of Amami's villages.[3] A mountain location called Amandhi demonstrates this topography in the north of the island. This mountain is one of the main freshwater sources in Amami and is said to be the most sacred and powerful spot, marked by a shrine where the creators of the island, the goddess Amamiko and god Shinireku, fell from heaven. After ceremonies had taken place, the priestesses would return the gods to Neriya-kanaya, a paradise at sea said to bring bountiful harvests. The Setta Tategami rocks in Setta Kasari-chō, a trio of boulders said to be a parent with its child and grandchild, mark one of the locations where the sea gods would arrive and depart from the island. The rocks sit on the edge of a coral reef that fringes Amami, signifying the boundary between the land of the gods and that of the human, a boundary also distinguished by the forests that blanket the mountains (Amami Park, 2017). This is the scene one approaches when arriving at the Amami airport today. It is also the place where officials from the Ryūkyū Kingdom would disembark from their ships.

Amami's indigenous religion was suppressed by the Meiji government (1868–1912), which intended to "civilize" Japan's "wilder" regions. Amamian women, for example, historically wore elaborate hand tattoos (figure 5.13)—protective markings that connected them with family, nature, and the spiritual world—but these were banned in 1876, although the practice continued for some time

Figure 5.11 *Two noro priestesses displaying 450-year-old regalia, 1951–52. Douglas Haring Papers, University Archives, Special Collections Research Center, Syracuse University Libraries, Syracuse, New York.*

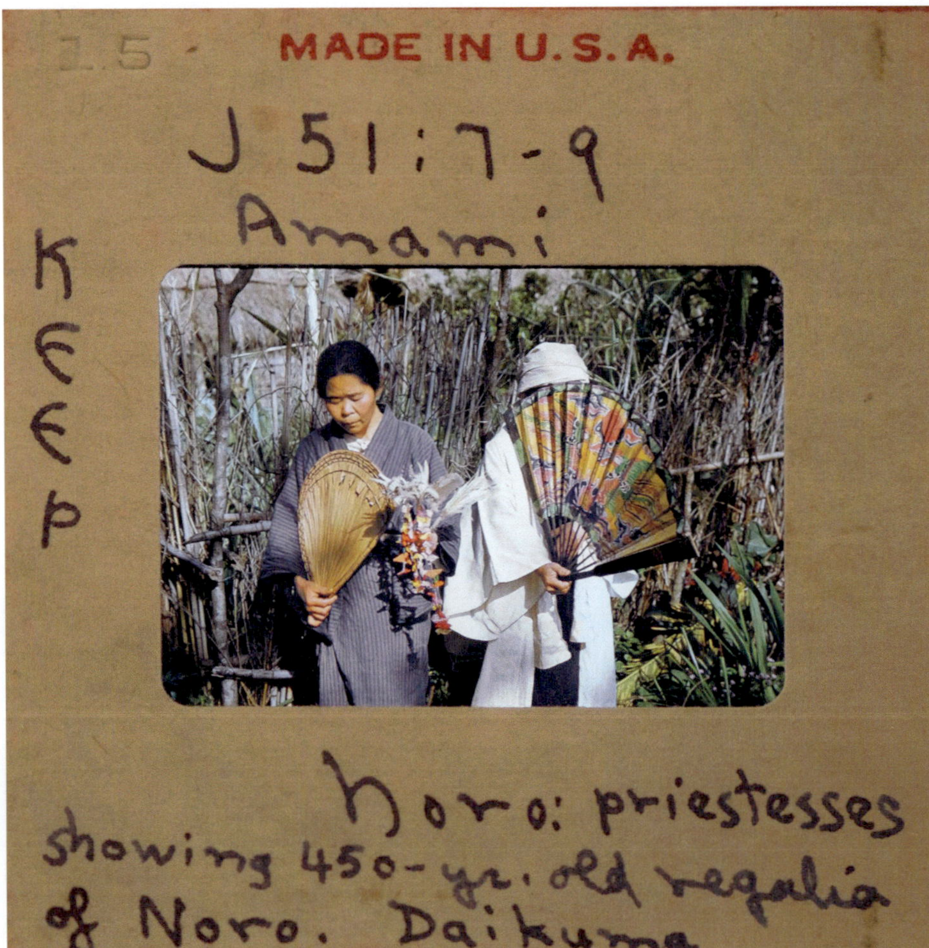

Figure 5.12 *A noro ceremony, 1951–52. Note the loom in the background. Douglas Haring Papers, University Archives, Special Collections Research Center, Syracuse University Libraries, Syracuse, New York.*

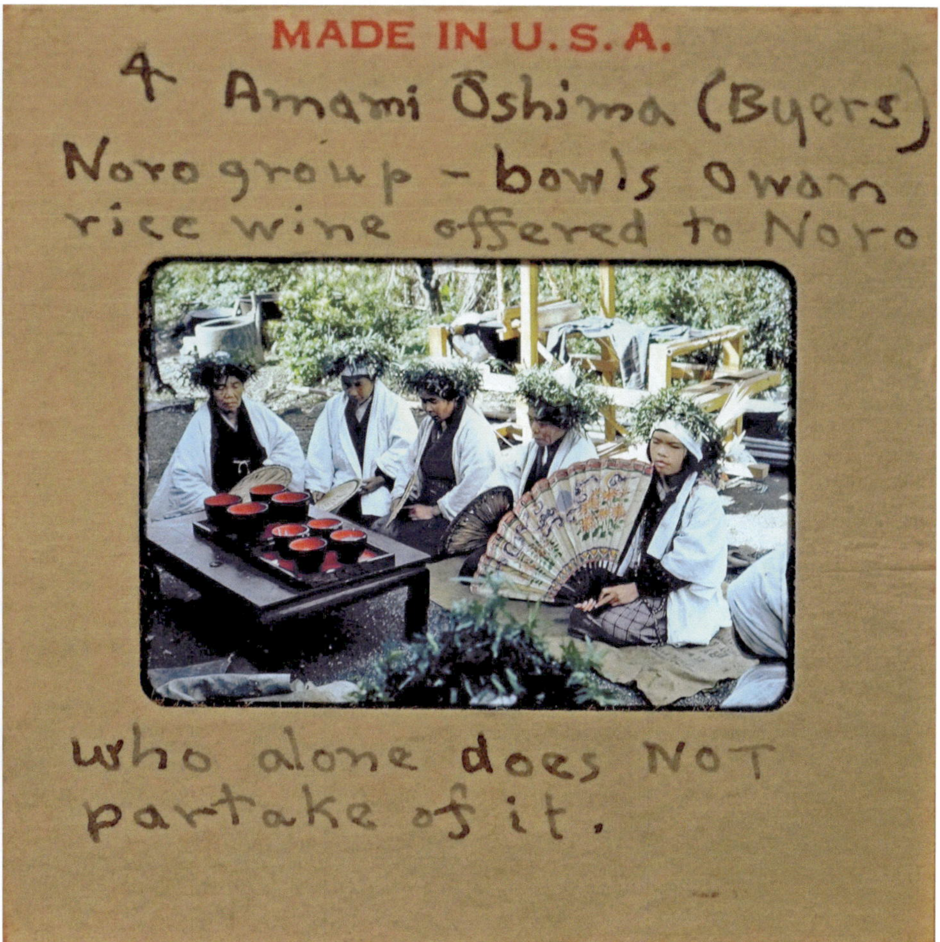

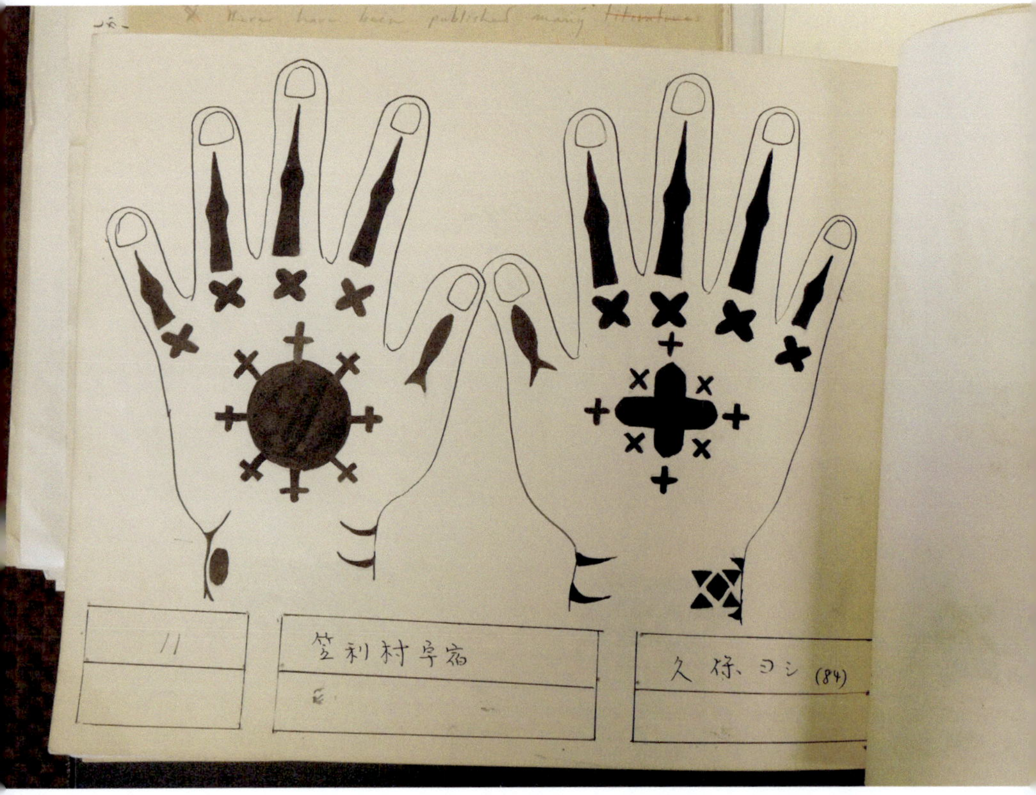

Figure 5.13 *Drawings of Amamian hand tattoos collected by Fumitake Yamashita in the 1950s. Douglas Haring Papers, University Archives, Special Collections Research Center, Syracuse University Libraries, Syracuse, New York.*

despite threat of police arrest (F. Yamashita 1952, 13–14). As imperialism progressed, John Clammer (2001, 224) explains, State Shinto, which was introduced to and enforced upon the Japanese people with a desire to control, stressed "ancestor worship, the religious systemization of patriarchy and the recognition of the emperor as a living *Kami* or deity." He says it was an "attempt by the State to impose a systemized and bureaucratized framework . . . on the amorphous, localized and diversified forms of Japanese folk religion" (218). While State Shinto was enforced in Amami until the end of the war in 1945, with shrines erected (at the cost of the village) and tended to by schoolchildren (Hardacre 2017, 357), it never took hold on the island, with most shrines quickly abandoned with the new constitution (Haring 1952, 57). There is little wonder, because for centuries the noro and yuta were deified as *kamisama*, meaning that women across Amami held equal respect to men. Spiritual ceremonies meanwhile were intimately linked with local geography, having little to do with the state or emperor. In Douglas Haring's field notes, for example, there is a record noting the popularity of a water deity named Nahabue-gami (with *Nahabue* representing "a place midway between heaven and earth") who is worshipped six times a year in the upper courses of a river, primarily by women, who leave offerings.[4] Amamians also favor an element of autonomy, perhaps because of their history of perpetual invasion and subsequent forced labor (see chapter 6). Even today there is an air of resistance regarding state authority, an attitude colloquially termed Amami *sutairu* (Amami style) among my friends. This was most frequently encountered through the bending or breaking of Japanese laws, particularly on Amami's roads, making driving at times a hazardous experience.

Haring claims that by the 1950s the local police's and government's success in weakening the influence of the noro and yuta was demonstrated by public confusion regarding the structure and purpose of this faith. Yet fear of black magic and cursing still lingered, with Haring (1952, 67–70) recording killing methods such as combining horse and human dandruff. Today, what was a complex religious practice continues to mystify. While fear of black magic might have been confined to the past, concerned friends warned me against visiting the notoriously secretive (Haring 1953) historic noro stronghold of Uken village alone, where they said my car tires might be slashed. Many people visit the yuta, who today work as mystics, speaking with the dead or future-telling for a small fee, a bag of sea salt, and a bottle of shōchū or calling upon them to resolve any supernatural occurrences or concerns. Yet what has remained strong are Amami's varied and plentiful *matsuri* (festivals) centered on the lunar calendar and strongly linked to agriculture. Islanders participate in the festivities of the annual *hatchigatsu odori* (August dances), tie pine ikebana (flower arrangements) to door posts at the New Year, wake at dawn and return at dusk to participate in *shōchōgama* (figure 5.14), and wrestle at the October sumo tournaments (figure 5.15).

I visited a sumo tournament in the Kasari area with Koki and Akiyo. It was held on the grounds of a large sports center, but historically these tournaments would have been located in the village miya, directly connecting sumo with the gods. Our motive to attend was to watch Kazuko's children, who had been training for mini sumo after school or nursery for weeks. Tournaments take place in each ward, with teams of men representing their village while children represent their school. The event was entertaining but also intense and moving—we were all brought to tears when the girls defeated the boys.[5] As a result, we were exhausted when we returned to the car, and Koki was overwhelmed. He thought this was because the large numbers of people participating and spectating created an intense force of energy beneath the sumo buildings. It was the first tournament

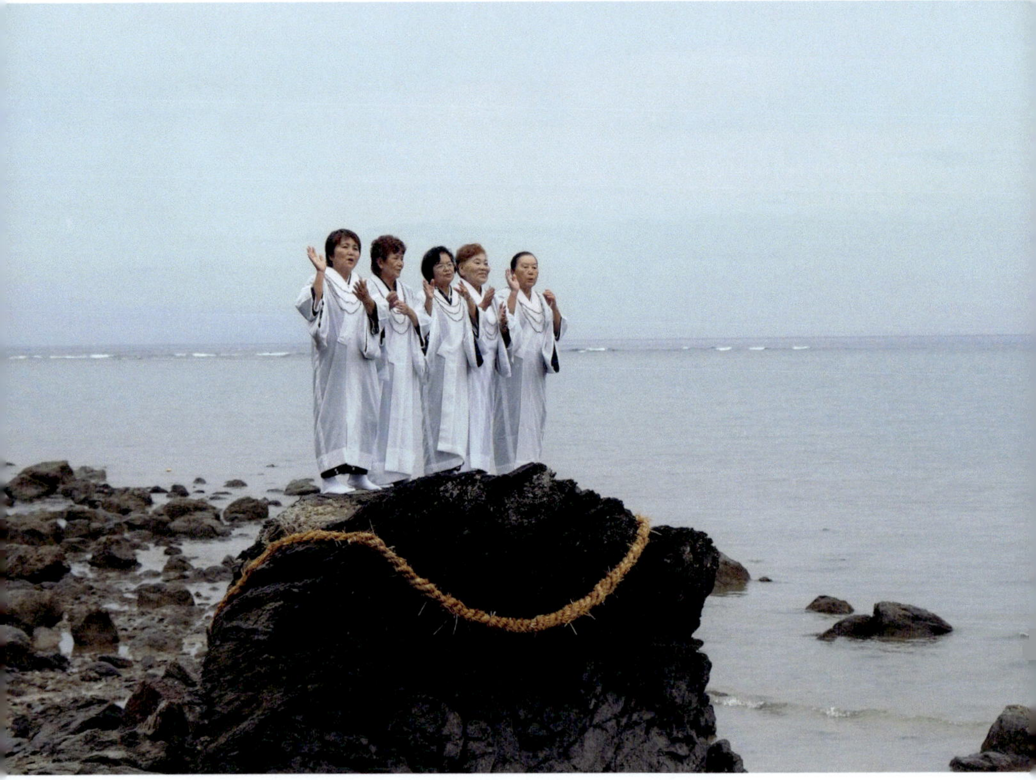

Figure 5.14 *Singing the ancestors back to Neriyakanaya at the* shōchōgama *ceremony held during Obon. The women's robes are of a style historically worn by Amami's priestesses. The rope strung around the rock is a* shimenawa, *indicating the presence of kami.*

he had attended despite living in Amami for three years. He explained that when he first arrived, he avoided village events—or any situation where he might have to socialize with other I-turners. Having lived in big cities his whole life, he was still learning how to calibrate his own social position in Amami. But now he saw why these types of rituals were so important, as they appeared to promote community bonding, collectively reenergizing the crowds. Kazuko often complained about the obligation to attend village events on weekends, but usually on Monday would enthusiastically elaborate about whom she had socialized with and what she had learned about Amamian culture.

Whether or not people continue to "believe" in the old or new religions, the existence of spirits, or kami, and the necessity of ritual practice is perhaps beyond the point. As anthropologist Inge Daniels explains, rituals continue to play important social roles: "In the Japanese context, the personal and collective are

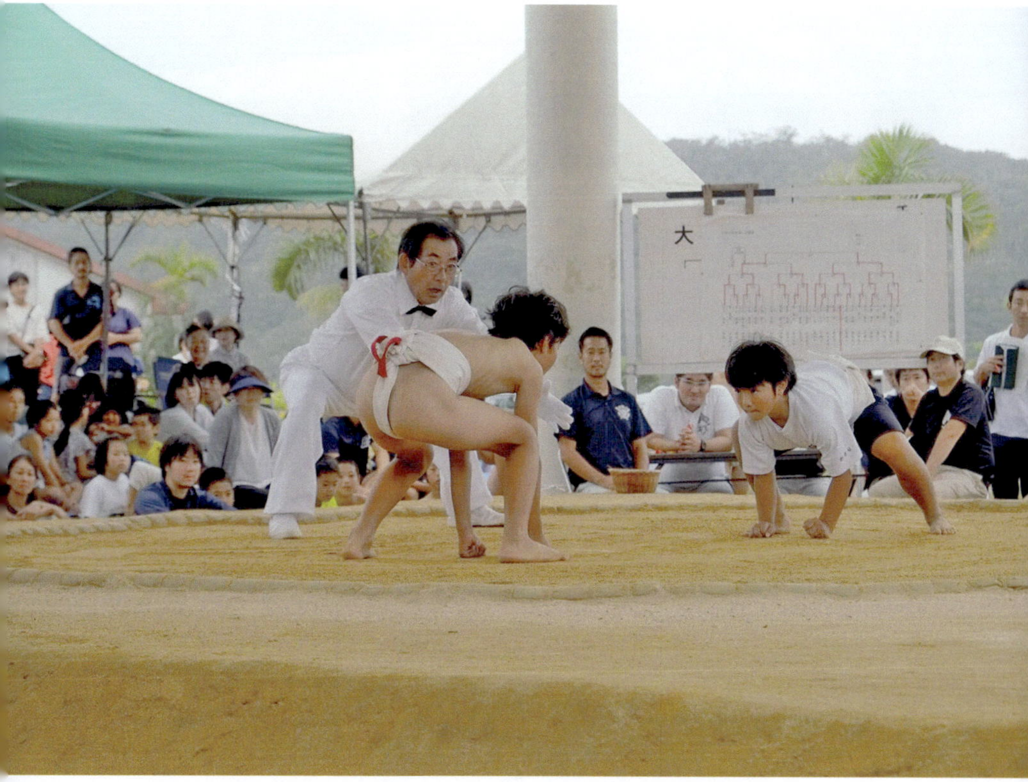

Figure 5.15 *A girl wrestles a boy (and wins) at the mini sumo tournament.*

considered complementary, and the notion of concern is integrated in the everyday lives of people through the enactment of rituals that recognize and maintain connections with others; whether with other people, dead or alive, with deities or with the inanimate world" (2009b, 154). On my second day in Amami at the beginning of November 2018, I attended a matsuri called a *taneoroshi* (village festival) in Toguchi village, and on my third day another in my own village of Sedome. The whole community enjoyed traditional dancing, songs, and drumming. The party moved from house to house where we received food—*onigiri* (rice balls), fruits, and mochi (sweet rice cakes)—and drank beer and Yakult late into the night. These festivals were held in line with the lunar calendar to ask the gods for a good harvest in the forthcoming year. But their contemporary purpose was to celebrate each household's paying of taxes, the amount of which was announced by an Amamian-style town crier, received with cheers and applause. These payments contributed to a fund put aside for village infrastructural maintenance, such as the repairing of low-lying electrical cables that likely took a hit during typhoon season. They were also incredibly fun, and both I and other tourists were welcomed with Amami's generous hospitality.

In line with Daniels's research, my fieldwork shows that in Amami "enactment of rituals" continues to support the community's spiritual, physical, and economic health. When living and working with the elements, the adoption of religious practice as a protective mechanism doesn't necessarily require "inner belief"—something so personal it is difficult to ascertain anyhow (Daniels 2009a, 166). Daniels, for example, describes the reverence given to traditional Japanese dolls, ritually gifted during rites of passage to absorb bad luck. These dolls were treated with "special care" until their useful lifetime had expired, when they were ritually burned during a Shinto shrine ceremony called *kuyō* (163), because, as one of Daniels's participants puts it, "one never knows . . . and it doesn't hurt" (167). At Kanai Kougei, Yukihito-san hoped that the maintenance of their kamidana would counteract the nonchalance of the Shachō and Nagata-san, who frequently worked with a cigarette pursed between their lips. The presence of this mundane ritual—replacing freshwater, shōchū, and sakaki leaves—perhaps served as a reminder not to be complacent. On an island such as Amami, where threats to life, home, and places of work are encountered daily—from habu to typhoons, fires, and even dangerous motorists—the "one never knows" attitude can help in dealing with uncertainty. As Clammer explains, "Animism is not the worship of nature, and the function of ritual Shinto is not so much to get things done . . . as to affirm, exemplify and to continually keep open the channels to a metaphysical and ontological reality" (2001, 238). Ritual practice is used to mitigate against uncertainty—but while the kami may be asked for protection, the question remains as to whether this relationship is reciprocated.

Spatial Boundaries Between Nature and the Village

Under the rule of the noro and yuta, the beaches and forests were considered the boundaries between the land of the gods—the mountains, sea, and sky—and the land of the humans, who were confined within the village. These boundaries were inhabited by a multitude of Amamian *yōkai* (supernatural beings) and kami. In the forests lived yōkai called *kenmun*—small, hairy-faced, naked forest sprites wearing plates on their heads—that one can today find visually rendered across the island. The sad rumor I heard in Amami was that kenmun were in fact the abandoned children of incest, born with physical deformities. Haring recorded many stories that warned of the kenmun's mischievous and mythical nature, with people convinced of their veracity. According to his notes, they tended to appear most frequently to drunk men, who would need to outsmart the sprites to avoid wrestling or being dragged around all night. The following anecdote comes from an informant who, Haring hastens to add, was "well-educated" and who described the trees the kenmun liked to dwell in: "Certain trees, usually banyan and sometimes pines, are *kiranki* [trees we don't cut]; ginkgo are *kiranki*; so, for that matter, is any large, fearsome tree. If you cut one you fall ill. Gods and *kenmun* live in big trees; some trees are inhabited by *ujigami* (tutelary deities). A tree spirit will take the form of a woman and seduce the unwary, then carry him away into the mountains and he never comes back." The noro and yuta forbade clearing the forest, except for those areas designated as common ground (Haring 1952, 68). As a result, Megumi Takarabe and Akira Nishimura claim, during the reign of the Satsuma clan in the period before 1859, the clan began a systematic campaign of oppression, decrying the authority of the noro and yuta as folk superstition. The Satsuma saw the noro and yuta as an obstruction to the expansion of *kokutō* (black sugar) agriculture, which at the time was a significant industry in southern Japan (Takarabe and Nishimura 2013, 16). While the country had not yet opened to trade in cheap sugar produced by enslaved people in the Caribbean, the "ideology of improvement" (Bhandar 2018, 8) that sought to maximize the productivity of the land and people had begun to breach the borders of Japan from the West. Haring explains that oppression continued into the Meiji era, demonstrating how the land was turned to profit: "Amami Oshima was covered with magnificent strands of virgin timber. According to popular belief trees were sacred to the gods and could be cut only with religious ceremonies. Japanese capitalists, however, acquired Oshima land and conducted large-scale lumbering operations. The gods took no apparent vengeance and the taboo against cutting trees was relaxed, but still holds among some of the peasants" (1952, 5).

Amami's mountains continue to be forested and are largely undeveloped, although the majority is secondary growth planted under the guidance of forestry experts during the Edo and Meiji eras (USCAR 1952, 33). This secondary growth is the source of most of Kanai Kougei's techigi, because the forests were replanted with economically useful species (see chapter 6). Virgin forest is now found only in the mountains at the center of the island, in an area designated a UNESCO World Natural Heritage site. These are some of the most sacred of Amami's mountains, but they are also the least accessible, found far from any village. Even today, the roads to Kinsakubaru Virgin Forest, a national park and "special protection zone," are challenging for drivers. Toguchi is outside of these special zones, in the northeast of the island, and isn't subject to restrictions regarding cutting trees and collecting wild plants and animals (except those that are endangered). The forest remains sacred (or threatening) to many islanders, the consequence of mythologies around kami and yōkai alongside the omnipresent threat of poisonous snakes, resulting in a taboo preventing many from entering. But I would propose that an invisible boundary based on historical land use and cosmologies around nature separates the village—where people today live and work—from the mountains, forest, and sea, shepherding the way people in Toguchi continue to use their resources. This hypothesis might explain the presence of both a reverence for nature and polluting practices.

For example, opposition to the development of environments historically associated with Amamian spirituality was documented as early as the 1970s, when plans to build a central gasoline storage unit on the island of Edatekujima (a former noro stronghold) were abandoned because of environmental activism (Kuwahara 2011). In 1995 plans to build a golf course were scrapped after a lawsuit was brought over concerns that it would threaten the endangered Amami black rabbit's mountain habitat (see chapter 4). During my fieldwork, Japan's Ministry of Tourism asked Amami to facilitate the docking of huge cruise ships, but plans to construct new quays have been repeatedly dropped because the authorities "couldn't gain the understanding of residents" (Sado 2019). There has also been concern about military expansion, a consequence of China's and North Korea's hostility in Asia. While various Japanese army sites have been constructed without public consultation, the threat of American influence looms large, Amamians knowing too well the social and environmental impact that US military bases have had on neighboring Okinawa.

Whereas cruise ships and army barracks cause both a visual blight and a verifiable environmental impact, it should not come as a surprise that a low level of environmental recklessness occurs in the backyards of residents' properties, something that might also be attributed to a question of scale. Scholars have shown that even if a society respects nature, there will always be a human tendency to engage in ecological destruction, as occurred historically when societies were considered less secular (Hanley, 1997; Ellen 2021). While the practice of recycling is known to be "precise and detailed" across Japan (Kanatsu 2013, 303), attitudes toward recycling were observed to be inconsistent in Amami and fly-tipping common. Amamians also love to burn things, which Kazu-san even jokingly suggested was the Shachō's hobby, despite the fact that bonfires are technically illegal in Japan. Typically, agricultural and gardening waste is burned, and this is generally accepted, yet what you will routinely notice across the island is the black smoke of burning plastic, a habit the Shachō had adopted that angered Yukihito-san. It should be noted, however, that prior to at least 1960, there were no local-authority waste incinerators accessible to the island, perhaps accounting

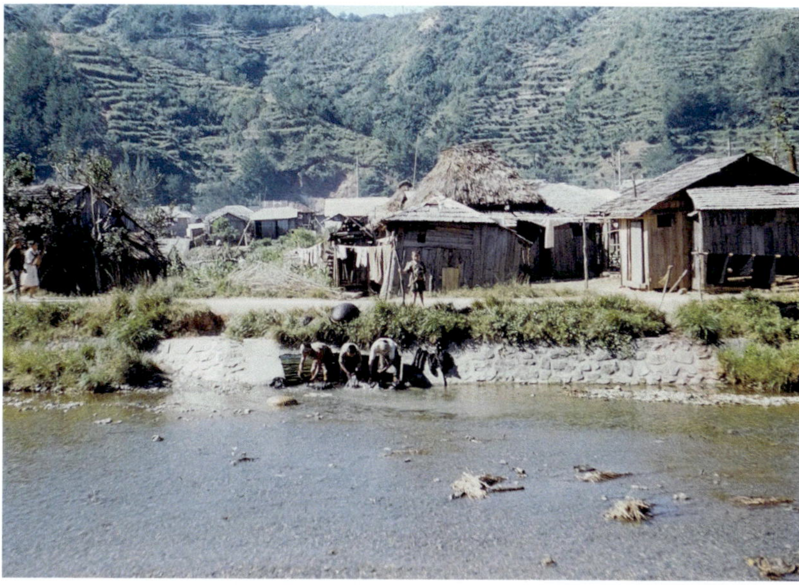

Figure 5.16 *Dyers washing yarns in the river, 1951–52. Douglas Haring Papers, University Archives, Special Collections Research Center, Syracuse University Libraries, Syracuse, New York.*

for this enduring habit (Ministry of the Environment of Japan 2012, 6), while the cost of removing unwanted domestic appliances is high on an island where incomes are typically low.

The disposal of dye chemicals also happens within the workshop's walls, the waste flowing to the river via concrete drains in the village before heading out to sea. The Shachō explained that dyehouses were always located near the river (figure 5.16), because in the past, drainage infrastructure and water mains didn't exist. As in many countries, rivers were (and still are) the sinks that transport waste to the sea, given that, by their very nature, rivers are self-cleansing and the mere scale of large water bodies disperses pollution. Recent news reports in the UK, for instance, highlight that this remains a global condition, as research has revealed that private water utility companies frequently (and illegally) discharge raw sewage into local rivers and onto coastlines.

This conceptualization of the river in Amami was brought to the fore when Kanai Kougei was experiencing a rat problem—a serious issue because rats attract dangerous snakes—and I observed the Shachō nonchalantly throw a rat attached to a plastic glue trap into the water. Given the island's spatially segregated cosmology, where nature and the gods inhabit the mountains, sea, and sky and humans the village, this is perhaps not surprising. Although no longer held on Amami, each spring the island would hold ceremonies called *hamaore*, the Amamian version of the Japanese tradition *mushi-okuri* (sending off insects) (Ivy 1995, 136), in which harmful pests were collected in agricultural fields, loaded onto leaves or small hand-carved canoes, and expelled from the community on the tide. Mary Douglas ([1966] 2001), in her classic work on pollution, states that, whether secular or spiritual, as time passes, classifications that create order in our lives should be updated to account for changing practices.[6] But confidence often lies with past experience, meaning that "uncomfortable facts which refuse to be fitted in" are "ignor[ed] or distort[ed] so that they do not disturb these established assumptions." "Dirt," whether toxic chemicals or pests, material entities that threaten to disrupt systems of order and power, must be expelled from the village because pollution occurs when "matter [is] out of place" (Douglas [1966] 2001, 38). So in this configuration, is washing a rat or a chemical downriver simply a way of rejecting pollution, ritual or otherwise, in the modern era?

"That's Natural Because It's Chemical"

For the first five months of my time working at Kanai Kougei, I assumed its wastewater was being treated at a sewage works. But it was not until I made a comparative visit to Takarajima Senkou, a natural dyeing studio in Chikugo on the mainland island of Kyūshū, that I began to question this assumption.[7] The owner, Ogomori-san, was dyeing apparel for customers in the same network as those who commissioned Kanai Kougei, but the area is renowned for traditional *Kurume gasuri* (ikat) production.[8] In the past, yarns for this popular cloth would have been dyed using a plant-based indigo pigment. But dyers have the option of using a chemical variant first synthetized in Germany in the late nineteenth century, which is the basis for global industrial indigo production today. Whether natural or synthetic, indigo molecules (indican) are essentially the same, but the depth of color achievable between natural and synthetic variants is vast, and methods of dyeing differ. Like Kanai Kougei, Ogomori-san uses caustic soda and hydro for dyeing with Indian indigo (obtained from the plant *Indigofera tinctoria*) for economic efficiency. But, as she explained, a pH of 9 will kill fish, and it is therefore essential to lower the pH of the very alkaline waters of the dyebath (around pH 10–11.5) before they enter the drainage. She told me that, when establishing her studio, she researched whether to use tap or groundwater, and how wastewater should be disposed of, by observing the setup at other dyeing studios and following local government standards. She installed

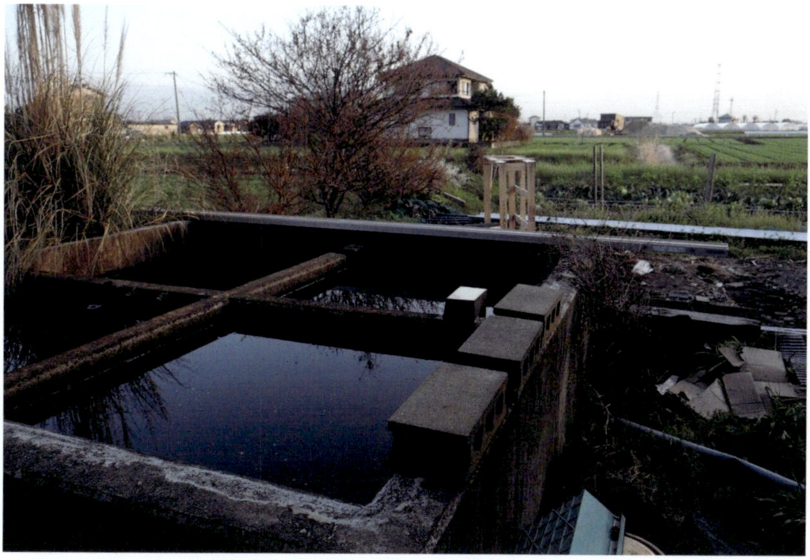

Figure 5.17 *Wastewater tanks at the Takarajima Senkou studio.*

a twenty-three-ton-capacity wastewater tank system (figure 5.17) to filter impurities for sewage treatment and released the remainder into the drainage only once the pH had neutralized and become reoxygenated.

Ogomori-san lamented that local dyers needed to take more responsibility for water disposal, because the studios she visited were doing nothing or else their tank systems were too small to have any purpose. She explained that many dyers claimed this wasn't a problem because they used *sukumo* ai (obtained from *Polygonum tinctorium*), a low-impact but expensive Japanese indigo paste that uses a composting method produced on Shikoku Island. Before the introduction of synthetic indigo and chemical agents to Japan in the early twentieth century, indigo vats were naturally fermented. In the place of hydro, bacteria remove oxygen. The naturally occurring bacteria in the bath must first be cultured over a number of weeks, then kept warm and fed a diet of locally available foodstuffs. In Amami, Yukihito-san had a sukumo vat that he kept for "special projects." Its pH was raised with wood ash from Kanai Kougei's own furnace, and it was wrapped in a quilted blanket and fed with shōchū and *miki* (an Amamian fermented sweet potato and rice drink). Natural vats are literally alive, so this method takes time and care, demanding vigilance equivalent to keeping a pet. Natural indigo vats are the ideal; they are what people imagine indigo dyeing consists of. But in an industrial setting, chemical baths using Indian indigo or synthetic German pigment are the compromise to this ideal, as they are cheaper, quicker, and stronger in color than natural vats. As Ogomori-san explained, dyehouses cannot break even if they use sukumo alone. She reported she'd witnessed empty boxes of "indigo pure" (a synthetic pigment) lying around local dye studios, suggesting that a dyer's claims of using only sukumo obscured the mixed use necessary to be economically sustainable.

The actions of the Kurume dyers and those I observed in Amami are what I believe my colleague Kazuko would call "really Shōwa," indicating the attitudes of those born and reaching adulthood between 1926 and 1989, a period named after the reigning emperor Hirohito. *Really Shōwa* first arose in conversations we shared around the additive *amino* (MSG, or monosodium glutamate), an amino acid responsible for umami flavors occurring naturally in foodstuffs such as cheese or seaweed. It was chemically isolated and promoted as a condiment at the turn of the twentieth century in Japan, and today it is ubiquitous in junk food globally. Kazuko told me her mom uses it liberally, believing it natural because it's (chemically) derived from cane sugar and was advertised during the Shōwa era to "make *any* dish delicious." This uptake of new materials occurred during the "Chemical Century" (Langston 2010), a time when industrialization and the two world wars furthered scientific advancement, resulting in products for expanding consumer markets that brought convenience to everyday tasks. War led to global shortages of chemicals essential for dyeing but also for photographic supplies and drug manufacturing (Beer 1959). These shortages kick-started home chemical industries, which developed military-grade substances but also products for the dyer, home cook, and agriculturalist. Governments, meanwhile, wanted to boost public welfare and the economy, so they allowed industry to flout environmental regulation in the name of progress.

Postwar government policy in Japan, for example, embraced the rhetoric of the Green Revolution by encouraging the use of chemicals and field consolidation in agriculture, processes that between 1946 and 2012 reduced farmers' work hours by 86 percent, increasing yield by 60.7 percent (Katayama et al. 2015, 75). But the use of toxic chemicals, such as the rice fungicide organic mercury, resulted in serious health consequences for humans and the environment (Katayama et al. 2015). The acceleration of industrialization during the Meiji era, and again during the rebuilding of the economy after World War II, saw a general disregard for the environment by government and industry that has filtered down to the farthest corners of the country (see chapter 3 of this book).

This pattern of industrialization is seen as a compromise by those in power, a resolution equivalent to that depicted by anthropologist Anna Lora-Wainwright (2017) in her study of everyday experiences of pollution in industrialized rural

China. Lora-Wainwright describes how China's "development strategy" affects communities subject to rapid development who suffer from "weak pollution regulation." Local authorities may ignore industrial negligence because they "face hard trade-offs between long-term sustainability and short-term needs to provide employment and support public services" through taxation (2017, 4). As a result of international pressure and its economic implications, in the 1970s Japan introduced laws to curb environmental damage, reforming them again in the 1990s. But the devastating 2011 nuclear disaster in Fukushima—the combined consequence of earthquake, tsunami, and human error—suggests Japan's environmental issues remain unresolved. While these issues have been widely discussed (B. Walker 2010; Kanatsu 2013), as Lora-Wainwright (2017, 6) writes, such content often focuses on places where environmental pollution produces "clear health effects." But by examining pollution as part of the "daily grind," she reveals the "slow process through which environmental plight may become embedded and normalized" (6–9).

Textiles provide a familiar reference point for comprehending how industrial chemicals have become part of the "daily grind." The global textile industry has become reliant on synthetic chemistry to design low-cost performance-based materials at speed in a fantastic array of colors, while reducing the labor of care carried out by producer and consumer (Schneider 1994, 4; Küchler and Oakley 2014). Yet this shift from potentially benign natural resources such as wool, cotton, and natural dyestuffs to petrochemical materials has come with significant environmental consequences.[9] Equally, knowledge of textile production has mostly been erased from public knowledge, at least in the Global North. In recent years, the media has focused on the environmental and health impacts caused by synthetic textiles (Crang et al. 2020) and their microfiber (plastic) filaments (Greenpeace UK 2019). But light has also been shined on the production and use of less visible per- and polyfluoroalkyl substances (PFAS), which have gained a wide-ranging utility, including improving the stain, water, and fire resistance of textiles (Renfrew and Pearson 2021, 146). Invented in the United States during World War II to repel oil, water, and heat, these "forever chemicals" are increasingly being recognized as damaging to human health because they resist degradation and bioaccumulate in the body, while the scale of their environmental impact is alarming.[10] Anthropologists Daniel Renfrew and Thomas Pearson (2021) describe how companies such as DuPont and 3M, the latter of which developed the well-known brands Teflon and Scotchgard used for textiles, were aware of the dangers in the 1960s but concealed in-house research to protect business interests. Because the US government encouraged self-regulation, only recently did the Joe Biden administration take action to address the situation (Renfrew and Pearson 2021, 152–53; Reuters 2023). The use of PFAS in the manufacture of domestic items (including most recently the controversy surrounding Thinx period underwear) highlights their troubling nature in that they remain invisible until their "slow violence" (Shapiro and Kirksey 2017, 488) presents itself (Choy 2020; Gupta 2023). Science and technology are notoriously exclusive (Shapiro and Kirksey 2017, 486), meaning that performance chemicals have seamlessly glided from the lab to the coating of a textile and into our bloodstreams and waterways without the public's awareness of their presence or knowledge of their impact. The chemical industry has thus brought an unimaginable level of convenience and temporal and financial efficiency to production processes and everyday tasks that, while liberating, might also be reframed as an economic and ethical bind.

Conscientious consumers are consequently beginning to reject synthetics in favor of natural materials that reflect their environmental consciousness and connoisseurship, the result of wider societal change setting them apart from previous generations. Yet my research shows the extent to which the petrochemical industry has seeped into our material culture and how rejecting one material over another is not a simple solution. At Kanai Kougei, short-term fixes have been sought in new materials to speed up the production of naturally dyed textiles and improve performance. This has allowed the company to remain competitive and to reach a level of economic sustainability despite environmental risks. This became apparent in a conversation I had with Eriko Kanai. She told me about a meeting between Yukihito-san and Motoji-san, an Amamian kimono cloth seller with a shop in Tokyo's exclusive Ginza neighborhood. Motoji-san had been invited to an exhibition held at Kamawanu, a client of Kanai Kougei's, that sells hand-printed, hand-dyed *tenugui* (hand towels). Eriko-san explained: "I heard Motoji-san was happy to be introduced to Kamawanu people by Yukihito and he thought, 'Both Kanai-kun and I [Motoji-san] will have to change the way we think continuously.'" She elaborated with an example: "In the old days, the typical *Oshima tsumugi* was black, right? When white obi [wide belts worn with kimono] became fashionable, we had a customer complain that tsumugi stained the obi. We could tell them it's the real Oshima tsumugi—the color comes off. But we cannot say that now. Apparently, Motoji-san told Yukihito, 'You guys have to think about why the color comes off and how you can prevent that.'"

Before industrial chemicals were introduced to Japan, production was slower, meaning the longevity of a color could be conserved by resting items, or "putting them to sleep" (*nekaseru*) to increase the bonds between dye and fiber and improve their colorfastness. Indigo garments were typically kept in the dark for one to two years before they were worn, to let the indigo "mature." However, such time frames do not suit the immediacy of the fashion calendar today, where four collections might be designed, developed, manufactured, and sold in one year. Rather than using time to improve the performance of natural dyes, Kanai Kougei has evolved its craft in line with contemporary living by seeking new solutions to old problems. Chemical assistants such as hypren NFS, a silicone-urethane resin emulsion bought from a Kyoto-based textile materials supplier, are used as a barrier to maintain colorfastness on apparel products (see chapter 2). Staff told me that Kanai Kougei also uses pretreatments to help textiles absorb color and softening agents labeled with a "chemicals toxic to aquatic wildlife" hazard symbol. As one worker explained, expressing concerns about the environment, "Many customers tell me Kanai Kougei products are amazing, with less color fading than other natural dyes. That's natural because it's chemical."

These temporal fixes have allowed the company to attract customers who can pay a premium—high-end designers and artisans with an interest in craft, tradition, and the environment—but who also expect speed and a high level of standardization and color stability. The contemporary use of natural dyes should conform to what one considers "craft"—including the materials and methods of production carried out by skilled laborers—but the product's performance should conform to the vagaries of modern lifestyles: washing machines, personal hygiene products, and pale-colored soft furnishings. The irony is that the high tannin content of techigi liquid used in dorozome creates a textile with some water and stain resistance while also improving the tensile strength of the fibers. Indigo carries this property, too, and has antibacterial and antifungal qualities, just one of the reasons—alongside its mass production by enslaved and indentured laborers—that blue became popular for workwear in the nineteenth century. Nevertheless, knowledge of these inherent properties, which reduce the need for excessive laundering and increase the lifespan of a garment, have largely been forgotten by designers and members of the public who focus on aesthetics, while a reconfiguration of time remains largely absent from sustainability discourse in commercial fashion. Yet if time and money were invested in their manufacture and knowledge of aftercare embraced, naturally dyed garments could offer real sustainability to the fashion industry.

"The Amamian Way"

Observing the "daily grind" as a member of staff at Kanai Kougei gave me the opportunity to examine water management across a year. After I had returned from Ogomori-san's studio in Kyūshū, I casually began asking questions, prompting

Yukihito-san to instruct employees to dilute used indigo before disposing it to lessen its impact. Yukihito-san later told me that drainage was an area where Kanai Kougei was "not adequate with [its] work." During discussions with colleagues, I heard that Yukihito-san had suggested installing septic tanks, but his father, the Shachō, had refused, saying "it was not the Amamian way." As Yukihito-san explained:

> What is needed is for the [dyebath] to be poured into the drainage only once it is oxidized and neutralized [and] some solvents need to be filtered and scrapped. We would need the tool for filtering and the space to operate it. We should set it up. But the Shachō and the tsumugi industry lean toward the industrious way of doing things. I understand they do not want to add more cost. The tsumugi industry's wages won't change, right? So, they cannot make the move to invest in setting up such a system. I understand that they operated without it so far but . . . with the case of techigi, there shouldn't be any problem because we simply use what we take from the trees—it only colors the water. But with the case of ai, I know what is actually being used—we would need to take care of that.

At Kanai Kougei, it is not the pursuit of untold profit that accounts for decision-making, because wages and turnover are low and the industry's future remains precarious. Yet economic gains have historically come at a cost to the environment, and this appears to have been the case as recently as the early 2000s, when the company diversified. Before this time, I was told that the Shachō outsourced his indigo work to a natural indigo-dyeing studio in Amami. After this closed in the 1990s, he set about dyeing with sukumo ai himself. Synthetic and chemically assisted indigo was eventually embraced for economic efficiency—yet without additional infrastructure to account for the risk of pollution. While Ogomori-san was able to build her studio in line with current environmental debates and local government regulations, Yukihito-san explained that the Shachō has simply followed "the Amamian way" since Kanai Kougei was founded in 1982, when the materials he was using were considered low-impact. The Kanais' attribute a reluctance to implement change more recently to two factors.

First, the prefectural authorities still consider Kanai Kougei's work distinct from industrial processes, so they do not enforce regulations. While they fall beneath the fifty cubic meters of water usage per day that is subject to compulsory industrial wastewater management stipulated by the Japanese government, I was told that Kanai Kougei, located within a residential village, abides by local regulations (Kagoshima Prefecture, n.d.). In addition, it appears that Kagoshima Prefecture, unlike more industrialized areas, does not implement its own regu-

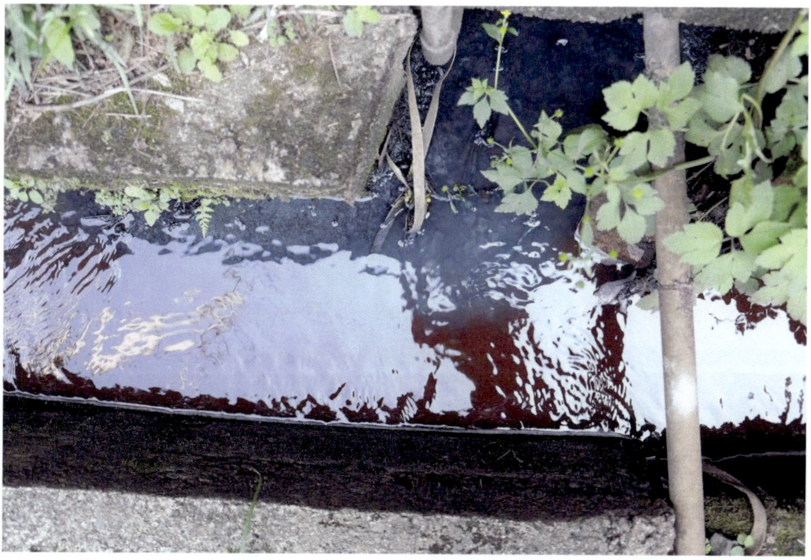

Figure 5.18 *Wastewater from the two workshops—aizome (blue) and dorozome (red)—merges before heading to the river.*

lations for dyeing, perhaps a result of its textile industries having contracted to such a great extent and to the outdated assumption that natural dyeing is "preindustrial." Amami might also be said to be afflicted by infrastructural lag. Being on an island, residents rely on septic tanks, but in some villages they use nonflushing toilets and channel wastewater from baths and washing machines out to sea. With a declining population, particularly in rural areas, Japan's water utility companies, predominantly run by the prefecture or local municipality, are facing ominous economic prospects, as there isn't adequate tax revenue to invest in infrastructural updates (Urakami et al. 2021).[11] The central government's relaxed approach to regulating big industry, meanwhile, has hardly set an example for smaller industrial users such as Kanai Kougei.

Second, the workshop was built around an existing drainage system, meaning Kanai Kougei would need to cover not only the cost of the tank itself but also the remodeling of the whole workshop, an expense that would outweigh their ability to generate income. My case study parallels the experience of producers in low-income countries such as Bangladesh, where Maiko Sakamoto et al. (2019) claim that government legislation that demands factories construct effluent treatment plants has failed. While this demonstrates how the challenge of seeking sustainability traverses national borders, the extent of the problem in

Bangladesh is extreme. The government has declared three rivers in the Dhaka region "biologically dead" (Chowdhury 2019), while effluent containing dye chemicals and heavy metals from textile factories floods agricultural fields and contaminants find their way into local food markets (Sakamoto et al. 2019, 2). Authorities blame noncompliance on inadequate monitoring and enforcement, but Sakamoto et al. argue that the major barrier to implementing effluent treatment plants is the lack of information about which system to buy and the cost of importing, installing, and running equipment (6). While large companies, those subject to compliance pressure from international commissioning agents, can cover costs to avoid losing business, smaller companies cannot make the short-term investment. Consequently, fines were given to the smaller companies, who often took unrecorded piecework outsourced from the larger companies. If the government were to crack down further, these smaller companies would lose their competitive edge and be forced to close, with wider implications for the workforce. "Small-scale" is often assumed to be more sustainable because low production quantities will have less environmental impact, and increased intimacy between workers, materials, and place "should" result in better care (Thomas 2020, 732). However, this example and my own research challenge this assumption. Small companies are often able to pass under the radar, and even if they wanted to institute change, they often lack the resources or agency to do so. Consequently, at Kanai Kougei the running of the workshop, the employment of craftspeople, and the continuation of tradition were prioritized above the environmental consequences of their practices of disposal.

This highlights one of the key issues with the route toward sustainability, that solutions to the use of toxic chemicals or the overarching problem of overconsumption are sought at the level of singular actions with definitive, ends-oriented goals. "Technoscientific solutions" (Gibson-Graham et al. 2019, 7), such as filtration systems or the pushing of regulation oversight onto local authorities, are production-level strategies adopted to maintain economic growth rather than to promote ongoing, adaptive, structural change. Even sustainability frameworks such as life cycle assessments, developed by scientists in the 1960s and widely used by government and industry, do not always capture inconsistencies. Life cycle assessments analyze a product's environmental impact from "cradle to grave," or from raw material extraction to production, transportation, use, and disposal (see Geyer 2021). Yet given their scope, life cycle assessments can't account for the vagaries of human behavior, embedded cosmologies, social conflicts, infrastructural breakdowns, or economic pressures that account for environmental neglect. It should also be stressed that the desire for sustainability—often sought by urban elites—transfers the time, labor, and responsibility it requires onto others within "an uneven geography of power" (Yamada et al. 2022, 8). This often occurs without the necessary knowledge or finances to enable those ultimately responsible to guarantee a product's safe manufacture, use, or disposal (Gregson et al. 2016; Zhang 2019).

In Bangladesh, clients made demands on factories as a way to offset their own ethical responsibilities without taking into consideration the unique set of circumstances that would make their adoption challenging. Yukihito-san, meanwhile, has inherited the legacies of twentieth-century industrial capitalism while striving to sustain the future of the family business, which supports local employment and Amamian tradition—a lot to ask of an individual. He is aware of the potentially negative impact textile chemicals have, and to avoid making spurious claims, he has expressed a desire to make the necessary changes. But in recent years his reputation as a craftsman has grown, meaning he is now so overworked that he lacks the time to put words into action (see chapter 2). While it could be said that his father was subject to the same pressures, the role of the craftsperson has fundamentally changed in Yukihito-san's lifetime. In previous generations, craftspeople in Japan (such as the tsumugi dyers) would spend their careers perfecting and taking responsibly for a defined set of processes (known as *bungyō*) within a close-knit community of production overseen by an external body. But since the late 1990s, the business of craft across Europe and North America, but also in Japan, has necessitated an embrace of flexibility, innovation, and entrepreneurship, with the craftsperson being responsible for other areas of business, including sales, publicity, management, and design, as well as for the manufacture of the craft items themselves. While localism is essential to the authenticity and functioning of craft, the uptake of advanced communications means this entrepreneurial style of business relies on dispersed national and international supply chains and global trading networks. Yet commissioning agents from afar cannot easily grasp an understanding of geographically defined resource extraction, production processes, and contextual time frames, meaning that the conditions that define sustainable practice in one context cannot necessarily be imprinted onto another.

Making Settlements

The myth of sustainability, which can be understood via the imaginaries of "tradition" and "nature," has been perpetuated at Kanai Kougei in order to maintain the status quo. These imaginaries are rooted in a nostalgia for an era before industrial capitalism, conveniently sidestepping the reality of twenty-first-century production. What is troubling about certain industrial chemicals and materials is their invisible nature—with their misuse or improper disposal rendering them "secular spirits of the Anthropocene," which Nils Bubandt (2017, G124) suggests emerge when nature collides with industrial capitalism, producing an "aporia," or sense of uncertainty outside of one's control. This indicates that chemicals themselves are not always at fault, because the uncertainty they produce is the result of human action. If the chemicals needed to prepare synthetic dyebaths are handled correctly through make, use, and disposal, a case could be made to defend them when compared with a natural indigo bath prepared with sukumo. While sukumo seems more environmentally friendly at the dyeing and disposal stage, in a comparative study one would need to ascertain how sustainable sukumo production is, from seed to dye paste, examining pesticide and fertilizer use in cultivation, water runoff, and labor conditions. This highlights the complexity of assessing sustainability, demonstrating how the quantity of harmful materials, context of their use, or ineffective disposal are all potentially damaging factors. At Kanai Kougei, commissioning agents take the services offered on face value, tending not to question the origins of materials, conditions of labor, and use and disposal of natural resources, especially when, as I frequently observed, companies squeeze the workshop on turnaround time and price.[12] The costs of natural dyeing remain high, despite access to groundwater, cheap labor, and a reliance on fossil fuels and materials with ambiguous origins. Yet without these conditions, coloring textiles in this way on this island wouldn't be deemed financially viable at all.

Nevertheless, the pressure to uphold the image that natural dyeing is sustainable will only intensify as the climate and biodiversity crisis worsens, meaning production processes in polluting industries like textiles will be subject to increased scrutiny, regulation, and cost. Change may occur if local authorities implement or fund infrastructural updates or increase regulation or if individuals seek resolutions that align with the responsibilities they wish to uphold toward their own bodies, families, and conceptions of community, whether or not that conception stretches to nonhumans. Koki demonstrated this in his village of Sakibaru, where all household wastewater is washed out to sea. While toilets are dry, the drains empty onto Tomori beach, popular with tourists but also nesting sea turtles. When Koki realized this, he switched his detergents to more expensive, eco-friendly alternatives, prioritizing the issue despite his low income. Koki's background and his exposure to the global circulation of ideas meant he sought what sociologist Kevin Hetherington calls a "settlement" for the "haunting" generated by failed disposal. Hetherington (2004, 172) claims we make such settlements with ourselves but also with "others in terms of our memories, a sense of tradition, and through our relations not only with our contemporaries but also with our ancestors and future generations." Kazuko, too, refused to work with the ai after she became pregnant with her third child. At first the smell didn't agree with her morning sickness, but she later read online that hydrosulphates can be harmful to unborn babies. Like the respect paid to spiritual beings that reside in inanimate objects or landscape features, the "one never knows . . . and it doesn't hurt" (Daniels 2009a, 167) attitude was adopted.

Further from our discussions that revealed the environmentally conducive actions his peers at Takarajima Senkou are taking and the uncertainty about the impact of their practices of disposal, Yukihito-san has quietly gone about improving the drainage situation at Kanai Kougei. Yet instituting change is by no means straightforward, because polluting practices in Amami have become what Lora-Wainwright (2017, 9) calls "embedded and normalized." This is the result of decades of habit instituted by the Kanais' ancestors and contemporaries within the tsumugi community, where the flow of water has been used to dispose of ritual pollution but also industrial waste. In the final chapter, I show how community dispossession of land and resources, as an impact of geopolitical and economic forces, has led to the breakdown of ecological knowledge of using and conserving ecosystems like the river. Bubandt claims that "in the Anthropocene, both climate science and biology seem to bring spirits, once thought to have been killed by secular thought, back to life" (2017, G125). As I have demonstrated, Amamian spirits have not been "killed off"; they have simply taken new forms, adapting to contemporary circumstances. So one might ask, Like the wildlife discussed in chapter 4 that have become revered totems in Amami, how might the river be shown the same respect?

6

Dyeing with the Earth

Arriving at Kanai Kougei one day in April, Kazuko showed me a sprig of *sharinbai* (yeddo hawthorn) blossoms she had picked by the *dorota* (figure 6.1). This enabled me to identify the slow-growing evergreen throughout Amami's villages, planted in the yard of the Tatsugo power station and dotted wild throughout the forest or by the sea—a position it favored most. *Techigi* is the Amamian name by which both the tree and the liquid used for *dorozome* is known. Although found all over Japan and Korea, the species remains valued in Amami; Kazu-san explained that its fleshy black berries were eaten in times of famine—his mother used to eat them, and he remembers snacking on them, too. Kazuko tried them on my behalf when I was back in the UK and the berries returned to season: "THIS IS NOT FOOD!" she typed. "It tastes like a weed or flower we don't eat." During dorozome, techigi's red tannins—molecules that protect trees from bacteria, fungi, and pests—bind with the iron that occurs naturally in Amamian mud, fixing color to the cloth (figures 6.2 and 6.3). But techigi is also a strong

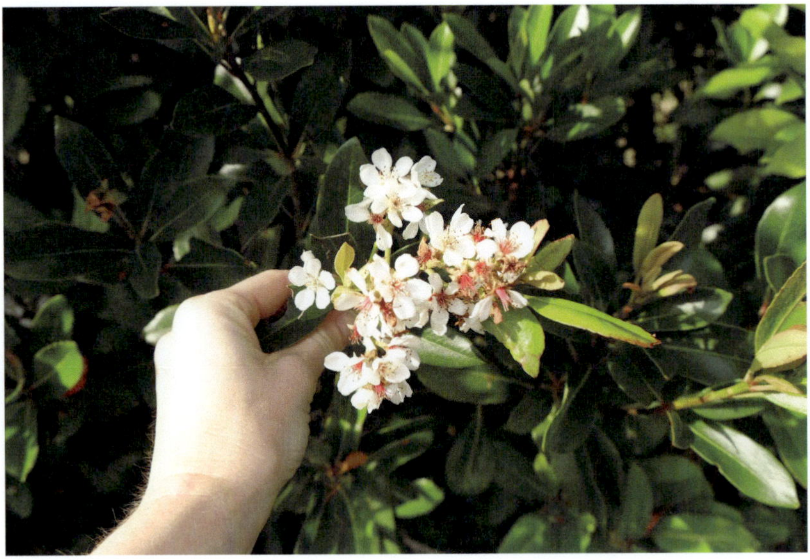

Figure 6.1 *Blossoms of the sharinbai tree in spring.*

colorant, because the density of tannins means a textile can be changed from white to pink to red to brown or, with repeated applications and the assistance of iron, to black. The majority of techigi timber the workshop sources today comes from the clear-cutting of local forests; the woodcutters set techigi aside as "waste" and ship the other felled trees to the mainland for processing into paper. As techigi tannins are red in color, the trees are unusable in the paper industry because they would contaminate and tint the pulp.

Every few weeks, around six hundred kilograms of techigi would arrive at Kanai Kougei, but it took me almost a year to establish exactly where the trees came from. The contemporary dependence of Amami's natural dyeing workshops on the waste products of the forestry industry, and the illicit and informal processes required to obtain them, slowly became apparent. In the first few months of my time at the workshop, logs would arrive in the back of a beaten-up silver hatchback driven by the enigmatic Tanaka-san, often accompanied by his girlfriend.[1] On one occasion, the Shachō told Kazuko that Tanaka-san had brought us a stolen tree. "Stolen?" I asked, a little surprised. "Yes," said Kazuko, "he took it from someone's mountain without gaining permission." As we chatted, Eriko-san emerged from the office with a bunch of thousand-yen notes. Sometime after the New Year, I heard that Tanaka-san had died unexpectedly after suffering a heart attack while hunting octopus. After he passed away, the

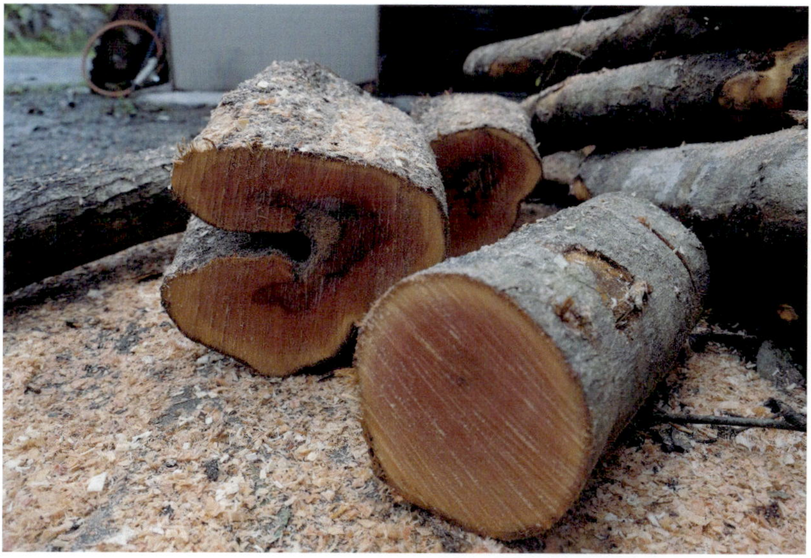

Figure 6.2 *A cross section of wood shows the deep color of techigi tannins.*

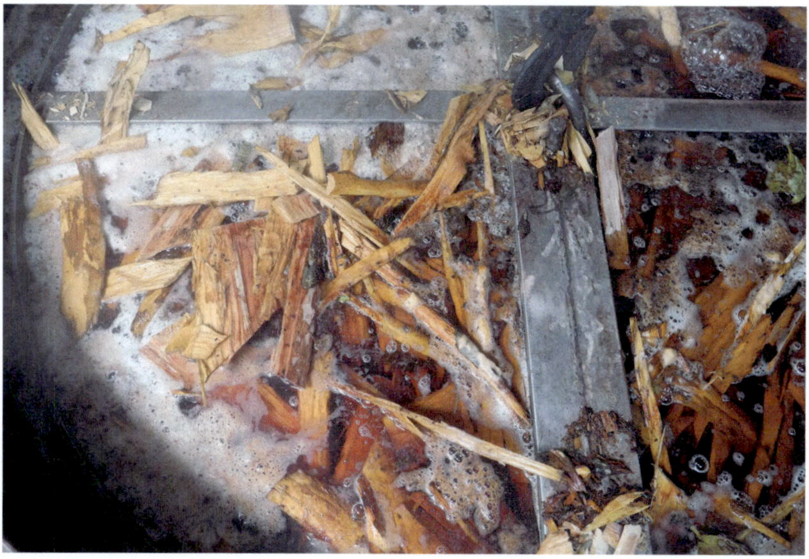

Figure 6.3 *Extracting techigi tannins during boiling.*

job of collecting techigi fell to the craftsmen. Takahito-san and Yuske-san, the youngest male members of staff, did the collection for a while, but after Yuske-san left the workshop, the female dyers would also take turns, returning looking exhausted. Obtaining techigi was clearly becoming increasingly precarious, presenting a little-acknowledged threat to the future of Amami's textile traditions that are already subject to economic strain. Equally, this precarity represents significant shifts in the local consciousness around techigi and its place in Amamian material culture.

In this chapter, I examine in depth how and why a resource with a wide-ranging utility has been devalued to the extent that it is considered "waste," with residents, including craftspeople, struggling to ascertain its "real worth." I use ethnography to reveal the "messiness of practice" (Law 2004, 18–19) and demonstrate how dyeing work and the wider textile industry in Amami is built on a foundation of low-wage labor and materials with ambiguous origin. I use the craftsperson's relationship with nature via trees and land to argue that regimes of privatization and centralized resource management have dispossessed local communities of access to materials—and knowledge of how to use and sustain those materials—which contradicts the imperative to preserve both the environment and tradition. I undertake an examination of how this situation has occurred by exploring the history of resource management on the island and changes in property law at the national level. I consider how, prior to the 1950s, Amamian residents relied on the utility of their environment, so they understood the material, economic, and spiritual value of sustaining natural resources. Yet after World War II the "improvement" of land and bureaucratic frameworks that governed it led to dispossession, meaning that Amamians today are unable to steward natural resources in a way that is beneficial for a wide conception of community.

Techigi is an important case study, as its story reveals how mutable and interchangeable the concepts of "waste" and "value" are that have formed between the nineteenth and twenty-first centuries. These concepts and their material and logistical formalizations have disrupted the ways that local natural resources are accessed, used, and cared for in Amami. Significantly, I pinpoint the impact this has had on a geographically specific and culturally important craft process that is being framed as a sustainable fix to environmentally damaging mass production in times of uncertainty. By focusing on trees little considered beyond the Ryūkyūs, I demonstrate how in supply chain capitalism value can be salvaged from waste and valorized through handcrafted labor, which repackages it as a commodity with a "traditional" and "green" veneer.

This very local case study prompts one to ask whether a divorce from the land is, in some respects, responsible for the contemporary ecological crisis. Although this question goes beyond the scope of this book, I use the context of Amami to show how locally specific social, economic, and cultural conditions and histories might affect a wider ability to tackle ecological crisis. I question how this situation might be addressed by reconfiguring models of land management but remain skeptical about the authorities' desire and will to bring about collaborative change.

Salvaging Value from Waste

As part of his ethnographic survey, Douglas Haring undertook an examination of Amamian industry, including forestry, and noted: "The stands of sharinbai [techigi] planted by the Japanese forest service are not being maintained. Amami foresters say that natural reproduction of these trees will suffice; the tsumugi dyers, however, complain that the supply of dyewood is shrinking" (1952, 5). Haring's report was influential, and postwar investment by the occupying Americans and the Japanese government tackled the supply issues with techigi, meaning that by the 1960s the textile industry could respond to a boom in demand for *Oshima tsumugi*. By creating a system to industrially fell techigi and deliver it to chipping stores, Amami's sixty dyeing workshops received a ready supply of timber, allowing them to meet peak production of 290,000 rolls of kimono cloth in 1972. In 1982, when the Shachō established Kanai Kougei, the increasing trend toward Westernized clothing, and later the burst of Japan's economic bubble, meant that *tsumugi* production was already in decline, as was the role of the chipping stores. The Shachō consequently purchased the same chipping machine he uses today and relies on his own social networks to obtain enough techigi to sustain his workshop. Kanai Kougei is one of only four companies that continue to produce tsumugi yarns, and only two of these companies, including Kanai Kougei, accept regular work. The industry faces a precarious future, but Kanai Kougei's diversification means that while other workshops have maintained a skeleton staff, Kanai Kougei has more work than its team of four tsumugi dyers and six apparel dyers can accept. The workshop has struggled to attract committed young apprentices to carry out this labor-intensive yet satisfying traditional craftwork, which demands a six-day working week (see chapters 1 and 2). The situation at Kanai Kougei reflects a wider problem across Amami of shortages of people willing to do low-wage manual labor. Securing access to techigi is therefore another burden on the time but also the bodies of the workers.

Near the end of my fieldwork, I followed the Shachō on the drive to collect techigi from the forested area of Uken in southern Amami. The fact that it took so long for me to experience this trip was explained by the unpredictability of

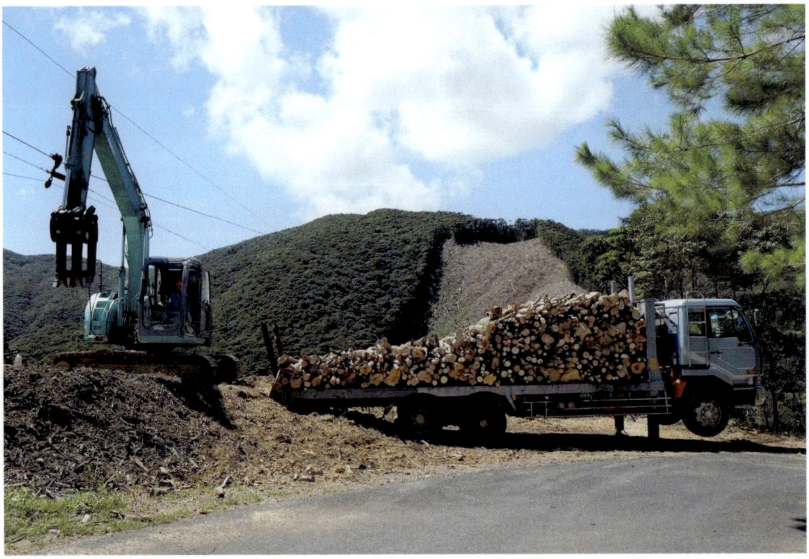

Figure 6.4 *Mixed-species wood is loaded onto a truck for export to the mainland.*

the arrangement by which Kanai Kougei was able to source techigi following Tanaka-san's death. When techigi is available, the woodcutters working on land being clear-cut sell it for cash on the side. The woodcutters phone the Shachō, and a member of Kanai Kougei staff is sent to pick up the techigi. Climbing through the mountains, we drove for several miles down a poorly maintained road. A great brown scar in a landscape blanketed with forest identified the clear-cut site. The simple skyline logging technology—a wooden tripod hoist suspending a pulley of steel wires attached to a gasoline-fueled motor reel to drag trees off the mountain—demonstrated both a lack of investment and the remote location's resistance to more advanced infrastructure (figure 6.4). The woodcutters, two men over fifty, welcomed us. As they loaded up the Shachō's truck with techigi, the suspension buckling under the weight, I confirmed with them that the "low-grade" mixed broadleaf forest—*shii* (Okinawan chestnut), *sarusuberi* (crepe myrtle), and *matsu* (pine)—was cut in rotation every forty years and extracted for making paper pulp (figure 6.5).

During tsumugi's boom period the trees' roots were extracted from the ground, because the tannins located there are concentrated, making them highly valued by dyers, but today the roots are left in the earth. Amami's climate, which provides high annual rainfall and sunlight hours, means deforested trees will re-sprout or self-seed, seeing forests regrow with little human input, making their

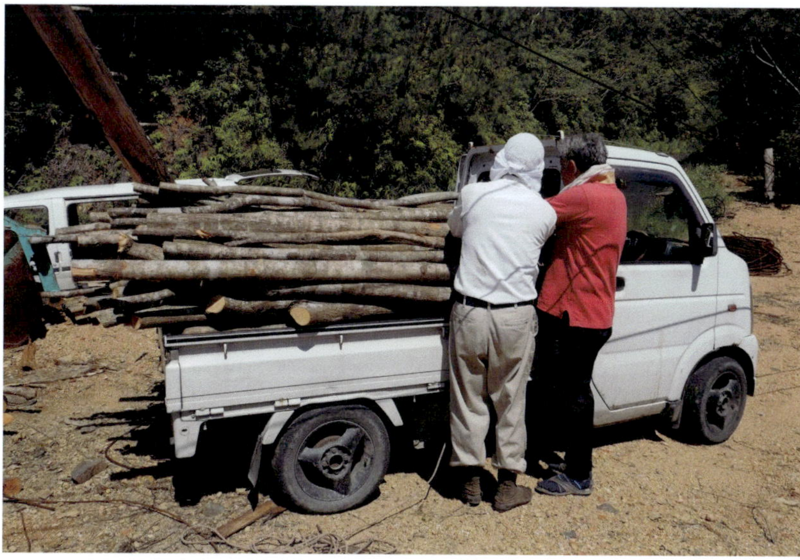

Figure 6.5 *Techigi being loaded onto the Shachō's* keitora *(minitruck).*

management and logging economically efficient (Nakatsuhama 2007). It is likely, too, that the speed of logging, as opposed to the more intensive process of root extraction, is prioritized, relying on the woodcutters' knowledge to presort and codify contaminants as waste. As anthropologists Nicky Gregson et al. argue, "Sorting discarded goods into categories is the means by which value is created in resource recovery.... The more sorting... work that occurs then the higher the purity [and price] of the resultant materials" (2016, 546). Felling rather than extracting also has the advantage of sustaining the long-term supply of techigi through regrowth. As a result, for Amami's remaining dyeing workshops, there is little concern about techigi resources depleting; rather, the question of access to local trees generates uncertainty.[2] Despite the fact that techigi is endemic to Southeast Asia, Amami lies 210 nautical miles from mainland Japan, so importing trees from elsewhere would be costly. Besides, this overlooks the point that techigi remains cheap because of local conditions, which I shall describe, that keep overhead low for dyers, who operate on tight profit margins. This is exemplified by the cash price; if the craftspeople collect the techigi, the woodcutters charge ¥10,000 (about sixty-four dollars) for one truckload. If they have it delivered to Kanai Kougei, a two-hour round trip, it costs three times as much.

The processes that surround techigi highlight, on a small scale, the workings of supply chain capitalism that are necessary to create value where initially there is perceived to be none. As Amamian wood is used for industrial paper, it fetches a low market price. In order for a landowner to profit from its sale, the cost of its extraction—technology and labor power—must also be kept low. These circumstances recall Anna Tsing's (2013, 25) work on the informal economies of matsutake mushroom supply chains in which she explains, "Labor and natural resources are costs to be reduced by finding someone willing to take care of these issues for less." Tsing's ethnography was conducted with Thai and Vietnamese migrants and Vietnam War veterans in the United States who lack access to social care, avoid taxes, and often forage for mushrooms on federal and private property without permits, risking considerable fines. Tsing (2015, 78) states that these pickers "act as if the forest was an extensive commons . . . [doing] their best to ignore questions of property." I asked the dyers who owns the forests where the techigi grow. They vaguely explained that they were owned by small or large landowners or managed by the state or prefecture. Oshima tsumugi, still one of Japan's most luxurious textiles, overseen by Amami's powerful tsumugi union, relies on this ambiguous regime where private and public property coalesce. As Tsing says: "Elite firms turn to supply chains to . . . cut the costs of managing natural resources by allowing poorly regulated suppliers to steal, salvage, or forage raw materials. . . . Suppliers lower their costs by taking advantage of the privatization of what once were public or common domains; taking raw materials from such domains is a kind of stealing. Such arrangements raise urgent questions about private property as a precondition of capitalist commodities. What does it take to turn stolen, salvaged, and foraged materials into commodity value?" (2015, 26).

Techigi was variously described as "waste" by my participants when speaking English and *amatta mono* in Japanese, which translates as "surplus" or "remainder." This linguistic choice draws attention to the fact that techigi's value is defined by a socioeconomic construct rather than a material reality. Like Tsing's mushrooms collected on private land, when techigi was felled from another's property and taken without permission, it was defined as "stolen," imbuing the tree with illicit connotations. Yet as a surplus resource that lacks value in one context and will go to waste if not utilized, value is recuperated that reflects resource efficiency, resonating with feelings of *mottainai* (chapter 3). Even if techigi's acquisition is cloaked in a certain ambiguity, this example of resource recovery retains a positive facade of frugality or circularity that, in itself, has value for Kanai Kougei's more eco-conscious customers. These are medium- to high-end designer brands that invest in the process's place-based, sustainable, traditional, and "natural" image. This efficiency continues once techigi arrives at Kanai Kougei's workshop, where a circular system is employed that makes use of both the raw material and its by-products (figure 6.6). Logs are chipped, loaded into a cage, and lowered into a cauldron containing groundwater and techigi wood ash, an alkali that raises the pH to draw out tannins. The tannins dissolve in water heated to 176 degrees Fahrenheit by a furnace. After being boiled for two days, the wood chips are removed, dried, and reused as fuel for the furnace.[3] The cooled liquid is transferred to large barrels to mature for a week before it is ready to be used for dyeing. Tsing (2013, 26) states that "raw materials must be translated into private, and thus alienable, commodities," an extensive process of valorization evident in techigi's division across multiple stages of production in the dorozome technique. But translating "stolen" or surplus resources into a material central to generating a new product with commodity value also requires the social relations that remove the material from the forest; the truck loaded beyond its legal weight that transports it to the workshop; and the low-wage or free labor of the Kanai family to check on the dyestuff preparation outside of working hours.

The need for techigi arises early in the tsumugi supply chain, and Yukihito-san explained that the tsumugi union, which oversees production and represents the industry's interests, is unlikely to interfere while this informal system functions. As he told me: "I do wonder if we could cover [techigi acquisition] more industrially. But the land where we harvest trees from are privately owned mountains. It would be easier for the craftsmen to do their work if [the tsumugi union] supported it. [The craftspeople] won't lose their time dealing with such issues—their full-time job is only to dye. Techigi is not owned by the dyers. They are Amami's. It would be good for anyone to cut and take it." With the disappearance of a formal industry-wide system for reproducing and extracting techigi, the ability to access it today relies on personal relationships. Techigi suppliers build connections with specific dyehouses so that each company can maintain its supply without competition. This builds obligation into the system, as seen when Kanai Kougei purchased a "stolen" tree from Tanaka-san, who might otherwise have sold it elsewhere. Using social relations as a pathway, such spatially embedded obligation and commitment circumvents the competitiveness of the open labor market and the regulation of labor defined by the state. Tanaka-san seemed to be one of many established residents and newcomers to Amami living off "free" natural resources, foraging for shellfish, collecting rare wildlife for the black market, or hunting dangerous snakes for the local authorities. But many of these activities are embedded with personal risk, highlighting the precarity of this form of labor and the potential exploitation of an undocumented workforce. Tanaka-san, for example, died from a heart attack while hunting octopus, a risky job for someone who I guessed was in his

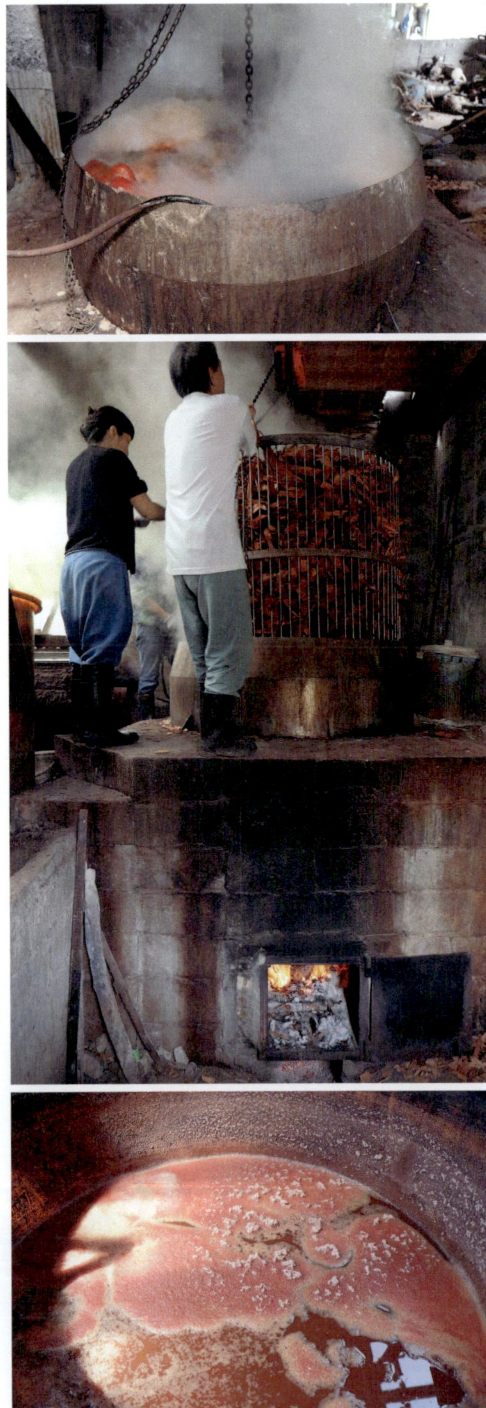

Figure 6.6 *Preparation of the techigi liquid.* Top to bottom*: Boiling the techigi; removing wood chips from the vat; the furnace that heats the water; and the techigi dye left to ferment.*

seventies. In their ethnography of recycling processing in the UK and Belgium, Gregson et al. (2016, 543) explain that recycling is framed as "clean and green"—or as in my case study, "sustainable and circular"—but resource recovery relies on low-skilled, migrant labor to carry out work that is "dirty, often demeaning, physically demanding," frequently "dangerous," and unappealing to the local workforce. Similarly in Amami, Tanaka-san's death identified a weakness in the supply chain: there are a limited number of people who are willing to do this form of work or have the specific ecological knowledge to carry it out safely and efficiently. I asked the tsumugi dyer Kazu-san about the divisive subject of the availability of techigi. He answered: "Right now, with regard to this workshop, there is not enough techigi. Maybe it would be enough if we were only doing Oshima tsumugi. . . . I mean, there are plenty of trees, but it's not easy to fell them. The problem is whether there are enough woodcutters. . . . Sometimes people from the workshop have to do the woodcutting ourselves."

Uncertainty therefore resides not in the availability of trees but in the ability to obtain them. The 2015 census put the number of forestry workers in Amami at 145, a tiny fraction of the island's population of around sixty thousand people (Kagoshima Prefecture 2018, 124). What will happen when there are no longer any woodcutters? Or if the form of paper production that underpins their official employment is deemed financially unsustainable? Techigi will be fixed in the landscape as private property and access will be restricted, forcing dyers to go to more extreme lengths to obtain resources, putting the future of this regional traditional craft in jeopardy. As Tsing explains, "Through incorporating non-capitalist social relations, capitalism achieves its creative strength. . . . Such incorporation, however, is not something finished and under control. . . . It is an everyday problem. Capitalism thrives from it—but it also makes capitalism weak" (2013, 38). The availability of techigi had become a contentious subject between the tsumugi and apparel dyers at Kanai Kougei. Since the early 2000s, apparel orders have economically sustained the business, but at the same time, these orders required a lot of techigi. Craft production is assumed to be the opposite of what Karl Marx imagined as alienated labor. But when techigi would arrive in the back of a vehicle as a commodity, its life as a tree was erased; so, too, were the ecosystem from which it was gathered and the necessary labor that led it to the workshop. Being a "mobile asset" (Tsing 2015, 6) sourced from "improved" land, the younger craftspeople who were engaged in apparel dyeing had experienced alienation from their craft materials. It was not until the younger dyers collected the trees themselves that they better understood Kazu-san's perspective. As Takahito-san explained, "Recently, we've started having the experience of going and cutting the techigi. When you do that you realize—'Wow, this is really tough.' And you start to want to really scrimp with things like washing with the *ni-ban* (no. 2 liquid) [a combination of fresh and recycled techigi]. In that sense I feel like I've realized the real worth of the techigi." These issues of alienation from the source of craft materials and the precarity of accessing them raise the important question of why techigi has been devalued to the extent that it is designated as waste by woodcutters and by regular members of the Amamian community, who often give techigi felled on their land to Kanai Kougei for free.

The Postwar Improvement of Forestry "Waste Lands"

Whenever I would plan a hike in Amami's forests, I was told "*Abunai-ne*!" ("Dangerous!") by locals and advised not to go alone but to hire a nature guide. I would more frequently see guided tourists on rough mountain roads in 4x4s than encounter local residents. This paradox was often explained by the risks posed by habu, which were responsible for around 11 percent of Amami's fatalities before the availability and effective delivery of antivenom (White and Meier 2017; figures for 1898–1903). Yet Amami's forests are both beautiful and hugely biodiverse, and in July 2021 the virgin forests were awarded a UNESCO World Natural Heritage designation. While tourists visit Amami with the intent of seeing rarities, many Amamians seem content to enjoy their wildlife through the proliferation of visual and material forms of companionship via photos, cartoons, and mascots infiltrating the built environment and local media (chapter 4). While I encountered a widespread ecological awareness among the public, ecological engagement tended to be confined to the agricultural fields, beaches, and green spaces of the villages, while schoolchildren had little exposure to hands-on nature activities (Shimizu 2019, 28–29). There are of course exceptions, such as people who enjoy wildlife conservation activities or who gain materially from working, collecting, and foraging in the mountains. The Shachō and Kazu-san, for example, have favorite hunting grounds for matsutake mushrooms and mountain crabs (figure 6.7)—seasonal produce that sustains social relations and their connection with the land.

Nevertheless, the situation today is in stark contrast to how people lived before the 1950s, when Ryūkyū islanders maintained a strong reliance on local materials for construction, medicines, cosmetics, clothing, fuel, food, tools, building transportation, fertilizers, and more. Today, construction timber is shipped in from the mainland, and imported commodities have almost exclusively replaced local materials for everyday use. Evidence for these changes is apparent in the contrast between my own ethnographic data and the records held in forestry bulletins

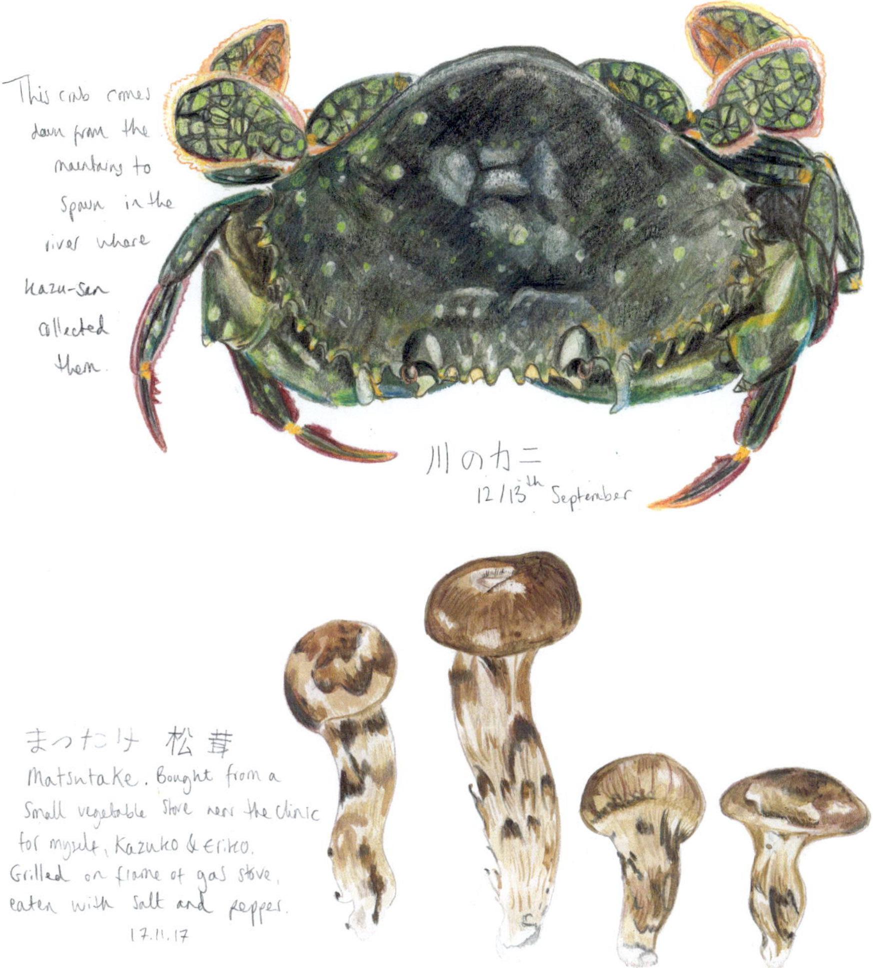

Figure 6.7 *A mountain crab and matsutake mushrooms.*

produced by the US Civil Administration of the Ryukyu Islands (USCAR), the administrative and governmental body that replaced the US military government in 1950 and lasted until Okinawa's return to the Japanese state in 1972. Collated by American and Japanese forestry experts, the bulletins (USCAR 1952, 1953) detail the island's soil types, property distribution, forestry history, and 207 native trees and their wide variety of uses. Alongside its use as a dyestuff, historically techigi was prized for its berries, its pink and white flowers, and its strength in construction and wind protection—essential qualities for a community exposed to annual extremes of subtropical weather. The aim of the bulletins was to establish the economic potential to "improve waste lands" by implementing reforestation and its management across the Ryūkyū archipelago, so that the islands could be economically self-sustaining upon their revision to Japanese control (USCAR 1953, 12). The addition of maps, statistics, and photographs to the bulletins provides an impression of "colonial science," a method Americans learned from European colonization and "imitated" (McNeill 2009, 476) in their own imperial history in the Pacific and Caribbean but also Korea and the Philippines.

Trees have always been important to territorial expansion and wealth accumulation, from the mahogany enslaved people felled on Caribbean plantations in the seventeenth century for European luxury furniture markets (Funes Monzote 2008) to the ornamental species planted along geometric lines that were seen to "bring order" to colonial cities in the tropics (Mrázek 2002, 66). To the European sensibility, such order was necessary to tame "foreign" landscapes defined by what historian David Arnold (2005) calls their "tropicality"—a threatening presence that encompassed extreme weather, disease, poisonous animals, aggressive weeds, vivid colors, "natives," and supernatural forces. Arun Agrawal's (2005, 34) archival and field research in Kumaon in northern India is exemplary in demonstrating how the British colonial authorities constructed an enduring and hegemonic "representation regime" that defined the status of trees, vegetation, and soils by numerical calculus and erased previous ideas held by local people. By restricting access, criminalizing trespass, and simplifying ecological diversity, authorities also aimed to reduce the social diversity of those who relied on rich ecosystems for sustenance (5). Legal scholar Brenna Bhandar (2018, 8) has shown how legal frameworks have dispossessed people of their land using a justification based on the "ideology of improvement," where increased productivity of the land will lead to an improved society to benefit the "greater good." This thinking can be traced back to the work of Enlightenment philosopher John Locke (1632–1704), who believed that if "wastelands" are made more productive via improvement, the rights to access and own that

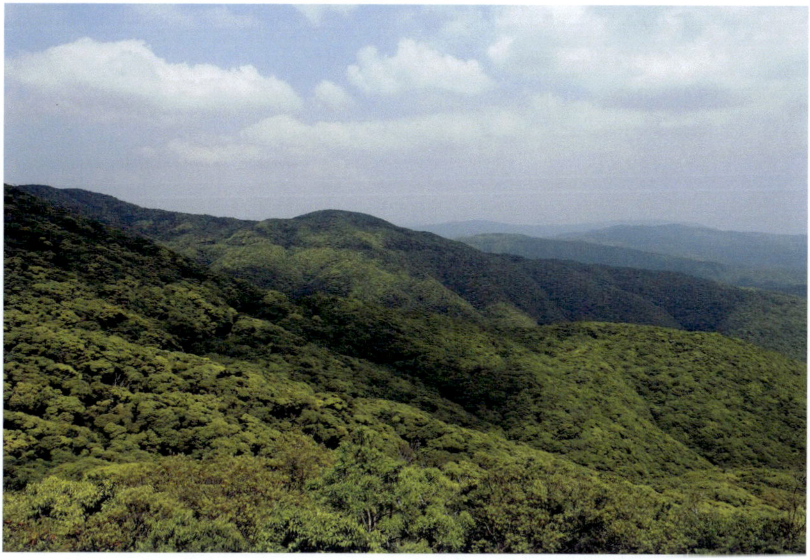

Figure 6.8 *The forest as seen from Mount Yuwan-dake.*

land as property are legitimized (Prudham 2011, 84–86). As Agrawal (2005, 201) explains with his case study in India, the command-and-control method instituted by a centralized authority was initially so successful at increasing profit that it allowed colonists to "[remake] nature."

The United States adopted this logic of improvement when it took possession of the Philippines from Spain in 1898 in the knowledge that the Philippine forests could solve timber supply issues caused by the overexploitation of American forests (Bankoff 2009, 480). Under the instruction of Gifford Pinchot, whom environmental historian Greg Bankoff calls "the 'father' of professional forestry in the United States" (479), American foresters set out to implement scientific management plans developed in the United States in very different environmental (and cultural) conditions in Southeast Asia. Forest residents who used slash-and-burn techniques were criticized by the administration because their "land use system . . . did not conform to American ideals of individual land ownership" (Roberts 2014, 219). Authorities therefore cleared areas in order to force "shifting agriculturalists" to settle and "bring all Philippine forest users into an ideal of forest modernity" (218). Whereas the conflicting laws and interests that governed US property reduced the possibility of implementing widescale regulation at home (Bankoff 2009, 485–86), under colonial conditions the Philippine forests were both conserved and exploited by implementing no-cut zones and establishing national parks, while commercial lumber was better accessed via improved infrastructure. Timber exports consequently rose from "94,000 to 2.5 million cubic meters between 1901 and 1940" (Bankoff 2013, 543).[4] Arriving in the Ryūkyūs in 1945, experts trained with the US Forest Service encountered similar problems to those initially observed in the Philippines of low productivity and a style of highly localized and distributed forest management that was seen as an obstruction to the industry's potential.

Japan is considered a "tree culture" (*ki no bunka*) (Knight 1998) and has historically relied heavily on wood for domestic consumption, from the production of chopsticks and sandals to the interior and exterior construction of houses, temples, and shrines. Wood was also a safe construction material in the event of earthquakes, while its availability and utility made it convenient for rebuilding in the aftermath of natural disaster (Hanley 1997, 54). Prior to the Meiji era (1868–1912), foreign trading was severely prohibited, so to meet demand, Japan established a sustainable timber industry (Totman 1989, 4–5). But after World War II, forests across Japan were being cut at a rate faster than they could naturally regenerate. Colonial expansion, the war effort, and rebuilding of bombed-out cities led to unsustainable resource exploitation. This led the United States to organize the import of American and Philippine hardwoods, while the Japanese government encouraged the use of alternative materials, disrupting long-established material practices and supply chains. Concrete and steel were used for building, and imported fossil rather than wood fuel was to be used to run vehicles, cook, and heat homes (Matsushita 2015, 92). Imported chemical fertilizers facilitated the goals of the Green Revolution by replacing forest products that had supported agriculture for millennia (Takahashi et al. 2019). Yet despite changing material needs, Japanese forestry was still deemed critical for future economic and environmental sustainability. The American ideal saw the local management of forests replaced by "a unified national program" overseen by state-level bureaucrats (USCAR 1953, 36).

This was the case in Amami, where forest management at the village level was said to be in part "good" (USCAR 1953, 37) and soil and resource conservation "instinctive," but US foresters expressed frustration with residents who, "in the absence of strong control," overcut immature trees close to the village and "engaged in the destruction of timber resources" (5). Amamians used coppicing for charcoal production (figure 6.9) that followed the *satoyama* model (Sugimura 2021, 48), a style of land management that bridges the village and the mountains, and the practice of *okuyama*, where large trees were individually selected from the mountains to construct houses or dugout canoes (Sugimura 2021, 48). These sustainable practices, which have been proven to be beneficial to both people and wildlife (Takeuchi et al. 2003), were displaced by a program of improvement that went hand in hand with legislation that governed land access and property ownership. This was administered under American supervision by the Ryukyu Forestry Bureau, which set out to map forests, replant useful species, improve access, educate rangers and locals, build roads, police trespassers, establish boundaries, institute formal sales policies, and fell old growth—the latter of which was deemed "decadent," "defective," and "going to waste" (USCAR 1953, 22). In contrast with current thinking in environmental and scientific circles where old growth is considered both "beautiful and biologically rich" (Prudham 2011, 94), large trees during this period were deemed economically unproductive because they restricted surrounding growth. This approach ignored embedded material stewardship and the animist cosmologies that had governed Amamians' relations with their environment for centuries.

Before there was commercial interest in large trees, the trees could be cut only with permission from the *noro* and *yuta* because they were considered home to spiritual beings, designating them *kiranki*—"trees we don't cut" (Haring 1952, 68; see also chapter 5 of this book). By the time Haring visited Amami in 1952, suppression by successive rulers who wished to exploit a landscape rich in natural resources and plentiful labor meant that the priestesses' authority had been degraded and many rituals were no longer practiced, yet belief in spiritual entities and black magic still held strong (see chapters 4 and 5 of this book). As Bhandar explains, "If the possession of land was (and remains) the ultimate objective of colonial power, then property law is the primary means of realizing this desire." As a means to legitimately dispossess a community of land and ecological knowledge, "laws of property" were needed to "reflect and consolidate language, ways of seeing, and modes of subjectivity that render indigenous and colonized populations as outside history, lacking the requisite cultural practices, habits of thought, and economic organization to be considered sovereign, economic subjects" (Bhandar 2018, 3). Failure to understand alternative "ways of seeing" in the Ryūkyūs is reflected in USCAR's (1953, 36) special bulletin 2, in which an "expert consultant" writes: "The present forest law divides responsibility between the central government and the prefectural governors and fails to provide competent systems of inspection and control. The disadvantages are serious. Divided responsibility prevents the creation of a unified national program. It subjects the application of the law to 46 interpretations. . . . It places in the hands of locally-elected officials the task of regulating the acts of their own electors in the interest of public good. Japan cannot hope for effective administration of a forest law unless full responsibility for carrying out its provisions is placed upon the central government."

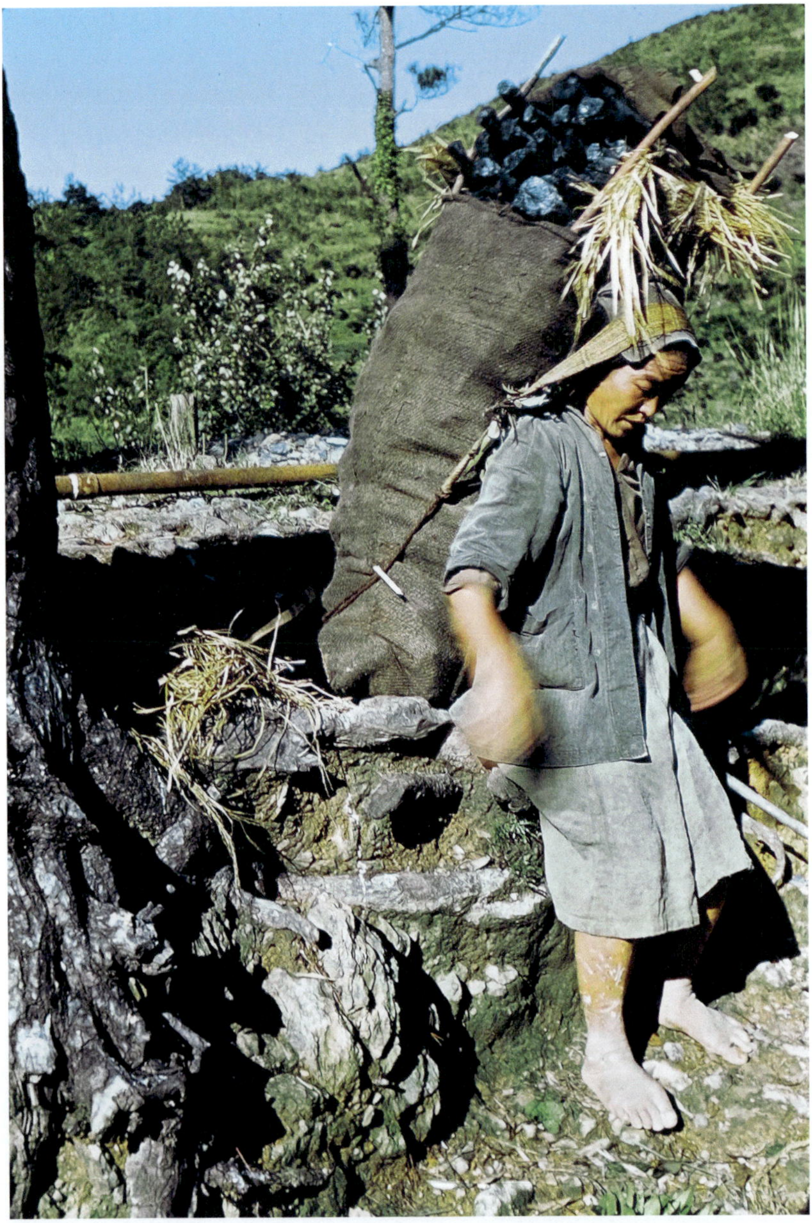

Figure 6.9 *Woman carrying charcoal, 1951–52. Douglas Haring Papers, University Archives, Special Collections Research Center, Syracuse University Libraries, Syracuse, New York.*

This racialized and paternalistic view, instrumental to the formation of the settler colonial narrative, has become hegemonic in "the intimate bond between state property and private property ownership" (Bhandar 2018, 18). Although these ideas have a history embedded in Western scholarship, after the Meiji Restoration (1868) they were increasingly imported into Japan as a means of "modernization."

The Laws of Property

While property laws diverge in every country, tracking the history of land rights and access in Amami demonstrates how, to prioritize economic development, legal frameworks have become increasingly uniform at the global scale, lacking the diversity that suited the welfare of local populations and their distinct geographies. I have suggested that changes in local consciousness about the utility of Amamian natural resources occurred, most significantly, in the post–World War II period. Amami became accessible to global commodity markets, and increased wealth and living standards displaced subsistence farming and foraging practices. However, Amamians were incrementally dispossessed of land and ecological knowledge much earlier, the result of changing political regimes and corresponding economic policy that cemented dominant conceptions of property and land access in the public imaginary.

Prior to the Meiji Restoration in 1868, the Japanese people lived under feudalism, where territory was controlled by a *han* (domain) system of powerful landlords called *daimyō*. The domain provided villagers with access rights, with taxes payable in agricultural produce, which was mainly rice but also in the Ryūkyūs crops such as sweet potatoes. Between the fourteenth and twentieth centuries, these rights were based on a *warichi* (split-land) system, and while warichi differed in every region (P. Brown 2002), in Amami (where the system was termed *wariyama* [split-mountain]) "house lots, paddies, upland fields, and mountain land" were redistributed every three to five years among adults (USCAR 1953, 6). This meant that land was "roughly comparable to holding shares of stock" in the village (P. Brown 2002, 42), with no individual "owning" the best land and tax being paid as a village unit. Accordingly, it was in the collective interest of the village to care for the landscape holistically. In addition to tenurial rights, local authorities across Japan expanded use rights and restrictions to forests and commons to lock villagers into social contracts of mutual responsibility across large tracts of land and periods of time. Historian Conrad Totman's *Green Archipelago* (1989) details how the Japanese supported the country's burgeoning population that swelled from 18 million to almost 35 million people (Hanley 1968, 622) across the Tokugawa era (1603–1867) by moving from clear-cutting virgin timber, which resulted in deforestation, to "regenerative forestry," which facilitated plantation silviculture and naturally seeded forest management, arising independently from similar German practices established during this time (Totman 1989, 4–5). The aim was to both stabilize Japan's poor mountain soils that, because of deforestation, were plagued by erosion, flooding, and landslides; maintain peace between individuals with land "rights"; and productively maximize yields (174). Despite reforestation being expensive and risky, these factors were offset using "corvée duty"—compulsory village labor that was bartered for tax reductions, profit share, or wages or imposed as trespass penalties (136–37). Totman claims, however, that these partnerships eventually dissolved, since the daimyō could enclose land at will and landowners moved increasingly toward more profitable monoculture forestry, which lacked the biodiversity that sustained the village (178).

Arable land is scarce in Amami, and as the population swelled land became highly divided under the wariyama system. Added to this burden, forced cropping and payment of tax in sugar to the Shimazus—the powerful rulers of the Satsuma domain, current-day Kagoshima Prefecture—was introduced in 1745. By 1820 the Shimazus instructed that rice paddies be drained and replaced by sugarcane to implement monocropping (Hellyer 2009, 95–96). This "Black Sugar Policy" (USCAR 1952, 52) led to deforestation as trees were used to fertilize and improve the soil (Nakatsuhama 2007, 51) and made way for *sotetsu* plantations, whose poisonous seeds prevented starvation (see chapter 4). Despite these efforts, crop failure—a frequent occurrence due to extreme weather—led to debt and widespread famine. As a result, many residents became *yanchu* (slaves or indentured laborers) in the households of village heads who acted as officials, suggesting that these households ultimately grew in people but also in land as individuals surrendered wariyama rights (Hagihara 1974, 248–49).[5] The resulting profits from sugar brought wealth and power to the Shimazus, funding their overthrow of the Tokugawas to establish "modern" Japan, starting the Meiji Restoration (Haring 1952, 77).

After 1868, laws were passed to transform landownership from a "feudalistic landlord" system to a "farmer-owner" system alongside a record of title registration. Amamians gained the right to own private land in 1869 (Takigawa 1972). Wariyama, meanwhile, was outlawed in 1873, taxes were tied to the value of a *specific* parcel of land (P. Brown 2002, 46), and common land became the property of communities but under municipal or prefectural management (Takigawa 1972, 305). Whereas in earlier eras sustainable forestry developed to meet local needs, beginning in 1897 nationwide Forest Acts were established, allowing a united Japan to meet the demands of industrialization, colonial expansion, and military action. A stream of laws that were becoming increasingly centralized and nationalistic in character meant that the productivity of the land provided cash profit and tax revenue prior to industrialization, supporting public services, agricultural development, and ultimately the founding of the nation-state (Takahashi et al. 2019, 1021–22).[6]

It is helpful here to introduce a direct beneficiary of this "modernization," the "Boss of Kagoshima," businessman Yohachiro Iwasaki (1902–1993), founder of the Iwasaki Sangyo Corporation (*Fortune* 1992). Iwasaki made his fortune by supplying railway sleepers to the Japanese government after the Great Kanto earthquake in 1923, before moving into postal services and, after an export ban was lifted in 1930, gold mining (Iwasaki Group, n.d.). In 1943 Iwasaki bought twelve thousand hectares of land in the Uken mountains (the area I visited with the Shachō), equivalent to 10 percent of Amami's forests (Sugimura 2021, 48). My fieldwork participants informed me that the large trees on Iwasaki's land were extracted and sold to the government for railway construction in Japan's colony of Manchuria, a narrative supported by environmental scientist Ken Sugimura (48–49). Although it is only supposition, because without further archival research one cannot know the conditions of sale, one might assume that the Japanese government supported this land sale at a moment when it needed funds but also the services and materials supplied by private timber merchants for military expansion.

After World War II, the occupying Americans directed an overhaul of agricultural landownership to tackle the problem of "absentee landlords"—mostly city-dwelling nonfarmers (Hagihara 1974). Laws were instituted that reduced individual landownership to one hectare, with any excess sold to the government and then on to tenant farmers. The push for these reforms aligned with the writing of the 1947 Japanese constitution, penned by American authors and based on "the Western theory of natural rights" that found their origins in John Locke's philosophy (Repeta and Jones 2015, 314). American influence was not just material but also epistemological, embedding the Lockean sense of freedom and the rights of the individual into the Japanese legal system. In Amami, however, historian Shigeru Hagihara (1974, 259) claims that the reforms failed because "parasitic landlords" either registered land exceeding one hectare in a family member's name or signed land over to tenants with unrealistic loan conditions knowing they would default. Yet many of the Amamian families with whom I researched owned their houses and house lots, and most had access to small fruit groves, vegetable plots, or parcels of land in the mountains which their families had relied on for subsistence. They explained the land was purchased in the first half of the twentieth century, but they were all unsure exactly how it came into their families' possession.

When discussing landownership with my participants, issues were often raised about the *tōki*, or *fudosan tōki* (real estate registration), which details the owners of land and/or buildings on a central registry providing official documentation. Despite land registration existing in some form since 1869 (Takigawa 1972), I was told that transfers of ownership were in the past done orally in Amami, without paperwork but built on a system of trust. The Shachō told me that when his neighbor sold a parcel of land that the Shachō thought belonged to him, the neighbor explained that many years ago the Shachō's family had exchanged the land to the neighbor's family for pigs. Since there was no tōki, the Shachō took his word. Kazu-san recalled a similar problem, explaining that when the authorities wanted to buy part of a road his family had built, all the owners of the land couldn't be identified, making the sale challenging. Kazu-san offered a second example by explaining that when the state undertook a significant project to establish landownership in Amami around 2015, the boundaries of his land were queried, so he had to pay again for land he believed he already owned. While issues surrounding local landownership, such as spaces located within the village, can be resolved, it is more difficult in the case of forestry, where land might be highly divided and located deep in the mountains. This is exemplified by large off-island landowners such as the Iwasaki Sangyo Corporation, as local people are unsure where its land is even located, and when they do know, access is prohibited. My participants elaborated that when villages suffered from significant landslides or typhoon damage in the past, Iwasaki Sangyo would not grant access through its land when the public right of way had been blocked. For reasons such as these, the company is hugely unpopular with Amamians but also, I was told, throughout Kagoshima Prefecture.

The history of landownership in Japan demonstrates how land is a means to accrue wealth and therefore power, a factor that postwar land reforms instituted by Americans attempted to address by bestowing the "rights to life, liberty and property" (Repeta and Jones 2015, 314–15) to individual tenant farmers. Yet in the Japanese context, liberty can be achieved by the individual, but scholars such as John Clammer (1995, 109) would argue, only when supported by the structure of the community. Clammer claims that, because the Japanese are taught from childhood that "social power is dispersed," the individual (in theory) will be a cooperative "subject who can be a 'we' as well as 'I'" (111). As he explains, "Individuality and individualism are not the same, and individualism is not a necessary condition of individuality. Community also need not mean collectivism, since there are many ways to being community-orientated" (110). The cooperative nature of Japanese society has of course been tarnished by the negative associations of "groupism," and it is certainly a condition not without conflict (see chapter 3). But while the "group" from the outside might be imagined as a powerful (even threatening) social unit, groupism also describes complex sociality, where the system gains its strength from the relations that exist between individuals (Clammer 1995, 102). The history of warichi and wariyama demonstrates this well, as in some areas it was still occurring after the land reforms of 1947–49, despite being "illegal in principle." Philip Brown (2002, 46) explains that many villages that felt the system functioned well ignored or manipulated the law in order to maintain it. One might imagine, in an ideal scenario, that a practice such as wariyama encourages individuals to take responsibility for the environment to maintain social order and village health but also for more selfish reasons, because uncertainty about the future and the land one will at some time be designated might promote sustaining processes in the present. Residents have been concerned with preserving the health and productivity of the landscape to meet both their immediate material needs and those of future generations. Although wariyama encountered problems—overpopulation meant land was in short supply, for example—it is helpful to consider the possibilities of models of land stewardship that offer alternatives to private ownership, the model that has come to dominate globally.

The legal frameworks of private ownership and land taxes have disadvantaged small landowners today, because in the past, levels of literacy were low and cash was in short supply while social relations took preference over paper documents. But essentially, the reforms failed to understand the role of the village in Japan as an independent, bureaucratic unit that conceptualized the landscape—the mountains, forests, village, and sea—holistically as part of the community (see chapter 5). The fractured nature of landownership, meanwhile, has made collective decision-making—whether to exploit or protect the environment—challenging in the present. Private ownership of forest land is as high as 90 percent in Amami, a number that exceeds the average of the whole of the country (Kagoshima Prefecture 2018, 118). But it is important to stress that postwar reforms were directed only at agricultural land, not at forest land, which explains how Iwasaki Sangyo continues to control a sixth of Amami's forests (Sugimura 2021, 51). Because trees were seen as a resource necessary to benefit the "greater good," the rights to access communal forests were not considered worthy of protection, and large-scale ownership was left untouched (Takigawa 1972, 290).

State, Private, or Community Management?

Since the 1950s, the Japanese government has instituted a range of forestry laws to secure future sustainability and make Japanese timber competitive by better using common land for profit-driven exploitation and easing the way for privatization (Takahashi et al. 2019, 1022). In addition, laws initiated by Americans meant that between 1951 and 1963 all of Japan's public and private forests were subject to "compulsory [silviculture] regulations" (Matsushita 2015, 103), with many forests on the mainland replaced by monoculture plantations of Japanese cedar and cypress (Knight 1998). Community relationships with forest ecosystems, their broad utility, and cosmologies were severed from the everyday functioning of social and material life. While dependency on forests would still be paramount, an economic understanding of the value of trees, which was mutually beneficial for both local communities and the state, came to dominate.

In many rural areas such as Amami, residents practiced a subsistence lifestyle into the 1950s, harvesting forest products as a whole-family pursuit (including children), carried out based on the agriculture calendar to supplement income (USCAR 1953, 26). People's relationships with natural resources were bounded by both a spatial and a temporal proximity—accounting for the material development of processes such as dorozome and the weaving of Oshima tsumugi. But converting forestry into an industry introduced mobility, meaning the state could siphon capital through untapped natural resources—solving supply issues on the mainland—while subsistence farmers would become tax-paying laborers. In addition, professionalizing forestry and the construction industry (on which forestry relied to improve infrastructure) would provide wage labor for men for whom migration to Okinawa or the mainland had become a necessity (Haring 1952, 8). Regulating forestry as both a long-term capital project and a means to relocate labor according to such temporal cycles is an example of capitalism's need to be fixed in a territory or economic unit while allowing capital and labor to move "beyond the boundaries of the space or region in which it was generated" (Jessop 2006, 147). In the Ryūkyūan forests, it could be argued that USCAR and the Japanese government created the conditions for what David Harvey (2001) terms a "spatiotemporal fix" by using geographic expansion and temporal deferment as a method of absorption of surplus capital (trees going to "waste" in the mountains) and labor (high levels of unemployment in rural areas).

Yet the authorities did not account for imminent changes in market conditions and the resulting instability caused by the mobility of capitalism. The example of Japanese forestry demonstrates "one of the central contradictions of capital, that it has to build a fixed space (or 'landscape') necessary for its own functioning at a certain point in its history only to have to destroy that space (and devalue much of the capital invested therein) at a later point in order to make way for a new 'spatial fix'" (Harvey 2001, 25). Industrialization, market expansion, and urbanization degraded the industries of forestry and agriculture, increasing Japan's dependency on imports. By the early 1970s timber from the Philippines and the United States accounted for 60 percent of Japan's softwood market (Cox 1987, 35), a source replaced in the 1980s when Japanese trading companies undercut local timber by dealing with the corrupt Indonesian government to harvest tropical rainforests (Tsing 2005, 14–16). While the costs of imports remained low, Japanese forestry also suffered from destructive pine nematodes that were brought in with US timber and a declining workforce due to out-migration from rural areas (Cox 1987, 37). As Harvey would claim, "spatiotemporal fixes" are helpful for as long as they are profitable. Sugimura (2021, 53–54) writes that by the 1980s, state and prefectural forestry in Amami that was logged for paper and biofuel products was running a "negative profit," but the industry was able to draw income by accruing government subsidies to rebuild old and construct new mountain roads to improve logging access. So rather than providing profitable material reserves, the role of forestry had become a means to support the local economy through job creation—a type of labor no longer desired today—at the expense of the dispossession of the community's ecological stewardship and environmental destruction.

After World War II, forestry and Oshima tsumugi were highlighted as areas for innovation and investment by the occupying Americans. While forestry plans withered, the nostalgia for traditional kimono that swept across the country with the nation's rising wealth meant that Oshima tsumugi could employ twenty thousand islanders at peak production in 1972. In the 1960s, the Japanese state proactively created regional boundaries as a way to bolster domestic tourism and investment in national heritage. Because the state sought to maintain "structured coherence," a region's "capacity to impose relatively firm boundaries on otherwise porous and unstable geographical edges" (Jessop 2006, 154), capital and labor were fixed in Amami not through forestry but by the boundaries of tradition. Quality and authenticity were tied to local hand labor, intangible skills, and folk traditions that were geographically fixed. Oshima tsumugi—designated a *dentō kōgei* (traditional craftwork) by the government in 1974—was able to thrive in the 1970s by taking advantage of the cheapness of forest products such as techigi, following the economic devaluation of local forests and the removal of these products from everyday circulation.

The private sector also moved on from forestry. My participants explained that after Iwasaki Sangyo felled large, profitable trees it "abandoned" much of its least accessible land because there was no benefit to ongoing investment, an argument supported by Yasuteru Nakatsuhama (2007, 52). While the sheer scale of its ownership had dispossessed the community of access, Sugimura (2021, 51) claims that "extracting," then "abandoning," has had the unintended consequence of protecting the island's old-growth forests from logging. This is because it was not until the 1990s that the local authorities began to reject clear-cutting of virgin timber on sites under their management and instead recognized the value of conservation, which could be capitalized on for nature tourism (90–91). Although Iwasaki Sangyo continued logging operations—including clear-cutting for paper pulp—in 1948 its main business shifted to tourism and transportation, building hotels, golf courses, and establishing ferry services to remote islands such as Yakushima and Amami. In 1992, at the age of ninety, Iwasaki's approach to business, which he claimed was in speculating on the future value of land, gave him billionaire status, making him the 115th richest man in the world at that time (*Fortune* 1992).

In 2017 in preparation for Amami's recognition as a UNESCO World Natural Heritage site, the Japanese government converted the island's old-growth forests (initially earmarked for logging by USCAR in the 1950s) into a national park and acquired the surrounding area from individual landowners as an environmental buffer zone. This is a practice that legitimizes the acquisition of property under the guise of preservation and conservation, using legal frameworks to promote but also sustain natural environments to benefit "the greater good" (Mollett 2011). Although centralized initiatives of conservation, preservation, and resource management are often imagined with good intentions, the opening of a World Natural Heritage site could be framed as yet another economic "fix." As Sugimura (2021, 90–91) stresses, critical decision-making on the future of forestry in Amami has always been "top-down," without a full understanding of the "complexity of the situation," which should include "biological, silvicultural, social, geographical and historical factors." Commentators stress that the balance between "protection" and "utilization" should be maintained in consultation with the local community, and the environmental education of children should be prioritized (Nakatsuhama 2007; Kuwahara 2011; Shimizu 2019). While there were efforts to consult with the community on the World Natural Heritage process, on the ground there was little evidence this had an impact on everyday life, leaving the dyers again concerned about access to resources.

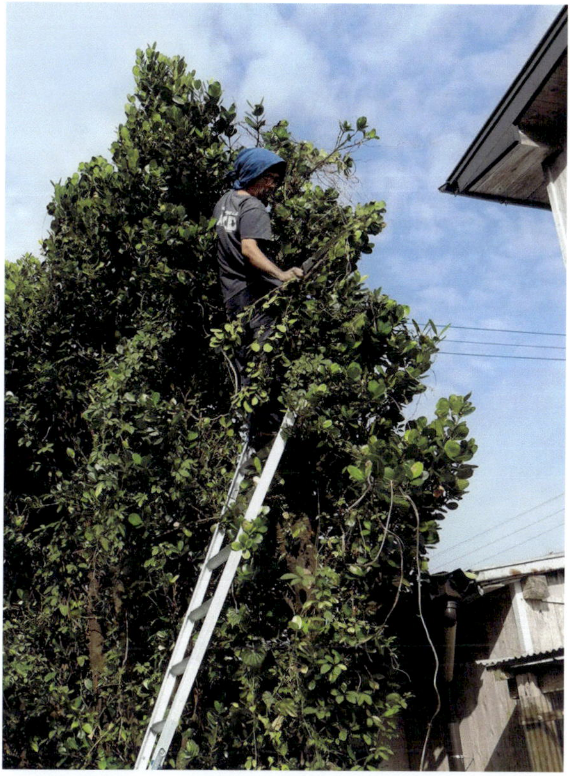

Figure 6.10 *Yukihito-san carrying out his hedge-cutting service and getting fukugi in return.*

World Natural Heritage as Contemporary Resource Management

Figure 6.10 shows Yukihito-san precariously perched on a ladder with a *nokogiri* (handsaw) performing his "hedge-cutting service" in Toguchi village. He comes to this orchard, which backs up to a *kominka* (traditional wooden private house), and to other houses when called on by neighbors or when he needs *fukugi* (common garcinia), whose plant materials yield a bright lemon-yellow dye. This source of the dyestuff is convenient but only yields limited quantities of material per cutting. It is chipped and bagged at the workshop, boiled, strained, and used within days.

Fukugi also came from the mountainside in Takahito-san's village of Yamato-son, which borders the buffer zone of the World Natural Heritage site. During my fieldwork in 2018, restrictions on cutting trees had already been enforced in

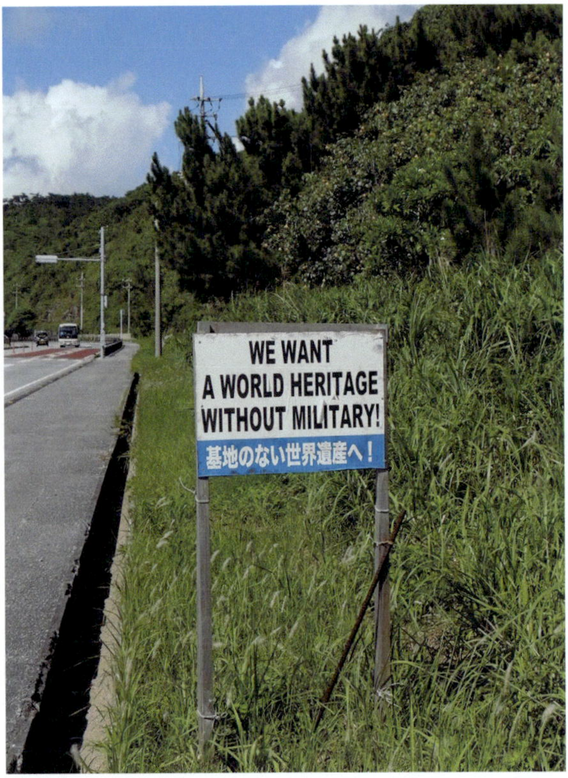

Figure 6.11 *A protest sign in Okinawa, where relations between residents and the American military have remained contentious since the US invasion in 1945. Prioritizing English on the sign suggests its message is aimed at American military personnel and tourists.*

the area, meaning this second source of fukugi was no longer sustainable. Maiko-san (Yukihito-san's sister) explained that if Amami achieved recognition, "lots of different fukugi trees might just arbitrarily become banned from being cut down, so we won't be able to make fukugi anymore." Whether or not this was true, the statement indicated a sense of uncertainty about the World Natural Heritage designation in regard to access to resources—even those found in one's own backyard.[7] For small production runs, the trees from a kominka would suffice, but for larger quantities such as garments and yarn dyed for the Japanese brand 45RPM (found in department stores countrywide), Kanai Kougei would have to stop production or raise the price significantly. Maiko-san explained, "This is why Yukihito is actually against [Amami] becoming a World Heritage site."

Before heading to Amami I presumed that World Natural Heritage recognition would be unanimously desired. When I arrived, I saw posters mounted on walls and pasted to the sides of buses and car bumper stickers supporting the recognition. But when in June 2018 the decision was delayed and the application put on hold, many locals expressed a collective sigh of relief. There was general concern about the damaging potential of nature tourism—as had been initially experienced by the neighboring island of Yakushima, which achieved recognition in 1993 (see Song and Kuwahara 2016). But global conservation schemes implemented at the local level often restrict people's ability to use their land responsibly. Geographer Sharlene Mollett (2011, 101) has worked with Indigenous groups who have struggled to maintain "customary property rights" in "ancestral domains" in a UNESCO biosphere reserve in Honduras, where 20 percent of the country is enclosed in protected areas. She writes that "critics of global environmentalism argue that its hegemonic norms have appropriated 'Third World' natural resources into a global commons and that leaders in the Global North have both discursively and materially assumed leadership over this commons despite the needs of the people on the ground" (102).

While this critique is valid, she also argues that it is local government that ultimately has the power to exploit conservation initiatives, meaning that conservation becomes less about what is beneficial for local people and nature and more about what it can do for nation-building. This was highlighted in the *Japan Times* by Philip Brasor when he reported that the World Natural Heritage application had been delayed until 2020 because UNESCO and scientists from the International Union for Conservation of Nature had raised concerns about the sites and wanted these concerns addressed in what might be seen as a power play with the Japanese government. Brasor (2019) writes: "Japan is upfront about seeking World Heritage status for cultural and natural assets in order to boost tourism, a purpose UNESCO doesn't encourage. The issue with this purpose is whether attracting visitors to help domestic business works against UNESCO's primary aim, which is conservation." What was interesting about the delay was the gossip that circulated regarding these concerns, which were not initially reported in the local press, revealing issues the Amamian community already had with local and national government. These ranged from the recent building of a Japanese army base and missile store to the possibility that the Americans might build a military base in Amami and the potential for geological disposal of nuclear waste that would be buried in the mountains at the heart of the World Natural Heritage site. But two more likely reasons that circulated, and did turn out to be true, were the exclusion of an area of land in Okinawa that was previously used by the US military that UNESCO wanted regenerated, and ongoing concerns about "alien" species such mongoose, cats, and goats (figure 6.12). This latter issue was already being addressed in regard to the introduced Indian mongoose, brought to Amami in the 1970s to control habu. While mongoose have now mostly been eradicated, the issue of stray cats persists. These unwanted pets and feral populations have been ravaging endangered species,

Figure 6.12 *A public information flyer reads, "Cute but . . . cats are an alien species! A cat management plan for ecosystem conservation in Amami Ōshima." Courtesy of the Amami City local authority.*

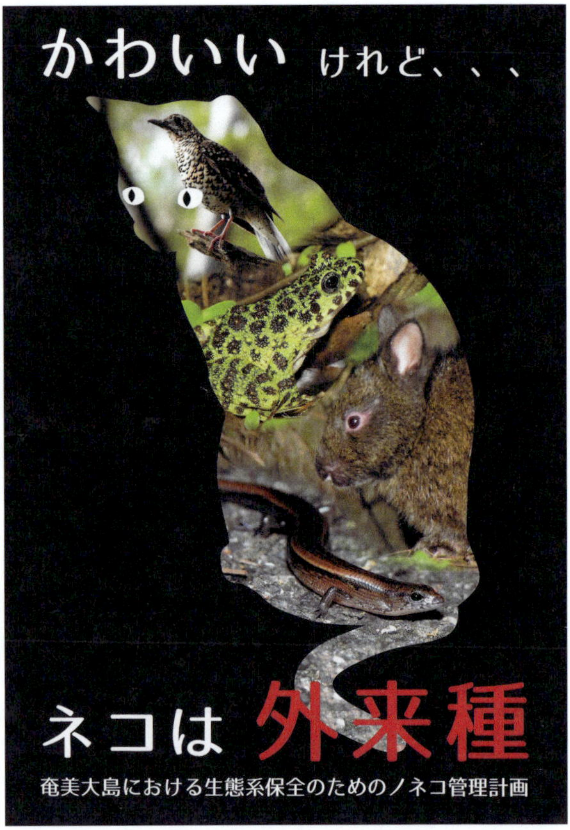

including the Amami black rabbit. A trap/neuter/release and adoption program was in effect during my fieldwork, as was an education campaign and an appeal to residents to keep pets indoors. But a cull program had also been initiated, much to the ire of animal rights groups, causing local concerns about the right to keep cats—an animal formerly respected as kami in Amami.[8] Despite the concerns of international conservation organizations, Brasor (2019) quotes an Amamian nature guide who explained: "Amami rabbits have more to fear from urban development, of which tourism is one form. More are killed by cars than by predators." It is far easier for the government to eradicate problem cats than to attempt to reduce road traffic by improving public transport and restricting the number of tourist vehicles on the road—especially those seeking to view an endangered rabbit.

Yet the paradox that increased tourism inflicts damage on sensitive landscapes does not fit the plan for the sustainable economic development and "market environmentalism" (Mollett 2011, 108) that governments seek. By establishing World

Natural Heritage sites and gaining "territorial authority" (109), the Japanese government is able to legitimately dispossess the community of prior access rights to land and resources, which are already severely degraded, in order to accommodate the mobility of capitalism—that across this chapter has jumped from rice to sugar, textiles, and forestry, back to textiles, and now to tourism in Amami. So how might the community regain some autonomy to reestablish the Amamian forest's "real worth"?

In a 2013 paper, environmental philosopher Mitsuyo Toyoda (2013, 279) proposes a return to the commons by combining traditional knowledge with innovative practice to "re-establish sustainable resource management" in rural areas. Toyoda addresses critics of the commons—most prominently Garrett Hardin (1968)—who believe the commons cannot work, because by their selfish nature humans are "rational beings" who will always "seek to maximize [their own] gain" at a cost to others (Toyoda 2013, 281). Yet Toyoda has joined other scholars of common property rights (Ostrom 1990; Gibson et al. 2000) by suggesting that rather than having an agenda set by external authorities such as academics, scientists, bureaucrats, or corporate partners, there could be a democratic approach that employs community decision-making with input from experts. Japan has a wealth of experience with community-driven environmental restoration and management projects (Takeuchi et al. 2003; Satsuka 2014), and Toyoda uses the example of such a project on an estuary on the Sea of Japan where the local fishing industry, but also municipal infrastructures, had caused water pollution. Key to the project's success was the inclusion of multiple stakeholders and generations, because for older fishermen "the concept of sustainability [was] too abstract and [could not] be connected with their everyday concerns" (Toyoda 2013, 290). But by involving local children, the fishermen were able to imagine a future for the estuary. Toyoda suggests that it is "crucial to consider how to re-identify values in the natural surroundings and turn them into important resources that people care about and care for" (291). Arun Agrawal's (2005, 93) research carried out in India for several decades also supports the effectiveness of community management, which he describes as an intimate form of regulation that "operates more constantly, consistently, effectively, and transformatively on its . . . village residents," while also being "less costly," "more autonomous," and "more humane" than external regulation. He explains, "Localities and their residents become participants in conservation on the basis of a transformation in the understanding of the place of forests in social life" (103).

These examples demonstrate that if provided with agency and support, local communities are more suited to environmental management: first because they have self-interest; second because social pressure encourages self-governance;

and last because residents tend to have ethical, genealogical, and/or spiritual connections with things and places that prompt the adoption of sustaining processes, whose flexibility cannot be matched by external management.[9] The ability to enact care based on informed ecological knowledge was apparent when I asked Kazu-san if age or growing location affected the color of the techigi dye. He told me: "The best place to grow techigi is on the coast because sunlight reaches it. Deep in a mountain forest . . . the tree grows big, but it has to mature quickly in order not to be in the shadow of the surrounding trees, which makes the color of the dyeing liquid thinner, compared to coastal techigi trees. When you break off the coastal techigi's twigs, they are already red-colored inside. The ones on the mountainside are whitish in color." Reengaging the community in forest management in Amami would require a new paradigm for the laws that govern property and a shift in mindset among the population. While gaining access to trees in the village forests, land known as *kaihō yama* (open mountains), is still possible in Amami, village heads tend to be responsible for negotiating logging with private companies on residents' behalf (Nakatsuhama 2007, 51). Although instituting changes to management appears to be a huge undertaking, the fact that property ownership was challenged in order to establish the World Natural Heritage site shows just how important protected zones of international interest are to the "national" project. Yet it remains to be seen whether there is a will to implement such seismic change in management that could directly benefit the everyday needs of the local community and reconfigure local relations with the forest.

As has been demonstrated, dispossessing a community of a close relationship with the land because of the need for economic expansion leads to the dispossession of ecological knowledge. This has a direct impact on local cultural practice, restricting the capacity of a community to take responsibility and develop caring capacities, while the ability to access even individual trees is precarious, perhaps even pushing the boundaries of legality. Throughout the twentieth century a rational approach has been taken to industry, whether textile dyeing or forestry. To improve productivity and maximize profits, industrialists have attempted to reduce risk by simplifying processes, materials, and environments using scientific management. But what I have shown with both dyeing and forestry is that a somatic approach that relies on a wealth of dispersed knowledge and privileges care above efficiency is more sustainable in the long run. For example, by leaving textiles to rest (*nekaseru*) between dye applications, the color of the textile will last longer. But this step is also carried out in the knowledge that the color will eventually fade through use, a property of workwear that is highlighted, not hidden (see chapter 2). Yukihito-san obtains fukugi by establishing a tree-cutting service that cares for the local community and its infrastructure, the trees having been planted decades ago to reduce damage caused by typhoons. Ensuring the dorota doesn't become polluted with waste *ai* is an act of care for both the color of tsumugi yarns and the endangered wildlife living in the dorota (see chapter 5). One might also imagine that knowing the location of techigi trees and being aware of their ability to produce edible berries during times of social hardship would add motivation to take only the timber that was needed or to leave the roots to allow regrowth. Traditional processes accept that uncertainty will always be present rather than try to eliminate risk. By implementing practices of care that are environmentally, socially, and materially embedded, uncertainty is mitigated.

I asked the Shachō whether he felt that increased tourism would change Amami. He agreed that the number of tourists was increasing, but in his opinion, it was just a movement of traveling to small islands in Japan that wouldn't last long, three to five years, perhaps. Although it is hard to say how long the current tourism boom might last, and whether it will be bolstered by World Natural Heritage recognition, the Shachō is quick to recognize (having lived through the tsumugi boom) that local communities, societies, and ecosystems that might enjoy the benefits of temporary prosperity created by a "spatiotemporal fix" are ultimately left with bust.[10] Foregrounding the economic value of cultural assets and the processes that bring them into being—whether Oshima tsumugi, dorozome, or a site worthy of World Natural Heritage status—risks breaking the threads that connect people with nature. But maintaining or reestablishing these threads leads to an acceptance that the future is unknown.

In November 2021, an article first published in an Amamian local newspaper found its way onto Japan's *Yahoo! News* (2021). The article explained that because of the shortage of woodcutters, there is a shortage of accessible techigi trees in Amami, a labor issue "causing a headache" for dyeing craftspeople that constitutes "a major problem for the survival of Oshima tsumugi, a traditional national craft." After the article's publication, Kanai Kougei was inundated with calls (even from the neighboring island of Tokunoshima) and visits from locals carrying logs in their vehicles, felled from their backyard, their own forests, or places where they knew techigi grew. It is impossible to know what propelled such a public response without recording individual motivations, but the reaction suggests that the community, like the younger craftspeople of Kanai Kougei, didn't realize techigi's "real worth." The news report altered their conception of waste and value by highlighting techigi as a material essential to a local tradition and demonstrated the tree's potential monetization. When the news broke, those who did know its value—the woodcutters—called the workshop to inform them that they had been "busted" by their employers for selling the wood on the side.

The loss of agency over the stewardship of Amami's land and forests and the associated ecological knowledge consequently threatens the future stability of a much-treasured traditional craft that is important to both the island's identity and its economy. While the demand for traditional kimono continues to decline, the demand for contemporary textiles that are assumed to be environmentally friendly increases. The question remains whether a sustainable source of techigi can be acquired to meet this demand in the future and, perhaps more vital, whether this access is embedded in truly sustaining processes that entwine Amami's environment and the lives of the island's inhabitants.

Conclusion

Throughout the year I spent in Amami there was ongoing construction work to the Toguchi River, which I would pass on my way to Kanai Kougei. The workmen were slowly moving down the river toward the sea, using heavy machinery to widen the riverbed and concrete the banks—raising defenses after a typhoon had led to bad flooding in the village some years before (figure C.1). Farther into the mountains the river ran wild, but at intervals it was intercepted by aging, moss-covered concrete walls and tunnels, previously erected in an attempt to manage the risk of heavy rainfall. Week after week I watched the workmen progress, coming ever closer to a stretch of road from where I could observe what they were doing over the steering wheel of my car. On those many trips to and from Toguchi, I pondered whether the engineers' work was necessary and what impact it would have. This thought came not without reason. To aid regional development and create jobs, riparian control and coastal defense via "hard" infrastructure projects exploded across Japan in the post–World War II period,

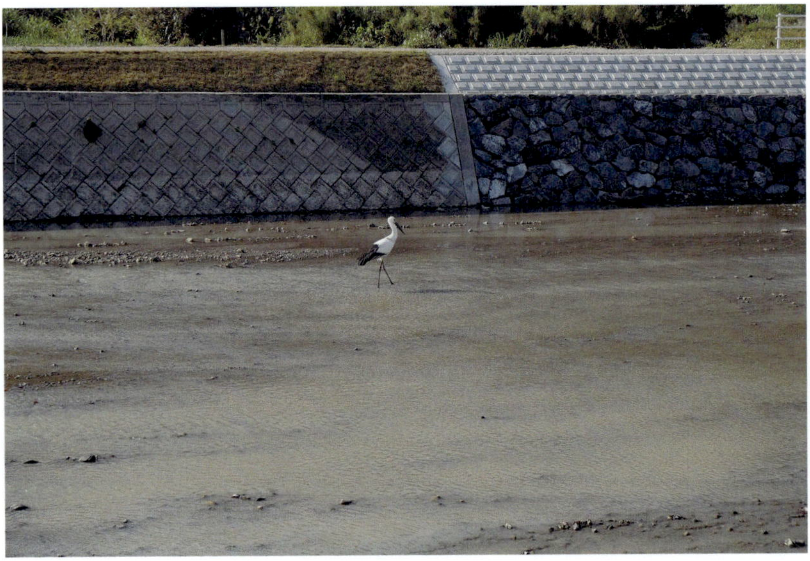

Figure C.1 *An endangered Oriental stork (*Ciconia boyciana*) fishing in the Toguchi River with its concrete-enforced banks.*

and many of these public works have produced unintended and destructive consequences.[1]

The industrial and mechanical scale of the work on the river seemed far removed from the careful handwork I witnessed and participated in across the workshops at Kanai Kougei—yet the proximity between the two endeavors resonated on other levels. For one, the river ran parallel to the workshop's valuable *dorota,* a sensitive ecosystem that both relied on the continual presence of groundwater brought to the surface with an electric pump and seemed intensely vulnerable to flooding. The raising of the riverbanks offered a level of security for Kanai Kougei, and the concrete drains built around the workshop's foundations in the 1980s provided free and convenient wastewater management. However, the natural state of the river farther into the mountains also played a fundamental role in the dyeing process. Cloth and yarn were washed in the fast-flowing, clear, pristine waters in an upland location made accessible by the feet of the dyers, who trampled the overgrowth carrying heavy boxes of textiles. Between the dorota and the riverbanks were fertile *hatake,* where bent-over residents with Amamian *teru* baskets would take a shortcut through the workshop's grounds to their patch of Amamian vegetables (figures C.2 and C.3). The workshop's cats and resident buzzards, meanwhile, would seek food or hunt snakes and lizards in the scrub that grew between neat rows of sweet potatoes, spring onions, tomatoes, and *handama* (a local bicolored spinach).

The workshop relied on the control of nature via concrete infrastructure, pipework, electric pumps, and the roads that defined the path into the mountains. But equally, the serendipity of the site and unpredictable local microclimate made Toguchi a prime area for the production of an esoteric dyeing process like *dorozome*. What became increasingly apparent to me during my fieldwork was the *permeability* of Kanai Kougei—at a structural level, in the workshop's active use of natural water sources, atmospheric conditions, and fertile soils for dyeing or crop growing, and on a more abstract level, through its adaptability and improvisation around its relationship to shifting conditions and access to resources, labor, and the market. While this book has taken the workshop and its traditional practice of natural dyeing—specifically dorozome—as its core, I have done so with the understanding that such craft practices operate alongside industrial processes through the shared underlying need to extract economic value from material resources and labor. The visual proximity I experienced daily between the concreting of the Toguchi River in the background and the dorota in the foreground seemed exceptional to me because, within a tight geographic boundary, nature, infrastructure, industry, cultural practice, sustenance, and sociality collided in the open. But this boundary was permeable to the elements, nature, pollution, spiritual forces, the community, and the influence of craftspeople and bureaucrats both local and from farther afield. Kanai Kougei might provide a metaphor for the shared ground of uncertainty apparent in the microprocesses of natural dyeing and the unpredictable force of river hydrology. I have attempted in this book to offer an entrance point for understanding the distinct ways in which Kanai Kougei navigates such uncertainty and the perspectives this may offer for increasingly urgent discourses around sustainability.

The Impact of Controlling Nature

Japan is vulnerable to the effects of around twenty-five typhoons annually (Japan Meteorological Agency 2020), with Amami often lying in their path. But the frequency of typhoons in Amami amounts to a consistency of extreme weather that didn't register with me until after I arrived on the island. In fact, there were only two or three typhoons in 2018 that were violent enough for me to bolt the front door—most prominently Typhoon 21 in September, which caused the significant damage at Kanai Kougei that I mentioned in the introduction (figure C.4). My experience of typhoons was mostly marked by inconvenience:

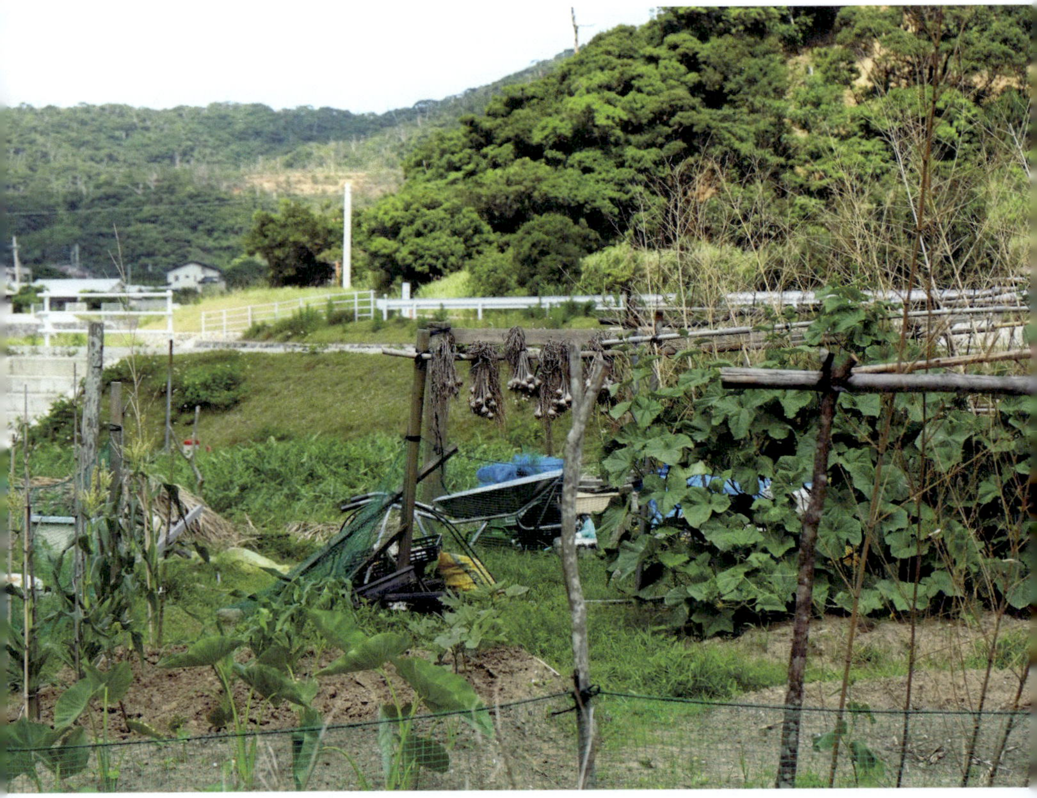

Figure C.2 *Village residents use hatake to grow vegetables that help make Ryūkyū residents some of the longest-lived people in the world.*

torrential rain, a disturbed night's sleep, canceled flights, and disappointment that I couldn't swim in the sea. But that is not to say I didn't check in with friends or they with me to be sure everyone was safe. As I have described, typhoons are considered part of Amami and as such people take them in their stride. When they know an imminent typhoon might be strong, they take precautions, with schools and nurseries closing and the sound of hammering nails resounding through the villages. I had wondered why it was only now that the river was being reengineered; the Shachō had told me that the strength of typhoons had been worse in the past and flooding therefore more likely. Perhaps, like the unprecedented tsunami that smashed through the seawalls in Tohoku on March 11, 2011, the power of nature has become a more dispersed and shared concern across Japan's population in recent years, and what havoc this power could create in the future is seen as increasingly unpredictable.

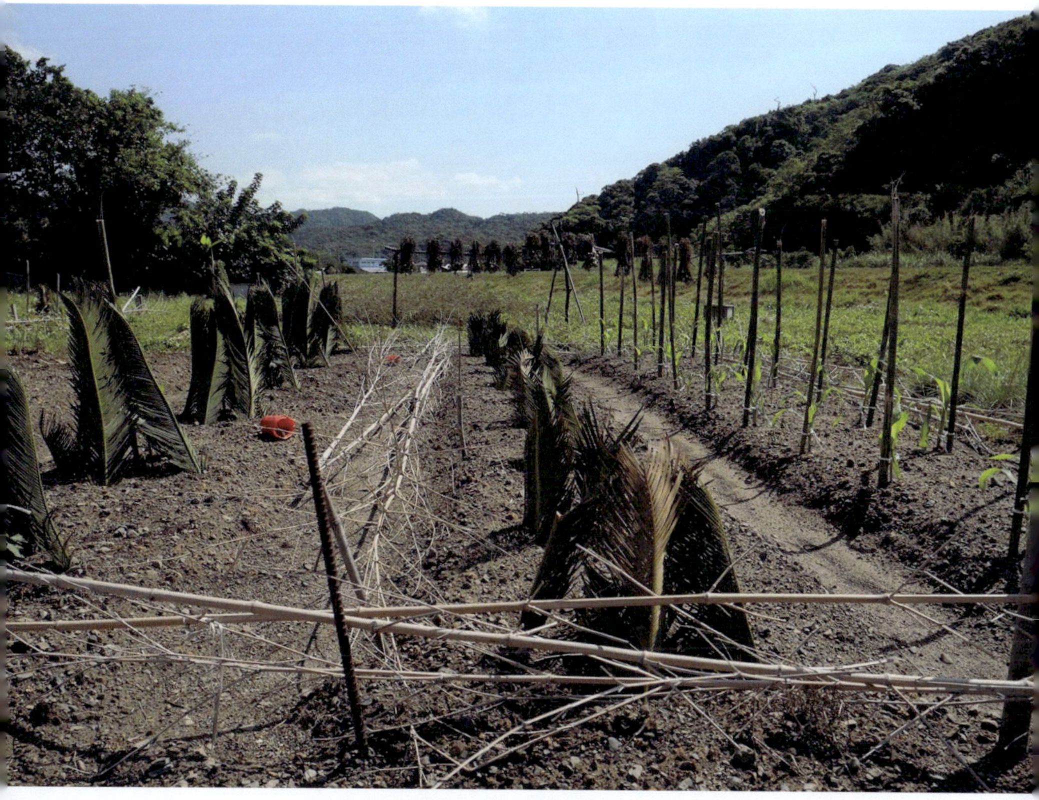

Figure C.3 *Sotetsu fronds protect seedlings from the wind.*

Such a concern for the future played on my mind as I asked how climate change might affect a small island like Amami, where weather and water are so present in the lives and livelihoods of its residents. This dependence was certainly the case for the dyers, who I have shown are both reliant on natural materials and resources but also restricted by atmospheric conditions, at times needing to adapt their workflow daily. But the answers I got from residents, who didn't seem overly worried and, similar to the Shachō, perceived typhoons to be lessening in their severity, actually aligned with what many climate scientists are currently saying about the region. Although much of their work is based on modeling, scientists believe that due to the rise in sea temperatures typhoons are shifting farther west and heading north to Honshu, to mainland Japan, away from Amami. In some instances, storms are proving to be not as strong as in previous years, but they are capable of carrying a heavier rain load and lasting for

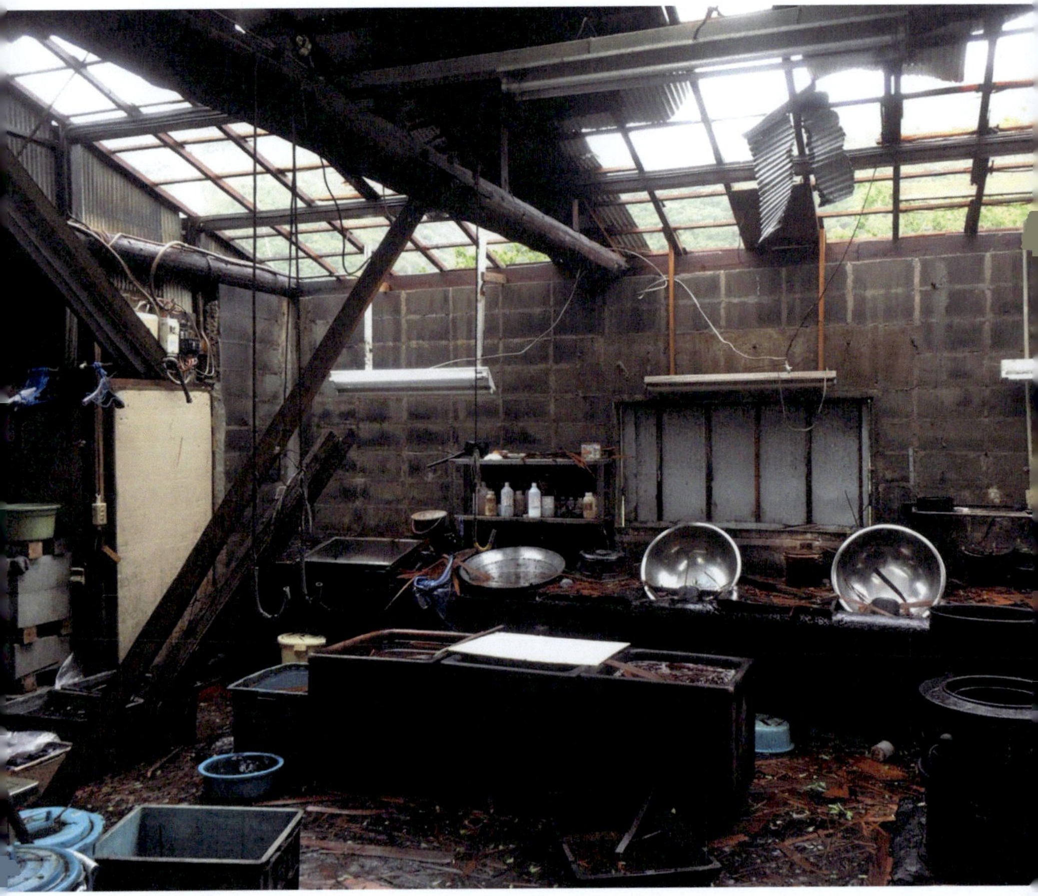

Figure C.4 *The dorozome workshop after 2018's Typhoon 21. Photo by Yukihito Kanai.*

longer, which causes flash flooding and landslides—already a deadly problem throughout Japan (Sousounis 2019). My participants suggest that because of the lack of human intervention—trees are no longer coppiced and thinned for daily use—forests have become thick and dense, leading to an increase in landslides as roots uplift the thin soils that cover the mountains. The combination of human intervention (or lack thereof) and the shift in the predicted path and the changing nature of typhoons is causing significant anxiety about the ability of infrastructure to cope; this became apparent after Typhoon 21, when Kansai Airport, which serves Kyoto and Osaka (and provides daily flights to Amami), suffered extensive damage. But more frequent, more violent, and longer-lasting storms hitting more populated mainland areas will also have a significant economic impact, with insurance premiums rising to account for damage but also disruption. It is unknown how extreme weather will impact Amami directly, but as an island heavily reliant on state funding and corporate infrastructures, it is likely that mitigations and crisis measures at the national level will have knock-on effects economically and socially. This is the case around the world, where the impacts of the climate crisis will range from extreme national drought to localized flooding. Newspaper articles and blog posts suggest that rather than addressing the source of the problem by reducing its carbon output, Japan, like most developed countries worldwide, is seeking to engineer its way out of trouble. The contradictions inherent in Amami, between local experiences and adaptations and national anxieties and mitigation measures, suggest that while the climate emergency is a relatively new struggle, the uncertainty it generates and the solutions being sought are not unfamiliar.

These historical patterns lead one to ask how local conditions are controlled to manage uncertainty when outside forces are beyond control. How do the actions of bureaucrats and state agencies differ from or even conflict with local methods, and what impact does this conflict have? While addressing the vast uncertainties generated by global climate change goes beyond the scope of this book, I have tried to account for the way that particularly economic and environmental uncertainty experienced at a national level weaves its way into the lives and work practices of my participants in Amami, particularly in regard to commodity production and consumption. The majority of this book has addressed the question of uncertainty that individuals and communities feel as a result of friction between nature and economics. Chapter 1 told the history of *Oshima tsumugi* and the unstable market the industry has increasingly dealt with, addressing the often-opposed approaches of preservation or innovation that aim to sustain the skills of artisans locally. By considering the *longue durée* of textile production in Amami, I have shown how processes of industrialization have applied advancing technology to traditional techniques to gain a competitive edge. But at the stage when technology matched the quality of handwork or a local industry could no longer compete with global prices, a crisis of labor, space, and identity has been resolved through the halting of innovation and the fixing of labor, materials, and traditions to local geographies. This worked in favor of the nostalgia boom that occurred in Japan in the post–World War II period, where the symbolic potential of "traditional Japan" was used to promote national identity, and traditional commodities such as kimono were used to offset social anxiety caused by rapid industrialization and urban migration. Typically, these dynamics have been managed by outside bureaucrats in order to maintain cultural boundaries and local economies. Yet by examining the history of Oshima tsumugi one can appreciate that this approach of fixing labor, materials, and traditions to geographic spaces only works when there is demand (see Harvey 2001, 25). I used Kanai Kougei to show an alternative approach to fixity, that of innovation and diversification, that welcomed the flow of ideas, materials, technologies, and people from outside the community to better manage local conditions. Instead of being threatening, outside forces were reconceptualized by Kanai Kougei as an opportunity to obtain social and economic sustainability using the power of nature and tradition as tools for promotion. But rather than being singular solutions, I suggested that both routes—preservation and innovation—are precarious and therefore require an adaptive touch, that they borrow from each other, if craft processes are to endure.

Chapters 2 and 3 looked at how the precarious labor market and the environmental pollution in Japan motivated some of my participants to relocate to the countryside, where they felt they could find more agency regarding their career, lifestyle, and relationships with their community and the natural environment. I argued that rather than reframing this move as a retreat, problems became more tangible in rural contexts, where my participants felt they could develop the skills, networks, and knowledge associated with craftmanship to enable them to make a difference locally. In chapter 2 I explored how the alchemy of producing color allows for these aspirations to be realized, because natural dyeing ties one to one's local geography and community through atmosphere, nature, and history. The metropolitan mobility of a younger generation of dyers and their entrepreneurial outlook, meanwhile, allows them to take advantage of global networks of craftworkers and enthusiasts and to engage multinational corporations. This makes their lifestyle economically viable, while supporting the wider island economy. Nevertheless, I highlighted that this approach to business requires compromise: It comes at the cost of reliance on industrial materials and infrastructures and exploits the craftsperson's love for their profession to solve the problem of financial deficit and industrial timing, resulting in potentially exhaustive labor regimes.

Chapter 3 began to delve into the ethics of the environmental impact of the production and consumption of commodities. I have shown how, at Kanai Kougei, production and consumption have been blurred through the public workshop model that enables people to "dye it themselves," but also how my participants' past consumption practices inform how they live their lives and consume in the present. I discussed how many of my participants were drawn to Amami partly in response to a history in Japan of prioritizing economic growth over the health of citizens and the environment. My analysis followed the narrative of food security, an issue heightened since 3.11 when anxiety caused by

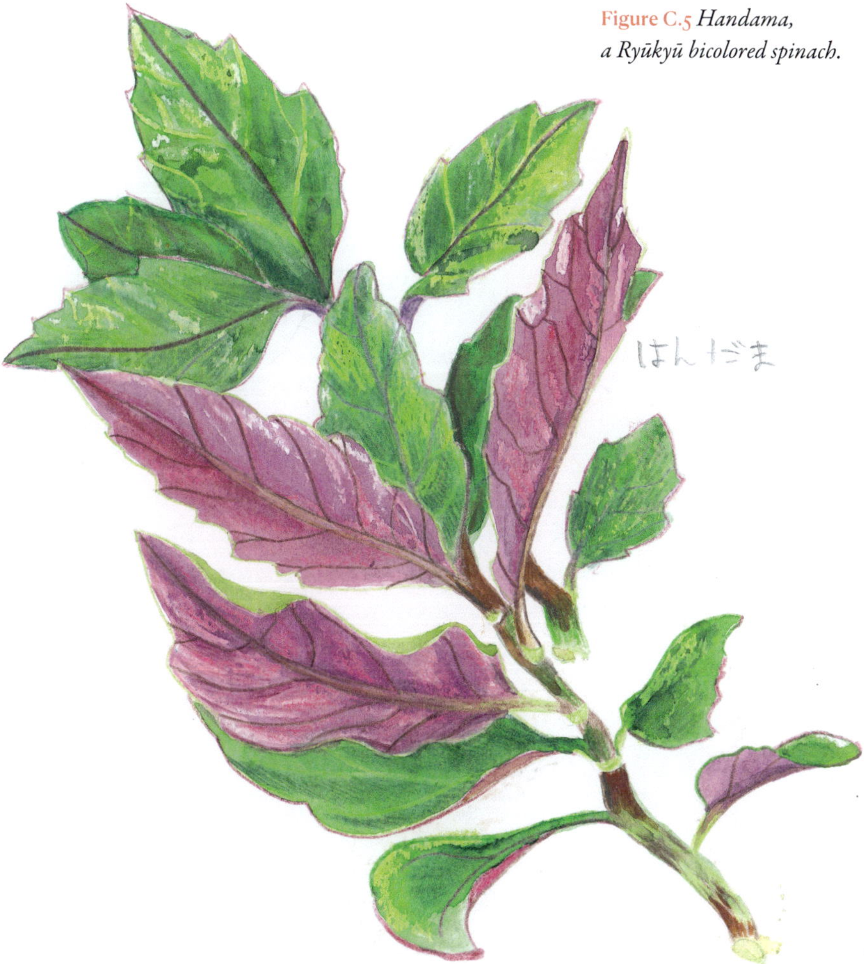

Figure C.5 *Handama, a Ryūkyū bicolored spinach.*

radiation created at least two "secular spirits" of the Anthropocene (Bubandt 2017, G124). The first of these spirits is radiation's invisible potential to cause significant health problems; the second is the bureaucratic failings that led to a loss of trust in public health advice issued by the state. In order to regain control of these aporetic forces, many of my participants reassessed their work-life balance by moving to the countryside to reestablish stronger connections with nature and local food systems (figure C.5). I have suggested that as a result of lower incomes and an increased sensitivity to seasonality on the island, my participants were redefining the meaning of affluence and reevaluating waste through practices associated with the Japanese term *mottainai*. The address of a waste of life, waste of time, and waste of materials coalesced in Amami through sharing, exchange, and reuse economies, leading me to ask whether everyday practices could actively facilitate lasting redefinitions of value. The first discussion I had about mottainai was with Kazuko when we both noticed that outside a weaving school many fallen *tankan* fruits weren't being collected. Mottainai expresses "shame" because it highlights something that has value in the broadest sense but isn't being accessed as it might. Mottainai might have reflected the loss of economic value because these citrus fruits could be sold with good market value. But on another occasion, Kazuko told me that her kids were out of the house because they had accompanied her neighbors to pick the family's tankan grove. This activity could be defined as highly social, educational, free, and fun—and it would mean the boys would return home with bags of tankan that would last several weeks. Value, then, is not concentrated on the economic but distributed in far more novel ways. Rather than the countryside being seen as a historical repository, its residents, traditions, and local ecological knowledge might just posit an idea of a more sustainable future. Nevertheless, these practices might be offset by more wasteful habits that go unacknowledged, particularly those described in the second half of the book, where water pollution, a reliance on fossil fuels, and industrial forestry are reflective of practices enforced by national policies that sever conceptualizations of circularity within resource use.

The first three chapters worked toward answering my central research question: Can local craft processes and ecologies of production sustain a community socially, economically, and environmentally? In many respects the answer would be a tentative yes, but as I have shown, the situation is complex and precarious. As discussed in the introduction, sustainability, as an interconnected set of practices and rhetorics, necessarily functions at a scale that is global and universalizing, with impact often felt at smaller scales through targets tied to ends-oriented change. Imperatives toward reaching the goal of "sustainability" are often divorced from conditions experienced at local levels, with defined sets of protocols instituted by an outside authority or the expectations of an ethically driven corporate brand. The ideology of sustainability, not unlike heritage or other preservation initiatives, largely serves to define "low-impact" small-scale craft processes as niche and geographically and temporally bounded. In *Dyeing with the Earth* I have turned my gaze away from *sustainability* and instead toward *sustaining processes*, what I define as those small actions that my participants carry out on the ground in order to maintain resources, whether cultural, economic, or environmental, while being subject to pressure from local hierarchies, municipal bureaucrats, or commissioning designers.

While I have argued that *kusakizome*, at least in Amami, relies on local materials, environmental conditions, and traditional knowledge, my research has shown that craft processes, craft materials, and craftspeople are always on the move, adapting to circumstances as they present themselves. This suggests that the adaptability—not only the fixity—of craftwork should be highlighted. This is because craft cosmologies can redefine the concept of innovation: Ideas do not necessarily need to be new to respond to modern-day problems. The Shachō's and Yukihito-san's work in redefining the potential of dorozome (chapters 1 and 2) demonstrates this well, while the embrace of mottainai, as described in chapter 3, illustrates a wider practice of recycling old ideas to answer contemporary problems among creative communities. As I have argued, Kanai Kougei is a permeable entity that absorbs difference, reconceptualizes disruptions, and uses innovation to problem solve. But it is also clear that this permeability has its boundaries—water literally seeps into every aspect of Kanai Kougei's work, yet its disposal practices seem to sever a connection to water at the point it meets the workshop's drains. My understanding of "sustaining processes" therefore needs to encompass actions that appease uncertainty through willful avoidance, or even neglect. These actions can perhaps be gauged in terms of proximity—the issue of water pollution is considered distant enough not to impact the workshop in a way that would outweigh other considerations related to sustaining itself, its environment, and its community. Contradictions and compromises that tend to lower production costs rather than benefiting the environment have to be accepted. Such compromises are sought to sustain local social relations (even within the confines of the workshop) and to appease high-profile clients farther afield.

Yukihito-san often told me that working in apparel differed from working in *tsumugi*, because the business was heterarchical rather than hierarchical. In some respects, this was true—he was in a position to negotiate terms or refuse work if it did not align with his vision, unlike in the tsumugi industry, which remained very much top-down. Yet I watched as a bystander as designer brands would take advantage of the workshop's generosity regarding payment procedures or use the promise of big orders or public relations exposure to pressure Kanai Kougei on cost, timing, or aesthetics. Having worked in the fashion industry, I know how to recognize these tricks of the trade from a distance, and I offered my opinion when asked. This was certainly a benefit of my methodological approach, as I stood in the unique position of being both expert and novice. Rather than asking how reaching economic sustainability might positively impact craft communities and ecologies, an alternative perspective on these conflictual conditions may stem from asking how craft communities, their ways of life, and their epistemologies might disrupt capitalist frameworks of consumption.

Chapter 4 began to focus on local resource extraction, setting the tone for the remaining chapters by bringing to the fore the wider theme of control and impact that ran through the first but also the second half of this book. From the microprocesses of natural dyeing to the macroscale of wildlife conservation, I have highlighted man's desire to control nature and the negative (but sometimes positive) impact such actions have. I have tried to account for the contradiction between discourse and practice, where Amamians have a strong connection with, and respect for, the natural environment—but where, like most advanced capitalist societies globally, environmental ethics are inconsistent. In chapter 4 I used the case study of bird conservation in Japan as a historical example, guided by the *mejiro* bird kept as a pet at Kanai Kougei. Grounded in the period during and immediately after World War II, a time when Japanese conceptions of nature collided with Western ideals and a period of widespread modernization ensued, I demonstrated in the local context the geopolitical, social, and ecological dynamics that either allow or resist the ability of global environmental movements to take hold. During this period, the abundance of nature was commodified to sustain the population in times of scarcity. But the occupying Americans in the postwar period brought into sharp relief what Japanese elites had been saying for decades: that the consumption of birdlife was ecologically unsustainable. I suggested reasons why conservation was successful, despite wild bird consumption being culturally important. Birds consequently reverted from commodity to "companion," as human populations were alerted to the interdependent dynamic of their relationship. Bringing the wildlife conservation debate into the current day, I explored how Japanese Shinto cosmologies integrate animism into daily life and discussed how "spiritual" narratives tend to incorporate practical knowledge of living in relative harmony with other beings. I suggest, however, that postwar rationality in the form of technoscientific development and the use of industrial materials has tended to obscure these narratives and break the threads of connection that tie people to the land. I argue that without a physical land-based connection, kami and therefore nature became an abstraction. But by imbuing the material world with visual symbols of kami and also endangered wildlife, a contemporary form of totemism or visual companionship occurs, creating a connectedness that bridges the distance between internal thought and external representations of nature. These totems promote care and responsibility—at least in theory. This case study, that considered natural resource extraction in Japan but also Amami, set the scene for a closer look at Kanai Kougei's ecologies of production in chapters 5 and 6.

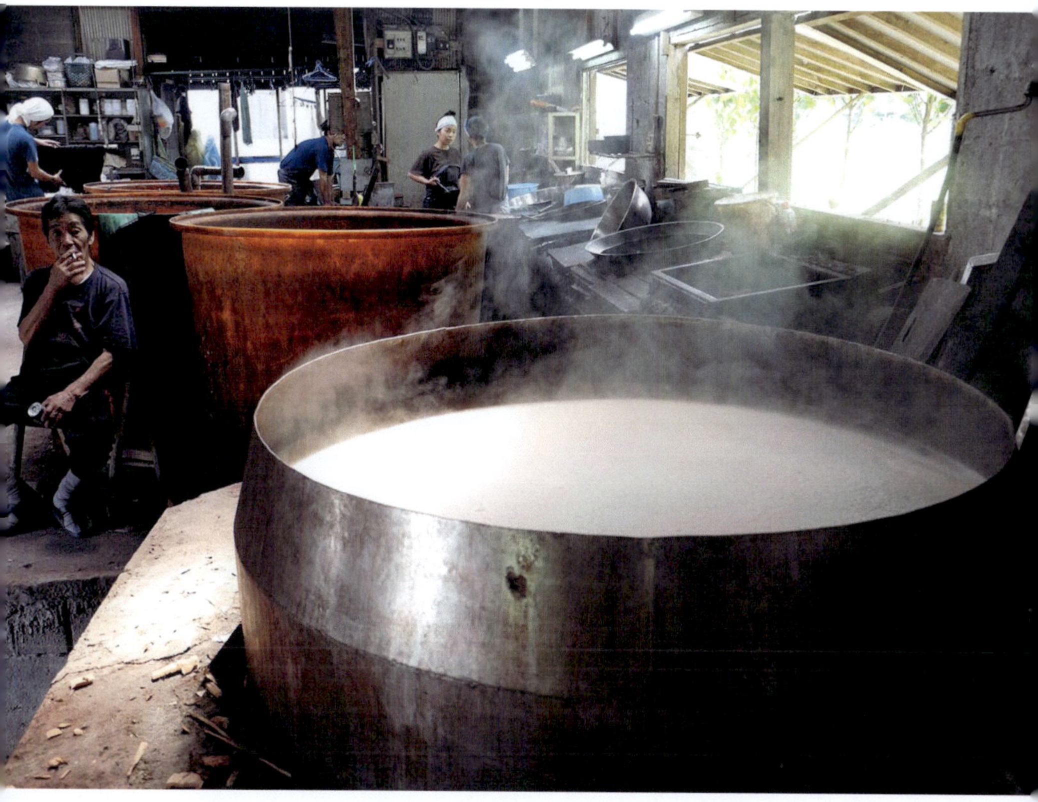

Figure C.6 *Nagata-san rests and watches over the hot techigi liquid.*

Chapter 5 sought to understand water pollution at Kanai Kougei as a generationally defined happening, resulting from financial limitation, and as a clash between traditional practice and industrial capitalism. Through an analysis of water sources used by the workshop, I argued that water is a central binding force enmeshing history, ecology, utility, and capital at Kanai Kougei. But I also revealed practices of disposal, where waste dye and chemicals are put into the drains, washed into the Toguchi River, then out to sea. I used a discussion of Amamian spirituality to suggest water pollution results from a continuation of geographically embedded beliefs where nature and spiritual beings are considered to reside beyond the boundaries of the village. Within the village, embedded habits of disposal have not been updated to account for industrial materials. I highlight the complexity of instituting sustaining processes and the economic and social limitations to seeking resolutions that offset individual but also collective uncertainty.

Chapter 6 delves into reasons why nature has become increasingly abstract by exploring land and forest access in Amami and the historical events that have led to an increasing disconnect with the land and loss of traditional ecological knowledge. I argued that nature's reduction to data, a conceptualization that exists within a history of Western knowledge systems, where the control of nature has been seen as a tool to improve society, has been forced by economics mostly instituted by colonial and imperial forces. By making nature easier to govern and understand, humans have been better able to control it and thereby increase productivity, a method applied to both natural environments and communities of people, plants, and animals. By focusing on trees essential for dyeing textiles in Amami, I highlighted the impact that this control has had in the realm of forestry, where the ability to access even individual trees is precarious and obtaining them in the future uncertain. But more importantly, I suggested that the control of nature has meant that craftspeople are not able to conceptualize a tree's "real worth" and thereby implement practices of care. This is because the trees are seen only as an economic unit and not an element existing within an ecosystem and within a culture. I explained how this has been allowed to occur, as communities have increasingly been dispossessed of land and property laws made more hegemonic in the context of geopolitical interventions. I suggested that although the aims of conservation, preservation, and resource management—centralized initiatives organized at the state, prefecture, or NGO scale—are often imagined with good intentions, foregrounding economics to promote but also sustain natural environments or craft processes often increases risk. Instead, it might be argued that with guidance, local people are better able to manage and self-govern their environment by adopting sustaining processes that benefit a wide conception of community.

In the introduction I posed the argument that Japan's cultural and natural properties are exploited by the ideology of improvement, making them subject to appropriation by the government and market as assets. By demarcating these assets as special, they can be put to profit, with their "natural" qualities being particularly valuable during this current period of environmental crisis. This bounding of property is important because it works toward a greater understanding of current heritage models, which might offer fresh insight. The Japanese system of craft preservation via the Intangible Cultural Property scheme is held in such high esteem because, unlike UK models that have historically focused on preserving objects, the Japanese model aims to preserve the skills of individual craftspeople and collectives of craftspeople, resulting in prestige and finance. This model is lauded because, in theory, it encourages the transference of intangible knowledge across generations so that the same item can be made anew in fifty, one hundred, or three hundred years' time. Yet much in the way that nature conservation focuses on a particular space, what I have shown is that while craft preservation aims to maintain skills, it ultimately still fixes these skills within the object—whether it is Oshima tsumugi, Onta pottery, or *sukumo* indigo. However, it is the *permeability* of the skills of craftspeople, and their ability to adapt to environmental and economic conditions, that makes dorozome possible in a context such as Amami. Nevertheless, the skills that are highlighted within schemes such as the Intangible Cultural Property scheme, but also in the marketing literature of companies using Kanai Kougei's services, reflect unchanged practices and perfected outcomes of a technique that emphasizes continuity, a fallacy that is marketed for profit. I have also shown that the tsumugi union and those with a stake in tsumugi work toward preserving the skills of dorozome or techniques such as weaving but have little interest in securing the future of *techigi* trees—even though they are essential for the dyeing process. Similarly, the methods of washing yarns in the rivers and obtaining groundwater are vital for achieving the approved shades of Oshima tsumugi, yet it is unlikely that anyone but the dyers considers the importance of the river.

Promoting low-impact craft processes as sustainable is also a worthless pursuit if interconnecting processes, materials, infrastructure, and labor are not taken into account. This problem, on a broader scale, was demonstrated by the Japanese government's promotion of mottainai as part of its sustainability initiative for the 2020 (2021) Tokyo Olympics. Various waste and recycled materials were adopted, including renewable energy, recycled rainwater, podiums made from recycled plastic, and medals made of recast precious metals from postconsumer electronics (Tokyo 2020, 2018.). But the construction of the Olympic stadium itself came under fire. Structurally, it used Japanese wood together with concrete panels to create the look of a cliff face. Yet these panels were made using cheap plywood, the production of which had been sourced to timber harvested from South Asian tropical rainforests with unknown origins (Neslen 2018).

My central argument here is that embracing, promoting, and preserving traditional craft skills is of little value if the process is not considered holistically. Instead, throughout this book I have shown that craft processes and craft communities of natural dyers are entangled in complex, geographically specific entwinements of nature, cultural practice, and economics. These entanglements accrue across multiple temporalities; in the case of Amamian dorozome, they are influenced by feudalism, land-based belief systems, postwar state reforms, and contemporary patterns of migration. Craft processes use intangible knowledge of local materials and resources garnered via social relationships established across many generations and also gain those from farther afield, through communication with crafting communities across Japan and internationally. They access informal economies that allow the craft to continue, while taking advantage of international markets and state financing. Craft cosmologies exist alongside ecosystems of companion species that assist in the production of commodities, whether it is the trees and plants that provide colorants, the bacteria that ferment indigo baths and techigi dye, or the mejiro that pollinate tankan blossoms to provide sustenance for the dyer.

Ecologies of (Textile) Production

When I have given talks about my research, textile enthusiasts have been frustrated when I haven't explained exactly how the *shimebata* loom works (chapter 1). Those who work in textile conservation, meanwhile, want to know why the iron mordant used in dorozome doesn't destroy the fibers, as it is widely acknowledged that ferric oxide eventually eats away at textiles that rely on similar chemistry. While my research is embedded in the Amamian textile industry, my participant apprenticeship methodology might not allude to a traditional ethnography of making. Unlike the work of anthropologist Maureen MacKenzie (1991), it forgoes details on technique; neither does this book follow the path laid by Tim Ingold (2013) or Trevor Marchand (2010), who bring to the fore somatic knowledge. I believe aspects of this work are embedded throughout the chapters and reflected in my use of design, apprenticeship, and visual methods. But the heart of the book is located in the natural world, somewhere a reader who is expecting to learn principally about textiles may be surprised to find themselves.

I headed to Amami with a desire to learn more about the materiality of natural dyeing and to explore those "natural" credentials and what they might mean for discourses around sustainability. The reality, then, that dyeing cosmologies expanded into the forests, mountains, skies, rivers, and seas should not be a surprise to any anthropologist. *Dyeing with the Earth* offers a new perspective on the study of textiles and the study of the environment, because I demonstrate the point where these two disciplines meet through economics and resource extraction, in what I term "ecologies of production." These are spaces shaped both by humans and other species that collectively work in a productive capacity both within and outside of capitalist systems. They may be the rivers used to wash yarns, the biodiverse dorota whose mud is aerated by the boots of dyers, the monoculture forests where techigi grows, or the boundary *fukugi* trees of old *kominka* houses that shield fruit groves from the wind while offering up a

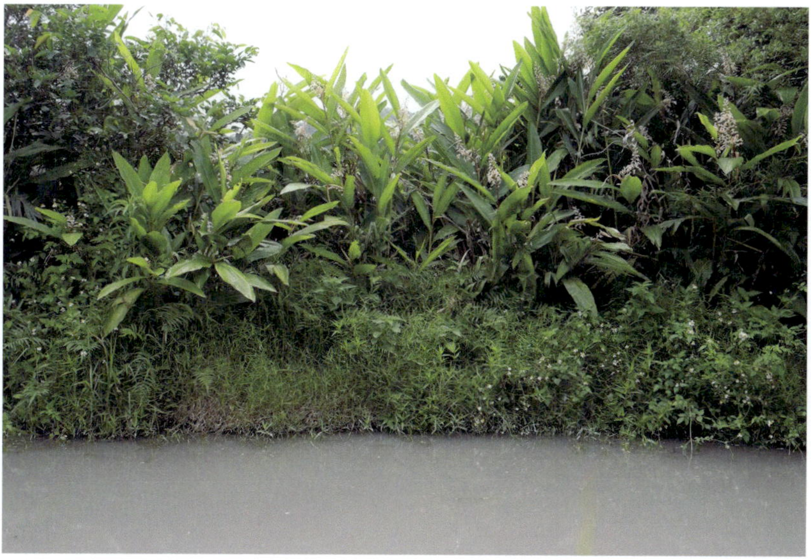

Figure C.7 *Kanai Kougei's dorota.*

brilliant shade of yellow. Like in the *satoyama* (mountain-village) ecosystems of Japan—where cultivated and uncultivated areas in the mountains, valleys, forests, and seas provide ideal habitats for a variety of species that are helpful to humans—in ecologies of production, there is also interdependence. A variety of species embedded in the landscape are interconnected through material and infrastructural needs, yet as I have shown, there is also a breakdown of understanding of this level of dependence among craftspeople, a reality that does not bode well for more sustainable futures. I argue that understanding how ecosystems that support craft production function environmentally, socially, culturally, and economically is key to establishing sustaining processes that could have wider implications for the future of craft and other production-based industries.

Much of this book was written during the UK's COVID-19 lockdowns, a time when the world faced an unprecedented period of uncertainty. Initial panic concentrated on the health of oneself and one's family, friends, and wider community, but beyond anxiety about catching the virus, it was interesting to observe how uncertainty that started from afar moved into the domestic sphere. As the virus impacted geopolitics and supply chains, I was left worried whether I would be able to buy Seville oranges at the grocery store or post letters to friends in Japan, seeing uncertainty relocated to the contents of one's fruit bowl in no time at all. What I have argued throughout is that while uncertainty and disruption stimulate anxiety, uncertainty in daily life might be reconceptualized as a necessity—because it makes you do things that you might not otherwise. As Mathijs Pelkmans (2013, 31) says, the "important point is that the future will remain unknown, and it is this uncertainty that provides the stimulus for continuation." Uncertainty leads one to question the politics of the everyday, since there are many things that are beyond our control but others that should be within our grasp. We should be able to say whether the water of a river, lake, or coastline is safe for swimming. If not, why not, and who is responsible for its care? When life was disrupted during the COVID-19 pandemic, issues that might have seemed superfluous or monolithic were thrust into the public spotlight. It has made societies globally question what John Law (2004, 13), after Annemarie Mol, suggests are "different realities" and when one might choose to adopt "*political* reasons for preferring and enacting one kind of reality rather than another." In many instances these realities are chosen based on a need to implement change, but my work has shown a contradiction at play: that good intentions, motivated by either a genuine desire to implement processes of care or else a desire to perform them, do not always result in direct action. It is often the case that communities are restricted by a lack of finance, by social norms, by the pressures of time, or by the inability to organize, resulting in compromises to reach a resolution.

As I have shown throughout this book, traditional craft provides its own reality—different stories of make and use that can be adapted by the craftsperson or commissioning agents to fulfill a purpose. Craft processes—such as natural dyeing—are thought to have a low environmental impact, support cultural continuity, and offer enriching vocations. The practice has therefore entered the discourse as a fix to contemporary problems of resource extraction, production, use and disposal of commodities, and associated discussions around labor. In this respect, natural dyeing is an example of the universalizing tendencies present in sustainability rhetoric, where designers and brands latch on to the knowledge—or hope—that it will assuage anxieties (their own or others') and encourage consumers to buy their products. Capitalism is, after all, ends oriented, locating the quickest route to generating capital. But throughout this book I have tried to show that natural dyeing and traditional craft processes more widely are not the panacea for the challenges faced by the fashion and textiles industry. I have shown that natural dyeing is a process full of contradictions, entangled in histories, societies, ecologies, and markets of varying scales and ethics. Perhaps more tellingly, it is at the apex of problems surrounding resource extraction, materials stewardship, land access, and exploitative labor as issues that exist on a historical continuum rather than simply contained by concepts of modernity.

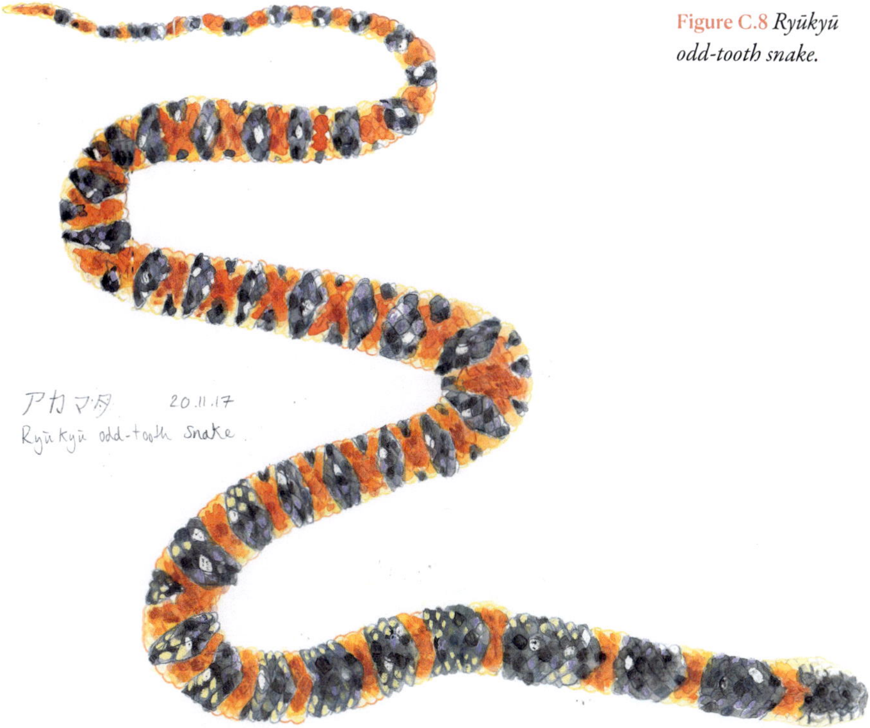

Figure C.8 *Ryūkyū odd-tooth snake.*

Accordingly, I have endeavored to highlight the pitfalls of extracting the methodologies and practices that Kanai Kougei works with as solutions to concerns around sustainability. Such a logic renders solutions through bounded conceptions of space and time—the uniqueness of place that yields privileged access to materials and that of history that produces cultural specificity—rather than addressing the uncertainties, absences, and frictions that exist within the dynamics of control and impact felt in an environment. Instead, I suggest that the workshop may be considered as a heuristic device for complexifying the way we think and produce knowledge around concerns of sustainability and how this spans geographies and temporalities. Among its wealth of techniques, skills, and aesthetics, what can be learned from Kanai Kougei is how the embrace of a lack of control, and the acceptance of uncertainty, is responsively built into local epistemologies. Traditional craft is not a fixed system of practices and relations—seen outside of the imperative to preserve, it is rather a daily encounter with the very issues that lie at the heart of our ability to exist sustainably.

Acknowledgments

This book would not have been possible without the generosity and support of Kanai Kougei and the wider community in Amami Ōshima. The Kanais welcomed me into their workshop, an extension of their family, and introduced me to friends who have shared and continue to share their knowledge while bestowing care and kindness. Particular thanks go to Yukihito, Reiko, Eriko, and Kazuhito (Shachō) Kanai; Akiyo and Koki; Maiko-san; Satoko-chan; Kazu-san; Nagata-san; Takahito-san; Yuske-san; Kōji-ani; and Yumiko-san. I continue to work with and appreciate the brilliance of Kazuko, who has become a great friend and makes each return to Amami a homecoming. Thank you also to Sayaka in New York for introducing me to *dorozome*, and to the craftspeople I met in Okinawa and Kyūshū who took the time to share their experiences of dyeing with me.

My husband, Richard, encouraged me to study anthropology and has given feedback on almost everything I've ever written. I am eternally grateful for his patience, input, care, and faith in me and, most importantly, for having him by my side. My friend and mentor Professor Inge Daniels, whose dedication to her students is unsurpassed, continues to inform my academic thinking and method of "mushrooming" while always offering her critical eye to my writing. I am grateful to Professor Lucy Norris, Professor Anna Lora-Wainwright, and Dr. Eiko Soga, who contributed valuable help and feedback during the writing of this book, and the two anonymous peer reviewers selected by Duke University Press for their generous comments on the book manuscript. I thank those at the University of Oxford who extended their learning as professors, teachers, and classmates of anthropology and who have more recently become valued friends and colleagues. Professor Kei Kawai and Professor Sueo Kuwahara in Japan continue to support my research and provide invaluable insights into Amamian human and nonhuman worlds.

Many thanks to the funders of my studies and fieldwork: the Arts and Humanities Research Council, Wolfson College and the School of Anthropology and Museum Ethnography at the University of Oxford, the Pasold Research Fund, the British Association of Japanese Studies, the Folklore Society, the Great Britain Sasakawa Foundation, the Sainsbury Institute for the Study of Japanese Arts and Culture, and the Daiwa Anglo-Japanese Foundation. Generous funds for the color printing of this book were received from All Souls College and the School of Anthropology and Museum Ethnography at the University of Oxford, the Great Britain Sasakawa Foundation, the Association for Asian Studies, and the Pasold Research Fund. At Duke University Press, Ken Wissoker, Kate Mullen, James Moore, and the editorial and design teams, including Lisa Lawley and Courtney Leigh Richardson, have made the publishing process a pleasure—thank you.

Aspects of this book have appeared as journal articles and book chapters. Thank you to the editors of those volumes and to the anonymous peer reviewers for helping strengthen the content and argument of those works. An earlier version of chapter 1 appeared as the article "'Making It for Our Country': An Ethnography of Mud-Dyeing on Amami Ōshima Island" in *Textile: The Journal of Cloth and Culture* 18, no. 3 (2020): 250–277. A previous version of chapter 4 titled "The *Mejiro* Bird: Between Commodity, Conservation and Companion" was included in *Animals Matter: Resistance and Transformation in Animal Commodification*, edited by J. Dugnoille and E. Vander Meer (Leiden: Brill, 2022), 56–84. An earlier version of chapter 6 was published as "Re-Evaluating a Tree's 'Real Worth': The Historical Dispossession of Ecological Stewardship and Its Legacy for a Japanese Textile Tradition" in the journal *History and Anthropology* (2022): 1–24.

My family, friends, and ex-colleagues in the UK and United States have supported my winding route to academia, extended their love of the natural world, and engaged in discussions about Japan, sustainability, and textiles that have informed my thinking. Finally, I thank Amami, an island whose people, nature, and culture are uniquely special. This book is written in the hope that it contributes to respect for the island's complexity and the lessons it can teach us—increasing awareness of the vulnerability of its human and nonhuman worlds rather than fueling their exploitation.

Glossary

Key Japanese Terms

ai	indigo
ai-doro	indigo overdyed with dorozome
aizome	indigo dyeing
akane	madder
boro	rag; tattered clothes
chikyū	Earth
daitai	approximate; rough
dasuki	spinning machine for wet textiles
dentō kōgei	traditional craftwork
dorota	mud field
dorozome	mud dyeing
fudosan tōki	real estate registration
fukugi	common garcinia
furusato	old village; home; native place
habu	pit viper
hanami	cherry-blossom viewing
hatake	agricultural field, but closely resembling an allotment in this context
hebi	snake
ie	physical house, or the household line

ikiru yorokobi	joy of living
inaka	countryside
izakaya	restaurant-bar
kami	god, a deity
kamidana	god-shelf
kasuri	cloth with resist-dyed yarn that is realigned during weaving, creating a blurred pattern
kawa	river
kawaii	cute
keitora	minitruck
kenmun	Amamian forest sprite, or yōkai
kiranki	"trees we don't cut"
kiruto	quilt; blanket
kokutō	black sugar
kuchinashi	Cape jasmine
Kurume gasuri	kasuri from Kurume
kusakizome	plant and tree dyeing
matsuri	festival or party, both traditional and modern
mejiro	Japanese white-eye
mejirooshi	white-eye huddle; signifies abundance
mingei	folkcraft
mochi	sweet or savory rice cake
mottainai	"what a waste"
mukei bunkazai	Intangible Cultural Property
mushi	bugs
nekaseru	to put to sleep
nihonjinron	theories of Japaneseness
noro	the highest-ranking Amamian priestesses
okayu	rice porridge
omiyage	souvenir
onigiri	rice ball
ontayaki	Onta pottery
orimoto-san	weaving company
Oshima tsumugi	Amamian kimono cloth
rurikakesu	Lidth's jay
Ryūkyū ai	Ryūkyū indigo
sakura	cherry blossom
sararīman	salaryman; white-collar worker

satoyama	mountain village associated with a unique ecological system of human-nonhuman cohabitation
shachō	company president
sharinbai	yeddo hawthorn
shima	island
shimayumuta	Amami dialect of the Japanese language
shima-uta	island music
shimebata	loom developed in Amami that wraps the yarn before dyeing to create areas of kasuri resist
shizen	nature
shōchū	sugarcane rum produced in Amami
sotetsu	cycad; *Cycas revolute*
sukumo	Japanese composted indigo pigment
tan	counting unit for cloth
tanbo	rice paddy
tankan	crossbred fruit of tangerine and navel orange grown in Amami
tanmono	roll of cloth for one kimono
techigi	Amami dialect for yeddo hawthorn; used for the tree, wood, and dyeing liquid
tenugui	multiuse hand towel
teru	Amamian back-strapped basket
tsukumogami	tool kami
umeboshi	aged, pickled plums
yōkai	supernatural being or phenomenon; ghost
warichi	split-land system
wariyama	split-mountain system
yuta	lower-ranking Amamian priestesses who today work as mystics

Notes

Introduction

1. Kanai Kougei refers to its name using this romanization. But as a rule, this book follows the Hepburn system when anglicizing Japanese.

2. All participants mentioned or quoted throughout were aware of my position as a researcher and gave consent to record their words and real names, unless stated otherwise.

3. Although the "fashion" and "textile" industries are two distinct entities, I use them interchangeably because their dependence makes them difficult to prize apart.

4. The levels of global water pollution that the fashion and textile industries are responsible for is difficult to quantify, but it is thought to be high (Wicker 2022).

5. Kelly et al. (2019) document how auditing and compliance via corporate social responsibility policies has swelled into a multimillion-dollar industry. Yet the report's authors show these policies are motivated by the mitigation of reputational risk rather than a desire to protect workers or environments. See De Neve and Prentice (2017) for a comprehensive discussion on the health and well-being of sweatshop workers.

6. Although *shachō* translates as "company president," more colloquially it can be understood as "boss." Kazuhito Kanai was known by this term at work, and even his family used it.

7. In Japan, the honorific *-san*, using either first name or surname, is equivalent to *Mr.*, *Mrs.*, or *Ms.*, while *-chan* is used for female children, friends, or pets and *-kun* for male counterparts. When participants were acquaintances or people for whom I wish to stress a level of respect, I have used *-san*. However, my friendships with Koki, Kazuko, and Akiyo, for example, moved beyond honorifics.

8. Previously part of Okinawa's Ryūkyū kingdom, Amami is today bureaucratically attached to Kagoshima Prefecture.

9. I use the term *community* interchangeably to refer to residents bounded by geography—in this case, the island of Amami and the villages of diverse people who share local issues and concerns—and groups within those communities, i.e., those who have migrated to Amami who share a lived experience (see chapter 3). But I also use it when

speaking of dispersed individuals, both in Japan and internationally, who share a passion for craft and are motivated to develop their practice for similar reasons.

10. Alternatively, manufacturers are pursuing innovative and sustainable solutions such as waterless dyeing or dyeing with microbes (Willis 2023).

11. Anthropological research on textile dyeing is scarce, and what exists tends to take a historical perspective focusing on materials and cultural impact (see Schneider 1987; Taussig 2008). Indigo dyeing, however, has been documented ethnographically (Hoskins 1989; Balfour-Paul 2011; Douny 2015).

12. It should be noted that mass production using natural dyes was also environmentally damaging and used exploitative labor practices. See Nenadic and Tuckett (2013) on Scotland's nineteenth-century Turkey red industry.

13. See Luckman and Thomas (2024) for an extended discussion on the community of craft practice.

14. I studied Japanese for one year prior to my fieldwork, and although English was common given the international education and experiences of my fieldwork participants who were happy to translate, including during interviews, a basic level of Japanese was required for taking instruction at the workshop, communicating with visitors, and getting by in daily life.

15. Japan was overtaken by China, which took the number 2 spot in 2010.

16. To maintain anonymity, I have purposely not referenced the designer's name.

1. The Mud Dyers of Amami Ōshima

An earlier version of chapter 1 appeared as "'Making It for Our Country': An Ethnography of Mud-Dyeing on Amami Ōshima Island," *Textile: The Journal of Cloth and Culture* 18, no. 3 (2020): 250–77.

1. The ages given for participants reflect their ages in January 2018.

2. There is evidence to suggest that sericulture existed in Amami until the 1950s, but today silk yarn is imported from China.

3. Kanai Kougei recently began selling bags of dyeing liquid in its gallery under the label Dye It Yourself, meaning that one can also do Amamian dorozome at home.

4. By this I infer the Shachō means patience and willingness to commit to one thing over many years.

5. Kurume gasuri was used for workwear called *monpe*, a style of women's (and later men's) pants made popular during World War II, when women were encouraged to break from kimono to assist the war effort (Horikiri 2016, 129).

6. During Douglas Haring's (1952, 42) time in Amami, a tanmono cost around ¥6,000 (forty dollars).

7. *Orimoto-san* is a local term combining two kanjis: 織 (*ori*), meaning to weave, and 元 (*moto*), taken from *iemoto*, meaning a family company. The honorific *-san*, used to show respect to individuals, is also extended to tradespeople.

8. The shima system is a "co-op" but differs significantly from my understanding of a co-op because profits are not evenly distributed. Rather it follows the *Oxford English Dictionary*'s definition of "working together or with others to the same end."

9. The translation of *kimono* is "thing to wear."

10. Thank you to Dr. Eiko Honda, who described to me the meaning of the aphorism "A nail that sticks out must be banged down."

2. The Alchemy of Producing Color

1. Susan Parman's (2005) research in 1970s Lewis, Sharon Macdonald's (1997) research in 1990s Skye, and my own ethnographic research (Linton 2016) and that of Joana Nascimento (2023) in the Outer Hebrides similarly documents incomers moving to depopulated Scottish islands.

2. See also Hoey (2005) for lifestyle migration in North America; Korpela (2014) in India; and Høyer Leivestad (2018) in Sweden and Spain.

3. In Japan, lifetime employment is guaranteed employment with the same company for life.

4. When I returned to Amami in 2023–24, the cost of living remained stable, but property prices were experiencing a boom.

5. A middle-class lifestyle was defined by full-time employment and home and private car ownership.

6. See Luckman and Thomas's edited volumes *Craft Economies* (2018) and *Craft Communities* (2024) for an extended discussion on the entrepreneurial potential and social value of craft from the global perspective.

7. As with dyeing in Amami, Okinawans historically would have used crushed coral as an alkali.

8. This is a poetic Japanese term for the shiny bubbles that form on the surface of a fermented indigo vat. The bacteria produced in fermentation draw oxygen from the water and release it to the surface, creating bubbles.

9. See, for example, the *mejiro* birds discussed in chapter 4.

10. See, for example, the Onomichi denim company based in Hiroshima Prefecture, which sends its jeans to manual laborers—fishermen, carpenters, citrus farmers—to wear before they are sold to customers for ¥48,000 (around $310).

11. When I returned to Amami in 2023, Kanai Kougei had installed fabric steamers to improve colorfastness and reduce the amount of hypren required.

3. "*Mottainai!*" What a Waste!

1. See the popularity of Marxist academic Kōhei Saitō's (2022) book on degrowth, first published in Japan in 2020, which has sold over half a million copies in Japan (Gardels 2023).

2. See, for example, the *tsukumogami* (tool kami) in which the power of a tool is linked with the spirit of its maker, who may possess the object, or after one hundred years of service it may receive its own soul (Reider 2009).

3. In central Honshu, sakura blooms coincide with the start of the new academic and financial year.

4. See Kuwahara (2012) for details on the acts of parliament that have channeled huge levels of capital to the Amami Islands via public works projects since the 1950s.

5. *Becquerels* are units used to measure radioactivity, while the prefix *tera* represents a trillion (Obe 2012).

6. Kazuko shared details of a California-based health food store called iherb.com that shipped dry goods to Japan for free with a fifty-dollar spend. We used this service to access affordable organic foods that dramatically undercut Japanese producers and importers of organic foodstuffs.

7. I listed, for example, gifting, language exchange, foraging, fermentation, pollination, and car maintenance.

8. I reference the "ordering" that seasonality inflicts regarding the individual, but Daniels (2009b, 175) references Ackermann to make a darker point that "throughout Japanese history the ruling elite has drawn on these natural representations linked with correct social behavior in order to establish their authority."

9. Koki has more recently established a name for himself making beautiful patchwork art pieces using colored silk from discarded kimono. Kazuko, meanwhile, has established her own brand and dyeing workshop in Amami under the name Meeraboo, and Satoko-san has similarly set up workshop called Midori.

4. The *Mejiro* Bird

A previous version of chapter 4, titled "The *Mejiro* Bird: Between Commodity, Conservation and Companion," was included in *Animals Matter: Resistance and Transformation in Animal Commodification*, edited by J. Dugnoille and E. Vander Meer (Leiden: Brill, 2022), 56–84.

1. The Wild Bird Society of Japan was also established in 1934 by Godo Nakanishi, a Buddhist monk and poet responsible for selecting the prefectural birds of Japan in 1963.

2. The mejiro, for example, was introduced to Hawaii in the 1920s for insect control, but its success as a forager has made it a threat to native bird populations, and it is categorized as an invasive species.

3. This relates to jays in general, as the Lidth's jay is not listed in *The Birds of Japan*.

4. Because conservation efforts to eradicate the mongoose have been successful, the status of the Lidth's jay was downgraded in 2008 to vulnerable.

5. An Amamian historian more recently told me that black rabbits were routinely eaten by women after childbirth to restore strength.

6. Inge Daniels told me that many of her (mature) participants staunchly defended eating whale, as did those who discussed the matter with anthropologist Peter Wynn Kirby (2010, 192).

7. Japan has a rich cultural history of visualizing absent natural and supernatural phenomena that are geographically bound and reflect community identity. Today, anime and manga perform a similar role. Anne Allison (2006, 27) has claimed that kids and adults seek out a sense of "companionship" with animist "fantasy fare," as demonstrated by Pokémon or characters from Studio Ghibli.

8. Although this may seem radical, it should be noted that companies and corporations are treated as legal persons, providing them the same legal rights as individuals.

9. Rachel Carson's *Silent Spring* (1962) raised alarm among the public about the damage pesticides such as DDT, commercially developed by the chemical industry during

World War II, were inflicting on ecosystems, especially for birds. Japan banned DDT in 1969 and the United States followed suit in 1972.

5. "The Industrious Way of Doing Things"

1. When I invited Kanai Kougei to the UK in 2019 to carry out dorozome workshops, we found that dye colors changed significantly between sites—the heavy metals from London pipes, the calcium and magnesium that make the water "hard," and the sterilizing chlorine produced results that were brighter and redder in some locations than others.

2. *Sotetsu* literally translates as "revive-iron" (蘇鉄). The soils are said to be mineral rich in Amami because the island was impacted by an ancient meteorite.

3. Some miya have been replaced by schools or village halls, while others host *matsuri* and sumo tournaments.

4. These data were recorded in 1951 by Fumitake Yamashita (1952), a prominent local historian who worked with Haring.

5. Boys must participate between the ages of four and sixteen, while girls can participate optionally.

6. A participant also told me they had returned plastic trash (some of which was name-labeled) to their eighty-plus-year-old neighbor after it washed up on the village beach. Not seeing a problem, she explained that she dumped it in the river while it was running fast because it would deposit the trash far out to sea.

7. Takarajima Senkou was also present at MONO JAPAN, where I first encountered Kanai Kougei and KITTA (see the introduction to this book).

8. My discussion with Ogomori-san was kindly translated by Dr. Yasuhiro Ota, who organized a tour with Kurume craft producers.

9. It should be noted that natural fibers frequently come with their own environmental and ethical issues, for example, intensive water and agrochemical dependence, labor and animal rights abuses, and widespread fraud.

10. See Wicker (2023) for a discussion on the health impact of toxic dyes and finishes.

11. This is a problem in postindustrial areas with declining populations globally, as in the case of the widely discussed polluted tap water of Flint, Michigan.

12. It should be noted this is not exclusively the case. Many companies work to establish these facts, while corporations hire whole teams to ensure supplier compliance. Nevertheless, the complexity of supply chains means issues often evade detection.

6. "Dyeing with the Earth"

An earlier version of chapter 6 was published as "Re-Evaluating a Tree's 'Real Worth': The Historical Dispossession of Ecological Stewardship and Its Legacy for a Japanese Textile Tradition," *History and Anthropology* 2022, 1–24.

1. Tanaka-san is a pseudonym.

2. Kagoshima Prefecture (2018, 132) claims that the tsumugi industry uses forty-seven tons of Amamian techigi annually but does not quote its sources.

3. Maiko-san, the Shachō's daughter, told me that when she and her siblings were children, the Shachō would tell them "every hour [to] just go and check the *kama* and put some water in if its boiling hard!"

4. This biodiverse resource led the Japanese to capture the Philippines in 1941, but the islands were reclaimed by the Americans after the war and gained independence in 1946.

5. In 1905 the "Yanchu liberation decree" (Hagihara 1974, 250) ended decades of Amamian slavery, releasing residents into an emerging labor market with the development of Japanese capitalism.

6. The 1897 Forest Act was enacted to conserve and protect Japanese forests in response to industrialization. The 1907 act built on these foundations to regulate "use and control of land and establish forest owners' cooperatives." The 1951 Forest Act meant that revisions to ensure "sustainable growth and improvement of productivity" were put in place (FAO 2010).

7. This concern is not without precedent; craftspeople with whom I met in Okinawa needed to obtain permission to collect a species of bamboo from Yambaru National Park to make a tool needed for processing banana fibers for the textile *bashō-fu*.

8. According to Akiyo's elderly neighbor, cats were considered kami in Amami and after death were put in a basket and hung in a tree to be worshipped. Haring's field notes also record an informant explaining: "Cats (*maya*) grow old, become ghosts, kill master; especially black cats. A three-color cat if male foretells the weather; there is one such cat in 1000. Give a cat as a present, expect to receive copper money or nails in return."

9. See also John Knight's (1998, 197–200) research with foresting families on Japan's Kii peninsula, in which he asserts that while postwar forestry had become dominated by economics, "a rich set of ideas, beliefs and associations" are attached to trees, with foresters considering their practice in a way analogous to child-rearing.

10. Although tourism slowed during the COVID-19 pandemic, when I returned to Amami in 2023 the tourism boom that I had first discussed with the Shachō in 2018 had accelerated, evidenced by the building of new hotels and an influx of English-speaking visitors.

Conclusion

1. See McCormack (1995) for a critique of wasteful public works across Japan and Kuwahara (2001) and Linton (forthcoming) for the environmentally and socially destructive impact of construction on Amami.

References

Ackermann, Peter. 1997. "The Four Seasons: One of Japanese Culture's Most Central Concepts." In Asquith and Kalland, *Japanese Images of Nature*, 36–53.

Addie, Jean-Paul D., and James C. Fraser. 2019. "After Gentrification: Social Mix, Settler Colonialism, and Cruel Optimism in the Transformation of Neighbourhood Space." *Antipode* 51 (5): 1369–94.

Agrawal, Arun. 2005. *Environmentality: Technologies of Government and the Making of Subjects; New Ecologies for the Twenty-First Century*. Durham, NC: Duke University Press.

Ahmed, Monisha. 2002. *Living Fabric: Weaving Among the Nomads of Ladakh Himalaya*. Bangkok: Orchid Press.

Aldous, Christopher. 2015. "A Tale of Two Occupations: Hunting Wildlife in Occupied Japan, 1945–1952." *Journal of American–East Asian Relations* 22 (2): 120–46.

Allison, Anne. 2006. *Millennial Monsters: Japanese Toys and the Global Imagination*. Asia—Local Studies/Global Themes 13. Berkeley: University of California Press.

Allison, Anne. 2013. *Precarious Japan*. Durham, NC: Duke University Press.

Amami Park. 2017. "Description of the Exhibits in the General Exhibition Hall." Handout in English. Amami Ōshima, Kagoshima Prefecture, Japan.

Amano, Masatoshi. 1999. "Industrial Development in the Daimyo Domain and Economic Modernization of Japan—With Special References to the Awa Indigo Industry in the Province of Awa-Tokushima from the Tokugawa Period to the Meiji Period." *Japan and the World Economy* 11 (2): 225–41.

Anand, Nikhil, Akhil Gupta, and Hannah Appel, eds. 2018. *The Promise of Infrastructure*. Durham, NC: Duke University Press.

Appadurai, Arjun. 1990. "Disjuncture and Difference in the Global Cultural Economy." *Theory, Culture and Society* 7 (2–3): 295–310.

Arnold, David. 2005. *The Tropics and the Traveling Gaze: India, Landscape, and Science, 1800–1856*. Delhi: Permanent Black.

Arvidsson, Adam, and Bertram Niessen. 2015. "Creative Mass: Consumption, Creativity and Innovation on Bangkok's Fashion Markets." *Consumption Markets and Culture* 18 (2): 111–32.

Aso, Noriko. 2014. *Public Properties: Museums in Imperial Japan*. Durham, NC: Duke University Press.

Asquith, Pamela J., and Arne Kalland, eds. 1997a. *Japanese Images of Nature: Cultural Perspectives*. Richmond, VA: Curzon.

Asquith, Pamela J., and Arne Kalland. 1997b. "Japanese Perceptions of Nature: Ideals and Illusions." In Asquith and Kalland, *Japanese Images of Nature*, 1–35.

Assmann, Stephanie. 2010. "Reinventing Culinary Heritage in Northern Japan: Slow Food and Traditional Vegetables." In *Japanese Foodways, Past and Present*, edited by Eric C. Rath and Stephanie Assmann, 243–56. Urbana: University of Illinois Press.

Assmann, Stephanie. 2013. "Reassessing Food Safety, Risk and Globalization in China and Japan: An Overview of Emerging Research Trends." *Food, Culture, and Society* 16 (1): 7–19.

Assmann, Stephanie, ed. 2016. *Sustainability in Contemporary Rural Japan: Challenges and Opportunities*. London: Routledge.

Austin, Oliver L., and Edythe Austin. 1978. Interview by Steve Kerber, August 30. University of Florida Oral History Project. Digital Collections, George A. Smathers Libraries, University of Florida. https://ufdc.ufl.edu/uf00005958/00001.

Austin, Oliver L., and Nagahisa Kuroda. 1953. *The Birds of Japan: Their Status and Distribution*. Cambridge, MA: Harvard Museum of Comparative Zoology.

Aves, Alex R., Laura E. Revell, Sally Gaw, et al. 2022. "First Evidence of Microplastics in Antarctic Snow." *Cryosphere* 16 (6): 2127–45.

Balfour-Paul, Jenny. 2011. *Indigo: Egyptian Mummies to Blue Jeans*. London: British Museum Press.

Bankoff, Greg. 2009. "Conservation and Colonialism: Gifford Pinchot and the Birth of Tropical Forestry in the Philippines." In McCoy and Scarano, *Colonial Crucible*, 479–88.

Bankoff, Greg. 2013. "'Deep Forestry': Shapers of the Philippine Forests." *Environmental History* 18 (3): 523–56.

Bear, Laura. 2015. *Navigating Austerity: Currents of Debt Along a South Asian River*. Stanford, CA: Stanford University Press.

Beck, Ulrich. 1999. *World Risk Society*. Cambridge: Polity.

Beer, John Joseph. 1959. *The Emergence of the German Dye Industry*. Champaign: University of Illinois Press.

Befu, Harumi. 1992. "Symbols of Nationalism and Nihonjinron." In Goodman and Refsing, *Ideology and Practice in Modern Japan*, 26–46.

Bennett, Jane. 2001. *The Enchantment of Modern Life: Attachments, Crossings, and Ethics*. Princeton, NJ: Princeton University Press.

Benson, Michaela, and Karen O'Reilly. 2009. "Migration and the Search for a Better Way of Life: A Critical Exploration of Lifestyle Migration." *Sociological Review* 57 (4): 608–25.

Berg, Achim, Karl-Hendrik Magnus, Sara Kappelmark, et al. 2020. *Fashion on Climate: How the Fashion Industry Can Urgently Act to Reduce Its Greenhouse Gas Emissions*.

New York: McKinsey and Global Fashion Agenda. https://www.mckinsey.com/~/media/mckinsey/industries/retail/our%20insights/fashion%20on%20climate/fashion-on-climate-full-report.pdf.

Bhandar, Brenna. 2018. *Colonial Lives of Property: Law, Land, and Racial Regimes of Ownership*. Durham, NC: Duke University Press.

Blake, William. (1862) 2000. *Poems of William Blake*. Hoboken, NJ: BiblioBytes.

Blatman-Thomas, Naama, and Libby Porter. 2019. "Placing Property: Theorizing the Urban from Settler Colonial Cities." *International Journal of Urban and Regional Research* 43 (1): 30–45.

Brandt, Kim. 2007. *Kingdom of Beauty: Mingei and the Politics of Folk Art in Imperial Japan*. Asia-Pacific. Durham, NC: Duke University Press.

Branwell, Eleanor, Megan Schuknecht, Beth Rattner, Natasja Hulst, and Brian Dougherty. 2020. *The Nature of Fashion*. Missoula, MT: Biomimicry Institute. https://cdn.prod.website-files.com/661d02928b04b93a6a97251c/6673abfca91563d5df871023_The%20Nature%20of%20Fashion_2021.pdf.

Brasor, Philip. 2019. "Of Cats and Rabbits: UNESCO World Heritage Candidate Caught in a Bind Over Tourism Drive." *Japan Times*, September 14.

Brazil, Mark. 1991. *The Birds of Japan*. London: Christopher Helm.

Brightman, Marc, and Jerome Lewis, eds. 2017. *The Anthropology of Sustainability: Beyond Development and Progress*. New York: Palgrave Macmillan.

Brown, Kate. 2017. "Marie Curie's Fingerprint: Nuclear Spelunking in the Chernobyl Zone." In Tsing et al., *Arts of Living on a Damaged Planet*, G33–50.

Brown, Philip C. 2002. "Harvests of Chance: Corporate Control of Arable Land in Early Modern Japan." In *Land, Property, and the Environment*, edited by John F. Richards, 38–70. Oakland, CA: ICS Press.

Brumfiel, Geoff. 2011. "Fallout Forensics Hike Radiation Toll." *Nature* 478 (7370): 435–36.

Bubandt, Nils. 2014. *The Empty Seashell: Witchcraft and Doubt on an Indonesian Island*. Ithaca, NY: Cornell University Press. Project MUSE.

Bubandt, Nils. 2017. "Haunted Geologies: Spirits, Stones, and the Necropolitics of the Anthropocene." In Tsing et al., *Arts of Living on a Damaged Planet*, G121–41.

Bunn, Stephanie. 2010. *Nomadic Felts*. London: British Museum Press.

Bunn, Stephanie. 2011. "A 'Making Point of View': Deep Knowledge from Local Practice, with Special Reference to Felt-Makers in Kyrgyzstan." *Journal of Museum Ethnography*, no. 24, 23–40.

Bunn, Stephanie, and Victoria Mitchell, eds. 2020. *The Material Culture of Basketry*. London: Bloomsbury Visual Arts.

Burgess, Rebecca. 2019. *Fibershed: Growing a Movement of Farmers, Fashion Activists, and Makers for a New Textile Economy*. White River Junction, VT: Chelsea Green.

Burke, Joan. 1989. "Becoming an Insider-Outsider." *Journal of the Anthropological Society of Oxford* 20 (3): 219–27.

Callicott, J. Baird, and James McRae, eds. 2017. *Japanese Environmental Philosophy*. New York: Oxford University Press.

Carr, Chantel, and Chris Gibson. 2016. "Geographies of Making: Rethinking Materials and Skills for Volatile Futures." *Progress in Human Geography* 40 (3): 297–315.

Carrington, Damian. 2024. "Microplastics Found in Every Human Placenta Tested in Study." *Guardian*, February 27.

Carson, Rachel. 1962. *Silent Spring*. Boston: Houghton Mifflin.

Castree, Noel. 2003. "Commodifying What Nature?" *Progress in Human Geography* 27 (3): 273–97.

Checker, Melissa, Cindy Isenhour, and Gary McDonogh, eds. 2015. *Sustainability in the Global City: Myth and Practice*. New York: Cambridge University Press.

Chowdhury, Tanvir. 2019. "Bangladesh's Garment Factories Pollute Rivers." *Al Jazeera*, July 1. https://www.aljazeera.com/news/2019/07/bangladeshs-garment-factories-pollute-rivers-affecting-residents-health-190701090533205.html.

Choy, Jessian. 2020. "My Menstrual Underwear Has Toxic Chemicals in It." *Sierra*, January 7.

Clammer, John. R. 1995. *Difference and Modernity: Social Theory and Contemporary Japanese Society*. Japanese Studies. London: Kegan Paul International.

Clammer, John. R. 2001. *Japan and Its Others: Globalization, Difference and the Critique of Modernity*. Melbourne: Trans Pacific.

Clark, Rodney. 1979. *The Japanese Company*. New Haven: Yale University Press.

Coleman, William, ed. 2011. *Property, Territory, Globalization: Struggles Over Autonomy*. Vancouver: University of British Columbia Press.

Cox, Thomas R. 1987. "Coping with Gaizai: Japanese Forest Cooperatives and Imported American Timber." *Environmental Review* 11 (1): 35–54.

Coy, Michael W. 1989. *Apprenticeship: From Theory to Method and Back Again*. Albany: State University of New York Press.

Crang, Philip, Katherine Brickell, Laurie Parsons, Nithya Natarajan, Thomas Cristofoletti, and Naomi Graham. 2020. "Discardscapes of Fashion: Commodity Biography, Patch Geographies, and Preconsumer Garment Waste in Cambodia." *Social and Cultural Geography* 23 (4): 539–58.

Culver, Annika A. 2017. "Saving the Birds: Oliver L. Austin's Collaboration with Japanese Scientists in Revising Wildlife Policies in US-Occupied Japan, 1946–1950." *Endeavour*, n.s., vol. 41 (4): 151–65.

Cwiertka, Katarzyna. 2005. "Culinary Culture and the Making of a National Cuisine." In Robertson, *A Companion to the Anthropology of Japan*, 415–28.

Daniels, Inge. 2003. "Scooping, Raking, Beckoning Luck: Luck, Agency and the Interdependence of People and Things in Japan." *Journal of the Royal Anthropological Institute* 9 (4): 619–38.

Daniels, Inge. 2009a. "'Dolls Are Scary': What Constitutes Japanese Religious Activity?" In *Religion and Material Culture: the Matter of Belief*, edited by David Morgan, 153–70. London: Routledge.

Daniels, Inge. 2009b. "Seasonal and Commercial Rhythms of Domestic Consumption: A Japanese Case Study." In Shove, Trentmann, and Wilk, *Time, Consumption and Everyday Life*, 171–87.

Daniels, Inge. 2011. *The Japanese House: Material Culture in the Modern Home*. Materializing Culture. Oxford: Berg.

De Neve, Geert, and Rebecca Prentice, eds. 2017. *Unmaking the Global Sweatshop: Health and Safety of the World's Garment Workers*. Philadelphia: University of Pennsylvania Press.

Descola, Philippe. 2013. *Beyond Nature and Culture*. Chicago: University of Chicago Press.

Douglas, Mary. (1966) 2001. *Purity and Danger: An Analysis of the Concepts of Pollution and Taboo*. London: Routledge.

Douny, Laurence. 2015. "Wild Silk Indigo Wrappers of Dogon of Mali: An Ethnography of Materials Efficacy and Design." In Drazin and Küchler, *Social Life of Materials*, 101–18.

Drayton, Richard Harry. 2000. *Nature's Government: Science, Imperial Britain, and the "Improvement" of the World*. New Haven, CT: Yale University Press.

Drazin, Adam, and Susanne Küchler, eds. 2015. *The Social Life of Materials: Studies in Materials and Society*. London: Bloomsbury Academic.

Durkheim, Émile. (1915) 2008. *The Elementary Forms of the Religious Life*. Translated by Joseph Ward Swain. Mineola, NY: Dover.

Dusinberre, Martin. 2012. *Hard Times in the Hometown: A History of Community Survival in Modern Japan*. Honolulu: University of Hawaii Press.

Ellen, R. F. 2021. *Nature Wars: Essays Around a Contested Concept*. New York: Berghahn Books.

FAO (Food and Agriculture Organization of the United Nations and Regional Office for Asia and the Pacific). 2010. "Asia-Pacific Forestry Sector Outlook Study II." Working Paper No. APFSOS II/WP/2010/30.

Fletcher, Kate. 1998. "Design, the Environment and Textiles: Developing Strategies for Environmental Impact Reduction." *Journal of the Textile Institute* 89 (3): 72–80.

Fletcher, Kate, and Mathilda Tham. 2019. *Earth Logic: Fashion Action Research Plan*. London: JJ Charitable Trust. https://earthlogic.info/wp-content/uploads/2021/03/Earth-Logic-E-version.pdf.

Forsythe, Diana E. 1980. "Urban Incomers and Rural Change: The Impact of Migrants from the City on Life in an Orkney Community." *Sociologia Ruralis* 20 (4): 287–307.

Fortune. 1992. "The Billionaires," September 7.

Friedman, Vanessa. 2015. "Kering Becomes Luxury's Activist." *New York Times*, May 20.

Fukuoka, Masanobu. (1978) 2010. *The One-Straw Revolution: An Introduction to Natural Farming*. New York: New York Review of Books.

Fukushima Prefecture. n.d. "Japanese Standards on Radioactive Substances in Food and Overseas Indexes." Fukushima Revitalization Information Portal Site. Accessed July 14, 2020. https://www.pref.fukushima.lg.jp/site/portal-english/en01-03.html.

Funes Monzote, Reinaldo. 2008. *From Rainforest to Cane Field in Cuba: An Environmental History Since 1492*. Chapel Hill: University of North Carolina Press.

Furukawa, Yuki, and Rei Kansaku. 2020. "Amabié—a Japanese Symbol of the COVID-19 Pandemic." *JAMA* 324 (6): 531–33.

Galvin, Shaila Seshia. 2018. "The Farming of Trust." *American Ethnologist* 45 (4): 495–507.

Gardels, Nathan. 2023. "Degrowth in Japan: Mending the 'Metabolic Rift' of Capitalism." *NOĒMA*, May 5. https://www.noemamag.com/degrowth-in-japan.

Geschiere, Peter. 2016. "Witchcraft, Shamanism, and Nostalgia: A Review Essay." *Comparative Studies in Society and History* 58 (1): 242–65.

Geyer, Roland. 2021. *The Business of Less: The Role of Companies and Households on a Planet in Peril*. London: Routledge.

Gibson, Clark C., Margaret A. McKean, and Elinor Ostrom. 2000. *People and Forests: Communities, Institutions, and Governance*. Cambridge, MA: MIT Press.

Gibson-Graham, J. K. 2014. "Rethinking the Economy with Thick Description and Weak Theory." *Current Anthropology* 55 (S9): S147–53.

Gibson-Graham, J. K., Jenny Cameron, Stephen Healy, and Joanne McNeill. 2019. "Roepke Lecture in Economic Geography: Economic Geography, Manufacturing, and Ethical Action in the Anthropocene." *Economic Geography* 95 (1): 1–21.

Ginsberg, Alexandra Daisy, and Natsai Chieza. 2018. "Other Biological Futures." *Journal of Design and Science*, September 11. https://jods.mitpress.mit.edu/pub/issue4-ginsberg-chieza/release/5.

Gkartzios, Menelaos. 2013. "'Leaving Athens': Narratives of Counterurbanisation in Times of Crisis." *Journal of Rural Studies* 32 (October): 158–67.

Goodman, Roger. 1992. "Ideology and Practice in Modern Japan: Towards a Theoretical Approach." In Goodman and Refsing, *Ideology and Practice in Modern Japan*, 1–25.

Goodman, Roger, and Kirsten Refsing, eds. 1992. *Ideology and Practice in Modern Japan*. London: Routledge.

Goto, Kazuko. 2013. "Policy for Intangible Cultural Heritage in Japan: How It Relates to Creativity." In *Handbook on the Economics of Cultural Heritage*, edited by Ilde Rizzo and Anna Mignosa, 567–85. Cheltenham: Edward Elgar.

Government of Japan. 2017. "Nomination of Amami-Oshima Island, Tokunoshima Island, The Northern Part of Okinawa Island, and Iriomote Island for Inscription on the World Heritage List." Accessed September 24, 2019. https://www.env.go.jp/en/nature/wh/amami/wh_list.html.

Graham, Fiona. 2003. *Inside the Japanese Company*. London: Routledge Curzon.

Greenberg, Miriam. 2013. "What on Earth Is Sustainable? Toward Critical Sustainability Studies." *Boom* 3 (4): 54–66.

Greenoak, Francesca. 1997. *British Birds: Their Names, Folklore and Literature*. London: Christopher Helm.

Greenpeace Germany. 2021a. *Self Regulation: A Fashion Fairytale. Part 1: Progress of Detox Committed Brands on Hazardous Chemicals and Slowing the Flow/Closing the Loop*. Hamburg: Greenpeace Germany. https://www.greenpeace.de/sites/default/files/publications/20211122-greenpeace-detox-fashion-fairytale-engl-pt1.pdf.

Greenpeace Germany. 2021b. *Self Regulation: A Fashion Fairytale. Part 2: Evaluation of Detox Committed Brands, 2021–the Ten-Year Milestone*. Hamburg: Greenpeace Germany. https://www.greenpeace.de/publikationen/20211122-greenpeace-detox-fashion-fairytale-engl-pt2_0.pdf.

Greenpeace International. 2011. *Toxic Threads: The Big Fashion Stitch-Up*. Amsterdam: Greenpeace International. https://www.greenpeace.org/static/planet4-denmark-stateless/2018/10/de1f42ec-de1f42ec-121120_toxic_threads_the_big_fashion_stitch-up.pdf.

Greenpeace UK. 2019. *Upstream: Microplastics in UK Rivers*. London: Greenpeace UK. https://www.greenpeace.org.uk/wp-content/uploads/2024/07/plastics_v08.pdf.

Gregson, Nicky, Mike Crang, Julie Botticello, Melania Calestani, and Anna Krzywoszynska. 2016. "Doing the 'Dirty Work' of the Green Economy: Resource Recovery and Migrant Labour in the EU." *European Urban and Regional Studies* 23 (4): 541–55.

Gupta, Alisha Haridasani. 2023. "What to Know About PFAS in Period Underwear." *New York Times*, January 30.
Hagihara, Shigeru. 1974. "Study on Transition of Farm-Land System at Amami-Oshima." [In Japanese.] *Bulletin of the Faculty of Agriculture, Kagoshima University*, no. 25, 243–68.
Hani, Yoko. 2001. "Easing the Way for U and I." *Japan Times*, October 14.
Hanley, Susan B. 1968. "Population Trends and Economic Development in Tokugawa Japan: The Case of Bizen Province in Okayama." *Daedalus* 97 (2): 622–35.
Hanley, Susan B. 1997. *Everyday Things in Premodern Japan: The Hidden Legacy of Material Culture*. Berkeley: University of California Press.
Haraway, Donna J. 2004. *The Haraway Reader*. New York: Routledge.
Haraway, Donna J. 2008. *When Species Meet*. Minneapolis: University of Minnesota Press.
Hardacre, Helen. 2017. *Shinto: A History*. New York: Oxford University Press.
Hardin, Garrett. 1968. "The Tragedy of the Commons." *Science* 162 (3859): 1243–48.
Haring, Douglas G. 1952. *The Island of Amami Ōshima in the Northern Ryūkyūs*. Scientific Investigations in the Ryukyu Islands Report 2. Washington, DC: Pacific Science Board, National Research Council.
Haring, Douglas G. 1953. "The Noro Cult of Amami Ōshima: Divine Priestesses of the Ryūkyū Islands." *Sociologus* 3 (2): 108–21.
Harrod, Tanya. 2001. "Picturesque Pleasure." *Crafts*, no. 172, 36–39.
Harvey, David. 2001. "Globalization and the 'Spatial Fix.'" *Geographische Revue*, no. 2, 23–30.
Hathaway, Michael J. 2013. *Environmental Winds: Making the Global in Southwest China*. Berkeley: University of California Press.
Hayward, Philip, and Sueo Kuwahara. 2012. "Sotetsu Heritage: Cycads, Sustenance and Cultural Landscapes in the Amami Islands." *Locale: The Australian-Pacific Journal of Regional Food Studies*, no. 2, 26–46.
Hellyer, Robert I. 2009. *Defining Engagement: Japan and Global Contexts, 1640–1868*. Cambridge, MA: Harvard University Asia Center.
Hetherington, Kevin. 2004. "Secondhandedness: Consumption, Disposal, and Absent Presence." *Environment and Planning D: Society and Space* 22 (1): 157–73.
Hickel, Jason. 2021. "What Does Degrowth Mean? A Few Points of Clarification." *Globalizations* 18 (7): 1105–11.
Hobsbawm, Eric J., and Terrance O. Ranger. 1983. *The Invention of Tradition*. Past and Present Publications. Cambridge: Cambridge University Press.
Hoey, Brian A. 2005. "From Pi to Pie: Moral Narratives of Noneconomic Migration and Starting Over in the Postindustrial Midwest." *Journal of Contemporary Ethnography* 34 (5): 586–624.
Horikiri, Tatsuichi. 2016. *The Stories Clothes Tell: Voices of Working-Class Japan*. Lanham, MD: Rowman and Littlefield.
Hoskins, Janet. 1989. "Why Do Ladies Sing the Blues? Indigo Dyeing, Cloth Production, and Gender Symbolism in Kodi." In Weiner and Schneider, *Cloth and Human Experience*, 142–64.
Howe, Clifton Durant. 1915. "Service of the Birds to Horticulture." In *Twelfth Annual Report of the Vermont State Horticultural Society*. St. Albans: Vermont State Horticultural Society.

Høyer Leivestad, Hege. 2018. *Caravans: Lives on Wheels in Contemporary Europe*. London: Bloomsbury Academic.

Igeta, Midori. 1983. "The Image of Woman in Sermons: Anju in 'Sanshō Dayū.'" *Japanese Journal of Religious Studies* 10 (2–3): 247–72.

Inglehart, Ronald. 1995. "Public Support for Environmental Protection: Objective Problems and Subjective Values in 43 Societies." *PS: Political Science and Politics* 28 (1): 57–72.

Ingold, Tim. 2011. *The Perception of the Environment: Essays on Livelihood, Dwelling and Skill.* London: Routledge.

Ingold, Tim. 2013. *Making: Anthropology, Archaeology, Art and Architecture*. London: Routledge.

Ishida, Ken. 2014. "Lidth's Jay." *Bird Research News* 7 (4): 4–5.

Ivy, Marilyn. 1995. *Discourses of the Vanishing: Modernity, Phantasm, Japan*. Chicago: University of Chicago Press.

Iwasaki Group. n.d. "About Iwasaki Group." Accessed March 16, 2022. https://www.iwasaki-group.com/recruit/aboutus.

Jacoby, Russell. 1977. *Social Amnesia: A Critique of Conformist Psychology from Adler to Laing*. Hassocks: Harvester.

Japan International Labour Foundation. 2022. "Japan's Middle Class in Crisis." Email magazine, no. 374, October 19. https://www.jilaf.or.jp/en/news/20231016-2855.

Japan International Research Center for Agricultural Sciences. 2024. "Trends and Outlook of Food Self-Sufficiency Ratio—Toward Revision of the Basic Law on Food, Agriculture and Rural Areas." January 31. https://www.jircas.go.jp/en/program/proc/blog/20240131.

Japan Meteorological Agency. 2020. "Normal Statistics for Tropical Cyclones with Maximum Wind Speeds of 17.2 m/s or Higher Forming Over the Western North Pacific." Accessed December 20, 2024. https://www.data.jma.go.jp/gmd/cpd/longfcst/en/tourist_tc.html.

Jepson, Paul. 2010. "Towards an Indonesian Bird Conservation Ethos: Reflections from a Study of Bird-keeping in the Cities of Java and Bali." In *Ethno-Ornithology: Birds, Indigenous Peoples, Culture and Society,* edited by Sonia Tidemann and Andrew Gosler, 313–30. London: Earthscan.

Jessop, Bob. 2006. "Spatial Fixes, Temporal Fixes and Spatio-Temporal Fixes." In *David Harvey: A Critical Reader*, edited by Noel Castree and Derek Gregory, 142–66. Malden, MA: Blackwell.

Johnson, Leslie M., and Eugene S. Hunn. 2009a. "Introduction." In Johnson and Hunn, *Landscape Ethnoecology*, 1–11.

Johnson, Leslie M., and Eugene S. Hunn, eds. 2009b. *Landscape Ethnoecology: Concepts of Biotic and Physical Space*. New York: Berghahn Books.

Johnson, Leslie M., and Eugene S. Hunn. 2009c. "Landscape Ethnoecology: Reflections." In Johnson and Hunn, *Landscape Ethnoecology*, 279–97.

Johnson, Leslie M., and Iain Davidson-Hunt. 2011. "Ethnoecology and Landscapes." In *Ethnobiology*, edited by E. N. Anderson, D. Pearsall, E. S. Hunn, and N. Turner, 267–84. Hoboken, NJ: John Wiley and Sons.

Kagawa-Fox, Midori. 2012. *The Ethics of Japan's Global Environmental Policy: The Conflict Between Principles and Practice*. London: Routledge.

Kagohashi, Taka'aki. 2002. "The Amami 'Rights of Nature' Lawsuit." *Social Science Japan*, no. 23, 14–16.

Kagoshima Prefecture. n.d. "Drainage Standards." [In Japanese.] Accessed March 27, 2020. http://www.pref.kagoshima.jp/ad05/kurashikankyo/kankyo/suishitu/odakuboshi/haisuikijun.html.

Kagoshima Prefecture 2018. "Current Status and Issues of the Amami Islands (Forestry)." [In Japanese]. Accessed January 10, 2022. http://www.pref.kagoshima.jp/ac07/documents/63688_20180121161149-1.pdf.

Kakiuchi, Emiko. 2014. "Cultural Heritage Protection System in Japan: Current Issues and Prospects for the Future." *GRIPS Discussion Papers* 14 (10): 1–12.

Kalland, Arne. 1998. "The Anti-Whaling Campaigns and Japanese Responses." In *Japanese Position on Whaling and Anti-Whaling Campaign*, edited by Institute of Cetacean Research, n.p. Tokyo: Institute of Cetacean Research. https://users.emmanuelchanel.com/whaling-library/icr_camp_kalland.html.

Kalland, Arne, and Brian Moeran. 1992. *Japanese Whaling: End of an Era*? Scandinavian Institute of Asian Studies Monograph Series 61. London: Curzon.

Kanatsu, Takashi. 2013. "Killing Three Birds with One Stone: Possibilities of Achieving Environmental Success in Conforming Societies—What Japanese Experiences May Suggest to China." In *Nature, Environment and Culture in East Asia: The Challenge of Climate Change*, edited by Carmen Meinert, 283–318. Leiden: Brill.

Kant, Rita. 2012. "Textile Dyeing Industry an Environmental Hazard." *Natural Science* 4 (1): 22–26.

Katayama, Naoki, Yuki G. Baba, Yoshinobu Kusumoto, and Koichi Tanaka. 2015. "A Review of Post-War Changes in Rice Farming and Biodiversity in Japan." *Agricultural Systems*, no. 132, 73–84.

Kelly, Ilona, Ilana Winterstein, Christie Miedema, and Ben Vanpeperstraete. 2019. *Fig Leaf for Fashion: How Social Auditing Protects Brands and Fails Workers*. Amsterdam: Clean Clothes Campaign.

Kelly, William W. 1986. "Rationalization and Nostalgia: Cultural Dynamics of New Middle-Class Japan." *American Ethnologist* 13 (4): 603–18.

Kenji, Kaneko. 2007. "The Development of 'Traditional Art Crafts' in Japan." In *Crafting Beauty in Modern Japan: Celebrating Fifty Years of the Japan Traditional Art Crafts Exhibition*, edited by Nicole Coolidge Rousmaniere, 10–11. London: British Museum Press. Exhibition catalog.

Kirby, Peter Wynn. 2010. *Troubled Natures: Waste, Environment, Japan*. Honolulu: University of Hawai'i Press.

Kirby, Peter Wynn. 2019. "Slow Burn: Dirt, Radiation, and Power in Fukushima." *Asia-Pacific Journal: Japan Focus* 17 (19–3): 1–19.

Kitta. 2017. "Interview 08." *KŌSA*, October 20. https://kosaten.net/int08_en.

Klepp, Ingun Grimstad, and Tone Skårdal Tobiasson, eds. 2022. *Local, Slow and Sustainable Fashion: Wool as a Fabric for Change*. Cham: Palgrave Macmillan.

Klien, Susanne. 2016. "Reinventing Ishinomaki, Reinventing Japan? Creative Networks, Alternative Lifestyles and the Search for Quality of Life in Post-Growth Japan." *Japanese Studies* 36 (1): 39–60.

Klien, Susanne. 2019. "Entrepreneurial Selves, Governmentality and Lifestyle Migrants in Rural Japan." *Asian Anthropology* 18 (2): 75–90.

Klien, Susanne. 2020. *Urban Migrants in Rural Japan: Between Agency and Anomie in a Post-Growth Society*. Albany: State University of New York Press.

Klink, H., M. Potschin, B. Tress, G. Tress, M. Volk, and U. Steinhardt. 2002. "Landscape and Landscape Ecology." In *Development and Perspectives of Landscape Ecology*, edited by Olaf Bastian and Uta Steinhardt, 1–47. Dordrecht: Springer Netherlands.

Knight, John. 1997. "The Soil as Teacher: Natural Farming in a Mountain Village." In Asquith and Kalland, *Japanese Images of Nature*, 236–56.

Knight, John. 1998. "The Second Life of Trees: Family Forestry in Upland Japan." In *The Social Life of Trees: Anthropological Perspectives on Tree Symbolism*, edited by Laura M. Rival, 197–220. Oxford: Berg.

Kondo, Dorinne K. 1990. *Crafting Selves: Power, Gender, and Discourses of Identity in a Japanese Workplace*. Chicago: University of Chicago Press.

Kopytoff, Igor. 1986. "The Cultural Biography of Things: Commoditization as Process." In *The Social Life of Things: Commodities in Cultural Perspective*, edited by Arjun Appadurai, 64–92. Cambridge: Cambridge University Press.

Korpela, Mari. 2014. "Lifestyle of Freedom? Individualism and Lifestyle Migration." In *Understanding Lifestyle Migration: Theoretical Approaches to Migration and the Quest for a Better Way of Life*, edited by Michaela Benson and Nick Osbaldiston, 27–46. London: Palgrave Macmillan.

Koyama, S. 2015. "History of Bird-Keeping and the Teaching of Tricks Using *Cyanistes varius* (Varied Tit) in Japan." *Archives of Natural History* 42 (2): 211–25.

Kronenberg, Jakub. 2014. "What Can the Current Debate on Ecosystem Services Learn from the Past? Lessons from Economic Ornithology." *Geoforum* 55 (August): 164–77.

Küchler, Susanne. 2018. "Materials and Design." In *Design Anthropology: Object Cultures in Transition*, edited by Alison Clarke, 23–37. London: Bloomsbury.

Küchler, Susanne, and Daniel Miller, eds. 2005. *Clothing as Material Culture*. Oxford: Berg.

Küchler, Susanne, and Peter Oakley. 2014. "New Materials and Their Impact on the Material World." In *Objects and Materials: A Routledge Companion*, edited by Penny Harvey, Eleanor Conlin Casella, Gillian Evans, et al., 82–91. London: Routledge.

Kuwahara, Sueo. 2001. "The Galapagos of the Orient: Amami Oshima." In *Beyond Satsuma: Satsunan Islands Accepting the 21st Century Challenge*, edited by Toru Aoyama, 64–77. Kagoshima: Kagoshima University Research Center for the Pacific Islands.

Kuwahara, Sueo. 2011. "Development and Conservation Issues Relevant to the World Natural Heritage Listing of Amami." *South Pacific Studies* 31 (2): 81–92.

Kuwahara, Sueo. 2012. "The Development of Small Islands in Japan: An Historical Perspective." *Journal of Marine and Island Cultures* 1 (June): 38–45.

Kyodo News. 2018a. "Average Land Price in Japan Posts First Rise in 27 Years on Back of Tourism Boom." *Japan Times*, September 18.

Kyodo News. 2018b. "Endangered Turtle Dies as Oil Reaches Japan's Coastline After Iranian Tanker Collision." *Japan Times*, February 9.
La Berge, Leigh Claire. 2019. *Wages Against Artwork: Decommodified Labor and the Claims of Socially Engaged Art*. Durham, NC: Duke University Press.
Lane, Ruth, and Matt Watson. 2012. "Stewardship of Things: The Radical Potential of Product Stewardship for Re-Framing Responsibilities and Relationships to Products and Materials." *Geoforum* 43 (6): 1254–65.
Langston, Nancy. 2010. *Toxic Bodies: Hormone Disruptors and the Legacy of DES*. New Haven, CT: Yale University Press.
Latour, Bruno. 2004. "Why Has Critique Run Out of Steam? From Matters of Fact to Matters of Concern." *Critical Inquiry* 30 (2): 225–48.
Latour, Bruno, and Steve Woolgar. 1986. *Laboratory Life: The Construction of Scientific Facts*. Princeton, NJ: Princeton University Press.
Lave, Jean. 2019. *Learning and Everyday Life: Access, Participation, and Changing Practice*. Cambridge: Cambridge University Press.
Lave, Jean, and Etienne Wenger. 1991. *Situated Learning: Legitimate Peripheral Participation*. Cambridge: Cambridge University Press.
Law, John. 2004. *After Method: Mess in Social Science Research*. London: Routledge.
LeBlanc, Robin M. 1999. *Bicycle Citizens: The Political World of the Japanese Housewife*. Berkeley: University of California Press.
Linton, Charlotte. 2016. "Wool-Work in the Outer Hebrides: Harris Tweed, and the Intersecting Productive Forces and Frictions of Brand and Authenticity." Master's thesis, University of Oxford.
Linton, Charlotte. Forthcoming. "Saving Katoku: How Dysfunctional Economic and Environmental Policy Is Risking the Health of Communities and Ecosystems in Japan." *Asia-Pacific Journal: Japan Focus*.
Littlejohn, Andrew Lewis. 2017. "After the Flood: The Politics of Reconstruction in Post-3.11 Tōhoku." PhD diss., Harvard University.
Lora-Wainwright, Anna. 2017. *Resigned Activism: Living with Pollution in Rural China*. Cambridge, MA: MIT Press.
Love, Bridget. 2013. "Treasure Hunts in Rural Japan: Place Making at the Limits of Sustainability." *American Anthropologist* 115 (1): 112–24.
Luckman, Susan, and Nicola Thomas, eds. 2018. *Craft Economies*. London: Bloomsbury.
Luckman, Susan, and Nicola Thomas, eds. 2024. *Craft Communities*. London: Bloomsbury.
Macalister, Terry. 2011. "Background: What Caused the 1970s Oil Price Shock?" *Guardian*, March 3.
Macdonald, Sharon. 1997. *Reimagining Culture: Histories, Identities and the Gaelic Renaissance*. Oxford: Berg.
MacKenzie, Maureen Anne. 1991. *Androgynous Objects: String Bags and Gender in Central New Guinea*. Chur, Switzerland: Harwood Academic Publishers.
Makovicky, Nicolette. 2010. "'Something to Talk About': Notation and Knowledge-Making Among Central Slovak Lace-Makers." In Marchand, *Making Knowledge*, 76–94.
Manzenreiter, Wolfram, Ralph Lützeler, and Sebastian Polak-Rottmann, eds. 2020. *Japan's New Ruralities: Coping with Decline in the Periphery*. London: Routledge.

Marchand, Trevor H. J., ed. 2010. *Making Knowledge: Explorations of the Indissoluble Relation Between Mind, Body and Environment*. Hoboken, NJ: John Wiley and Sons.

Marchand, Trevor H. J. 2022. *The Pursuit of Pleasurable Work: Craftwork in Twenty-First Century England*. New York: Berghahn Books.

Massey, Doreen. 1995. "Places and Their Pasts." *History Workshop Journal*, no. 39, 182–92.

Mathews, Gordon. 1996. "The Stuff of Dreams, Fading: Ikigai and 'The Japanese Self.'" *Ethos* 24 (4): 718–47.

Mathur, Nayanika. 2014. "Of Tigeraphernalia and Talking Big Cats." *CRASSH* (blog), February 5. https://www.crassh.cam.ac.uk/blog/of-tigeraphernalia-and-talking-big-cats.

Matsushita, Koji. 2015. "Japanese Forestation Policies During the 20 Years Following World War II." In *Precious Forests—Precious Earth*, edited by Miodrag Zlatic, 83–112. London: IntechOpen.

McCormack, Gavan. 1995. "Growth, Construction, and the Environment: Japan's Construction State." *Japanese Studies* 15 (1): 26–35.

McCoy, Alfred W., and Francisco A. Scarano, eds. 2009. *The Colonial Crucible: Empire in the Making of the Modern American State*. Madison: University of Wisconsin Press.

McHattie, Lynn-Sayers, and Lindsey Stewart Sherrod. 2023. "Designing In-Between: Innovation from Field to Fabric." *Journal of Textile Design Research and Practice* 11 (1–2): 61–80.

McNeill, J. R. 2009. "Environmental and Economic Management." Introduction to McCoy and Scarano, *Colonial Crucible*, 475–78.

McRobbie, Angela. 1998. *British Fashion Design: Rag Trade or Image Industry*? London: Routledge.

McRobbie, Angela. 2013. "Fashion Matters Berlin: City-Spaces, Women's Working Lives, New Social Enterprise?" *Cultural Studies* 27 (6): 982–1010.

McRobbie, Angela. 2015. *Be Creative: Making a Living in the New Culture Industries*. Cambridge: Polity.

Milhaupt, Terry Satsuki. 2014. *Kimono: A Modern History*. London: Reaktion Books.

Miller, Daniel, and Sophie Woodward. 2007. "Manifesto for a Study of Denim." *Social Anthropology* 15 (3): 335–51.

Miller, Ian Jared. 2013. *The Nature of the Beasts: Empire and Exhibition at the Tokyo Imperial Zoo*. Berkeley: University of California Press.

Ministry of Foreign Affairs of Japan. 2016. "Cultural Heritage." February 21. https://www.mofa.go.jp/policy/culture/coop/unesco/c_heritage/index.html.

Ministry of the Environment of Japan. 2012. *Solid Waste Management and Recycling Technology of Japan: Toward a Sustainable Society*. Tokyo: Ministry of the Environment of Japan. https://www.env.go.jp/content/900453393.pdf.

Ministry of the Environment of Japan. 2017. "Wildlife Protection." Section 6 of Policies and Programs: Nature Conservation in Japan. https://www.env.go.jp/en/nature/npr/ncj/section6.html.

Ministry of the Environment of Japan. 2024. "Recycling Demonstration Project in Iitate Village." Accessed January 31. https://josen.env.go.jp/chukanchozou/facility/recycling/project_iitate/.

Miyazaki, Hirokazu. 2010. "The Temporality of No Hope." In *Ethnographies of Neoliberalism,* edited by Carol J. Greenhouse, 238–50. Philadelphia: University of Pennsylvania Press.

Moeran, Brian. 1984. *Lost Innocence: Folk Craft Potters of Onta, Japan*. Berkeley: University of California Press.

Moeran, Brian. 1985. *Ōkubo Diary: Portrait of a Japanese Valley*. Stanford, CA: Stanford University Press.

Moeran, Brian. 1997. *Folk Art Potters of Japan: Beyond an Anthropology of Aesthetics*. Richmond, VA: Curzon.

Mollett, Sharlene. 2011. "Contested Autonomy: Globalization and Miskito Customary Property Rights in the Río Plátano Biosphere Reserve." In Coleman, *Property, Territory, Globalization*, 101–21.

Morikawa, Jun. 2009. *Whaling in Japan: Power, Politics and Diplomacy*. London: Hurst.

Mousseau, Timothy A., and Anders P. Møller. 2014. "Genetic and Ecological Studies of Animals in Chernobyl and Fukushima." *Journal of Heredity* 105 (5): 704–9.

Mrázek, Rudolf. 2002. *Engineers of Happy Land: Technology and Nationalism in a Colony*. Princeton, NJ: Princeton University Press.

Muehlebach, Andrea. 2013. "On Precariousness and the Ethical Imagination: The Year 2012 in Sociocultural Anthropology." *American Anthropologist* 115 (2): 297–311.

Nakano, Lynne Y. 2018. "Women in Politics in Japan: Beyond Housewife Activism." *Asian Anthropology* 17 (2): 71–84.

Nakatsuhama, Yasuteru. 2007. "Amami ni okeru jizoku kanōna shinrin keiei ni kan suru shiron: Ukenmura ni okeru chippu kōjō sai ritchi o tegakari ni" [Sustainable forestry management in Amami: Hints from the relocation of a chip plant in Uken]. *Amami Newsletter*, no. 32, 50–57.

Nascimento, Joana. 2023. *Working the Fabric: Resourcefulness, Belonging and Island Life in the Harris Tweed Industry of the Outer Hebrides of Scotland*. New York: Berghahn Books.

Nenadic, Stana, and Sally Tuckett. 2013. *Colouring the Nation: The Turkey Red Printed Cotton Industry in Scotland, c. 1840–1940*. Edinburgh: National Museums of Scotland.

Neslen, Arthur. 2018. "Tokyo 2020 Olympics Confirms Use of Rainforest Timber in Stadium Build." *Climate Home News*, February 23.

Nieto-Galan, Agustí. 2001. *Colouring Textiles: A History of Natural Dyestuffs in Industrial Europe*. London: Kluwer Academic.

Niinimäki, Kirsi, Greg Peters, Helena Dahlbo, Patsy Perry, Timo Rissanen, and Alison Gwilt. 2020. "The Environmental Price of Fast Fashion." *Nature Reviews Earth and Environment* 1 (4): 189–200.

Norris, Lucy. 2004. "Shedding Skins: The Materiality of Divestment in India." *Journal of Material Culture* 9 (1): 59–71.

Norris, Lucy. 2010. *Recycling Indian Clothing: Global Contexts of Reuse and Value*. Bloomington: Indiana University Press.

Norris, Lucy. 2011. "Creating Fame and Fortune from the Ruins of Handloom in Kerala, Southern India." In *Textile Economies: Power and Value from the Local to the Transnational,* edited by Walter E. Little and Patricia A. McAnany, 285–306. Lanham, MD: AltaMira.

Norris, Lucy. 2019. "Urban Prototypes: Growing Local Circular Cloth Economies." *Business History* 61 (1): 205–24.

Obe, Mitsuru. 2012. "Radiation Release in Japan Higher Than Reported." *Wall Street Journal*, May 24.

Ocejo, Richard E. 2017. *Masters of Craft: Old Jobs in the New Urban Economy*. Princeton, NJ: Princeton University Press.

Oehlkers, Peter. 2016. "Bird Protection Between the U.S. and Japan in the 19th and 20th Centuries." Conference paper. Human Dimensions of Wildlife Group at Salem State University. https://medium.com/@oehlkers/bird-protection-between-the-u-s-and-japan-in-the-19th-and-20th-centuries-dd9630215708.

Ostrom, Elinor. 1990. *Governing the Commons: The Evolution of Institutions for Collective Action*. Cambridge: Cambridge University Press.

Otake, Tomoko. 2023. "Twelve Years After 3/11, Dispute Grows Over Fukushima's Radioactive Soil." *Japan Times*, March 10.

Palmer, Theodore Sherman. (1900) 2020. "A Review of Economic Ornithology in the United States." In USDA, *Yearbook of Department for Agriculture for 1899*, 259–92. Washington, DC: United States Department of Agriculture.

Paredes, Alyssa. 2018. "The Problem of Mechanization: Craft, Machines, and 'Centering' in a Japanese Mingei Pottery Village." *Journal of Material Culture* 23 (2): 133–50.

Parkes, Graham. 2017. "Kūkai and Dōgen as Exemplars of Ecological Engagement." In Callicott and McRae, *Japanese Environmental Philosophy*, 66–84.

Parkins, Wendy, and Geoffrey Craig. 2006. *Slow Living*. Oxford: Berg.

Parman, Susan. 2005. *Scottish Crofters: A Historical Ethnography of a Celtic Village*. Belmont, CA: Thomson/Wadsworth.

Parry, Richard Lloyd. 2017. "The School Beneath the Wave: The Unimaginable Tragedy of Japan's Tsunami." *Guardian*, August 24.

Paton, Elizabeth. 2022. "Why Does Fashion Love This Radical Anticapitalist Concept?" *New York Times*, November 17.

Pelkmans, Mathijs. 2013. *Ethnographies of Doubt: Faith and Uncertainty in Contemporary Societies*. London: I.B. Tauris.

Pharr, Susan J. 1992. *Losing Face: Status Politics in Japan*. Berkeley: University of California Press.

Phipps, Elena. 2013. "Global Colours: Dyes and the Dye Trade." In *Interwoven Globe: The Worldwide Textile Trade 1500–1800*, edited by Amelia Peck and Amy Elizabeth Bogansky, 120–35. London: Thames and Hudson.

Portisch, Anna. 2010. "The Craft of Skilful Learning: Kazakh Women's Everyday Craft Practices in Western Mongolia." In Marchand, *Making Knowledge*, 59–75.

Prata, Joana Correia, João P. da Costa, Isabel Lopes, Armando C. Duarte, and Teresa Rocha-Santos. 2020. "Environmental Exposure to Microplastics: An Overview on Possible Human Health Effects." *Science of the Total Environment* 702 (February): 1–9.

Prudham, Scott. 2011. "Making Forests 'Normal': Sustained Yield, Improvement, and the Establishment of Globalist Forestry in British Columbia." In Coleman, *Property, Territory, Globalization*, 80–100.

Puig de la Bellacasa, María. 2017. *Matters of Care: Speculative Ethics in More Than Human Worlds*. Minneapolis: University of Minnesota Press.

Purvis, Ben, Yong Mao, and Darren Robinson. 2019. "Three Pillars of Sustainability: In Search of Conceptual Origins." *Sustainability Science* 14 (3): 681–95.

Rath, Eric C. 2010. *Food and Fantasy in Early Modern Japan*. Berkeley: University of California Press.

Ray, Romita. 2022. "Unruly Indigo? Plants, Plantations, and Partitions." In *Landscape and Earth in Early Modernity: Picturing Unruly Nature*, edited by Christine Göttler and Mia Mochizuki, 181–208. Amsterdam: Amsterdam University Press.

Reader, Ian. 2005. "Historical, New, and 'New' New Religions." In Robertson, *A Companion to the Anthropology of Japan*, 429–51.

Reider, Noriko T. 2009. "Animating Objects: Tsukumogami Ki and the Medieval Illustration of Shingon Truth." *Japanese Journal of Religious Studies* 36 (2): 231–57.

Renfrew, Daniel, and Thomas W. Pearson. 2021. "The Social Life of the 'Forever Chemical': PFAS Pollution Legacies and Toxic Events." *Environment and Society* 12 (1): 146–63.

Repeta, Lawrence, and Colin P. A. Jones. 2015. "State Power Versus Individual Freedom: Japan's Constitutional Past, Present, and Possible Futures." In *Japan: The Precarious Future*, edited by Frank Baldwin and Anne Allison, 304–28. New York: New York University Press.

Reuters. 2023. "3M Pays $10.3bn to Settle Water Pollution Suit Over 'Forever Chemicals.'" *Guardian*, June 23.

Ricketts, Rowland. 2006. "*Polygonum tinctorium*: Contemporary Indigo Farming and Processing in Japan." In *Indirubin, the Red Shade of Indigo*, edited by Laurent Meijer, 7–22. Roscoff, France: Life in Progress.

Ritvo, Harriet. 1987. *The Animal Estate: The English and Other Creatures in the Victorian Age*. Cambridge, MA: Harvard University Press.

Roberts, Nathan. 2014. "U.S. Forestry in the Philippines: Environment, Nationhood, and Empire, 1900–1937." PhD diss., University of Washington.

Robertson, Jennifer. 1991. *Native and Newcomer: Making and Remaking a Japanese City*. Berkeley: University of California Press.

Robertson, Jennifer, ed. 2005. *A Companion to the Anthropology of Japan*. Hoboken, NJ: John Wiley and Sons.

Rosenberger, Nancy. 2017. "Young Organic Farmers in Japan: Betting on Lifestyle, Locality, and Livelihood." *Contemporary Japan* 29 (1): 14–30.

Sado, Michiyo. 2019. "Amami Announces Plans to Attract Thousands of Large Cruise Ships from China." [In Japanese.] *Epoch Times*, August 23.

Sahlins, Marshall. 1999. "Two or Three Things That I Know About Culture." *Journal of the Royal Anthropological Institute* 5 (3): 399–421.

Saitō, Kōhei. 2022. *Marx in the Anthropocene: Towards the Idea of Degrowth Communism*. Cambridge: Cambridge University Press.

Sakamoto, Maiko, Tofayel Ahmed, Salma Begum, and Hamidul Huq. 2019. "Water Pollution and the Textile Industry in Bangladesh: Flawed Corporate Practices or Restrictive Opportunities?" *Sustainability* 11 (7): 1–14.

Sanders, Katherine. 2018. "'Beyond Human Ownership'? Property, Power and Legal Personality for Nature in Aotearoa New Zealand." *Journal of Environmental Law* 30 (2): 207–34.
Satsuka, Shiho. 2014. "The Satoyama Movement: Envisioning Multispecies Commons in Postindustrial Japan." In "Asian Environments: Connections Across Borders, Landscapes, and Times," edited by Ursula Münster, Gunnel Cederlöf, and Shiho Satsuka, *RCC Perspectives*, no. 3, 87–93.
Schneider, Jane. 1987. "The Anthropology of Cloth." *Annual Review of Anthropology*, no. 16, 409–48.
Schneider, Jane. 1994. "In and out of Polyester: Desire, Disdain and Global Fibre Competitions." *Anthropology Today* 10 (4): 2–10.
Shapiro, Kenneth. 1989. "The Death of the Animal: Ontological Vulnerability." *Between the Species* 5 (4): 183–94.
Shapiro, Nicholas, and Eben Kirksey. 2017. "Chemo-Ethnography: An Introduction." *Cultural Anthropology* 32 (4): 481–93.
Shimizu, Maho. 2019. "Naihatsu-teki hatten-ron kara mita Amami no iji kanōna hatten no kadai to kanōsei" [Amami's sustainable development and potential seen from the theory of intrinsic development]. *Regional Initiative* 1 (1): 23–25.
Shove, Elizabeth. 2009. "Everyday Practice and the Production and Consumption of Time." In Shove, Trentmann, and Wilk, *Time, Consumption and Everyday Life*, 17–33.
Shove, Elizabeth. 2012. "The Shadowy Side of Innovation: Unmaking and Sustainability." *Technology Analysis and Strategic Management* 24 (4): 363–75.
Shove, Elizabeth, Frank Trentmann, and Richard R. Wilk, eds. 2009. *Time, Consumption and Everyday Life: Practice, Materiality and Culture*. Oxford: Berg.
Singleton, John. 1998. *Learning in Likely Places: Varieties of Apprenticeship in Japan; Learning in Doing*. Cambridge: Cambridge University Press.
Siniawer, Eiko Maruko. 2014. "'Affluence of the Heart': Wastefulness and the Search for Meaning in Millennial Japan." *Journal of Asian Studies* 73 (1): 165–86.
Siniawer, Eiko Maruko. 2018. *Waste: Consuming Postwar Japan*. Ithaca, NY: Cornell University Press.
Skabelund, Aaron Herald. 2011. *Empire of Dogs: Canines, Japan, and the Making of the Modern Imperial World*. Ithaca, NY: Cornell University Press.
Skov, Lise, and Brian Moeran. 1995. *Women, Media and Consumption in Japan*. Richmond, VA: Curzon.
Slater, David H. 2012. "Fukushima Women Against Nuclear Power: Finding a Voice from Tohoku." *Asia-Pacific Journal: Japan Focus* 10 (54): 1–5.
Song, Dajeong, and Sueo Kuwahara. 2016. "Ecotourism and World Natural Heritage: Its Influence on Islands in Japan." *Journal of Marine and Island Cultures* 5 (1): 36–46.
Sopranzetti, Claudio. 2018. *Owners of the Map: Motorcycle Taxi Drivers, Mobility, and Politics in Bangkok*. Oakland: University of California Press.
Sousounis, Peter. 2019. "How Climate Change May Have Made Typhoon Hagibis Worse." AIR Worldwide, October 28. https://www.air-worldwide.com/blog/posts/2019/10/how-climate-change-may-have-made-typhoon-hagibis-worse/.

Stenton, Marie, Joseph A. Houghton, Veronika Kapsali, and Richard S. Blackburn. 2021. "The Potential for Regenerated Protein Fibres Within a Circular Economy: Lessons from the Past Can Inform Sustainable Innovation in the Textiles Industry." *Sustainability* 13 (4): 1–18.

Sternsdorff-Cisterna, Nicolas. 2015. "Food After Fukushima: Risk and Scientific Citizenship in Japan." *American Anthropologist* 117 (3): 455–67.

Strathern, Marilyn. 2023. *Property, Substance, and Effect: Anthropological Essays on Persons and Things*. London: HAU Books.

Struck, Doug. 2001. "Tokyo's Winged Bullies." *Washington Post*, June 12.

Sugimura, Ken. 2021. *Wildlife, Landscape Use and Society: Regional Case Studies in Japan*. London: Routledge.

Takahashi, Takuya, Koji Matsushita, Yoshio Yoshida, and Tetsuji Senda. 2019. "Impacts of 150 Years of Modernization Policies on the Management of Common Forests in Japan: A Statistical Analysis of Micro Census Data." *International Journal of the Commons* 13 (2): 1021–34.

Takarabe, Megumi, and Akira Nishimura. 2013. "Amami Island Religion: Historical Dynamics of the Islanders' Spirit." In *The Islands of Kagoshima*, edited by Kei Kawai, Ryuta Terada, and Sueo Kawahara, 14–20. Kagoshima: Kagoshima University Research Center for the Pacific Islands.

Takeuchi, K., I. Washitani, R. D. Brown, A. Tsunekawa, and M. Yokohari, eds. 2003. *Satoyama: The Traditional Rural Landscape of Japan*. Berlin: Springer Science and Business Media.

Takigawa, Tsutomu. 1972. "Historical Background of Agricultural Land Reform in Japan." *Developing Economies* 10 (3): 290–310.

Tanaka, Shigeru, Masaho Sikano, Minako Suga, Masaki Matsushita, and Yoko Yamaguchi, eds. 2005. *Textiles Across the Seas: Amami, Kagoshima, Kurume*. Vol. 3. Tokyo: Textiles Across the Seas Executive Committee.

Tanaka Nao (website). n.d. Accessed June 7, 2018. https://www.tanaka-nao.co.jp/shop/206-107-30.html.

Taussig, Michael. 2008. "Redeeming Indigo." *Theory, Culture and Society* 25 (3): 1–15.

Taussig, Michael. 2009. *What Color Is the Sacred*? Chicago: University of Chicago Press.

Thomas, Kedron. 2020. "Cultures of Sustainability in the Fashion Industry." *Fashion Theory* 24 (5): 715–42.

Thomas, Nicola J., David C. Harvey, and Harriet Hawkins. 2013. "Crafting the Region: Creative Industries and Practices of Regional Space." *Regional Studies* 47 (1): 75–88.

Thornton, Gene. 1975. "Photography View: Minamata Victims Transformed." *New York Times*, May 11.

Tokyo 2020. 2018. *Tokyo 2020: Tokyo 2020 Olympic and Paralympic Games Sustainability Plan Version 2*. Tokyo: The Tokyo Organising Committee of the Olympic and Paralympic Games. https://gtimg.tokyo2020.org/image/upload/production/jyt3ocxciw8shkus9vqd.pdf.

Totman, Conrad D. 1989. *The Green Archipelago: Forestry in Preindustrial Japan*. Berkeley: University of California Press.

Toyoda Mitsuyo. 2013. "Revitalizing Local Commons: A Democratic Approach to Collective Management." *Environmental Ethics* 35 (3): 279–93.

Toyoda Mitsuyo. 2017. "Recollecting Local Narratives on the Land Ethic." In Callicott and McRae, *Japanese Environmental Philosophy*, 180–92.

Traphagan, John. 2020. *Cosmopolitan Rurality, Depopulation, and Entrepreneurial Ecosystems in 21st-Century Japan*. New York: Cambria.

Trentmann, Frank. 2007. "Before 'Fair Trade': Empire, Free Trade, and the Moral Economies of Food in the Modern World." *Environment and Planning D: Society and Space* 25 (6): 1079–102.

Trentmann, Frank. 2009. "Disruption is Normal: Blackouts, Breakdowns and the Elasticity of Everyday Life." In Shove, Trentmann, and Wilk, *Time, Consumption and Everyday Life*, 67–84.

Troll, Carl. 1950. "Die geographische Landschaft und ihre Erforschung." In *Studium generale: Eitschrift für die Einheit der Wissenschaften im Zusammenhang ihrer Begriffsbildungen und Forschungsmethoden*, edited by K. H. Bauer, L. Curtius, H. v. Einem, et al., 163–81. Berlin: Springer.

Tronto, Joan C. 1993. *Moral Boundaries: A Political Argument for an Ethic of Care*. New York: Routledge.

Tsing, Anna Lowenhaupt. 2005. *Friction: An Ethnography of Global Connection*. Princeton, NJ: Princeton University Press.

Tsing, Anna Lowenhaupt. 2013. "Sorting Out Commodities: How Capitalist Value Is Made Through Gifts." *HAU: Journal of Ethnographic Theory* 3 (1): 21–43.

Tsing, Anna Lowenhaupt. 2015. *The Mushroom at the End of the World: On the Possibility of Life in Capitalist Ruins*. Princeton, NJ: Princeton University Press.

Tsing, Anna Lowenhaupt, Heather Anne Swanson, Elaine Gan, and Nils Bubandt, eds. 2017. *Arts of Living on a Damaged Planet: Ghosts of the Anthropocene; Monsters of the Anthropocene*. Minneapolis: University of Minnesota Press.

Tsoi, Grace. 2023. "Fukushima Nuclear Disaster: Japan to Release Radioactive Water into Sea This Year." *BBC News*, January 13. https://www.bbc.com/news/world-asia-64259043.

Tsutsui, William M. 2003. "Landscapes in the Dark Valley: Toward an Environmental History of Wartime Japan." *Environmental History* 8 (2): 294–311.

UNESCO. n.d. "Amami-Oshima Island, Tokunoshima Island, the Northern Part of Okinawa Island and Iriomote Island." Accessed December 16, 2024. https://whc.unesco.org/en/list/1574/.

Urakami, Takuya, David Saal, and Maria Nieswand. 2021. "Industry Fragmentation and Wastewater Efficiency: A Case Study of Hyogo Prefecture in Japan." ADBI Working Paper 1218. Tokyo: Asian Development Bank Institute.

USCAR (United States Civil Administration of the Ryukyu Islands). 1952. *Preliminary Notes on the Use, Distribution, and Adaptability of Native and Introduced Trees Species*. Special Bulletin No. 1. Washington, DC: US Adjutant-General's Office. https://www.google.co.jp/books/edition/United_States_Civil_Administration_of_th/tKNHAQAAIAAJ?hl=en&gbpv=0.

USCAR (United States Civil Administration of the Ryukyu Islands). 1953. *Preliminary Notes on the Use, Distribution, and Adaptability of Native and Introduced Trees Species*. Special Bulletin No. 2. Washington, DC: US Adjutant-General's Office. https://www.google.co.jp/books/edition/United_States_Civil_Administration_of_th/tKNHAQAAIAAJ?hl=en&gbpv=1&dq=Preliminary+Notes+on+the+Use,+Distribution,+and+Adaptability+of+Native+and+Introduced+Trees+Species&pg=PP5&printsec=frontcover.

Valk, Julie. 2018. "Survival or Success? The Kimono Retail Industry in Contemporary Japan." DPhil diss., University of Oxford.

Valk, Julie. 2020. "The Smell of Shōwa: Time, Materiality and Regimes of Value in Japan's Second-Hand Kimono Industry." *Journal of Material Culture* 25 (2): 240–56.

Veracini, Lorenzo. 2010. *Settler Colonialism: A Theoretical Overview*. Basingstoke: Palgrave Macmillan.

Vivero-Pol, Jose Luis, Mattei Ugo, De Schutter Olivier, and Ferrando Tomaso, eds. 2019. *Routledge Handbook of Food as a Commons: Expanding Approaches*. London: Routledge.

Vlastos, Stephen. 1998. *Mirror of Modernity: Invented Traditions of Modern Japan*. Berkeley: University of California Press.

Wahl, Daniel Christian. 2020. "Sustainability Is Not Enough: We Need Regenerative Cultures." *Medium*, April 9. https://designforsustainability.medium.com/sustainability-is-not-enough-we-need-regenerative-cultures-4abb3c78e68b.

Walker, Brett L. 2010. *Toxic Archipelago: A History of Industrial Disease in Japan*. Seattle: University of Washington Press.

Walker, Daniela. 2015. "The Hipster Is Dead, Let's Start an Anti-Authenticity Movement." *Campaign*, September 29. https://www.campaignlive.co.uk/article/hipster-dead-lets-start-anti-authenticity-movement/1366143.

Warnier, Jean Pierre. 2012. "The Moral Economy of Authenticity and the Invention of Traditions in Franche-Comté (France)." In *Debating Authenticity: Concepts of Modernity in Anthropological Perspective*, edited by Thomas Fillitz and A. Jamie Saris, 78–90. New York: Berghahn Books.

Washitani, I. 2003. "Species Diversity in Satoyama Landscapes." In Takeuchi et al., *Satoyama*, 89–94.

Weiner, Annette B., and Jane Schneider, eds. 1989. *Cloth and Human Experience*. Washington, DC: Smithsonian Institution Press.

White, Julian, and Jurg Meier. 2017. *Handbook of Clinical Toxicology of Animal Venoms and Poisons*. Boca Raton, FL: CRC Press.

Wicker, Alden. 2022. "Nope, Fashion Is Not Responsible for 20 Percent of Global Water Pollution, Either." *Ecocult*, July 27. https://ecocult.com/fashion-20-percent-global-water-pollution/.

Wicker, Alden. 2023. *To Dye For: How Toxic Fashion Is Making Us Sick—and How We Can Fight Back*. New York: Penguin Random House.

Wilkes, Sarah. 2015. "Sustainability and the Co-Constitution of Substances and Subjects." In Drazin and Küchler, *Social Life of Materials*, 211–26.

Willis, Sofia. 2023. "How Sustainable Dyeing Is Changing the Textile Industry." Plug and Play Tech Center, April 28. https://www.plugandplaytechcenter.com/insights/how-sustainable-dyeing-changing-textile-industry.

Woodcock, Victoria. 2021. "There's Nothing Dull About the World of Natural Dyes: Why Designers Are Shunning Synthetic Colour for a More Sustainable Fix." *Financial Times*, November 1.

World Bank Group. 2024. *Gender Data Portal: Japan*. Accessed December 18, 2024. https://genderdata.worldbank.org/en/economies/japan#:~:text=10.3%25%200f%20seats%20in%20national,lower%20chamber%20held%20by%20women.

Yahoo! News. 2021. "At the Oshima Tsumugi Manufacturing Site, There Is a Shortage of Collectors of the Dorozome Dye Material Sharinbai." [In Japanese.] November 28. Accessed January 10, 2022. https://news.yahoo.co.jp/articles/4ce67aefdda6e074c204f3b668c8db7ccf0536da.

Yaich, Hela, Haikel Garna, Souhail Besbes, Michel Paquot, Christophe Blecker, and Hamadi Attia. 2011. "Chemical Composition and Functional Properties of *Ulva lactuca* Seaweed Collected in Tunisia." *Food Chemistry* 128 (4): 895–901.

Yamada, Shoko, Lav Kanoi, Vanessa Koh, Al Lim, and Michael R. Dove. 2022. "Sustainability as a Moral Discourse: Its Shifting Meanings, Exclusions, and Anxieties." *Sustainability* 14 (5): 1–17.

Yamanobe, Tomoyuki, and Kenzō Fujii. 1996. *Kyoto Modern Textiles, 1868–1940*. Kyoto: Kyoto Textile Wholesalers Association.

Yamashita, Fumitake. 1952. "Tattooing in Amami Ōshima." Unpublished manuscript. Douglas Haring Papers. University Archives, Special Collections Research Center, Syracuse University Libraries, Syracuse, New York.

Yamashita, Kazuhito. 2019. "What's Behind the Food Self-Sufficiency 'Crisis'?" *Japan Times*, September 5.

Yardley, Jim, 2013, "Bangladesh Pollution, Told in Colors and Smells." *New York Times*, July 14.

Yoneyama, Shoko. 2012. "Life-World: Beyond Fukushima and Minamata." *Asia-Pacific Journal: Japan Focus* 10 (42): 1–27.

Yoneyama, Shoko. 2019. *Animism in Contemporary Japan: Voices for the Anthropocene from Post-Fukushima Japan*. London: Routledge.

Young, Diana. 2018. *Rematerializing Colour: From Concept to Substance*. Canon Pyon: Sean Kingston.

Yuge, Masami. 2005. "The History of Amami Oshima Tsumugi Right up to the Present Day." In Tanaka et al., *Textiles Across the Seas*, n.p.

Zhang, Amy. 2019. "Invisible Labouring Bodies: Waste Work as Infrastructure in China." *Made in China Journal* 4 (2): 98–102.

Index

Page numbers in *italics* refer to figures.